The Origins of the Iranian-American Alliance

1941–1953

U. S. S. R.
TURKEY
Dzulfa
Urmia
Tabriz
AZERBAIJAN-E KHAVARI
CASPIAN SEA
U. S. S. R.
Hari
Resht
GILAN
Bandar Shah
KOPET MTS.
Meshed
KORDESTAN
IRAQ
TEHRAN
ELBURZ MTS.
SALT DESERT
Qum
Kermanshah
ZAGROS MTS.
IRAN
KHORASAN
AFGHANISTAN
BAGHDAD
Isfahan
Tigris R.
Yzad
KHUZESTAN
KERMAN
Euphrates R.
Ahwaz
BAKHTIARI
Kharramshahr
Abadan
Bandar Shahpur
Kerman
KUWAIT
Shiraz
Zahidan
NEUTRAL ZONE
Bushire
PAKISTAN
FARS
BALUCHESTAN
PERSIAN GULF
Bandar Abbas
SAUDI ARABIA
QATAR
GULF OF OMAN
NORTH
ARAB EMIRATES
50 0 50 100 150
MILES
OMAN

The Origins of the Iranian-American Alliance

1941–1953

Mark Hamilton Lytle

HOLMES & MEIER NEW YORK | LONDON

Holmes & Meier Publishers, Inc.
30 Irving Place
New York, N.Y. 10003

Great Britain:
1–3 Winton Close
Letchworth, Hertfordshire SG61 1BA England

Book design by Mark O'Connor

The maps that appear in this book
(pp. ii, 20, and 66) were drawn by
Sharon Griffith.

Library of Congress Cataloging-in-Publication Data
Lytle, Mark H.
The origins of the Iranian-American alliance,
1941–1953.
Bibliography: p.
Includes index.
1. United States—Foreign relations—Iran.
2. Iran—Foreign relations—United States. 3. United
States—Foreign relations—1933–1945. 4. United
States—Foreign relations—1945–1953. I. Title.
E183.8.I7L97 1987 327.73055 86-26931

ISBN 0-8419-1060-X
ISBN 0-8419-1061-8 (pbk.)

Manufactured in the United States of America

For
Walter LaFeber

Contents

Abbreviations

AIOC	Anglo-Iranian Oil Company (was originally APOC and is now BP or British Petroleum)
APOC	Anglo-Persian Oil Company
CCS	Combined Chiefs of Staff
FEA	Foreign Economic Administration (Lend-Lease)
FO	Foreign Office
FR or FRUS	*Foreign Relations of the United States*
FTC	Federal Trade Commission
IPC	Iraq Petroleum Corporation
JCS	Joint Chiefs of Staff
JICAME	Joint Intelligence Committee—Middle East
MI or MIS	Military Intelligence Service
MMRB	Modern Military Records Branch, National Archives
NEA	Office of Near Eastern and African Affairs
NKVD	Narodnyi Kommissariat Vnutrennykh Del (People's Commissariat of Internal Affairs)
OCI	Overseas Consultants Incorporated
OGPU (or GPU)	Soviet police, successor of the Cheka, predecessor to NKVD
OPD	Operations and Planning Division (War Department)
OSS	Office of Strategic Services
OWI	Office of War Information
OWM	Office of War Mobilization
PAW	Petroleum Administration for War
PIWC	Petroleum Industry War Council

PGC	Persian Gulf Command (originally Persian Gulf Service Command, renamed December 1943)
PRC	Petroleum Reserves Corporation
PSF	President's Secretary Files
SD	State Department
SONJ	Standard Oil of New Jersey
UN	United Nations
UNJ	*United Nations Journal*
UNO	United Nations Organization
WD	War Department
WDGS	War Department General Staff
WPA	Works Progress Administration
YUL	Yale University Library

Acknowledgments

Any author who spends fifteen years on a book acquires more debts than he can possibly recall or adequately acknowledge. I am sure that some of the people who have helped me along the way or offered constructive criticism have by now forgotten their own contributions. But I would like them to know that I am still grateful. Scholarship is, after all, more of a cooperative enterprise than we admit when we fix a single name to the title page.

This project began as a dissertation at Yale where I had the good fortune to find myself among scholars who were also teachers and a community of graduate students that included some of the most stimulating and decent people I have ever met. Gaddis Smith, my adviser, suggested the initial topic and then helped me sort out the kind of mess novice historians are likely to make. Gaddis directed me into a career I have never regretted. John Blum had an equally important impact. I came to see that his generous use of an editorial pencil on my prose was an invaluable gift. He taught me and countless others to see how good history, good writing, and clear thinking are interconnected.

Firuz Kazemzadeh was the first of a number of Persian scholars who made it possible for me to understand something of Iran's history and politics. During our conversations, he shared with me personal memories that involved many of the same events and personalities I was struggling to understand. His own scholarship had a formative impact on mine. In that way I am grateful also to Ervand Abrahamian and Rouhollah Ramazani, two men I have never met, but upon whose scholarship I have relied heavily. Bruce Kuniholm has helped, too. Although I disagree with some of his interpretations, I respect his scholarship and his constructive criticism of my manuscript at a crucial stage has left me with a much better book.

Along the way this book had many readers who offered their ideas and encouraged me to keep going. Geof Hewitt, Allan Winkler, Gavin Hambly, Eduard Mark, Thomas Paterson, and others commented on the manuscript in its earlier incarnations. Then during a middle stage, when I contemplated going on to other things, my friends and colleagues at Bard College encouraged me to finish the book. Joseph

Solodow, a first-rate classicist, showed that scholarly expertise is not parochial by reading and commenting on the entire manuscript, as did Iska Alter, a fine literary critic and editor. John Fout kept after me to finish, while proving that teachers at a small college can publish as well. Fred Crane, Leon Botstein, Christine Stansell, Carol Karlsen, Alice Stroup, Gannady Shkliarevsky, and Myra Young-Armstead, my history colleagues, talked, shared their ideas, and encouraged me. In his generous and tolerant fashion Robert Koblitz cleared up some of my muddled liberal ideas. Paul Connolly and the faculty of the Institute for Writing and Thinking at Bard have included me in their community of writers.

Two friends from my Yale graduate school days have stuck by me and this project ever since. My footnotes give only a hint of what I owe Michael Stoff. Our interests and sensibilities converge in so many ways that I am not always sure which ideas are his, which are mine. And if I were to say I had three children, Jesse, Kate, and this book, James Davidson is the godfather to all three. Twice he read the manuscript when I needed some sense of how to go on. Three times he agreed to coauthor other books with me. And in each case I have emerged a better writer and historian feeling more secure about the future for all my children.

All scholars are indebted to the many people and institutions that support our work. Judith Skiff at the Yale Archives, William Cunliffe at the Modern Military Records Branch, Ruth Darling in the State Department archives, and the staffs at the Princeton, Yale, Truman, Roosevelt, and Bard College libraries have all taken extraordinary pains on my behalf. The Council on International Relations at Yale, the Kellogg Foundation, and the Research and Travel Committee at Bard have supported my research. Marcia Johnson, as a freelance editor, showed me how to make the manuscript more readable and interesting to a nonprofessional audience. My mother, Mary Emily Lytle, and my grandmother, Frances Hickman Wilkins, read my work and encouraged me. My sister-in-law Anne Brueckner dug up much needed bits of information on many occasions, while my good friend Arthur Sack listened to me for more hours than is good for a person.

I have been lucky, too, to have Max Holmes as a publisher. The editorial support from Holmes & Meier has been invaluable. Barbara Lyons launched the manuscript and Kevin Davis rescued it when it floundered. No author could expect a more professional or sensitive reading than Kevin gave this manuscript. And I was delighted to have a copy editor who clearly has a strong historical background.

Finally, a comment on the dedication. Anyone with as good a family as mine should dedicate a book to them. My wife Gretchen has always been my first editor and intellectual conscience. I have been able to sustain my work, because Jesse, Kate, and Gretchen have made my home such a happy place. They understand, too, why this book is dedicated to Walter LaFeber of Cornell University.

Recently, my friend Sherman Cochran, another Cornell historian, remarked that anyone who taught with Walt could understand why he has such an impact on his students. When he is not writing or teaching, he has a steady stream of students in and out of his office. My career as a professional historian began that way. I first came to his office to ask him to direct my senior thesis. Since then, he has encouraged me on every step of my career. When I felt discouraged with this project, he gently urged me to finish it. When I needed some guidance, he gave it. From his books I found a way to make scholarship and moral conscience converge. This book would never have been finished without him. I hope he likes it.

Introduction

A study of the origins of the Iranian-American alliance between 1941 and 1953 affords a historian of American foreign policy a rare opportunity—a chance to begin at the beginning. It can easily be argued that before 1941 Iran and the United States had almost no relations whatsoever. The two nations did have nominal diplomatic representation, and a handful of citizens in each country had some familiarity with the other. But commerce between the two nations amounted to just a few million dollars annually. Because the United States had little direct interest in Iranian affairs, American diplomats in Iran did little more than monitor the policy of the major powers involved in the region—the Soviet Union, Great Britain, and Germany. Concern with the Persian Gulf region was defined largely by oil, but not Iran's oil. Up until 1954, American oil company holdings lay largely in the areas carved out of the old Ottoman Empire—Mesopotamia or Iraq, Saudi Arabia, and Bahrain Island.

Almost all the ties that bound Iran and the United States from 1954 to 1979 were established during World War II and the early years of the cold war. That meant that the objectives of American policy for Iran were generally defined by global policy concerns. To understand the reasons for American initiatives in relation to the microcosm of Iran is to gain insight into broad areas of American foreign policy: relations with the Soviet Union and Great Britain, efforts to define an international oil policy, the tension between military and political strategies during the war, the formulation of postwar national security policies, the continuities and discontinuities of diplomacy in three successive presidential administrations from Franklin Roosevelt to Dwight Eisenhower, the development of foreign aid and technical assistance programs, and, above all, the origins of the cold war.

Increased specialization has often caused historians to study these various topics in isolation from each other. But in this study those many strands are understood as intertwined. It is possible, for example, to see the ways national security concerns shaped the definition of foreign oil policy against the backdrop of the growing Soviet-American rivalry over Iran.[1]

As a result a study of Iranian-American relations has the same significance for historians that it had for many wartime British and American policymakers, namely as a "test case" for postwar Allied relations with smaller nations. Iran was after all the one nation where all three major powers had stationed troops. At the Tehran Conference in 1943, Roosevelt, Churchill, and Stalin had made an unusual pledge to respect Iran's territorial integrity and sovereignty. The State Department had hoped that its policy of stabilizing Iran with the help of American advisers would eliminate the traditional causes of big power rivalry there. That expectation gave an ironic twist to the Iranian crises of 1944 and 1945–46. In 1944 the prospect that an American oil company might win an oil concession in Iran led the Soviet Union to demand its own oil concession in northern Iran. This Allied dispute over oil was followed in 1945 by a Soviet attempt to promote the establishment of autonomous states in Azerbaijan and Kurdistan. Only then did Americans become aware of their nation's growing stake in Iran. And Iran's complaint to the United Nations Security Council in 1946 confronted the fledgling United Nations with its first case. Instead of policing the actions of the smaller nations, the Security Council became an arena for conflict between its most powerful members. Confrontation, not cooperation, made Iran a "test case."

No historian could reasonably suggest that the cold war began over Iran. There were too many other areas of the world where Soviet-American ambitions conflicted to single out one country or one issue as a determining cause. However, it can be argued that the Iranian crisis of 1945–46 offers a textbook case of the origins of the cold war. John Lewis Gaddis perceived a shift in American policy from an effort to accommodate the Soviets in the fall of 1945 to a hard line in the spring of 1946. This change paralleled the crisis in Iran. Most recently, the historian Bruce Kuniholm has argued that, "If Eastern Europe presented the [Truman] administration with models of how not to deal with the Soviets, the Iranian crisis served as a model of how it should deal with them."[2]

But history can be a fickle teacher. Each generation, each school of thought, derives its own meaning from the same events. Did American policymakers and the historians who have commended their efforts draw the correct lessons from the conflict over Iran? Did the Iranian crisis form a prelude to further Soviet efforts to dominate the Middle East? Did these events justify the Truman Doctrine, the stationing of a permanent naval task force in the eastern Mediterranean, and an aggressive American policy to contain the Soviet Union? Obviously a generation of policymakers and many historians have since answered yes to all those questions. Where else after all did Stalin more nakedly violate wartime agreements than he did in Iran—a loyal member of the wartime United Nations alliance? Whether motivated by traditional tsarist ambitions, communist imperialism, security fears, paranoia, or some combination of all of these, Stalin had clearly targeted Iran as a prize for the Soviet war effort. Russian diplomats thwarted almost every British and American attempt to reach an accommodation over Iran. From 1944 through 1947 the Soviets did periodically seek to intimidate the Iranian government into making political or economic concessions. Any historical explanation of the recurring international tensions over Iran in the postwar era must assign the Soviet Union much of the responsibility.[3]

Few historians have been similarly critical of the American role in Iran. With the exception of some of the revisionists of the 1960s and 1970s, most historians have portrayed the United States as a champion of underdog Iran, a defender of United Nations principles, or as a world power protecting its legitimate national security interests. Such interpretations do not adequately explain the origins of the Iranian-American alliance or the emergence of the United States as the dominant power in the Middle East. The State Department itself had dismissed America's prewar role in Iran as a concern "with little more than extending protection to American philanthropic and missionary activities and the assurance of the nominal exchange of goods." By contrast NSC–5, one of the early strategic papers of the National Security Council, in 1947 declared that the Middle East was vital to the security of the United States and that an independent Iran friendly to the United States was an essential barrier to Soviet expansion.[4]

In 1944 Walter Lippmann warned American policymakers against the temptation to undermine traditional British or Soviet security systems in the region. He predicted that if the United States or the Soviet Union "reaches out for allies within the orbit of the other," the regional systems that could secure the peace would not work. To illustrate his point he wrote, "No one questions our alliance with Mexico or Canada. But if Mexico made an alliance with the Soviet Union everyone would know the peace was troubled. If we made an alliance with Iran or Roumania, all the world would have the right to think the worst of our intentions."[5] This study attempts to show that American policymakers did just that—they formed a *de facto* alliance with Iran, the peace was troubled, and historians now have an obligation to take a more critical look at American policy in Iran.

Why were American policymakers unwilling to accept the idea of a neutral Iran, aligned neither with east nor west, serving as it had before the war as a buffer between rival empires? Or to put it another way, what persuaded American policymakers that "legitimate" security concerns justified an alliance that would bring Iran into the American orbit? There is a temptation to embrace one single explanation—oil. Since World War II no nation has played a greater role in the development of Middle Eastern oil than the United States. No foreign resource has contributed more to American wealth and power. During the war and the immediate postwar years, policy analysts stressed the importance of oil both to the security and the prosperity of all the industrial nations of the west. If the Soviet Union dominated Iran, it could easily deny the west access to the oil reserves in the Persian Gulf basin. The overthrow of Mohammed Mossadeq in 1953 opened Iran's oil fields to American companies. It is tempting to conclude that with the inclusion of American companies in an Iranian oil consortium the United States acquired what it had sought all along.[6]

Single causes, no matter how consequential they may be, do not adequately explain complex events. A historical model that equates American interests in the Middle East with those of the major international oil companies is too simplistic. If that simple equation was the only truth, why would Truman extend aid to oil-starved Greece and Turkey, while excluding oil-rich Iran? Why would he recognize Israel over the objections of many Arab leaders whose nations control most of the region's oil? It is equally naive to make an artificial distinction between public policy and the "private" business pursuits of the oil companies, as State Department officials often did. At times the oil companies did operate autonomously in Iran and elsewhere in the Middle East, but, as one government report concluded, "American oil operations are for all practical purposes instruments of our foreign policy toward these countries."[7] Policymakers always saw American control of Middle Eastern oil concessions, whether at government or private initiative, as central to their definitions of national security.

A recent article by the historian Melvyn Leffler suggests that the Iranian-American alliance and American Middle Eastern oil policy fit into a global conception of national security that defense planners adopted in the postwar era. Several of the factors he analyzes influenced the State Department's decision to support an Iranian alliance. Technological advances associated with the war—

especially long-range bombers and the atom bomb—necessitated a strategy of "defense in depth." To guarantee its security, the United States would have to maintain a string of overseas bases as well as military air transit and landing rights. Budgetary and political constraints would at times force planners "to rely on private airlines, which had to be persuaded to locate their operations designated essential to military air transit rights." Iran's location along air and land routes to Asia and the Soviet Union led the State Department to define these air routes as one important aspect of the Iranian-American alliance.[8]

More importantly, by the end of World War II, American strategic planners had become convinced that the United States could not allow any potential enemy to control the Eurasian land mass. Huge reserves of natural resources, industry, and manpower were at stake. Middle Eastern oil was the one resource that most concerned defense planners. Control of Iran would open that resource to the Soviet Union and greatly extend the Russians' "defense in depth." Bases in Europe and the Middle East could undermine the effectiveness of strategic air power upon which planners had increasingly come to rely. A domino theory adopted during the 1945–46 crisis designated Iran as the first line of defense. The fall of Iran might lead to the loss of the entire Asian subcontinent. That was one reason the State Department insisted on maintaining American military and police advisers in Iran after the war had ended.[9]

Leffler, too, argues that the American assessment of Soviet intentions underwent a transformation from the fall of 1945 to the spring of 1946. As the war ended, diplomatic and military planners were willing to concede that the Soviet Union had some legitimate security concerns and that negotiations might still achieve some useful accommodations. But events in Eastern Europe, the eastern Mediterranean, Asia, and Iran led to a reformulation of American assumptions about Soviet intentions. Soviet behavior no longer seemed to be based on rational security considerations. American policymakers came to believe that Stalin had set out to control the Eurasian land mass, to destroy capitalism, and to extend Soviet-directed communism throughout the world.[10]

Most historians agree that George Kennan's "Long Telegram" established the conceptual framework in which American leaders came to understand Soviet policy. What was most striking about Kennan's analysis was his assumption that paranoia or irrational fear underlay Soviet expansion. The United States could not reach useful accommodations with such a foe in an ordinary way. Only through military strength, constant vigilance, and support for our allies—through a policy of containment—could the United States frustrate Soviet ambitions. As Leffler concluded, Kennan's analysis, undertaken as the World War II alliance deteriorated, confirmed the widely held assumption that the Soviet Union had as its ultimate aim "Russian domination of a communist world." That belief became embedded in national security thinking. By 1948 NSC–7 stated what had become an American cold war gospel: "The ultimate objective of Soviet-directed world communism is the domination of the world."[11]

This study will show that State Department policy for Iran anticipated those conclusions by as much as five years. Although the war had created the circumstance that involved the United States in Iran, State Department initiatives—advisory missions, diplomatic representations to London or Moscow, commercial agreements, and an oil concession—always had as a primary goal the containment of Soviet ambitions in Iran. The architects of this American policy, especially Wallace Murray and Loy Henderson, shared most of Kennan's assumptions long before they were formulated in the "Long Telegram." The crisis of 1945–46 persuaded them that they had been right all along. Stalin was determined to bring Iran into the Soviet orbit. Only American willingness to back Iran through the United Nations had prevented a recurrence of events like those that had taken place in Roumania. A similar scenario would play itself out in the early 1950s. Once again American policymakers would persuade themselves that their timely intervention, this time through a clandestine intelligence operation, had preserved Iran as an independent barrier to Soviet global ambitions.

These are not the conclusions this study draws. The dynamic factor in Iranian affairs, indeed throughout the Middle East during and after World War II, was the United States, not the Soviet Union. As historian Lloyd Gardner once suggested, "Far from justifying the Truman Doctrine, the Iranian episode revealed that it was possible to extend American influence to the doorstep of the Soviet Union without effective challenge." Or as Leffler observed, "American policymakers seldom subjected their assumptions about Soviet ambitions to any real analysis: In their overall assessments of Soviet long-term intentions, . . . military planners dismissed all evidence of Soviet moderation, circumspection, and restraint."[12] The Iranian crises of 1944, 1945–46, and 1950–53 could have indicated to planners the limits of Soviet ambitions and the reluctance of Soviet leaders to take major risks to achieve their goal of "defense in depth." But as Soviet influence in Iran declined, American policymakers became even more persuaded of Stalin's expansionist ambitions. Their assumptions hardened into a cold war ideology.

Worse yet, the United States did not need an Iranian alliance to realize its national security objectives. By supporting a neutral Iran, the United States could have maintained the barrier it sought without trying to direct events in a country whose politics and culture Americans still find almost impossible to fathom. My analysis of the role of advisory missions to Iran during World War II reveals just how ineffective the State Department was in carrying out its plan for "nation-building." The United States lacked the knowledge, the resources, and the commitment to support a fundamental alteration of Iranian life, even with the cooperation of some segments of the Iranian elite. Most Iranians never believed that they received enough material benefits from the United States to compensate for the restrictions on their political autonomy and the disruption of their traditional culture caused by these policies. Simmering discontent eventually exploded in the Islamic Revolution. A more restrained policy could have spared us the trauma of "America held captive" in 1979–81. A neutral Iran could also have eased one recurrent source of Soviet-American tensions.

So far I have focused largely on the Iranian-American alliance in its cold war context. But no more than Castro's government in Cuba were the Iranians innocent or helpless pawns in that big power rivalry. They played a central role in the formation of the alliance with the United States. I have tried to pay close attention to internal and external political circumstances that led successive Iranian governments to create ties that would somehow commit the United States to the preservation of Iranian independence. Historian Rouhallah Ramazani has identified as Iran's "third power strategy" the attempt to attract support from nations whose geopolitical situations make them rivals of the two powers—Great Britain and Russia—who have historically interfered the most in Iranian affairs. After World War II, Iranian "third power" advocates had to contend with an alternative doctrine championed by nationalists like Mohammed Mossadeq—called "negative equilibrium." Mossadeq did not wish Iran to continue playing off the powers against each other by bartering concessions for political favors. He thought Iran could better secure its independence and sovereignty by minimizing all foreign influences. It was only with reluctance that he sought American aid in his struggle to establish Iran's control over the Anglo-Iranian Oil Company (AIOC) concession.[13]

The Iranian-American alliance was more a marriage of convenience than a true love affair. At the same time it was a union that both parties sought, though often for quite different and even contradictory reasons. The United States did not simply assume neocolonial domination over Iran. It was the Iranians, not the Americans, who urged the creation of economic and political instruments—oil concessions, advisory missions, and commercial agreements—that traditionally were the devices of imperialist penetration. Even during the period of the Anglo-Soviet occupation of Iran during World War II, skillful diplomatic maneuvering, which westerners often dismissed as deviousness, enabled Iranian leaders to maintain significant autonomy in their dealings with the major powers. Even if the Iranian-American alliance was not a partnership between equals, Iran's leaders often played a decisive role in defining the relations between the two nations.

The alliance might never have come into being had it not had the blessings of Great Britain. British Foreign Office records reveal that early in World War II British diplomats encouraged Iranian overtures to the United States. Aware of the empire's weakness, they, like the Iranians, saw an American role as a necessary counterweight to Soviet ambitions. They understood that the American presence would reduce their own influence, but they preferred a junior status to the prospect of a Soviet-dominated Iran. British and American diplomats discovered that they shared a wide range of assumptions. Between 1941 and 1953 the two countries cooperated during almost every dispute involving the Soviet Union. Only on the question of the AIOC concession did they ever have any real disagreements. The CIA operation that overthrew Mossadeq was first conceived by British Intelligence. In many ways, the Iranian-American alliance was as much a product of British as of Iranian and American diplomacy.[14]

I have emphasized the role of American diplomats, because the alliance with Iran was largely a State Department initiative. Neither Roosevelt nor Truman nor Eisenhower ever showed any sustained interest in Iran. Yet each president indicated at crucial moments that he approved the direction of American policy. American military leaders were initially reluctant to support the State Department's program. Only as they began to accept the idea of an independent Iran as crucial to American security did State Department policy become American policy. Thus, during the war years, bureaucratic rivalry as much as any rational perception of the national interest shaped American policy for Iran.

Finally, I should admit that history never presents us with a *tabula rasa.* American involvement in Iran after 1941 may have been a new departure, but it did not begin on a blank slate. American diplomats drew heavily on their experience in Latin America. Placed in the context of the Truman Doctrine and of U.S. commitments to other states in the region, the formation of an alliance with Iran was part of a process by which the United States in essence extended the Monroe Doctrine to the Middle East. There are remarkable similarities between the rationale for overthrowing Mossadeq in 1953 and the principles of Roosevelt's corollary. Eisenhower, in the spirit of Teddy Roosevelt, assumed that Mossadeq's mismanagement of Iran forced the United States to intervene. Instead of the canal, the United States now had strategic oil reserves to defend.[15]

In addition, to bureaucratic and security concerns, two ideological strands shaped the State Department's commitment to an Iranian alliance. The first of these was a profound mistrust of the Soviet Union and a hatred of communism. Historian Daniel Yergin has associated these views with the Soviet Service, a group of State Department specialists on Soviet affairs. Many of the diplomats who defined American policy for Iran either participated in the Soviet Service or shared the views of its members. That is one reason why the Iranian-American alliance was conceived in the context of an anti-Soviet and anticommunist ideology. Americans have traditionally defined themselves as much by what they reject as by what they believe.[16]

American diplomats were also imbued with a sense of their own national exceptionalism. Even though the concept has seldom received precise formulation and comprises a rather loosely held body of ideas and attitudes, C. Vann Woodward has identified three central notions—success, prosperity, and innocence—that have informed the way Americans view their relationship to other nations. Americans have traditionally defined their historical experience as morally and materially superior to that of other peoples. This self-perception accounts for the tendency of leaders like Woodrow Wilson to project their experience universally even though it may in fact have little relevance to the actual needs or circumstances of a nation like Iran. After 1941 American diplomats set out on a nation-building crusade, confident that the instruments of their exceptionalism—democratic political institutions, capitalism, and western technology and administration—would transform a traditional Islamic society into an oasis of material prosperity and stability. Faith in the "American way" persuaded them that they would succeed in uplifting Iran where the old imperial powers like Great Britain and Russia had failed. Not until 1978 would it become obvious that the United States was no more immune than its rivals to the forces of history—but that is another story.[17]

The four factors I have identified—the desire for secure Middle Eastern oil reserves, the State Department's efforts to incorporate Iran into a new conception of American security, the department's long-term efforts to contain the Soviet Union, and the faith in American exceptionalism—are what led policymakers to assume that the United States had a "legitimate" stake in an Iranian-American alliance. But this study will show that all these factors acted as blinders that often obscured the contradictions between policies that promoted a unilateral national security system and the kind of multilateral security system that many Americans had assumed would guarantee peace in the postwar era. Because of these contradictions, the United States must share responsibility with the Soviet Union for the confrontations they had over Iran during and after World War II. Once both nations set out to incorporate Iran into their regional security systems, conflicts became inevitable.

NOTES

1. For example, John Lewis Gaddis, *Russia, the Soviet Union, and the United States* (New York, 1978) mentions Iran briefly on six pages and in Gaddis, *Strategies of Containment* (New York, 1982) Iran receives barely more attention. Adam Ulam, *The Rivals* (New York, 1971) and *Expansion and Coexistence: The History of Soviet Foreign Policy, 1971–1973* (New York, 1974) gives only cursory attention to Iran and the Soviet-American rivalry there. The problem of specialization was driven home to me when I participated in a panel on Middle East oil at the 1978 Organization of American Historians meeting. The panel included Irvine Anderson who has written extensively on Aramco, Michael Stoff who has written on the Anglo-American Oil Agreement, myself who presented a paper on oil concessions and Soviet-American conflict in Iran, and commentator Mira Wilkins, a historian interested in multinational corporations. The comments and questions soon made it clear that the majority of the audience had come to hear about oil companies and had little immediate interest in the connection between foreign oil policy and the cold war. I do not mean to be critical, only to emphasize a significant problem deriving from specialization that historians confront.

2. For the idea of the shift in American attitudes toward the Soviet Union, see John Lewis Gaddis, *The United States and the Origins of the Cold War* (New York, 1972), pp. 290–315; Daniel Yergin, *Shattered Peace* (Boston, 1977), pp. 163–92. See also Bruce Kuniholm, *The Origins of the Cold War in the Near East* (Princeton, 1980), pp. 303–4.

3. Although this summation does little justice to Kuniholm's far more complex analysis, it represents the essence of his interpretation. My differences with his views will soon be made

clear, but for other similar views see Herbert Feis, *From Trust to Terror* (New York, 1970), pp. 63–70 and 81–87; or John Spanier, *American Foreign Policy Since World War II*, 6th ed., (New York, 1973), pp. 30–32. For a more precise statement of Kuniholm's thesis, see his "Comment" in the *American Historical Review*, 89, 2 (April 1984): 385–90.

4. For examples of postwar strategic thinking about Iran, see U.S. Department of State, *The Foreign Relations of the United States*, 1946, vol. 7, p. 515 and pp. 529–32. Hereafter citations from the *Foreign Relations* series will be cited as FR followed by the year, volume, page reference, and where useful, the author, recipient, and date. See also FR, 1947, 5, pp. 509ff., the section entitled "Pentagon Talks of 1947."

5. Walter Lippmann, *U.S. War Aims* (Boston, 1944), pp. 136–37.

6. The term "legitimate" is the key to Kuniholm's defense of American policy for Iran (see "Comment," *American Historical Review*, pp. 388–89). He can only sustain it by discounting two major American initiatives—the quest for oil concessions in 1944, which with the State Department's support included Iran, and the decision to send American advisory missions to Iran and maintain these army and police missions after the war.

7. Quoted in Barry Rubin, *Paved With Good Intentions: The American Experience and Iran* (New York, 1980), p. 75.

8. Melvyn Leffler, "The American Conception of National Security and the Beginnings of the Cold War," *American Historical Review*, 89, 2 (April 1984): 346–88. I am indebted to Professor Leffler for this global view of American defense planning. It confirmed my own view that the definition of the American stake in Iran was conceived in the context of a fundamental redefinition of national security. A memorandum written by Loy Henderson in August 1945 provides one good example of the kind of strategic thinking Leffler discusses, though *Foreign Relations* and the State Department files have extensive coverage of the question of air transit rights and civil air routes. Henderson was attempting to create a policy statement that would provide a rationale for continued American involvement in Iran after the war. See FR, 1945, 8, pp. 393–400, the memorandum by Henderson, 8/23/45. The conclusions of this study support Leffler's "Reply" to Kuniholm in their exchange—see Leffler, pp. 391–400.

9. Leffler, "The American Conception of National Security," pp. 349–56.

10. Ibid., pp. 365–72.

11. For Kennan's "Long Telegram," see FR, 1946, 4, pp. 696–709. For an alternate reading see the comment on Leffler's article by John Lewis Gaddis, ibid., pp. 382–85. See also John Lewis Gaddis, *Strategies of Containment*, pp. 19–53; and Yergin, *Shattered Peace*, pp. 168–71. For NSC-7 see National Archives (NA), Modern Military Records Branch (MMRB), National Security Council Files, "The Position of the United States With Respect to Soviet-Directed World Communism," A Report to the National Security Council, NSC-7, 3/30/48, p. 1.

12. Lloyd Gardner, *Architects of Illusion* (Chicago, 1970), pp. 210–15. See also Leffler, "The American Conception of National Security," pp. 368–69. This is clearly the area where my study of American-Iranian relations differs from that of Kuniholm. I see the Americans repeatedly exaggerating the Soviet threat as a way to justify a greater American involvement than popular or congressional opinion would otherwise have supported.

13. Since I do not read Farsi, I am much indebted to Professor Ramazani for his scholarship, which makes wide use of Iranian sources. For his conceptual treatment of Iranian foreign policy, see Rouhallah Ramazani, *The Foreign Policy of Iran, 1500–1941* (Charlottesville, Va., 1966), especially pp. 1–12 and 277–310. See also Ramazani, *Iran's Foreign Policy, 1941–1973* (Charlottesville, Va., 1975). In a similar way I have been most fortunate to have access to Ervand Abrahamian's *Iran Between Two Revolutions* (Princeton, 1982). Without that book and a draft of an earlier article that Professor Abrahamian kindly shared with me I could never have made sense of Iran's factional politics in this era. Anyone interested in the Tudeh Party could find no better study.

14. The role of British Intelligence, baldly disguised as AIOC, is revealed by Kermit Roosevelt, *Countercoup* (New York, 1979), p. 3. This reference is to the first version of the book in which Roosevelt attributed the actions of British intelligence to the Anglo-Iranian Oil Company. Under threat of a lawsuit from British Petroleum, the AIOC of today, Roosevelt corrected the original deceit.

15. For a good summary of the American approach to Central America, see Walter LaFeber, *Inevitable Revolutions* (New York, 1984), pp. 19–39.

16. On the Soviet Service and the Riga Axioms, see Yergin, *Shattered Peace*, pp. 19–41.

17. C. Vann Woodward, "The Irony of Southern History," in *The Burden of Southern History* (Baton Rouge, La., 1977), pp. 187ff.

The Origins of the Iranian-American Alliance

1941–1953

1 Prelude to American Involvement

World War II drew Americans to almost every part of the globe. They fought in Arctic cold, dense equatorial jungles, Asian mountains, and North African deserts. Before the war ended once-remote parts of the world had become familiar places. It was then that Americans for the first time had significant contact with Iran. Oil as well as its strategic location along the world's ancient trade routes attracted Americans to this Persian Gulf nation. At first the war effort dictated the nature of American involvement with Iran and her people, but as the war wound down, Iran's proximity to the Soviet Union and the vast new oil fields of the Persian Gulf basin led the United States to extend its wartime role into the postwar era.

On the eve of World War II few Americans could have imagined that just four years later their government would define Iran's independence as vital to American national security. In 1941 most Americans probably could not have located Iran on a world map, much less explained its importance to the United States. Only a handful of American missionaries, travelers, oilmen, and diplomats had visited Iran. Trade between the two nations amounted to about $15 million annually. In fact, there was little in the historical traditions of either Iran or the United States to draw the two together.[1]

As Iran became important to the Allied war effort, American diplomats confronted for the first time the problem of its chronic political instability. A combination of centrifugal and centripetal forces have contributed to that pattern of internal unrest. Ethnic, religious, and cultural diversity have always threatened to break the country into autonomous tribes and provinces. Weakness at the center has often led to uprisings among the Kurds, the Azeris, nomadic tribes, and other traditionally restive minorities. Persia has a history of harsh authoritarian rule under a centralized monarchy. From Tehran the government's authority radiates to the perimeter. Persia on the eve of the feudal era fell under a government of despotic monarchs and a small landholding aristocracy. No trace of the Hellenistic world's democratic tradition softened the oppression of Iran's peasant masses. They toiled in the service of the one thousand or so families that controlled Persia's wealth and most of its arable land.[2]

Standing at a crucial crossroads on the edge of the Orient, Europe, and the Persian Gulf, Iran has long been subject to foreign pressures and invasions. In the seventh century A.D. Arab armies imposed their Islamic faith on the country. But even then the Persians revealed a capacity to retain their distinctive traditions by adopting the schismatic Shiite tradition rather than the orthodox Sunni faith of the Arab invaders. All the same, despotism did not allow the monarchs to stem the steady loss of their country's territory, particularly as the Russians under the tsars expanded southward toward the Persian Gulf. By the twentieth century the once mighty Persian Empire had shrunk to its present size of 636,000 square miles—roughly three times the area of France or equal to the American southwest, with which it shares striking similarities in climate and topography.[3]

PERSIA AND THE POWERS

In the late eighteenth century, Iranian armies briefly halted the foreign incursions. Led by Nadir Shah, they drove the intruding armies from much of their territory. Nadir Shah even managed to retrieve Persia's once-glorious peacock throne from India. But he proved himself an ineffectual ruler at home. After his death, bloody intrigue surrounded the throne for fifty years until in 1794 the Qajar tribe established the last major dynasty. Under the decadent and increasingly weak Qajars, Persia shaped the pattern of its relationships to the powers of the modern world. As a vital crossroads between east and west, it became an arena for the growing rivalry between the expanding British and Russian empires. From the reign of Peter the Great the Russians sought to impose their civilization throughout central Asia. A warm-water port on the Persian Gulf became one of their major imperial aspirations. Toward that end they employed a dual strategy of armed conquest and support for separatist movements among dissident minorities along their borders.[4]

Ever fearful of the Russian drive toward the Middle East and India, the British came to view an independent Persia as a buffer state. They relied on diplomacy and commercial concessions rather than military pressure to expand their influence there. The Imperial Bank of Persia, for example, founded in 1889 by British investors, became the country's largest financial institution. The Qajars sometimes granted such concessions to appease the imperial appetites of the British and Russians, but more often they sold foreigners control over their resources to finance the excesses of the court. Imminent bankruptcy increased their vulnerability to foreign influence. To make matters worse, the British government of India saw the tribal minorities as the key to an effective defensive perimeter against further Russian expansion. That policy had the undesired side effect of further weakening the Qajars by making the tribal leaders virtual sovereign authorities.[5]

In the late nineteenth century the British Foreign Office determined that the empire's interest would best be served if both the government and the finances of Persia were put on a sound footing. Stability would not be possible without active Russian cooperation. The formidable task of arranging an Anglo-Russian entente on Persia fell in 1887 to Sir Henry Drummond Wolff, the newly appointed minister to Tehran. Wolff approached his Russian counterpart, Prince Nikolai Dolgorukov, to see if the rivals might establish an understanding about how best to "civilize" Persia. "It seems to me," he wrote Dolgorukov, "that by establishing the prosperity of this country, and by assisting in the development of her resources, her two neighbors will interpose between their frontiers, territory which, while profiting from their support and legitimate influence, would remove the friction which is the inevitable result of uncertainty."[6]

Wolff's initiative in no way eased Anglo-Russian tensions. Factors that promote big power rivalry over Iran to this day were at work even then. And the weak and corrupt Persian government had little desire to reform itself, particularly if reform meant increased foreign influence over the nation's internal affairs. But more important, as Sir Robert Morier, British ambassador to St. Petersburg, told Wolff, the Russians saw no advantage in a strong, stable Iran:

> Russia is bent on creating an utopia of her own within the ring fence of her Asiatic annexations. . . . She believes that she thus makes herself the cynosure of all neighboring Asiatic peoples who must sooner or later gravitate towards her. The worse the condition of these neighbors, therefore, the more helpless their squalor and decadence, the nearer she is to the attainment of her goal and the less she can look with equanimity at any attempts made to endow them with the blessings of civilization otherwise than as annexes of the Russian Empire; that Persians should go on stewing in their own gravy is the credo which she opposes for your simple prayer for joint energetic action.[7]

Even if we discount Morier's traditional British suspiciousness of the Russians, his appraisal of Russian motives had relevance even during World War II. Stalin's behavior toward Iran indicated that the Soviet Union maintained tsarist Russia's determination to prevent major foreign powers from establishing a foothold on its Iranian border. Stalin, too, seemed to have it as a fundamental tenant of his foreign policy that Iran should have a friendly government oriented toward Moscow. That did not mean, as many American national security managers came to argue during the cold war, that the Soviet Union would risk armed conflict or resort to overt military means to achieve this end. Stalin seemed mindful of Lenin's adage, "If you strike steel, pull back; if you strike mush, keep going." He would be aggressive in pursuing Soviet security interests, but recognition of the realities of power would temper his ambitions.

By the early twentieth century circumstances conspired to drive the Russians toward an entente with the British. Germany's rise as a military and imperial rival threatened both England and Russia. Revolution shook the tsar's throne. And, finally, humiliation in the Russo-Japanese war made the tsar more eager to secure his borders. Seldom had the Persians faced such a growing threat to their political independence. The perils of entente coincided with a crisis for the Qajars. Corruption at court and profligate spending had bankrupted the national treasury. The shahs had already alienated the country's most valuable concessions to foreign interests. In an attempt to stave off possible partition or direct colonization, a combination of nationalists, merchants, and large landowners in 1905 launched a constitutional revolution to restrict the monarchy's powers. By 1906 they had created the 136-member National Consultative Assembly, or Majles, to give Persia a constitutional monarchy. Nationalism, not liberalism, had been the driving force behind the revolution.[8]

But reform came too late to stave off Anglo-Russian interference. In 1907 the Russians accepted a British proposal under which the two powers formally divided Persia into spheres of influence. Entente spelled disaster for the Persian constitutional movement. The Russians exploited their new influence to intervene on behalf of the monarchy and against the Majles. Persian nationalists responded to the crisis by adopting a third power strategy. That meant strengthening ties with another power whose interests potentially conflicted with both the Russians and the British. In the early nineteenth century the Persians had flirted with France as a way to offset growing Anglo-Russian pressures. Reversion to that strategy after 1907 opened the possibility of ties to the United States. Americans had yet to establish a substantial presence anywhere in the Middle East and certainly not in Persia. It was not until 1882 that the United States opened a legation in Tehran. That step came at the urging of an Ohio congressman whose sister was then serving in Persia as a Presbyterian missionary. Diplomatic ties did not significantly increase contacts between Persia and the United States.[9]

All the same the Persians in 1910 took a small step toward establishing an American third power presence. The government hired Moran Shuster to act as a financial adviser and to reform its finances. Shuster came to Persia with prior experience working in the Philippines Custom Service. He lasted barely eight months. A combination of internal political factions resistant to reform and a Russian military incursion forced the government to terminate Shuster's mission. Russian policy, as Sir Robert Morier had observed, dictated that only Russian advisers could have a role in Iran's internal affairs. But even if his mission had lasted longer, it is unlikely that Shuster could have fulfilled the Persians' hopes for American investments or attention from the State Department. Those were the days of aggressive dollar diplomacy in Latin America and China. For the United States, Persia remained a remote backwater of little potential economic, political, or strategic value.[10]

The outbreak of World War I promised at first to preserve Persia's precarious independence by diverting British and Russian attention to Europe. Instead, the world crisis confronted the Persians with even graver threats to their sovereignty. The Admiralty's decision in 1914 to rely on the Anglo-Persian concession to fuel the fleet increased Britain's security interests in Persia. Despite Persia's formal neutrality, the Russians used Azerbaijan as a base from which to attack the Ottoman Empire.

By 1918 the Bolshevik Revolution gave a new meaning to Persia's role as a British buffer state. The civil war that engulfed Russia soon spilled across the Persian border. White Russians used Persia as a staging ground for raids against the Reds. British forces violated Persian sovereignty by conducting military operations against Bolshevik forces. Lord Curzon, the British foreign secretary, acted quickly to protect what he defined as British interests, especially as the Bolsheviks' preoccupations with internal conflicts allowed the British an unprecedented opportunity for unilateral action. In 1919 Curzon imposed on the Qajars terms that made Persia a virtual British protectorate. He believed that if British advisers reformed the government and rebuilt the economy Persia could serve as a barrier against the spread of the Bolshevik contagion.[11]

Curzon ultimately failed in his attempt to bind Persia to Britain's imperial system. The Bolsheviks' strategy of renouncing the inequitable concessions under which the Russians had traditionally exploited Persia appealed to Persian nationalists who resented Curzon's assault on their nation's sovereignty. By 1921 Persian communists had established a Soviet republic in the province of Gilan. Determined to protect Persia from further Bolshevik or British intrusions, nationalists led by army Colonel Reza Khan and Sayid Zia Tabatabai staged a bloodless coup that reduced the Qajars to impotent figureheads. When Reza Khan and Tabatabai quarrelled, Ahmed Qavam became prime minister. Qavam, who had grown up at the Qajar court, had played an instrumental role in devising the constitution during the revolution from 1905 to 1906. With large landholdings in Gilan, he had reason to oppose the spread of communism into Persia.[12]

In constructing his foreign policy Qavam hoped that, in contrast to its policy in 1910, the United States would now assume a third power role. The American commitment to the "Open Door Policy" appealed to Persian nationalists who feared their country might fall under the exclusive dominion of either British imperialists or Russian revolutionaries. In 1919 the United States had denounced Curzon's agreement with the Qajars as a violation of Persian independence. During the peace conference at Versailles, President Wilson had backed the Persian bid to recover its lands lost to imperial Russia. In 1921 Qavam turned to the United States for technical assistance, loans, and investments that would make possible a national bank.[13]

The Persians in the 1920s had a resource that Americans coveted: oil. In the hills east of Khuzistan, at a place called Masjid-i-Suliaman (the Mosque of Solomon), G. B. Reynolds, the field manager for oil promoter William Knox D'Arcy, in 1907 sank the well that successfully ended years of arduous searching for Persian oil. The gusher altered the fortunes of D'Arcy, Persia, the world oil industry, and the British Empire. In 1914 the British Admiralty under Winston Churchill bought a controlling interest in the Anglo-Persian Oil Company (APOC), which had been formed to develop Knox's Persian concession. As American domestic petroleum reserves declined during the First World War, oil companies began to look abroad for concessions. As part of his approach to the United States, Qavam granted Standard Oil of New Jersey (SONJ) a fifty-year concession to produce oil in northern Persia. That same concession had once been held by a Russian national, but the Majles had never approved it, and the Bolshevik renunciation of foreign concessions seemed to eliminate any further Soviet claims. Nevertheless, both the Russians and British objected to the intrusion of Americans into an area where they both claimed a preemptive interest.[14]

New circumstances soon quieted Anglo-Russian anxieties. Because northern Persian oil had no natural outlet except through the Soviet Union, Standard Oil decided to drop the concession. Instead, it turned its attentions to neighboring Iraq, where, with State Department assistance, it forced APOC and the British government to grant a group of American companies a 25 percent share in what became Iraq Petroleum Company (IPC). Once rebuffed by Standard Oil, the Persians offered the concession to maverick oilman Harry Sinclair (also of Teapot Dome fame). Since Sinclair was then negotiating several oil deals with the Soviets, his seemed the company most likely to develop the northern oil concession. But when his Russian ventures collapsed, Sinclair lost interest in Persian oil as well. No other American company asked for the concession.[15]

Qavam meantime appeased the Bolsheviks by extending a friendly hand to the new government in Moscow. Beset by hostile forces on all sides, the Bolsheviks in 1921 gladly signed a treaty with their Persian neighbors that assured that each nation would respect the other's territorial integrity. Under Article 6 the Persians granted the Soviets the right to send troops across the border if Persia ever became the base for hostile third powers. To clarify the scope of Article 6, Soviet Ambassador Theodore Rothstein assured the Persians in a covering letter that by hostile third powers the Soviets meant counterrevolutionary forces. During World War II, Article 6 would enter repeatedly into the controversies surrounding Soviet-Iranian relations.[16] Even though he was unable to attract American support by means of an oil concession, Qavam pursued his third power strategy after 1922 by hiring an American, Arthur Millspaugh, to serve under a private contract as administrator general of finances. Millspaugh had been in the State Department as an economic adviser, with particular expertise in the oil industry. The Persians expected Millspaugh to put both government finances and the economy on a sound footing. But, like Shuster before him, Millspaugh failed to overcome domestic opposition to his reforms or to attract significant investments from American sources. For five years he struggled while every proposal ran afoul of special interests or government officials whose livelihoods depended on the traditional system of graft. Millspaugh's ultimate downfall came when he antagonized the new force in Persian politics, Reza Khan.[17]

In 1923 Reza Khan assumed control of the government. Two years later he drove out the Qajars and placed himself on the Peacock Throne, the first member of what he hoped would be a Pahlevi dynasty. An army colonel, the son of a soldier, Reza Khan burst from the ranks to establish himself as the heir to the legacy of the once glorious Persian Empire. His career in the Persian Cossack Brigade had never taken him farther from Persia than neighboring Turkey. One observer later described him as "unlettered, uncultured, and brutal." Along with an imposing physical presence and an iron will, the backing of the military, not any popular acclaim, had made possible his rise. Nationalism and despotism became the main features of his rule. He was determined to modernize Iran and thereby reduce its vulnerability to foreign powers. And in his ruthless ambition to bring Persia into the twentieth century, he also reduced the Majles to a mere rubber stamp for his policies.[18]

As war minister, Reza Khan had supported Millspaugh; as the new dictator he grew jealous of the financial adviser's power. Both men were almost totally inflexible in pursuing their goals and a clash became inevitable. Predictably, a dispute over funding for the army precipitated the final confrontation. Millspaugh, on the basis of sound financial practice, refused to appropriate additional funds for Persia's costly military. The shah sought to expand his power by building up the army. Rather than abide by Millspaugh's opposition, the shah dismissed him. And with Millspaugh's departure any further attempt to develop a third power relationship with the United States ended.[19]

Nor could it be said that Reza Shah's ascent to the Peacock Throne in any way improved Persia's relations with the British or the Russians. In 1932 the shah shook the international oil companies by threatening to cancel APOC's concession. During its twenty-five years of operation, the company had operated with almost complete autonomy. It established its own relations with neighboring tribes, it built tanker ports and pipelines without consulting the government in Tehran, and it felt no compulsion to accommodate the shah's need for more revenues. But when faced with a showdown against Reza Shah, APOC finally agreed to make some largely cosmetic revisions of its concession terms: higher royalties, an agreement to promote Iranians to higher management positions, and renaming the company the Anglo-Iranian Oil Company (AIOC) to accommodate the shah's determination to call his modernizing nation Iran.[20]

As much as he resented the British, Reza Shah viewed his northern Soviet neighbor as the more serious threat to Iran and to his aspirations for modernization. Even though Moscow in the 1930s had reduced its formal diplomatic presence by closing most of its consular posts in Iran, it maintained a large network of agents among many of the restive minorities. The Soviets also continued to demand and to receive commercial concessions that were almost all disadvantageous to Iran.[21]

After Millspaugh's departure American-Iranian relations steadily deteriorated. One low moment came in 1935 when a Maryland policeman arrested the Iranian minister in Washington for speeding. The Iranians had little appreciation of American traffic laws and viewed this incident as a grievous insult. The State Department gradually assuaged wounded Iranian pride, until a Hearst paper reported that the shah had once been a stableboy at the British legation. Reza Shah understood no more about a free press than he did about local speed limits. To vent his wrath he summarily removed his minister from Washington.[22]

At the same time he found himself in a quandary, because he wanted another nation besides Britain involved in the production of Iranian oil. Only American companies had the necessary technology and market outlets to satisfy this goal. As a result, the shah in 1937 offered the Amiranian corporation, a small American subsidiary of Seaboard Oil Company, a concession in Khorasan province. Circumstances did not favor the Amiranian venture. The depression had left world oil markets glutted and oil prices low. At the same time the major internationals—Gulf, Standard of California, Texaco, and the Iraq Petroleum Corporation partners—had made extensive new discoveries around the Persian Gulf. Among those discoveries the fields in Kuwait, Saudi Arabia, and Bahrain Island would prove to be the richest in the world. The more isolated Iranian concession could not easily compete. Finding itself at such a disadvantage, Seaboard withdrew from the concession agreement. That rebuff only added to the shah's anti-American fury. As part of a campaign to reduce foreign influence in Iran, he expropriated the properties of the American Presbyterian missions. That left the United States and Iran after 1937 with virtually no relations at all. The atmosphere was so strained that matters could scarcely get worse.[23]

The shah could afford his confrontations with the British and the Americans because in the late 1920s he had begun to establish with Germany the third power ties Iran had been seeking. The Germans could readily provide the shah with the technical and industrial resources necessary to realize his designs for modernization. They, in turn, would acquire a foreign market to help replace those they had lost at Versailles. The shah even hired a German financial expert to replace Millspaugh. The key to Iranian modernization was a viable transportation network to replace its primitive system of roads. In 1928 the shah granted the Junkers Corporation, a German firm, the exclusive concession to operate internal air routes. German technology also made possible the construction of an internal railroad network, though Iran itself generated the necessary capital and undertook the operation of the new Iranian State Railroad (ISR).[24]

The ISR was a prodigious achievement. Along its 850-mile length it crossed 4,100 bridges and two mountain ranges, and went through 224 tunnels. Economic rationality would have dictated a network that tied a Persian Gulf port into a line running from Tabriz in the northwest, where a Russian spur terminated, to Zahidan in the southeast, where a British line ended. But the shah had no desire to further integrate Iran into either the Soviet or British economic system. He therefore ordered that the ISR run in the opposite direction from the southwest at Bandar Shahpur, on the Persian Gulf, to the northeast at Bandar Shah, a port on the Caspian Sea. That decision would later plague the Allies during World War II when the ISR became the final leg of the supply route to the Soviet Union.[25]

Germans also started playing a major role in Iran's commerce and industry. German engineers helped design, build, and equip textile mills, mines, foundries, munition plants, and other construction projects. As of 1933 Germany ranked just fourth among Iran's trading partners, behind the Soviet Union, Great Britain, and the United States. By 1937 only trade with the Soviet Union exceeded that with Germany. Between 1939 and 1941 Germany surpassed the Soviet Union as well. Reza Shah openly admired German industrial and military efficiency. He found, too, that Adolph Hitler and the Nazis suited his political tastes. Mohammad Reza Pahlevi, his son and political heir, justified his father's pro-Nazi sympathies as an application of Iran's third power strategy. Certainly he was correct, though disingenuous, in 1961 when he argued that "Germany had no conspicuous record of imperialism in Iran; she had seldom interfered in our internal affairs; and she was opposed to the two big inperialist powers who had for so long plagued us. . . ." By 1939 the community of German technicians and businessmen in Iran included a well-established espionage network.[26]

The Molotov-Ribbentrop pact of 1939 enormously complicated Iran's relations with the world powers. Although Reza Khan could not have known that in negotiating the pact Molotov had staked out a Soviet claim to border regions "in the direction of the Persian Gulf," the Iranians had always understood that the Russian drive for security and a warm-water Persian Gulf port posed the greatest single threat to their continued independence. And the Soviet Union's efforts to secure its borders through the absorption of the Baltic states and the partition of Poland boded ill for the shah's efforts to remain outside the Soviet orbit. But if the shah responded by gravitating toward the Berlin-Moscow axis, he risked provoking British military action, since the Molotov-Ribbentrop pact had joined two rivals whose ambitions clearly conflicted with British interests in Iran.[27]

OVERTURES TO THE UNITED STATES

The outbreak of war in Europe led Iran to look to the United States for assistance. The combination of formal U.S. neutrality and its distance from the European conflict made an American ally particularly attractive. Reza Shah understood that substantial inducements would be necessary to raise the level of American concern. He had already acceded to President Roosevelt's request in 1939 that he reopen Iran's legation in Washington. His government removed another potential irritant by agreeing to pay for the recently expropriated Presbyterian mission schools. The newly appointed minister to Washington opened preliminary discussions for a trade agreement as well as for financial credits, airplanes, and technical advisers.[28]

An oil concession appeared the most promising way to attract greater American involvement in Iran while at the same time reducing Iran's financial dependence on AIOC. In the fall of 1939 the Iranian government began discussions with Standard Oil of New Jersey about a possible oil concession. News of the negotiations provoked an immediate objection from the Soviet Union. The Iranian prime minister thus announced that "under no circumstance would the Iranian government consider granting the Standard Oil Company of New Jersey a concession which included an area of northern Iran. . . ." The Soviets soon made it clear that in fact they opposed any American concession anywhere in Iran. By 1940, however, the war had so disrupted the world oil markets that a new Middle East concession held little attraction. Despite signals from Iran in May 1940 that the matter might still be open, Standard Oil declined further discussions.[29]

That episode, no matter how incidental it might have seemed at the time, had important implications for future Soviet-American relations involving Iran. While the Iranian government obviously intended to use oil to secure an American third power role, Soviet leaders did not want to see the United States gaining influence near their borders. To Moscow, any concession in northern Iran, even a private commercial one, was unacceptable. Wallace Murray of the Near East Division of the State Department understood full well the connection between oil concessions and a third power strategy:

> In our opinion the Iranian government is thoroughly anxious to have American business interests acquire a stake in Iran which would call forth a corresponding interest from the United States government in the welfare and continued independence of Iran. In other words, the Iranians are eager to use us, if possible, to offset Russian domination.

Such a detached analysis of the interplay of politics and oil was possible in July 1940, when the United States had ample petroleum reserves in the western hemisphere. Three years later, as American oil reserves dwindled, the State Department would no longer maintain such a clear distinction between its political objectives and the need to secure new sources of petroleum.[30]

Wallace Murray, who headed the Near East Division, would soon emerge as the primary architect of a *de facto* Iranian-American alliance. His fondness for Iran had developed when he had served a tour in Tehran in the 1920s, during the era of Millspaugh's rise and fall. He was thus one of the few Americans in or out of government who had even a passing familiarity with that remote land. By 1941 he had become an influential figure in the State Department. In addition to his duties in the Near East Division, he served as political adviser to Secretary of State Cordell Hull. A large and intense man, Murray ran his division like an overbearing schoolmaster. His colleagues learned that he read practically every cable that came in or left. He had fixed opinions on many subjects and frequently gave detailed instructions even on routine matters. Despite his foibles, his colleagues admired him for his integrity and his ready grasp of diplomacy.

From the Iranian perspective, Murray was a worthy advocate within the American government. He believed the United States should support the shah's aspirations to modernize his country. More important, he shared the Iranians' mistrust of both the Soviet Union and Great Britain. He saw an American third power role in the area as being beneficial both to Iran and to the United States. But like so many westerners drawn to the Middle East or the Orient, he failed to see that the build-up of advisers, commercial ties, national security interests, and political involvement might earn for the United States the same resentment Iranians had so freely showered upon the Russians and the British. The United States could not simultaneously grow in influence and remain a third power. It would inevitably be drawn into the pattern of big power rivalry.[31]

As the United States and Iran worked to repair their diplomatic relations, the German invasion of the Soviet Union forced a dramatic revision of big power alliances. Great Britain immediately pledged to support the Russians' struggle to repel Hitler's forces. Both powers now found the presence of German nationals in Iran a direct threat to their vital interests. It was no secret among foreign observers in Tehran that two German agents, Fritz Myer and Roman Gamotta, had organized an extensive fifth column apparatus throughout Iran. German agents might readily slip across the Azerbaijan border to sabotage the Baku oil fields or threaten AIOC facilities in Khuzistan. The presence of potential German saboteurs became even more intolerable when Iran became a major corridor for supplies from Britain and the United States to the Soviet Union.[32]

Reza Shah had made no secret of his admiration for Hitler and Germany nor of his distaste for both his predatory northern neighbor and the imperialist British. When the British tried to arrest the Mufti of Jerusalem for broadcasting anti-British diatribes to the Middle East over German radio, he fled to sanctuary in Iran. In Iraq, a German-backed coup led by Rashid Ali briefly captured the government, until British troops regained control in May 1941. Ali and his followers, who were dubbed by the British "Ali and the Forty Thieves," escaped to safety in neighboring Iran. In the face of Great Britain's repeated military setbacks, the shah became openly contemptuous. Nazi sympathizers dominated the Iranian Army. Who in the dark days of 1941 could actually blame the shah for anticipating a quick Nazi victory in Russia and Europe, especially when many Americans had similar expectations?[33]

By July 1941 the shah faced a severe dilemma. The Russians and British had grown increasingly insistent that he expel most of the two to three thousand German nationals in Iran. Yet the Iranian economy now depended on German technical advisers and trade. To force the Germans out meant potential disaster, because the Soviet Union and Great Britain were in no position to compensate for the loss of these German resources. Faced with an impossible choice, the shah followed the traditional course of Iranian leaders under pressure from foreign powers: he procrastinated. As he clung stubbornly to his policy of formal neutrality, the British and the Russians became more adamant that four-fifths of the Germans had to be out, no later than mid-September.[34]

Failure to placate the Russians and the British led the Iranians to renew their bid for American support. On 11 August 1941 Mohammad Shayesteh, Iranian minister in Washington, told Wallace Murray "his country would certainly expect to receive moral support and even material assistance from this country." Murray offered the Iranian minister no hope that as of August 1941 the State Department had any intention of acting as a third power in Iran. The Roosevelt administration firmly believed that the defeat of Nazi Germany was vital to the security of the United States and the western hemisphere. Moreover, the British Foreign Office had carefully cultivated American support for its campaign to drive the Nazis out of Iran. At each step British diplomats had assured the State Department that they would guarantee Iran's sovereignty and territorial integrity, while soliciting similar guarantees from the Soviet Union.[35]

The shah had failed to move with sufficient dispatch to retrieve a deteriorating position. On 25 August Russian and British forces in concert swept into Iran. The Russian Army attacked key provincial towns across the north. Within a matter of hours their troops had occupied Tabriz and Pahlevi in Azerbaijan and Meshed in Khorasan. The Russian Air Force gave some Iranians a frightening introduction to modern warfare when its planes bombed cities in Gilan and Azerbaijan, as well as the outskirts of Tehran. The bombs created pandemonium among army units whose officers deserted as rapidly as their troops. Only the British forces commanded from India by General Archibald Wavell met any significant opposition.[36]

Within forty-eight hours the Iranian Army's vaunted "life and death struggle" had ended in a humiliating rout. The cabinet of Prime Minister Ali Mansur resigned and his successor, Ali Foroughi, immediately announced Iran's surrender. His communiqué acknowledged that it was hopeless for Iran to fight on. The invaders had been so efficient that the Anglo-Iranian Oil Company managers had continued operations without serious interruption. Once Foroughi announced the cease-fire, Moscow and London issued immediate guarantees that neither power would infringe on Iran's sovereignty or territorial integrity. Both pledged to withdraw, once the Nazi danger had been eliminated. That promise proved to be sufficiently elastic to stretch over the next four and a half years.[37]

The Anglo-Soviet occupation posed a danger to Iran more grave than either the entente of 1907 or the foreign intrusions of World War I. Even if Foroughi's government managed to negotiate a satisfactory treaty with the occupying powers, the Iranians believed more than ever that they needed an American third power presence. But the United States government to which they turned for help was in no position to render significant assistance. It lacked the foreign policy instruments, the intention, and the desire to offer the support Iran sought. The State Department did not even have a desk officer for Iran until 1942. The seven people in the Near East Division had, in addition to Iran, the responsibility for North Africa, India, and the remainder of the Middle East. The United States diplomatic apparatus in Iran had few resources for political reporting or analysis. The legation in Tehran had a staff of three to assist the minister. Two Americans operated a consulate office there and a single consul ran an office in Tabriz. That was the whole of it. And save for a few people like Wallace Murray, the State Department could find almost no one in or out of government who even knew where Iran was, much less who had the background to help formulate an intelligent policy. Nor could the department turn to American citizens in Iran. Only a handful of missionaries remained after Reza Shah's xenophobic campaigns.[38]

The heavy burdens thrust on the U.S. legation in Tehran in 1941 threatened to overwhelm the American Minister, Louis Dreyfus. For him the post had been another minor assignment in a relatively undistinguished Foreign Service career. Though Dreyfus had always worked hard and brought a measure of idealism to his posts, he did not have the temperament to manage the political pressures that now swamped the legation. He shared with Wallace Murray a concern for reforming Iran and a distaste for the ways in which the British and Russians had exploited the country. Like Murray, he was determined to promote closer Iranian-American ties. At the same time, he had difficulty accommodating his middle-class, Anglo-Saxon values to Iran's culture. The graft and corruption endemic to local Iranian politics offended his progressive notions of efficient government. He once proposed to attack the defects of the Iranian character by requesting a boy scout leader who could mold Iran's young men. His wife Grace earned much goodwill by running a clinic in one of Tehran's slum districts. During the war diplomatic correspondence between Washington and Tehran increased almost 1000 percent; the staff increased too, but not quickly enough to help Dreyfus.[39]

In the early years of the war, the State Department often took its cues on Iranian affairs from the British Foreign Office, except when disagreements arose or a vital American interest was at stake. Under the circumstances, it made good sense for the Americans to rely on their far more experienced British counterparts. The Foreign Office had been involved in the region for well over a century. In that time the British had established a wide range of both official and informal channels through which they operated. Compared to the lonely American consulate in Tabriz, for example, Great Britain maintained twelve consular offices in Iran's important provincial cities. The Imperial Bank of Iran, controlled by British financial interests, had branches in fourteen cities. Every city that had a branch bank also had a chapter of the Anglo-Iranian Relief Association, financed largely by the British government.[40]

During the war, the British had expanded their already extensive networks. To manage the distribution of scarce supplies and civilian goods throughout the Middle East, they had created the United Kingdom Commercial Corporation and the Middle East Supply Center. If Iran needed trucks, foodstuffs, or spare parts, it had to rely on such agencies to provide them. In Tehran, Victory House disseminated propaganda and published a daily newspaper. The Anglo-Iranian Institute and Church Missionary Society extended their good works into education and medical care. Over its thirty-five years of operation, Anglo-Iranian Oil Company had evolved a far-flung and efficient operation that went well beyond the production of oil. AIOC alone employed over thirty thousand Iranians. Only the Iranian government had more employees. The company assigned district managers to all cities and Iranian managers for the large towns. It maintained closer ties with many tribes than did the Iranian government.

British diplomats were generally far better equipped for service in Iran than were the Americans. No member of the U.S. legation spoke Persian, and few Americans in Iran even spoke French, the foreign language favored by the local elite. By contrast, Sir Reader Bullard, who became British minister in 1939, was an amateur Arabist. He knew two dead and eight modern languages including Farsi (Persian) and Russian. His staff included the noted Persian scholar Anne Lampton. When he assumed his post in Tehran in 1939, he had had almost thirty years of service in the Middle East and Balkans already, as well as four years in the Soviet Union. Historian Roger Louis has compared Bullard's view of Soviet affairs to that of George Kennan in both its breadth and its psychological and moral analogies.

In his dogged efforts to promote his country's interests Bullard generally managed to equate Britain's policies and Iran's greater good. He had no animosity toward the Persians, but neither did he hold much regard for their intelligence or character. "They are untruthful, backbiters, undisciplined, incapable of unity, without a plan," he once wrote the foreign secretary. Like the members of the State Department's Soviet Service he saw the Russians driven by a messianic communist ideology toward conquest. That persuaded him they would use any means to draw Persia into their orbit and, as a consequence, he was never above heavy-handed meddling when he thought the exercise of his office would keep Iran out of Moscow's predatory grasp. For that reason, Bullard actively encouraged Iran's efforts to establish an American third power presence.[41]

Despite its proximity to Iran, the Soviet Union had no extensive diplomatic or commercial presence there. Under Stalin, it was impossible for Russians to live so freely abroad. The Soviet foreign policy apparatus in Iran was wholly manned and operated by the government. Contacts between the Russian and the British and American legations remained infrequent, even during the war. Washington and London found it more satisfactory to deal directly with Moscow on many issues affecting Iran. In any case Stalinist controls virtually guaranteed that NKVD agents, tightly reined from Moscow, dominated the Soviet diplomatic corps. In the 1930s Stalin had closed most of the Soviet Union's consular posts in Iran.

Even with such self-imposed restrictions, the Soviet Union could exert great influence on Iran's internal affairs. The two nations, after all, shared a 1,300-mile border. Ethnic similarities that transcend such human conventions as political boundaries made it simple for Soviet agents to slip across the border undetected. After World War I the Soviet Union operated an extensive underground network in Iran concentrated largely among disaffected minorities like the Kurds and Azeris. Some Iranian dissidents hostile to the shah or the British acted as Stalinist agents. Political refugees from the repression of the communist uprising in Gilan and Azerbaijan in 1921 received indoctrination in the Soviet Union before returning to Iran. A variety of commercial concessions and trade agreements gave the Soviet Union considerable economic leverage.[42]

During World War II, the occupation forces of the Red Army became a powerful instrument for disseminating propaganda and for interference in Iran's domestic affairs. Under the encouraging eye of Soviet officials, Azeri separatists could publicly vent their wrath against the Tehran government. The Russians also promoted the growth of the pro-Moscow Tudeh Party. Most Iranian political parties were little more than factions gathered around notable individuals. The Tudeh thus had the advantage of being practically the only well-organized party. It generally followed the lead of the Soviet embassy in adopting its program. The embassy itself had the capacity to conduct clandestine operations. As a result, the Soviet Union did not need as extensive an apparatus as the British in order to wield a comparable influence.[43]

The United States in September 1941 had almost no means, much less any substantial reason, to compete with the Soviet Union or Great Britain over Iran. There was no tradition of Iranian-American friendship, nor had the United States established consequential economic or commercial interests there. Still, a number of far-ranging factors embedded in the traditions of American foreign policy as well as wartime circumstances determined that the United States would come to play a dominant role throughout the Middle East and especially in Iran. In the 1930s

American oil companies had acquired extensive Middle East oil concessions. Oilmen had begun to recognize that the region would supersede the western hemisphere as the center of the world's petroleum industry. The Roosevelt administration recognized the importance of the region's oil to American security when it acceded to the pressure of several international oil companies to assume part of their burden for the financial support of King Ibn Saud of Saudi Arabia.[44]

The ease with which the Nazis conquered Europe and threatened to extend their dominion into the Middle East, Africa, and Asia began to shake Americans out of their sense of free security. But it took Pearl Harbor to force them to recognize their interdependence with the rest of the world. The two ocean moats that had once seemed unbridgeable no longer guaranteed an adequate defense against the contagion of modern war and new weapons of destruction. As the war progressed and the weakness of the British Empire became more evident, American leaders came to understand that they could no longer count on their English cousins and the Royal Navy to maintain peace in what once seemed remote areas of the world. Clearly, events in the Middle East could directly affect the security of the United States. And if not the Nazis, another rival like the Soviet Union might be all too eager to bring Iran and the Middle East into its orbit. As a result, the State Department began to pursue policies that would make the United States the dominant power in the region. In that process lay the roots of the Iranian-American alliance.

NOTES

1. In this work I use Iran and Persia, Iranian and Persian, interchangeably. Persians have always known their country as Iran. It was the Greeks who first called the country after Fars, a province of ancient Persia. The Greek tradition remained common practice in the west until the 1930s when Reza Shah asked foreign governments to adopt "Iran" as the official name. The United States government did so, while the British persisted at least in internal communications in using "Persia." On Iran's relations to the great powers prior to World War II, see Rouhallah Ramazani, *The Foreign Policy of Iran, 1500–1941* (Charlottesville, Va., 1966). A less valuable source that indicates the level of American involvement is George Lenczowski, *Russia and the West in Iran, 1918–1948* (Ithaca, NY, 1949).

2. R. Ghirshman, *Iran* (Middlesex, England, 1961), pp. 206–341. See also Peter Avery, *Modern Iran* (London, 1965), pp. 24–30 and Ramazani, *The Foreign Policy of Iran, 1500–1941*, pp. 25–32.

3. Ghirshman, *Iran*, pp. 289–318. William S. Haas, *Iran* (New York, 1946), pp. 70–91. On the geography of Iran see U. B. Fisher, "Physical Geography," *The Cambridge History of Iran*, vol. 1 (Cambridge, 1972), pp. 3–32, 60–110. For a superficial view with good pictures, see William Graves, "Iran: Desert Miracle," *National Geographic*, 147, 1 (January 1975): 2–47. See also Nikki Keddi, *Roots of Revolution: An Interpretive History of Modern Iran* (New Haven, 1981), especially Ch. 1.

4. Ramazani, *Foreign Policy of Iran*, pp. 19–23 and pp. 33–80. The best source on the Anglo-Russian rivalry is Firuz Kazemzadeh, *Russia and Britain in Persia, 1864–1914* (New Haven, 1968).

5. Kazemzadeh, *Russia and Britain in Persia*, pp. 185ff.

6. Ibid., pp. 186 and 189.

7. Ibid., p. 225. This argument is obviously crucial to any analysis of Soviet-American relations. Historians disagree as sharply as policymakers about Soviet motives. I side with Kazemzadeh and Adam Ulam among others who argue that the Soviets are more often realists than ideologues in the conduct of their foreign policy.

8. Ervand Abrahamian, *Iran Between Two Revolutions* (Princeton, 1982), pp. 81–101.

9. Ramazani, *Foreign Policy of Iran*, pp. 81–86. Amin Banani, *The Modernization of Iran* (Stanford, Calif., 1966), pp. 195–212.

10. Abraham Yeselson, *U.S.–Persian Diplomatic Relations, 1883–1921* (New Brunswick, N.J., 1956), pp. 104–24. Kazemzadeh, *Russia and Britain in Persia* p. 409. Abrahamian, *Iran*

Between Two Revolutions, pp. 102–110; see also Morgan Shuster, *The Strangling of Persia* (New York, 1912).

11. Ramazani, *Foreign Policy of Iran,* pp. 139–67.

12. Abrahamian, *Iran Between Two Revolutions,* pp. 112–18.

13. Ibid., pp. 116–21; Ramazani, *Foreign Policy of Iran,* pp. 203–25.

14. Ramazani, *Foreign Policy of Iran,* p. 205. See also Lenczowski, *Russia and the West in Iran,* pp. 83–85. For a readable brief account of the establishment of the Anglo-Iranian Oil Company concession see Leonard Mosley, *Power Play* (London, 1973), pp. 14–28. See also E. P. Elwell-Sutton, *Persian Oil: A Study in Power Politics* (London, 1955).

15. Mosley, *Power Play,* pp. 48–50, 89–90. Anthony Sampson, *The Seven Sisters* (New York, 1975), pp. 70–103.

16. Ramazani, *Foreign Policy of Iran,* pp. 234–40. See also Lenczowski, *Russia and the West,* pp. 83–85. He also includes a text of the treaty in an appendix.

17. Ramazani, *Foreign Policy of Iran,* p. 211. Abrahamian, *Iran Between Two Revolutions,* p. 131. For an obviously biased, but interesting, account, see Arthur Millspaugh, *The American Task in Persia* (New York, 1925).

18. Abrahamian, *Iran Between Two Revolutions,* pp. 118–49.

19. Ibid., p. 143.

20. Mosley, *Power Play,* pp. 91–93. A good general study of a more scholarly orientation is Benjamin Shwadran, *The Middle East, Oil and the Great Powers* (New York, 1954). It was at this time that the State Department adopted "Iran," though characteristically British diplomats persisted in calling the country "Persia."

21. A fascinating and little-known source on the early development of Soviet Intelligence and its Middle East operations is George Agabekov, *OGPU–The Russian Secret Terror* (New York, 1931), pp. 112–80. Agabekov might be dismissed as an unreliable refugee except that later revelations confirmed many of his statements about the personnel and structure of OGPU. On Persian operations he wrote, "The origins of a secret service of Ogpu in Persia was now complete; it could take the place of legal service in case of the rupture of diplomatic relations or war. Persia thus became the center of espionage into India; Teheran became a second Berlin, for Berlin, you know, is the Ogpu center for Europe." Ibid., p. 178.

22. On the speeding episode see Bruce Hardcastle, "First Time Farce," *The New Republic,* 22 December 1979, pp. 17–19. While Hardcastle offers an amusing account of this incident, he recognizes fully its more consequential implications, particularly the disproportionate outpouring of Iranian nationalism in the face of an otherwise minor incident. American diplomats might have recognized then the potential Iran had for sudden explosive shifts in political attitude. See also FR, 1936, 3, pp. 342 and 356.

23. On the shah's oil policy, see Lenczowski, *Russia and the West,* pp. 84–85.

24. On the shah's relations with Germany and the German role in modernizing Iran, see Ramazani, *Foreign Policy of Iran,* pp. 277–88. Ramazani points out that the Shah hired a German to replace Millspaugh. See also Lenczowski, *Russia and the West,* pp. 152–57.

25. A good account of the construction of the railroad is in Richard Pfau, "The United States and Iran, 1941–1947, Origins of Partnership," (Ph.D. dissertation, University of Virginia, 1975), pp. 12–13. Pfau, too, sees this as the formative stage of a growing American involvement. He gives more attention to supply operations and sees less significance in the oil politics than I do.

26. Mohammed Reza Shah Pahlevi, *Mission For My Country* (London, 1961) p. 66.

27. Jane Degras, ed., *Soviet Documents on Foreign Affairs,* v.3, 1938–1941 (London, 1951), pp. 477–78. See also J. C. Hurewitz, *Diplomacy in the Near and Middle East* (Princeton, 1956), 2: 228–31, which includes the text of this document.

28. FR, 1939, 3, pp. 342ff.

29. FR, 1940, 3, pp. 660–62. See also U.S. Department of State, Decimal File, Record Group 59, National Archives, Washington, [hereafter cited as SD, file number/date], 891.6363 Standard Oil/430, 100, 5/5/40.

30. SD 891.6363/Standard Oil, 7/5/40, Wallace Murray to Sumner Welles.

31. My information on Wallace Murray came from a series of interviews and correspondence with Eugene Rostow, John Jernegan, Loy Henderson, and Charles Bohlen. See also William Roger Louis, *The British Empire in the Middle East* (New York and London, 1984), pp. 66–68. Louis is an excellent source for identification of British diplomats.

32. On German espionage, see B. Shulze-Holthus, *Daybreak in Iran* (London, 1954).

33. Rouhallah Ramazani, *Iran's Foreign Policy, 1941–1973* (Charlottesville, Va., 1975), pp. 25–28.

34. For American observations of the pressures on Iran, see FR, 1941, 3, pp. 383–97. See also Pfau, "The United States and Iran," p. 18.

35. Ibid., 393–94 and pp. 406–07. Louis Dreyfus believed that the British and Russians had exaggerated the German danger to create a pretext for their invasion. All the same he supported the invasion as necessary for the Anglo-Soviet cause.

36. On the invasion, see Ramazani, *Iran's Foreign Policy, 1941–1971,* pp. 30–33. Lenczowski, *Russia and the West,* pp. 168–70. On the actual military operations, see Pfau, "The United States and Iran," pp. 25–29 and Mosley, *Power Play,* pp. 131–36.

37. On the negotiations covering the occupation, see Ramazani, *Iran's Foreign Policy,* pp. 35–39.

38. Much of my information about the Near East Division and diplomatic apparatus in Tehran came from letters and interviews, particularly John Jernegan, letter to author, February 1972. See also Bruce Kuniholm, *The Origins of the Cold War in the Near East* (Princeton, 1980), pp. 155–57.

39. Jernegan provided some of this information, but it is also derived from reading his extensive communications to the State Department, a good sampling of which can be found in *Foreign Relations.* On the boy scout request see FR, 1942, 4, p. 239. Dreyfus later received some vindication when Loy Henderson took over at the Near East Division. Though his depiction of Bullard was inaccurate, Henderson wrote to Under Secretary Dean Acheson:

> Those of us who have been following events in the Middle East are inclined to agree that Bullard, the former British ambassador in Iran, is to large extent personally responsible for present developments [the postwar Iranian crisis with the USSR] because he laid the groundwork for present Soviet activity. This was foreseen by our former Minister to Iran, Mr. Dreyfus, who differed strongly with Bullard. Mr. Dreyfus persistently tried to warn of the danger of Bullard's policies. Bullard, however, was backed fully by Churchill and Dreyfus received no support from high sources in this government. When the British and American Legations in Teheran were raised to embassies, the British Government made Bullard ambassador. Our government made Dreyfus, who events have shown was right, minister to Iceland and brought in a new ambassador.

SD 891.00/7–3046, Henderson to Acheson. Henderson seemed unaware that Bullard had alerted Dreyfus to the dangers of Soviet ambitions in northern Iran. The two had differed largely over how to achieve stability in Iran.

40. "Machinery of British Control," Research and Analysis Branch (R&A), Record Group 226, Office of Strategic Services (OSS), Iran File, L50737, 12/15/44. All OSS files are available at the National Archives through the Modern Military Records Branch (MMRB) or State Department and are hereafter cited as OSS, file number, and date. In its conclusion the report suggested that "the British have, during the past 25 years, built up an unequalled organization for the collection and coordination of information about every aspect of Iran. The personnel mentioned . . . associate closely together, working through the banks and consulate."

41. To gain a fuller view of Bullard and the formation of his values, see his autobiography, Sir Reader Bullard, *The Camels Must Go* (London, 1961). Jernegan also provided much useful background on Bullard, with whom he became friendly after attending weekly staff meetings at the British Embassy and riding with Bullard to the Moscow Foreign Ministers Conference in October 1943 in the back of an unheated DC–3. See also Louis, *The British Empire in the Middle East,* pp. 59–62 for a useful analysis of Bullard's views.

42. Agabekov, *OGPU,* 112–80. Ramazani, *Foreign Policy of Iran* and Abrahamian, *Iran Between Two Revolutions* provide assessments of Soviet activities in Iran.

43. Anyone interested in the Tudeh Party should see Abrahamian, *Iran Between Two Revolutions,* pp. 281–418 for a thorough study. See also Sephir Zabih, *The Communist Movement in Iran* (Berkeley, 1966), p. 97 and Richard Cottom, *Nationalism in Iran* (Pittsburgh, 1964), pp. 118–26.

44. The best source for U.S. foreign oil policy is Michael B. Stoff, *Oil, War, and National Security* (New Haven, 1980) pp. 1–33.

2 A Third Power Role in Iran

From 1941 to 1943 the war effort, more than any other factor, shaped the Roosevelt administration's policy for Iran. It was Germany's invasion of the Soviet Union that triggered the Anglo-Soviet occupation of Iran, which, in turn, led the Iranian government to intensify its efforts to gain American support. But the State Department did not make substantial commitments until Iran's stability became critical to the war effort. The growing American involvement in Iranian affairs did not at first reflect any long-term objectives, any scheme to undermine the British, acquire valuable raw materials, or capture new markets. American policy evolved as the State Department took steps to ease the burdens of the occupation and of Allied operation of the supply route.

All the same, a widely recognized set of interests and assumptions influenced State Department policymakers as they began to establish a stronger American presence in Iran. Oil defined the dominant American interest in the Middle East region. The desire to protect access to that resource would make closer ties to Iran seem crucial. At the same time the war did little to moderate deep-seated American anticommunism and mistrust of the Soviet Union. Even if the war had made the Russians and Americans allies, most members of the State Department saw a need to contain possible postwar Soviet expansionism. A stable Iran would constitute a front-line barrier. In addition, faith in American exceptionalism persuaded many policymakers that the United States could transcend the self-serving imperialism that had previously shaped Iran's relations to the great powers. Finally, State Department policy for Iran served an institutional imperative. Increased American involvement in Iran established a major wartime role for diplomacy.[1]

IDEOLOGICAL ROOTS

From the moment the Bolsheviks seized power in 1917, most Americans viewed the Soviet government with a mixture of morbid fascination, fear, and loathing. Secretary of State Robert Lansing spoke for many conservatives when he said, "Bolshevism is the most hideous and monstrous thing the human mind has ever conceived." The circumstances under which the Bolsheviks seized power fixed that hostile view almost in perpetuity. Americans believed that the revolutionaries had betrayed the Allies and killed a liberal democratic government in its infancy. Soon after the war the Soviet leaders had established the Comintern to spread the plague of Bolshevism wherever chaos and unrest threatened. Perhaps worst of all, the atheist Bolsheviks suppressed organized religion, which the American people have always seen as one basis of a legitimate civil order. In 1920 Secretary of State Bainbridge Colby turned the initial anti-Bolshevik prejudice into a rationale for nonrecognition: "We cannot recognize, hold official relations with, or give friendly reception to the agents of a government which is determined and bound to conspire against our institutions."[2]

In the 1920s a group of American career diplomats began to shape those general attitudes into a more sophisticated analysis of Soviet behavior. Associating their views with the city in which they developed, historian Daniel Yergin has identified the "Riga Axioms," a series of ideas about the motives and objectives of Soviet policy. The axioms encompassed four central ideas: that the Soviets were committed to worldwide expansion and communist domination, that Soviet leaders were both fanatical ideologues and calculating strategists, that immorality and indifference to the value of human life made them untrustworthy, and finally, that Americans must be ever vigilant and tough in dealing with such a foe.

Those axioms are worth noting in this study of American-Iranian relations because Loy Henderson and George Kennan, who became central figures in this group, the Soviet Service, both played critical roles in defining a U.S. policy for Iran. Their analysis of Soviet behavior heavily colored the American understanding of events there during the war and the early cold war years. They warned that the United States had to contain what they perceived as a Soviet threat to Anglo-American interests in the Middle East—Kennan at first from the embassy in Moscow, then in 1946 as the author of the famous "Long Telegram," and finally from the policy planning staff. Loy Henderson was the postwar head of the Middle East Division before he became ambassador to Iran in 1951.

The assumption that Soviet leaders were committed to a doctrine of worldwide revolution and expansionism led the Soviet Service to see Bolshevism as an immediate threat to nations like Iran, that shared a common border with the USSR, and a more remote, but no less real, threat to countries as distant as the United States. Although they were Marxist ideologues, Soviet leaders were also cynical political realists with a master plan for world conquest and fully elaborated strategies to achieve that goal. In 1936 Henderson warned that the Soviets had before them "a series of definite objectives."[3]

What made the Soviets so dangerous from the perspective of the Soviet Service was their complete lack of morality or humane values. By the late 1930s Stalin's purges had hardened their conviction that the Soviet government was dominated by thugs, atheists, murderers, and other criminal types eager to profit from chaos and human suffering. George Kennan once remarked after seeing Stalin that "an unforewarned visitor would never guess what depths of calculation, ambition, love of power, jealousy, cruelty, and sly vindictiveness lurked behind this unpretentious facade." Kennan and his colleagues believed that for such simultaneously paranoid and aggressive leaders, warfare was constant and attack was a form of self-defense. All around the Soviet borders Soviet leaders saw hostile forces seeking to destroy their revolution and the nation.[4]

The Soviet Service concluded from these assumptions that the United States could never afford to drop its guard. It had to be prepared to meet force with counterforce. Even if they were momentarily frustrated, the Soviets would continue their inexorable movement toward conquest. The United States would survive only if it proved equally resolute. Nor could the United States ever hope to achieve a community of interests or a spirit of cooperation with the Soviet Union, as Franklin Roosevelt would attempt during World War II. "Approaches by Britain and the United States must be interpreted here as a sign of weakness," Ambassador Laurence Steinhardt wrote Loy Henderson from Moscow in late 1940. "As you know from your own experience, the moment these people get it into their heads we are 'appeasing them, or making up to them or need them;' they immediately stop being cooperative."[5]

It is not difficult to understand why the Soviet Service held such extreme views. The members of this service were generally conservatives who valued morality, religious sensibility, decorum, free enterprise capitalism, property, and order—precisely those things that the Bolsheviks repudiated. In dealing with the Soviet government they experienced directly its disregard for traditional niceties of diplomacy and suffered repeated indignities on matters both trivial and consequential. Still, nothing prepared them for the horrors of the purges. "So prolonged and incessant were the hammer-blow impressions, each more outrageous and heartrending than the other—that the effect was never to leave me," George Kennan recalled. "Its imprint on my political judgment was one that would place me at odds with official thinking in Washington for at least a decade thereafter."[6] And during Roosevelt's presidency, the Soviet Service could not be sure that its views were properly appreciated, because its members, along with the entire State Department, were relegated to secondary diplomatic roles. Their sometimes strident tone may have reflected an awareness that their warnings were not being heard.

More than most presidents, Franklin Roosevelt directed his administration's foreign policy. He mistrusted the conservatives who ran the shop down at old "Foggy Bottom." For important missions he preferred to send personal emissaries rather than rely on the traditional State Department chain of command. His decisions to do so were conceptual as well as political. He wanted representatives like Harry Hopkins, Averell Harriman, and Sumner Welles who were loyal to him or shared his views. Once he had decided to aid the Soviet Union, the assumptions of the Soviet Service would have been too confining for his purposes. As John Lewis Gaddis observed, Roosevelt concentrated "on the congruities of interests between the United States and the Soviet Union, not differences of principle."[7] The Soviet Service largely reversed that order. Without shared principles, they argued, the United States could find no legitimate basis for shared interests or for mutual accommodations. To Soviet Service members, Roosevelt's efforts to cooperate with Stalin in the forging of a postwar peace were at best naive, at worst dangerous to American interests.

The State Department did not passively accept its diminished policymaking status under Roosevelt. American diplomats chafed when decisions based on short-term military necessity ignored long-term political consequences. Officials in the State Department realized that an active policy in areas like Latin America and the Middle East allowed them to maintain some influence over foreign policy, so long as they could persuade other agencies that initiatives in those regions benefited the war effort.

The application of a "government politics" model might help to explain the bureaucratic infighting that accompanied the early phases of wartime American policy for Iran. This model, as described by Graham Allison, assumes that foreign policy decisions generally reflect bargaining among individuals and agencies. Decisions result most often from compromise rather than from clear-cut choices. Individual players may be as much or more preoccupied with advancing their personal and organizational agendas as with achieving some optimal policy outcome. When conflict arises, as it almost inevitably does, the contending parties seek to reach a consensus. In that process the political skill of the particular players may be as crucial as the policies or organizations they represent in determining the final policy outcome.[8]

In its efforts to promote American involvement in Iran, the State Department most often found itself at odds with the military departments. Control over the allocation of supplies sometimes gave the military a decisive role in the direction of foreign policy. A decision on the delivery of trucks might have more political consequences than endless diplomatic exchanges. Thus the State Department found itself in a difficult position when it set out on a nation-building plan in Iran. The British and American Combined Chiefs of Staffs accorded Iran a low supply priority, because they planned no major operations in the region. They saw little reason to divert scarce foodstuffs, personnel, and supplies to support a policy that required potentially unlimited resources to achieve results that could only minimally assist the war effort.[9]

American policy for Iran evolved in the pattern of what economist Charles Lindblom has described as incremental decision making. When State and War found that their goals clashed, they compromised on the level of American aid to Iran. The results satisfied no one. The State Department, supported by the Iranian government and the British Foreign Office, believed that inadequate supplies would leave Iran in a state of unrest threatening to Allied supply operations, and that in the long run political instability would increase the danger of Soviet expansion. Military leaders at first disagreed. They believed that the Iranian government was too weak and corrupt to make effective use of American assistance. Supplies should go where they were needed—to maintain the Russian front. Not until late in the war would military leaders see the danger of Soviet expansion as a sufficient cause to reorder their supply priorities. By then the State Department had begun to recoup its influence over the formulation of American foreign policy.[10]

Exceptionalism, the notion that the United States could transcend the histories of old world societies, gave American policy for Iran its ideological basis. As historian C. Vann Woodward has observed, the concept has seldom been subjected to systematic analysis and is, therefore, difficult to define with precision. Certainly it is not an American invention. Almost all groups or nations have some vision defining their special character. Woodward has identified abundance, success, and innocence as three elements of historical experience that have given American exceptionalism its particular force. Material abundance has reaffirmed for Americans their belief in the unique virtues of free enterprise capitalism and liberal democracy. Patriotic orators never tire of reminding us how the perfection of those institutions accounts for the dynamic growth of American wealth and power. Abundance also contributes to the myth of success. An almost unbroken string of historical achievements in creating wealth, subduing the wilderness, building a national society, and waging war persuaded Americans of the World War II generation, in the words of historian Arthur Schlesinger Sr., "that nothing in the world [was] beyond [their] power to accomplish." Or as Woodward remarked, "Success and victory are still national habits of mind."[11]

Abundance and success have supported the American illusion of innocence. From the first New England settlers, many Americans felt called to the new world to escape the sin and corruption of the old. In the new land, they hoped to found the "city upon a hill," "God's American Israel." Providence had selected this people to revitalize humanity and to return man to his state of innocence. Whether by

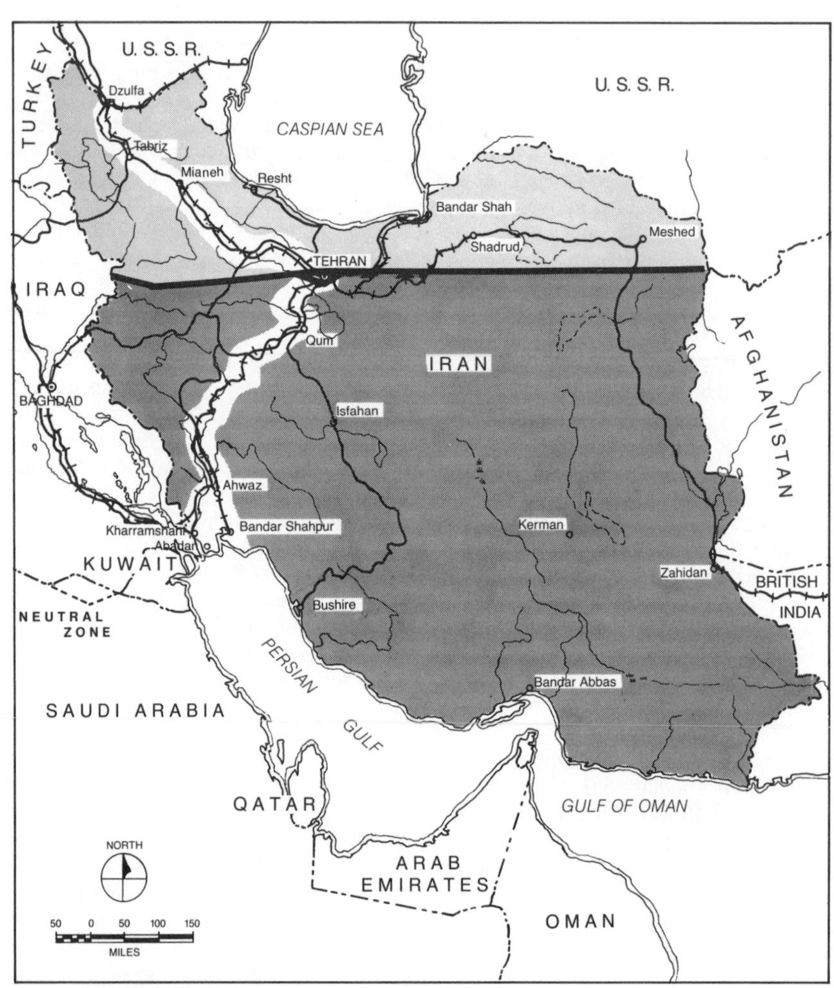

THE SUPPLY ROUTE 1941–1946

—— Major Roads

++++ Railroads

Russian Occupation Zone

British Occupation Zone

rejecting the corrupt church of Rome, the decadent aristocracies of Europe, or the Godless evil of communism, Americans have maintained a faith in their moral superiority to the old world.[12]

To justify the growth of American involvement in Iran the State Department drew on all three elements of this sense of exceptionalism. Wallace Murray and his colleagues in the Near East Division always embraced a robust nationalism. They translated the notion of innocence into "disinterestedness." Since the United States came to Iran without the imperial interests that drove the British and the Russians, and since it based its actions on a concept of the greater good, it could succeed in uplifting such a backward nation where the old selfish and self-interested powers had already failed. Greater material abundance for the Iranian people would eliminate the major causes of political unrest, thereby blunting the appeal of communism. As the American experience demonstrated, the development of free enterprise capitalism, liberal democracy, and other forms of western culture would create the necessary conditions for liberating Iran from its neocolonial dependence on Great Britain and the Soviet Union. Technical and military advisers, along with American diplomats, would be the bearers of the new American gospel.

American policy for Iran evolved from a complex, sometimes contradictory web of objectives and strategies. The war effort created the immediate circumstances to which the Near East Division responded. The need to enhance its policy functions gave the State Department an additional incentive to apply diplomatic remedies to ease chronic instability in Iran. Fear of Russian expansion led to the definition of a policy that would justify the continuation of an American presence there after the war ended. A sense of their own exceptionalism persuaded many Americans that they, unlike the British or Russians, could successfully end the traditions of rivalry that had long made Iran a pawn in big power politics. That faith masked for many policymakers one of the underlying ironies of this American involvement. In its efforts to block the ends envisioned by British and Russian imperialism, the State Department would adopt most of the means those powers had employed; commercial concessions, advisers, assistance programs, private investment, and diplomatic intervention in internal and external Iranian affairs became the instruments of American policy.

THE UNITED STATES, IRAN, AND THE WAR

The initial American involvement in Iran coincided with the low ebb of Allied military fortunes. Even after the United States entered the war, Allied forces had failed to stem the Axis onslaught. By the spring of 1942 the heroic, but doomed, Allied resistance on Corregidor and Bataan was the closest the Allies had come to a military success. The unexpected rapidity of the Japanese conquest had forced the Combined Chiefs of Staff to divert men and materials to the Pacific theater. For over a year the Soviet Union faced the brunt of German military might alone.

The enormity of the Allied military task dwarfed the problems of the Iranian occupation. At first just one potential nightmare brought Iran to the forefront of Allied planning. A worst case analysis could anticipate a German pincer movement, the northern arm of which would reach Stalingrad, conquer the city, then wheel southward toward the Caucasus oil fields and the Middle East. At the same time, the Afrika Corps might cross Suez and turn north. The two forces would then converge on Iran.

Allied victory hinged on the Russians' capacity to keep large German forces occupied until the British and Americans had mustered sufficient strength to open a second front in Europe. To that end Churchill and Roosevelt had pledged to deliver critical supplies to the Soviet Union. The inability to make good on that promise, in addition to the failure to open a second front before 1944 and the Allies' refusal to recognize Stalin's territorial demands in Eastern Europe, complicated Allied relations on all levels. The reverberations were particularly strong in Iran, the only nation where all three major Allies had stationed troops by the fall of 1942. Some of the Soviets' difficult behavior there may have reflected Stalin's larger dissatisfactions with his allies.[13]

As its primary goal, the Iranian government sought to limit the adverse effects of the occupation. That meant preserving some autonomy over domestic and foreign affairs. As a first step the Iranian government sought to limit the area of Russian occupation that engulfed all five northern provinces. Prime Minister Foroughi also asked the Russians and the British for a formal statement reiterating their respect for Iran's sovereignty and territorial integrity and, more important, their pledge to withdraw once hostilities had ended.[14]

To Foroughi's government also fell the difficult task of reviving Iran's third power strategy without Germany. Foroughi would prove himself an able advocate for his country, even though he assumed office at an advanced age and in frail health. Among Iranians he had a reputation as a teacher, a politician, and a diplomat who had served a term as president of the League of Nations General Assembly. His initial overtures to the United States in the fall of 1941, while far from promising, revealed that the State Department was at least sensitive to Iran's charge that the occupation violated the rights of "a neutral and pacific country." In response Secretary of State Cordell Hull had called upon London and Moscow to publicize their pledges to Iran, as reassurances to the Moslem world and to "small countries everywhere."[15]

Even that modest initiative revealed that Allied relations over Iran would be far from smooth. The British in this as in most cases were cooperative. Within a week after he had received Hull's request, Foreign Secretary Anthony Eden had given the desired reassurances in a public address. The Russians, by contrast, immediately aroused Anglo-American suspicions by refusing to make even this seemingly innocuous gesture. Vladimir Dekanozov, head of Soviet Near Eastern Affairs, replied that "in his opinion a reiteration of the Soviet government's position so soon after the note reaffirming its intentions might be misunderstood. . . ." Though he promised to consider Hull's note further, the State Department heard nothing more. Anglo-American diplomats treated that rebuff as characteristic of Soviet deviousness. Oliver Lyttleton, whose position at the head of British Middle East supply operations involved him in extensive contacts with Soviet officials, described a prevalent view of the Russians: "They are friendly and polite, but they don't do anything to ease three-cornered situations. They're past masters at the art of putting off with words."[16]

The Russians did in effect comply with Hull's request, though there is no evidence that the State Department ever knew of it. In a speech on 6 November 1941, Stalin said, "We have not and cannot have such war aims as the seizures of foreign territories of Europe or peoples and territories of Asia, including Iran." He never made a similar reference to any other country, though it is not clear he had Hull's note in mind when he made it. Just as likely, he was trying to facilitate current negotiations with Iran over a tripartite treaty of occupation. Certainly the Soviet Foreign Office made no attempt to make the State Department aware of Stalin's comment. All the same Stalin's reference indicated that satisfactory Iranian-Soviet relations would remain a Soviet priority.[17]

Hull's efforts to place the occupation on a sound moral footing marked a first step toward American involvement in Iranian affairs. President Roosevelt had earlier assured Reza Shah that the United States did respect Iran's independence and territorial integrity. By October 1941, Hull had begun to turn that passive assurance into a more active policy. In the spirit of the president's comment, the United States would monitor the behavior of its Allies to discourage either one from violating the terms of the occupation.[18]

The British and Iranian governments had already begun to cultivate American suspicions that the Russians had ambitions beyond the immediate need to expel the Germans and secure their southern border. Soon after the occupation Moscow had requested an oil concession around Kavir Khurian, which had been granted in the past to a Russian national. The Bolsheviks had repudiated the concession in 1918 and the Majles had never approved it anyway. After briefly reviving the concession in 1925, the Soviets failed to develop it. Most likely they made the new request in order to deny another foreign power access to resources in a traditional Russian sphere of influence. Negotiations the previous year between Standard Oil of New Jersey and the Iranian government may have triggered Russian suspicions, since the talks had encompassed the same area. Whatever the Soviet motive, whether to eliminate foreign intrusion or to establish a foothold for the postwar period, the Iranian government was certainly in no position to refuse further discussions.[19]

The oil bid was not the only cause of Anglo-American anxiety about Soviet intentions. As Russian forces assumed control, they severed communications with Tehran, leaving the capital awash in rumors of political intrigue and economic chaos in the occupation zone. Disruptions in that region threatened Iran's survival because the northern provinces produced more than half the nation's food and included some of the most restive minorities, like the Kurds and the Azeris. An American missionary arriving in the capital from Tabriz informed Louis Dreyfus, the American minister, that the Russians were encouraging movements of local autonomy among the Armenians. In Moscow the Iranian Ambassador, Mohammad Saed, complained to the American ambassador that the Soviets scarcely needed to hold a zone five times as large as the British. Saed was convinced that the Russians had no intention of withdrawing after the war.[20]

The lack of communication with the occupied northern provinces made it difficult to know just what the Russians were doing. The Nazi invasion had made them so desperate for food, supplies, and war materials from any source that they undoubtedly saw the occupation as an opportunity to seize whatever they could. They commandeered all the transportation systems that normally connected the region to Tehran and southern Iran. No doubt, as the Iranian, British, and American governments all suspected, the Soviets anticipated extending their influence in Iran, but in the fall of 1941 that could not have ranked high among the Kremlin's most pressing priorities. The war explained Russian actions well enough for the moment.[21]

Sir Reader Bullard, the archly anti-Soviet British ambassador, worried that the chaos resulting from Russian actions would threaten the operation of the supply route while opening up future possibilities for Soviet domination. As the British legation heard more stories from the north, London protested directly to the Kremlin. The State Department had been receiving similar reports from Louis Dreyfus. That inspired Cordell Hull to propose an American protest as well. Russian activities had in that sense encouraged the United States to become more interested in Iranian affairs.[22]

Much of the disorder that erupted would have occurred no matter what policy the Soviets had pursued. The combination of a weak government, corruption, and inflation that followed upon the occupation guaranteed a period of economic and political turmoil in Iran. With northern foodstuffs cut off, merchants began to horde scarce supplies. Most goods were available only at exorbitant black market prices. Automobile tires, for example, sold for as much as $2,000 each. Diplomatic personnel had to leave their cars under armed guard to protect the tires. Everywhere, particularly in the cities, food shortages and currency stringencies fueled inflation. Government warehouses seldom had more than a few days' reserves of wheat to provide bread, a staple of the Iranian diet. British and Russian forces made matters worse by obtaining their supplies locally. In addition, the war had ended Iran's trade with Germany. Replacement parts became scarce and many export goods had no market, since the Allies could not assume that trade in the same volume.[23]

Economic collapse was just one trial that befell the beleaguered Reza Shah. Its poor performance during the Anglo-Soviet occupation had destroyed the morale of his army. Dissident tribes like the Kurds and Qashqai saw new opportunities to challenge the government's authority. The army could no longer quell their rebelliousness. Iranian radio stations and newspapers broke the government censorship to openly criticize the shah's regime. Whether he was driven out by British-inspired propaganda or choosing a course to save the throne for his son, Mohammed Reza Pahlevi, the shah abdicated in September 1941. As the exiled shah left his country on a British freighter, the Allies agreed conditionally to accept the new ruler. The occupation had severely circumscribed Iran's political autonomy.[24]

The abdication did not just demonstrate the extent of Anglo-Soviet influence over Iran's internal affairs; it also introduced a period of unprecedented factionalism in the country. Under Reza Shah no real political parties had existed; only factions in the Majles, formed around important figures. None of the resulting cliques had ever achieved sustained political power or developed a permanent institutional structure with a coherent program. In short, Iran had no political parties in a modern sense. Many of the cliques had been receptive historically to foreign manipulations that had led to increased wealth or influence. The shah's fall had particularly emboldened the factions strongest among the old Qajar aristocrats like Ahmed Qavam who opposed the Pahlevi monarchy.[25]

Mohammed Reza Shah Pahlevi did not at first seem likely to fill his father's hobnailed boots. Dreyfus viewed him as "weak, incompetent, and pro-German." That judgment was only a bit harsh. Just twenty-one when he ascended the throne, the new shah was more a gentleman than a soldier. As the heir to an absolute monarch, he had had the opportunities for education and travel his father had never experienced. At school in Switzerland he became fluent in French, an avid skier, and an accomplished tennis player. He returned to Tehran in 1936 to complete his education at the national military college. There he met the officers who would provide the major backing for his regime. There too, he developed the passion for flying that eventually led him to seek to obtain the most advanced jet aircraft for the Iranian Air Force. Even though he married Princess Fawzia of Egypt in 1939, he remained something of a playboy. Then, as later, his westernized life-style alienated the fundamentalist Islamic clergy.[26]

By nature Reza Shah Pahlevi was cautious and speculative. His moods swung from exhilaration to despondency. In crises he was often racked by indecision. He leaned heavily on a few court favorites like Hussein Ala and the British and American ministers. Uncertain about his authority, he declared his intention to maintain a constitutional monarchy. That signaled a shift of power away from the throne to the Majles. His personal political base would rest, as had his father's, in the army, but in 1941 the army's loyalty and strength were untested. Pro-German sympathizers dominated the officer corps, while morale in the ranks remained at a low ebb. British and Russian troops assumed the primary responsibility for Iran's internal security. Despite the weakness of the army, it was still Iran's most powerful single organized force. As such, its support could make the new shah an important political factor.[27]

Internal political unrest made the selection of a prime minister and cabinet an uncertain process. Each candidate had to contend with a host of conflicting forces. The foreign powers backed some sympathetic factions and opposed others. The shah preferred figures who were personally loyal, like Foroughi, his foreign minister Ali Soheili, or Mohammed Saed, ambassador to the Soviet Union. Throughout the war, Iran's cabinets would rise and fall with remarkable rapidity. But one factor did hold the Iranian government together. Almost all the politicians, even those sympathetic to the British or Russians, looked forward to the day when foreign troops would withdraw. Each prime minister, encouraged by the shah, pursued a third power relationship with the United States. In this way Iran could protect its independence and retain some room for diplomatic maneuvering.[28]

By 1941 Wallace Murray of the Near East Division had determined that the assumption of third power status in Iran could benefit American interests. As an ardent Russo- and Anglophobe and an American nationalist, he looked forward to a realignment of big power relations in the region. He recognized, however, that the United States lacked both formal and informal channels through which to exert its influence. All that was at hand in 1941 was one of the oldest auxiliaries of American diplomacy—missionaries. The American missionary movement in Iran dated back to the 1830s when the Presbyterians had come to assist Armenian and Nestorian Christians living among Moslems. Reza Shah had expelled the missionaries in the 1930s and confiscated their property. Murray thought the new shah might be more receptive to a resumption of these missionary efforts. Iran had "fallen on evil days," he told the Presbyterian Board of Foreign Missions, and it desperately needed educational facilities. To his diplomatic colleagues, Murray revealed the true motives for this initiative: "The resumption of American educational work in Tabriz, in particular, would have a marked restraining effect upon Soviet separatist and ideological activities in the area. . . ." Close relationships between teachers and students would allow the missionaries "to obtain intimate and accurate knowledge of what is going on."[29]

In fact, Murray was probably the only person interested in the missionary scheme. Past experience had chastened the Presbyterian board, which insisted on a clear invitation from the Iranian government. When no such overture came, the board terminated its negotiations. In any case, the Iranian government sought a far broader commitment than that from the United States. It had its eye on material assistance programs, trade, advisers, commercial credits, military equipment, and a formal treaty.[30]

In the fall of 1941, the State Department was certainly receptive to stronger Iranian-American commercial ties. Though trade then stood at only $15 million a year, Wallace Murray warned his colleagues that "the occupation might well provide the opportunity for either Russia or Britain or both to enter into a trade agreement with Iran which could prove harmful to American trade in the postwar period."[31] With that in mind the State Department initiated negotiations that culminated in a trade pact signed in April 1943. It also promoted investment and trade prospects for American corporations and encouraged a few companies to seek markets in Iran. A greater American economic presence there promised at least three benefits: the United States would gain new markets and resources; the State Department would have more opportunity to support American interests; and finally, the Americans could erode British and Russian influence.

Eager to ensure these stronger ties, the Iranian government proposed in December 1941 that the United States adhere to the recently negotiated Tripartite

Treaty of Alliance. In return for Iran's acceptance of the occupation the Russians and British had agreed to compensate for any hardships they had caused and to withdraw their forces within six months after war with Germany ended. (The war with Japan had not yet begun). "American adherence would increase the value of the Treaty in Iranian eyes tenfold," Foreign Minister Ali Soheili assured Louis Dreyfus.[32]

The State Department was willing to lend its assistance, but not as a bilateral political agreement. An increased presence in the form of advisers, however, suited the intentions of both parties. Iran would have a more visible American presence; the State Department would have a new foreign policy instrument. The Iranian government had already indicated its interest in financial, municipal, and public health experts; the shah sought help in rebuilding his army; and in January 1942 the Iranians requested a police specialist to reorganize the gendarmerie along the lines of the American state police. Louis Dreyfus warned the department not to "miss the opportunity to improve our position." Wallace Murray suggested that a police specialist could serve the legation as a valuable intelligence source. To such practical arguments, Murray added his plea to assist Iran in its straitened condition. He implied that President Roosevelt's previous assurances to Reza Shah justified compliance with these requests for advisers.[33]

The British legation had been operating behind the scenes to encourage Iran's requests for American advisers. Sir Reader Bullard believed that the Soviets posed a far graver threat to British interests than the Americans ever would. Even if anglophobic and anti-imperial elements in the State Department sided with the Iranians against the British, American aid was the only possible antidote to the chaos that now threatened to engulf the country. The British Empire simply lacked the resources to sustain all its commitments throughout the Middle East. It was even providing Ibn Saud's bankrupt government with funds, though no British oil company held a concession in Saudi Arabia.[34]

The Foreign Office had no illusions about the reasons for Iran's growing interest in the United States:

> The Persian government's tendency to appeal to the United States for assistance is probably inspired (a) by the hope they will be able to benefit from the vast storehouse of America's wealth and production and (b) by the hope that as America is a long way away and has no territorial interest in Persia they will not have to concede the Americans any degree of control or influence over their policy.[35]

Recognition of Britain's weakness led the Foreign Office to accept the possibility that the United States might assume such a third power role in Iran.

The State Department did not so clearly appreciate the Iranians' intentions. Sumner Welles was reluctant to assist a government he saw as too corrupt to benefit from American aid. Rather than send advisers, as the Foreign Office urged, he suggested that the British and American ministers might better persuade the Iranians to appoint more capable public officials. Welles apparently did not mind meddling, but he did want to avoid burdening the United States with Iran's problems. Though corruption was one matter the British hoped American advisers would address, the Foreign Office thought Welles was misguided. As W. H. Young of the Eastern Department remarked, "If the appointment of American advisors to the Persian government is made conditional on their 'having the complete support of competent Iranian officials,' nothing will be done."[36]

The Iranian government placated Welles by removing some of its more objectionable figures. It then seemed to assume that increased American assistance would soon follow, since only the type and size of the American advisory missions remained undetermined. On 20 March the Iranian minister in Washington asked for a military officer to take charge of the army's finance and supply divisions, the equivalent of the quartermaster corps. Within two months the list had grown to include finance and aviation advisers and an army engineer, though the State Department had not yet found an army adviser.[37]

AMERICAN ADVISERS AND AID TO IRAN

Circumstances in the spring of 1942 conspired to bring Iran more centrally into Allied war plans. Springtime meant a renewal of the German offensive in the Soviet Union. German U-boats had so devastated shipping in the North Atlantic that the Allies began to reroute supplies through the Persian corridor. That gave the security of that route a higher priority. The British believed that only American advisers could train the Iranian Army to provide local security, since British or Russian advisers might provoke antiforeign elements. In a surprise about-face, Secretary of State Hull now agreed that American aid to Iran was needed to bolster declining British strength. The secretary had been encouraged in that view by reports from Dreyfus that American prestige in Iran had recently soared. Though a bit taken aback by the sudden State Department aggressiveness, the Foreign Office admitted that "from our point of view it is certainly all to the good."[38]

One stumbling block remained. The War Department opposed a large military mission. With all the theaters of the war clamoring for men and materials, military planners were reluctant to divert precious resources to Iran. An interdepartmental conflict now arose that only the president had the authority to resolve. The State Department defined the military mission as a political and diplomatic necessity; the War Department viewed it as an American intrusion into an area designated as a British responsibility. Resources sent to such a minor theater of the war would have little value. Since Roosevelt was not informed of the impasse, the two agencies were left to strike a compromise. In classic incremental fashion, the War Department agreed to a token mission; the State Department sent the mission anyway, but without sufficient resources to make it effective. In time the mission would come to symbolize American prestige in Iran. To preserve that prestige, the State Department would insist on more support for the mission. In short, the means would become an end.[39]

On 21 May 1942 the War Department assigned Major General John Greely to serve as an adviser on finance and supply for the Iranian Army. His appointment indicated no alteration in the military's thinking about Iran. It just happened that Greely had been stranded in Tehran while on a mission to the Soviet Union. Waiting for reassignment, he sought to take command of the scattered American supply and military units in the Middle East. Assigning him to the Iranian Army relieved the War Department of a growing embarrassment, while at the same time satisfying the State Department's request for a military adviser. Lest the State Department misconstrue Greely's appointment, General R. W. Crawford told department officials: "The United States Army does not contemplate undertaking operations in Iran, except for transportation of supplies to Russia, and it does not consider the country important to our war effort in any other respect."[40]

The State Department had no way to send a larger mission until Greely had evaluated the situation for the War Department. That news disappointed the British Foreign Office, where, as one official commented, "We have always considered the reorganization of the Persian army one of our most urgent tasks. . . ." Greely apparently agreed, for he decided on his own initiative that he would whip the army into fighting shape. Somehow he ignored the fact that Iran was neutral, that the

Tripartite Treaty excluded Iranian forces from a combat role, and that he had been assigned only as an observer. To begin his program Greely asked to have two hundred trucks diverted from Russian shipments so Iran's army would have more mobility. Although in March 1942 President Roosevelt had declared Iran along with Iraq and Saudi Arabia eligible for lend-lease assistance, authority for issuing the trucks and other supplies rested with the British.[41]

What had once been a squabble between the War Department and State Department now spilled over to the British and American lend-lease operations in the Middle East. At the time when Greely was seeking to assert his self-proclaimed authority, Lend-Lease officials were negotiating an agreement with Iran. His request for trucks threatened to confuse an already difficult situation. Such a usurpation of the chain-of-command was more than the War Department could abide and it ordered him home in July. Before he left, however, Greely offered a shrewd assessment of Iran's hopes for American aid. Like the British Foreign Office, he understood that the Iranian government did not want advisers to institute reforms; it expected "help, not advice." As a consequence, modest advisory missions would not work unless they had sufficient supplies.[42]

Greely's advice was lost on the State Department, which proceeded to organize a variety of missions without solving the problems of supply or assuring the competence of the advisers they sent. As a gesture to interbureaucratic harmony, the War Department provided several officers, but no materials. It recommended Col. H. Norman Schwarzkopf to head the Iranian gendarmerie. Schwarzkopf would prove in time to be one of the few capable advisers sent during the war. After graduating from West Point in 1917 he had left the army to head the New Jersey State Police until a dispute over his handling of the Lindbergh kidnapping case led him to resign. His experience in police work and in organizing a training regiment early in World War II gave him the background appropriate to his mission. In addition, he was one of the few Americans sent to Iran who spoke French. His tact and resilience in the face of repeated frustrations allowed him to achieve a modest success. It has since been suggested that his great legacy may have been the establishment of the CIA network for postwar Iran.[43]

The War Department also assigned Major General Clarence Ridley to replace Greely. General Ridley, unlike Greely, had no illusions about transforming the Iranian Army. Earlier duties in Puerto Rico and the Panama Canal Zone had given him some perspective on the limits of reform in an underdeveloped country. He stayed within the guidelines set by the War Department, which instructed him to appraise the value of a full-scale assistance program and advise the Iranian Army on supply matters. His orders did not, however, clarify his relationship to either Schwarzkopf or the American legation. In essence, the advisory program began with no one in charge.[44]

Unable to send a full-scale military mission, the State Department gave top priority to a finance mission. "We believe the Iranian government will agree that its success is vital to the Cabinet's policy of reform and reconstruction with American assistance," Welles wired Dreyfus. Had Welles listened to Greely or the British Foreign Office, he would have recognized that reform was not what the Iranians had in mind. Constant friction resulted from that misapprehension. The advisers resented Iranian resistance to their well-intended reform programs. The Iranians chafed at what they viewed as American interference in their internal affairs.[45]

The State Department compounded its problems when it selected Arthur Millspaugh to head the finance mission. On paper, Millspaugh seemed an inspired choice. Earlier service in Iran made him aware of the situation he faced. His economic expertise was in oil, an area where Iran would certainly need guidance.

Louis Dreyfus shared the department's enthusiasm: "I am personally of the opinion that the State Department has executed a grand *coup* in Millspaugh's appointment which will have favorable repercussions here."[46] Once again, however, the American failure to recognize Iranian intentions doomed this mission.

Even before Millspaugh's selection, the political climate in Iran had changed. The cabinet of the day was headed by seventy-year-old Ahmed Qavam, a wealthy tea planter from Gilan, a province in the Soviet-occupied zone. Qavam had long been a champion of constitutionalism and a foe of the Pahlevi dynasty. His opposition to Reza Shah had forced him into exile until the shah's abdication led him to return. He suited Iran's present needs because he was on friendly terms with the Soviets. Wallace Murray had urged the Iranians to find a more suitable prime minister, one sympathetic to American aims. Sumner Welles, who had warned Murray to avoid such meddling in Iran's affairs, gave him more latitude to express his views once Qavam assumed power. Welles feared that a prime minister friendly to Moscow would abet Soviet designs on Iran.[47]

Qavam had at first feigned satisfaction with Millspaugh's selection. Then he began to hedge. Millspaugh would have less authority than before, he told Dreyfus. For a month the State Department waited for word that the Majles had confirmed Millspaugh's appointment. Finally, the minister in Washington explained that Iran had a different kind of adviser in mind, someone with the stature of former Vice President Charles Dawes, whose prestige could greatly advance Iran's interests in Washington. The adviser did not even have to be a finance specialist, the minister admitted. Clearly the Iranian government and the State Department had conflicting views of the mission. Welles, however, chose not to clarify the misunderstanding. Since Millspaugh met the technical requirements of the assignment, he would be the department's choice. Qavam had almost no alternative but to accept. He was not willing to undermine Iran's third power strategy by alienating the United States over the selection of one adviser.[48]

Misunderstandings about the role of the finance adviser were not the only factors that would hamper Millspaugh. The situation he faced in 1942 called for a robust diplomat. The sixty-two-year-old Millspaugh would soon show he was neither diplomatic nor robust. Frequent illness sapped his strength. Inflexibility and tactlessness would alienate his American and Iranian subordinates. Inability to speak French or Farsi would limit his ability to explain his program. And whatever his qualifications as an economist, Millspaugh was a poor administrator in a position with extensive administrative responsibilities. One of his many critics remarked,

> Dr. Millspaugh during his first mission to Iran in the twenties dealt with an infant ready to take advice and be admonished; when he arrived for the second time twenty years later, he wanted to apply to Iran the same treatment as before; but he failed to notice that the infant had by now become an adolescent girl, independent, ambitious, and whimsical.[49]

It would be unfair to charge Millspaugh alone with the shortcomings of his mission. His failures often stemmed from a sincere desire to strengthen Iran. His programs attacked gross social and economic injustices. Widespread corruption hampered even modest reforms. His most fatal political mistake, a campaign to reduce the size and cost of the army, made good economic sense and had the support of many political factions. The poor qualifications of the Americans available to serve on his mission aggravated his administrative burden. All of these difficulties were complicated by the State Department's misunderstanding of why Iran wanted the missions.[50]

Millspaugh's appointment completed the initial organization of the American advisory program. Sumner Welles reported to President Roosevelt that the United States now had five missions in Iran. Besides Millspaugh, Schwarzkopf, and Ridley, the State Department had sent Joseph Sheridan as food and supply adviser and L. Stephen Timmerman as an urban police expert. For twenty years Sheridan had struggled with food shortages around the Middle East, while Timmerman had recently retired from the New York City police force. One American Welles overlooked, Lt. Col. Abraham Neuwirth, left his job producing typhus vaccine at Tehran's Pasteur Institute to become a health adviser. Welles used his report to state the case for a larger military mission. "I feel now more than ever that the United States mission to work with the Iranian army could in fact play an extremely important role. . . ," he told Roosevelt. But Welles still did not have the support of the War Department. Secretary of War Stimson reiterated the army's judgment that no program could appreciably benefit an organization as demoralized as the Iranian Army.[51]

The War Department had enough of a burden to bear in Iran without the army mission. It had recently undertaken the operation of the supply route through the Iranian corridor. Over the summer of 1942 Allied shipping losses on the Murmansk route had reached unacceptable levels. Of the eighty-four ships that left the United States between April and June, only forty-four actually reached Murmansk. Another fifty ships were stranded in Scotland. The Russians had accused the British of stealing their supplies. The Allies had thus turned to the Iranian route, even though it had a low tonnage capacity and ships on the 12,000-mile route could make just two trips a year. Soon, however, supplies were piled up on Iranian wharves while valuable shipping lay idled at anchor waiting to unload. The British were simply too overburdened to solve the problem. In September 1942 the Combined Chiefs of Staff turned the operation of the supply route over to a newly formed Persian Gulf Service Command (PGC) of the United States Army.[52]

Even though that decision would bring thirty thousand American troops to Iran, the combined chiefs never consulted the Iranian government. Considerable friction would arise over the status of these Americans, particularly when they violated Iranian laws. Command of the PGC went to Major General Donald Connolly, who was probably the choice of lend-lease overseer Harry Hopkins. After graduating from West Point and serving in the Army Air Corps, Connolly had worked for several New Deal agencies, including the Civil Works Administration and the WPA, where he and Hopkins became friends. The PGC faced a formidable task in expanding port and rail facilities, operating the Iranian State Railroad, and delivering massive quantities of supplies to the Soviet Union. The Allies could ill afford any delays that tied up scarce shipping. To complicate matters, because the nationalistic Reza Shah had built the Iranian Railroad without a direct link to the Soviet Union, trucks had to carry supplies on the final leg of the journey over almost impassable roads.[53]

The creation of a major military command in Iran could have created the possibility of cooperation between the State and War Departments. Connolly received vast quantities of materials that the advisers sent by the State Department could have used in their efforts to assist Iran. The army and gendarmerie were desperate for the trucks, radios, clothing, and other goods that the PGC possessed in abundance. Connolly's officers could have augmented the tiny staffs available to Ridley, Schwarzkopf, and Millspaugh. However Connolly shared his superior's conviction that the State Department program had no bearing on his mission or the war effort in general and felt that requests from the advisers for supplies served only to complicate his efforts to transport goods from the Persian Gulf to the Soviet Union. So intense was Connolly's commitment to his assignment that he disbanded his G–2 or Intelligence section, when he learned that Russian suspicions of its activities were impeding the work of his troops.[54]

Frustrated by Connolly's refusal to cooperate with their advisers, the legation in Tehran took to feuding with the PGC. The general's impatience with diplomats and their concerns did little to improve relations. But the real source of the conflict lay in Washington where the State Department and the War Department could not reach an agreement about Iran's relationship to the war effort. To a degree, both were correct in their basic assumptions. As the military argued, the desperate war situation in 1942 allowed for little room to pursue long-term political goals. Nor did Iran offer a promising environment for the kinds of social or economic development the department proposed. But State was also correct in arguing that the United States could not promote a stable peace if it ignored the plight of nations like Iran. All the same, the State Department should have understood from experience that except for their symbolic value, advisers were a weak instrument of foreign policy. The conspicuous failures of similar missions in Latin America should have made that fact amply clear. The pressures of war did not, however, lend themselves easily to reasoned political analysis or to the reconciliation of differences between diplomats and generals.

These difficulties did not dampen the enthusiasm with which Wallace Murray viewed the State Department's initiatives in Iran. "The obvious fact is that we shall soon be in a position of actually 'running' Iran through an impressive body of advisers . . . ," he told his colleagues. That was scarcely an accurate appraisal of what a handful of Americans without resources might be doing. Perhaps Murray was selling his program rather than offering an analysis of American policy. He was certainly eager to see the American role in Iran expanded. At a meeting with representatives from the War Department in August 1942 he argued that "in the future as in the past, the British would be unable to obtain Iranian cooperation in anything and sooner or later the United States would have to assume the dominant role in Iran." Here again he revealed both his anglophobia and his faith in American exceptionalism. Because of the superior position of the Americans, he thought the combined chiefs should have given them rather than the British the authority over the movement of supplies.[55]

That idea did not fall totally on deaf ears. There were those in the War Department who accepted the need for political as well as military planning. General Albert Wedemeyer, who shared Murray's antipathy to both Russian and British imperialism, agreed that if the United States had more authority over the supplies shipped through Iran, the British could not use them for their own imperial ends. The combined chiefs apparently did not agree, for they left the British in charge of supplies.[56]

Even if Murray had exaggerated the American position in Iran, by the end of 1942 the United States had begun to establish a presence there. Secretary Hull had made an informal commitment to guard Iran's sovereignty and territorial integrity. The advisory missions were in a position to influence Iran's internal affairs and to promote American interests. More than thirty thousand American troops would come to Iran to operate its internal transportation system. Although most of them would remember only the heat, the poverty, and the barrenness of the countryside, Americans and Iranians were no longer complete strangers.

The Americans arrived in Iran as the tide of war was turning. The State Department could begin to shift its planning from war to peace. The same four factors would shape American policy in Iran in the years ahead as had shaped it in the year that had passed. Middle Eastern oil would come to preoccupy policymakers in Washington more than ever before. In its efforts to define a policy for foreign oil, just as in its decision to send advisers, the State Department would spar with bureaucratic rivals. In that struggle the department would use the rhetoric of exceptionalism and the specter of Soviet expansion to promote its policies. Anticommunism would soften traditional American anglophobia and create an Anglo-American rapprochement on most issues involving Iran. As we shall see, all those strands came together in the first formal statement of an American policy for Iran that anticipated the United States playing a third power role there in the postwar era.

NOTES

1. My interpretation clearly puts me at odds with some of the major revisionists of the late 1960s; see, for example, Gabriel Kolko, *The Politics of War* (New York, 1968), pp. 298–300 and 307–13. Kolko and others err, I believe, in discounting the question of American national security and the expansionist character of Soviet policy. Both nations saw opportunities to achieve new influence in the Persian Gulf region by means of a stronger presence in Iran. Among the World War II American policymakers. Secretary of War Henry Stimson seemed best to grasp the consequences of what expanding American interests might mean: "By going into the Eastern Mediterranean we would run the risk of coming into rivalry with Russia. She is already nearer there than we are and could hardly fail to look with distrust at our actions," he wrote in his diary. I find myself in agreement with that view, though it does not explain why other policymakers ignored or discounted such prescient warnings. See Henry L. Stimson, "Diary," 47, 6/21/44, Yale University Library. Hereafter cited as Stimson Diary, volume, and date. Still, I would emphasize that on more general grounds I accept the revisionist critique that stresses the expansionist character of American foreign policy.

2. For a brief discussion of American responses to the Bolshevik Revolution, see John Lewis Gaddis, *Russia, the Soviet Union, and the United States* (New York, 1978), ch. 3. See also Christopher Lasch, *American Liberals and the Russian Revolution* (New York, 1962); and Robert Murray, *Red Scare: A Study in National Hysteria, 1919–1920* (Minneapolis, 1955).

3. Daniel Yergin, *Shattered Peace* (Boston, 1977), pp. 17–41.

4. Probably the most compelling treatment of the American diplomats' experience in Soviet Russia is George Kennan, *Memoirs, 1925–1950* (Boston, 1966). For this quotation, see pp. 278–80.

5. Yergin, *Shattered Peace,* pp. 37–38; see also Gaddis, *Russia, the Soviet Union, and the United States,* pp. 129–33.

6. Kennan, *Memoirs,* p. 70.

7. Almost all diplomatic historians of the Roosevelt era have made this observation. See, for example, Robert Dallek, *Franklin D. Roosevelt and American Foreign Policy, 1932–1945* (New York, 1979), pp. 532–33. For other corroborating views, see George Kennan, *Memoirs, 1925–1950,* pp. 182–84; Elting Morison, *Turmoil and Tradition* (New York, 1964), p. 499; and Gaddis Smith, *American Diplomacy During the Second World War* (New York, 1965), p. 53. On FDR's priorities in Soviet relations, see Gaddis, pp. 146–51.

8. Graham Allison, *The Essence of Decision* (Boston, 1971), pp. 1–9. On the politics model see pp. 144–84.

9. The best summary of early American policy for Iran is a memorandum prepared in early 1943, FR, 1943, 4, 386–88. The background and contents of this memorandum by John Jernegan will be the subject of the following chapter. On more general diplomatic and military thinking in 1941, see Dallek, pp. 269–313.

10. On Lindblom's incremental model, see Charles Lindblom, *The Intelligence of Democracy* (New York, 1965). A good source for military policy toward Iran is T. H. Vail Motter, *The Persian Corridor and Aid to Russia* (Washington, 1952), pp. 3–27 and 65–81.

11. C. Vann Woodward, "The Irony of Southern History," in *The Burden of Southern History* (New York, 1978). For the nativist strand of American exceptionalism, see John Higham, *Strangers in the Land* (New Brunswick, N.J., 1955), pp. 3–11.

12. Woodward, "The Irony of Southern History," pp. 167–71. Many diplomatic historians have referred to the "city upon a hill" and to John Winthrop as one source of America's sense of mission. See Edmund S. Morgan, *The Puritan Dilemma* (Boston, 1958), for an explanation of the sources of the concept.

13. Dallek, *Franklin D. Roosevelt and American Foreign Policy,* pp. 278–81, 292–99, and 336–38. See also Gaddis Smith, pp. 39–44; George Herring, Jr., *Aid to Russia, 1941–1946* (New York, 1973), ch. 1.

14. Ramazani, *Iran's Foreign Policy,* pp. 45–46 and 70–72. On Fouroughi, see Pfau, "The United States and Iran," p. 33.

15. FR, 1941, 3, p. 419, Shah to President Roosevelt; Memorandum of Hull's conversation with Soviet ambassador, pp. 434–35.

16. Ibid., p. 451, Winant to Sec. of State; Steinhardt to Secretary of State, ibid., pp. 453–54. Lyttleton quoted in Sir Claremont Skrine, *World War in Iran* (London, 1962), p. 88.

17. Joseph Stalin, *The Great Patriotic War of the Soviet Union* (New York, 1945), passim. This is a book of Stalin's wartime public speeches in which he made no reference to any other nation as he did to Iran.

18. FR, 1941, 3, pp. 446–47, Pres. Roosevelt to Shah of Iran, and ibid., p. 469, Hull to Ambassadors in London and Moscow. For a nice capsule sketch of Hull, see Stoff, *Oil, War, and American Security,* pp. 23–24. For an example of the Middle Eastern reponse to the occupation, see FR, 1941, 3, p. 427, Ambassador in Turkey (MacMurray) to Secretary of State. The Turkish foreign minister had said that "he personally considers the real reason for the Russo-British action was a strategic one of effecting a junction of their forces rather than any question of German agents." The historical record bears out that observation.

19. SD 891.6363/791, 9/10/41, Dreyfus to Hull. See also Lenczowski, *Russia and the West in Iran,* pp. 81 and 172.

20. Ramazani, *Iran's Foreign Policy,* p. 47; FR, 1941, 3, pp. 456–57, Steinhardt to Hull.

21. Much of this information about Soviet activities came from biased sources like Sir Reader Bullard. A good example of the view from the American legation is FR, 1941, 3, pp. 463–64, Dreyfus to Hull, 9/27/41. Ervand Abrahamian suggests, however, that at least in the early years of the occupation, the Soviets acted with restraint and refrained from interference in politics in their zone. See Abrahamian, *Iran Between Two Revolutions,* pp. 175–76 and 186–87. Much of the Anglo-American anxiety seems to reflect a concern more with what the Soviets could do if they chose rather than what their forces were actually doing, at least prior to 1944.

22. FR, 1941, 3, pp. 466–67.

23. A good first-hand account of conditions in Iran comes from the papers of Paul Atkins, Yale University Library. Atkins came to Iran with the Millspaugh finance mission. His evident hostility to Millspaugh may have colored his observations. See Atkins correspondence, Box 1, Yale University Library, New Haven, Connecticut.

24. FR, 1941, 3, p. 461. See also Abrahamian, *Iran Between Two Revolutions,* pp. 149–65 for an excellent analysis of Reza Shah's reign; Ramazani, *Iran's Foreign Policy,* pp. 43–44; Pahlevi, *Mission For My Country,* p. 74.

25. On Iran's internal politics see Abrahamian, *Iran Between Two Revolutions,* pp. 167–76.

26. On Mohammed Reza Shah Pahlevi's background and personality, see Donald Wilbur, *Contemporary Iran* (New York, 1962), pp. 103–4. See also Pfau, "The United States and Iran," p. 38.

27. Abrahamian, *Iran Between Two Revolutions,* pp. 176–85; also pp. 419–26 and 435–46. On command responsibility for the Allies, see MMRB, OPD (Operations Division), WD, 381, 8/21/42, Sec. of War Henry Stimson to Asst. Sec. of State Sumner Welles. A good source on the shah's reign and relations with the United States is Barry Rubin, *Paved With Good Intentions: The American Experience and Iran* (New York, 1980). In light of past allegations it might be worthwhile to comment on the charges of corruption levelled against the shah. Nothing in his character indicated any penchant for venality. He had mystical experiences in his youth and remained religious and conscious of his link to Persia's past. His drive for power was in large part a dream of restoring some of his nation's past glory. Certainly as he acquired both experience and power, the line between personal and national glory blurred. But his brothers and sisters were the main sources of family corruption. Denied any real role in governing Iran, they devoted themselves to amassing personal wealth and spending it in the style of the most decadent Qajar princes. The shah's failure to restrain them embarrassed the monarchy and contributed to its downfall.

28. Ramazani, *Iran's Foreign Policy,* pp. 45–62.

29. For this background, see George V. Allen, "Diaries," (unpublished manuscript), Harry S. Truman Library, Independence, Missouri, ch. 2. Allen's diaries are most useful for 1946–47 when he served in Iran as ambassador. They must be used with some caution since Allen recorded many events several years after. Once certain errors of chronology are corrected, the diaries generally correspond to official records. See also Yeselson, *United States-Persian Diplomatic Relations.* FR, 1941, 3, pp. 375–76. Memorandum by Wallace Murray. For another historian's view of Murray, see William Roger Louis, *The British Empire in the Middle East, 1945–1951* (New York, 1984), pp. 66–73.

30. FR, 1941, 3, p. 383. See also Public Records Office, London, (PRO), Foreign Office, File 371, 31438, E1705/888/34, Bullard to Foreign Office, 3/15/42. [Hereafter all Foreign Office records are cited as FO, file number, source, and date.]

31. Pfau, "The United States and Iran," 3 p. 24. FR, 1941, 3, p. 373 and FR, 1943, 4, p. 600.

32. FR, 1941, 3, p. 476. On Soheili, see Ramazani, *Iran's Foreign Policy,* p. 61n.

33. FR, 1942, 4, p. 263 and pp. 274–75. FR, 1941, 3, p. 475. For early contacts about advisers see FR, 1940, 3, pp. 638ff. For Iran's request, see FR, 1942, 4, p. 222 and pp. 223–34. See also Ramazani, *Iran's Foreign Policy,* pp. 70–72 for an explanation that outlines Iran's strategy.

34. FO, 31348, E917/888/34, 2/15/42, Note by C. W. Baxter; FO, 31348/ E1366/88/34, 2/28/42, Lord Halifax to FO; FO, 31348, E888/888/34, 2/4/42, Note by I. T. M. Pink. See also FR, 1942, 4, pp. 224–25.

35. FO, E888/888/34, Minute by I. T. M. Pink, 2/4/42.

36. FR, 1942, 4, pp. 224–25. FO, 31348, E1499/888/34, 3/9/42, Minute by W. H. Young (Eastern Dept.).

37. FR, 1942, 4, pp. 229 and 232.

38. FR, 1942, 4, pp. 227–38, 232–33, and 233–35. See also FO, 31348, E3352/888/34, 5/31/42, Minute by W. H. Young.

39. FR, 1942, 4, p. 235–36. See also SD (filed with) 891.24, 4/29/42, Murray to General Eisenhower.

40. Vail Motter, *The Persian Corridor and Aid to Russia,* pp. 77–81 and 165. The Iranian intendant general was equivalent to the American rank of quartermaster general. MMRB, OPD 210.68 Iran, 5/27/42, Stimson to Hull. SD 891.20.160, 6/5/42, Memorandum by Jernegan.

41. FR, 1942, 4, pp. 240–41. FO, 31348, E3657/888/34, 6/19/42, Minute by I. T. M. Pink. Vail Motter, p. 166–69.

42. Vail Motter, *The Persian Corridor,* pp. 167–69.

43. Ibid., pp. 167–68. Leonard Mosley (see *Power Play,* p. 214) has described Schwarzkopf as a member of OSS during the war and the organizer of the CIA operation in Iran. Kermit Roosevelt was denied the suggestion, but then, what self-respecting spy would do otherwise? After all, he covered up British intelligence activities by crediting them to AIOC. That neat little charade caused the recall of his book *Countercoup* (New York, 1979), in the wake of complaints from British Petroleum. Since it is widely accepted that the CIA relied heavily on police sources for information on Iran, Mosley's claim has great credibility. See Roosevelt, *Countercoup,* pp. 146–49.

44. SD 891.105A/11, 2/27/42, Murray to Berle; U.S. Department of State, *Bulletin* 11, 265, 7/23/44, p. 91. Skrine, *World War in Iran,* pp. 170–71; Vail Motter, *The Persian Corridor,* pp. 163 and 171. See also MMRB, OPD 210.684 Iran, 9/11/45.

45. FR, 1942, 4, p. 258.

46. Ibid., pp. 239 and 245.

47. SD 891.51A/515A, 3/3/42, Welles to Murray. See also Pfau, "The United States and Iran," p. 38. On Qavam, see Abrahamian, *Iran Between Two Revolutions,* p. 181.

48. FR, 1942, 4, p. 252–57.

49. Lenczowski, *Russia and the West in Iran,* p. 266.

50. See Ramazani, pp. 76ff. On Millspaugh's view, see Arthur Millspaugh, *American in Persia* (Washington, D.C., 1946).

51. Pfau, "The United States and Iran", pp. 87–89. FR, 1942, 4, p. 258. On the War Department's attitude, see MMRB, WD 381 (8–21–42) MS–E, 9/3/42; FO, 31348, E3657/888/34, 6/19/42, Minute by I. T. M. Pink.

52. Vail Motter, *The Persian Corridor,* pp. 174–211. On the higher-level decision making,

see Robert Sherwood, *Roosevelt and Hopkins* (New York, 1950), pp. 124–26 and Herring, *Aid to Russia, 1941–1946*.

53. Vail Motter, *The Persian Corridor,* pp. 174ff. To facilitate the Allied command structure, the PGC became an independent auxiliary of the British Persia and Iraq Command (PAI Force). PAI Force retained responsiblity for regional security and dealings that involved the PGC with the Iranian or Russian governments. British civilian agencies determined the allocation and movement of supplies; PGC controlled the operation of the supply route. See also Pfau, "The United States and Iran," pp. 44 and 67.

54. Vail Motter, *The Persian Corridor,* pp. 446–60.

55. FR, 1942, 4, pp. 190 and 242.

56. MMRB, Combined Chiefs of Staff File, 443, 12/8/42, Admiral Leahy to Hull.

3 *Defining an American Policy for Iran*

With victories at Stalingrad, El Alamein, Midway, and Guadalcanal, the Allies had by 1943 halted the seemingly relentless momentum of the Axis war machine. The danger had passed that German forces from Eastern Europe and North Africa might converge in the Middle East, and an eventual Allied victory, while it would demand long and bloody struggle, seemed inevitable. Thus the State Department could turn with greater confidence to planning for the postwar world, but it was far from clear in 1943 what the framework for the peace would be. Despite his public commitment to the Atlantic Charter, President Roosevelt indicated in his conception of the "four policemen" and by his territorial concessions to Stalin at the wartime conferences that he anticipated postwar regional security systems. Prime Minister Churchill had repeatedly stressed that his acceptance of Atlantic Charter principles would not mean the dismemberment of the British Empire. Ultimately, the charter would have little effect on Allied decisions about the shape of the peace.[1]

All the same, a few American officials like Under Secretary of State Sumner Welles and special presidential emissary Patrick Hurley invoked the charter to rationalize the United States' new commitment to Iran's political independence. In reality, however, the American interest in Iran sprang from the general consensus among officials in Washington that the United States could guarantee its security only by assuming a major role in maintaining the postwar peace, not from any commitment to the ideals set forth in the charter. The World War II generation had come to recognize the interdependence of the world's economic and political systems, and, after Manchuria, Munich, and Pearl Harbor, believed that aggression or political chaos even in remote areas of the world could no longer be ignored.[2]

AMERICAN POLICY AND ALLIED FRICTION IN IRAN

The State Department had already embarked by early 1943 on a series of initiatives that promised to open a new era in Iranian-American relations. Five advisory missions were in Iran to promote wartime stability through reform of key institutions. Secretary Hull had indicated that the United States would oppose any of its Allies' actions that violated the Tripartite Treaty. A trade agreement promised to increase commerce between the United States and Iran. Under lend-lease, American exports to Iran had already risen from $8 million before the war to over $20 million in 1943. The Persian Gulf Command, though operating strictly as a wartime agency, would leave a heavy American imprint on Iran's internal transportation network.[3]

All of these American initiatives were contingent on the war effort. Wallace Murray of the Near East Division was determined that wartime policy should establish a basis for continuing American involvement in Iran and the Middle East once the peace came. But planning for the peace required a rationale that would justify extending the new American role into the postwar era. Such a rationale could not readily acknowledge the State Department's fear of Soviet expansion or its desire for a larger policymaking role. It would have been poor politics in 1943 to warn of a Soviet danger. The American wartime propaganda machinery had worked diligently to overcome decades of anti-Soviet rhetoric and the heroic defense of Stalingrad had aroused widespread American sympathy for the Russian people. The president had stressed his intention to incorporate the Soviet Union into a new international system. Nor was the State Department's claim for its proper policymaking function likely to evoke much support from bureaucratic rivals. Secretary of the Interior and wartime petroleum administrator Harold Ickes had already staked his claim over foreign oil policy, while military planners had repeatedly rejected the department's requests to support political initiatives.[4]

The State Department needed to define a policy that embraced both the idealism of the Atlantic Charter and widely accepted notions of national self-interest. Exceptionalism, which tapped the wells of American idealism and nationalism, and the belief that a stable and independent Iran benefited American security interests provided the State Department with an effective and ideologically appropriate framework within which to justify its growing involvement in Iran. At the time, however, Iranian political leaders never had any intention of undertaking the extensive internal reforms the State Department sought. Sometimes by hints, sometimes by candid admissions, they indicated their belief that the U.S. advisers were almost solely instruments of their "third power policy" and conduits for American aid. They also believed that the presence of these missions would allow Iran some measure of autonomy in its relations with the great powers, despite the occupation. But most important, the Russians and the British gave little indication that they would assist the Americans in building a new Iran. Soviet actions in particular aggravated the very conditions the Americans hoped to alleviate. For the most part the American presence in Iran stimulated big power rivalries while immersing the United States in a totally alien political and cultural environment.

For Iranians the occupation brought about dislocations both large and small—food shortages, rampant inflation, political factionalism, and an irritating foreign presence. In 1942 and 1943 the shah made several attempts to curb the rebellious Qashqai tribes. Each foray ended in a further humiliation for the Iranian Army. Heavy Russian grain purchases disrupted the flow of food from the north to Tehran. With merchants hoarding scarce supplies and prices rocketing upward, bread riots filled the streets with angry protesters. The Iranian government pleaded with both the British and American governments to provide some form of relief. But since the Combined Chiefs of Staff accorded Iran a low supply priority, neither the State Department nor the British Foreign Office could offer any substantial assistance.[5]

The British legation saw an opportunity in Iran's adversity to resolve a number of nettlesome problems such as food hoarding, which artificially reduced supplies, and currency shortages, which hampered British purchases from local sources. The British also charged that German spies continued to operate throughout Iran. Sir Reader Bullard was determined to force the Iranian government to address these problems and to that end the British withheld wheat they had pledged to deliver to the Iranians during the winter of 1942–43. Louis Dreyfus thought that the use of food as a political weapon was more than the circumstances warranted and told the State Department that the current British actions were so excessive that they might actually be intended to create a situation that would serve as a pretext for occupying Tehran or establishing a puppet government. The fact that these British tactics did result in a new Iranian policy on foods and an expansion of currency did not comfort him.[6]

Dreyfus was convinced that the British would keep Tehran in turmoil until a more subservient government emerged. And shortly after the British made the decision to withhold wheat shipments, he received two secret British documents that seemed to confirm his suspicions. One proposed a new cabinet under Seyyed-Zia-ed-Din, known to all Iran as a British sympathizer. He would replace Ahmed Qavam, certainly no friend of British interests. The other recommended shifting authority from the shah to the American advisers. As the State Department sifted that information, the British, having pledged to leave Tehran unoccupied, marched troops into the city to combat food riots and other disorders. And a few days later, on 8 December 1942, they arrested a number of prominent Iranian citizens they believed to be German agents. Neither the American legation nor the Iranian government received advance warning of either action.[7]

Secretary Hull asked the Foreign Office to reconcile its behavior with earlier pledges to meet Iran's minimum economic requirements, to allow the Iranians to control their internal affairs, and to provide them with necessary grain. Further use of force or steps toward the creation of a puppet government threatened to undermine State Department efforts to stabilize Iran, he warned. On one level Hull was merely fulfilling his earlier promise to monitor Allied activities. On another level, however, his intervention marked a significant new step in American policy toward Iran. The United States had actively backed the Iranians in a disagreement with a foreign power.[8]

Hull must have sensed that his somewhat unusual action called for a fuller explanation, because he defined for the first time the principles guiding American policy. Favoring abstractions over concrete explanations of American interests, Hull stressed in his formulation that at present the Iranians bore such an animus toward both the British and the Russians that the United States alone could act to create conditions favorable to Allied operations. The State Department was particularly concerned that Allied actions might impede the advisers whose efforts to strengthen Iran would constitute an important American contribution to the war effort. Hull thus rejected any policy that by aggravating political or economic unrest threatened the operation of the Persian corridor.[9]

The Foreign Office took several steps to placate the Americans. Foreign Secretary Eden showed Ambassador John Winant secret files from the Tehran legation and from War Cabinet meetings to convince Winant that the British had acted out of necessity, not out of some sinister design. Nor did Eden accept Hull's suggestion that Sir Reader Bullard had instituted the offensive policies on his own initiative. The Foreign Office had given its full support to his actions, especially since Louis Dreyfus took so little initiative on behalf of the Allied cause. Regardless of any problems between Bullard and Dreyfus, Eden assured Hull that "the growing interest which the United States have shown in Persian affairs has been welcome to His Majesty's government. . . ."[10]

To assure Hull of Britain's good intentions, the Foreign Office sent Minister of State for the Middle East Richard Casey to Washington for talks with Wallace Murray. This visit allowed the two men to discover a wide area of agreement, including the need to work with the shah to correct the "generally weak moral fiber of the Iranian people." More important, they emphasized their common belief that Russian tactics had provoked much of the tension in Iran and that excessive Soviet wheat purchases had become the single largest source of political and economic unrest. Casey complained that even after the British and Americans had asked Moscow to refrain from imposing heavy burdens on Iranian food supplies, the Russians had failed to send normal grain shipments from Azerbaijan to Tehran. The British had had to bear the brunt of the ensuing crisis.[11]

Without directly criticizing British policy and to a degree ignoring the fact that when the Iranians failed to act on vexing issues, it always fell to the British, not the Americans, to bring them into line, Murray argued that the Allies might encourage more cooperation from the Iranians with Russian-style honey than with British vinegar. Accommodating policies, bolstered by propaganda, had firmly entrenched the Russians in their zone, Murray emphasized. "One of our reports had even gone so far as to say that a Soviet could be set up overnight, if the Russians gave the word." He reminded Casey that the Russians had used similar tactics in 1921 when they had eroded much of Britain's influence in Iran. Even though Casey and Murray did not agree on every point, such meetings between British and American diplomats smoothed over most differences.[12]

Similar meetings seldom occurred with the Russians. On many issues the two sides simply did not communicate. And in most cases the Russians and their Anglo-American allies lacked any common ground on which to compromise. The Russian aloofness in Iran might well have been a sign of Stalin's displeasure with his allies. In 1942, as historian Gaddis Smith has pointed out, Stalin had demanded three things from his allies: the recognition of his territorial demands, huge quantities of war materials, and a second front in Europe. On all three matters, Roosevelt and Churchill had left Stalin disappointed. It is worth noting that many of the Soviet demands on Iran that disturbed American and British diplomats were for resources that the Russians badly needed.[13]

One particular episode demonstrates the difficulty of interpreting Soviet actions. In 1941 Russian negotiators had pressured the Iranian government into a highly unfavorable arms contract and finance package. The agreement required Iran to provide capital and to pay stiff penalties if it failed to fulfill the contract's terms. The Russians, however, offered no provisions to pay for the arms. Both Dreyfus and Bullard viewed that arms deal as evidence of Soviet designs on Iran. As Dreyfus explained to the State Department, "Since one cannot accuse the Russians of a lack of practical common sense, the only conclusion to be drawn is that they signed the agreement to obtain a grip on the very heart of Iranian industry and prevent the plants from falling into British and American hands." That was of course one way to construe the contract, but it was not an interpretation that took into account the larger war picture. The Russians badly needed the guns, yet they probably could not have afforded to pay for them. Perhaps it was only their means and not their ends that warranted criticism. And had not the British been just as harsh on many occasions?[14]

In any case, Dreyfus considered that there was now sufficient cause for Washington to intercede. "The Soviet attitude might vitiate our entire adviser program," he warned Secretary Hull. Indeed, the Russians had imposed many hardships on American operations. The Soviet Embassy in Tehran had denied Colonel Norman Schwarzkopf, gendarmerie adviser, a permit to inspect posts in their occupation zone. Other American officials had experienced similar difficulties in obtaining visas or travel permits. Even General Connolly, whose command delivered much-needed supplies to the Soviet Union, could not acquire permits to establish facilities in the Russian zone. Bullard told the Foreign Office: "There are clear signs that the Soviet authorities dislike the presence of American advisors perhaps because the more successful the Americans are, the less amenable to communist propaganda the Persians will be. . . ."[15]

Soviet Ambassador Smirnov had underscored the appropriateness of Bullard's explanation when he publicly disparaged the American advisers, while praising the Russians as the "best administrators in the world." Dreyfus was particularly disturbed by reports that Smirnov had discouraged the Iranians from hiring more Americans. He did not find much comfort in Smirnov's explanation that his government chose to be uncooperative because the Americans had failed to notify them about the creation of the Persian Gulf Command, for as Smirnov surely knew, the British, not the Americans, were responsible for keeping Moscow informed. Yet even if the complaint was spurious, its general thrust did have merit. The Foreign Office and the State Department had taken a number of initiatives like the advisory missions without informing the Soviet Foreign Ministry.[16]

Secretary Hull was enough concerned about inter-Allied tensions that in March 1943 he sent Moscow a note explaining the broad outlines of American policy for Iran. Though for the most part intended to be simply a conciliatory gesture, Hull's action constituted something of a new departure in Soviet-American relations over Iran. In essence Hull was informing Moscow as he had earlier told the British that in its dealings with Iran, the Soviet Union must consider the United States an interested party. Hull dismissed the issue of the Persian Gulf Command as a problem for the Russians to take up with the British, who were responsible for Iran's security. He assured the Soviets that since the two countries had identical goals in Iran, they could work together toward a lasting peace. Perhaps Hull believed what he had said, but few others in the State Department shared his faith that the Soviet Union would participate in a Wilsonian peace.[17]

Before Hull's mediation efforts could have any results, the Soviets pulled off a propaganda coup that further fueled Anglo-American anxieties. Over the winter of 1942–43, the British and Americans had managed at enormous inconvenience to deliver grain to replenish Iranian supplies badly depleted by heavy Russian demand. The needs of the war effort seemed to justify such a sacrifice. But in April 1943 Ambassador Smirnov suddenly announced that his government would ship 25,000 tons of wheat to the people of Tehran. Now it seemed that the British and Americans had been played for suckers. They had struggled to make shipments so that the Russians could donate to the Iranians what was in essence their own wheat. And what made this gesture more galling was that wheat was no longer in short supply. Dreyfus was furious. "An obvious bid for Iranian sympathy prior to the Majles election," he fumed in a cable to Washington. "The Soviets, holding their punch to the last round, now come forth as the savior of Iran and make wheat available where the British and Americans are popularly believed to have failed."[18]

That episode, though of no great importance by itself, should have warned the State Department that the Russians would not allow the Americans a free hand, no matter how benevolent their intentions. Any plans the State Department had for nation-building would have to accommodate Soviet preoccupations with its security in the Caspian region. Nor were notes from Secretary Hull likely to ease Soviet suspicions. The Allies obviously needed to come to some broader understanding about their conflicting objectives in the area.

The Iranians caused almost as many headaches as the Russians. By early 1943

Iranian public figures had found it useful to make the American advisers scapegoats for a host of long-term problems aggravated by the war, the occupation, and internal factionalism. Some groups even publicly blamed the United States for the food shortages. Iranian-American friction first erupted in March 1943 when finance adviser Arthur Millspaugh sought to consolidate his authority under a sweeping "Full Powers Bill," granting him near dictatorial control over critical sectors of Iran's economy. Few politicians or merchants were willing to see their own influence so severely curbed. In a demonstration of both displeasure and political power, the merchants brought commercial life briefly to a halt by closing the bazaars.[19]

To make matters worse, American troops from the Persian Gulf Command, plagued by the oppressive heat, primitive living conditions, and boredom, came into the cities seeking relief. The Americans' notion of a good time—public boozing, womanizing, and riotous good fellowship—shocked conservative Muslims. Russian troops by contrast maintained a much lower visibility and comported themselves publicly under much stricter discipline. Since no treaty arrangements covered the presence of these American troops, each incident of public misconduct raised ticklish diplomatic issues.[20]

All of these problems eventually fell into the lap of the beleaguered Louis Dreyfus. "The goodwill manifested toward Americans for so many years is now at an all-time low," he told Secretary Hull. To an already long list of factors inhibiting the State Department's efforts in Iran, Dreyfus could now add the erosion of American prestige stemming from a general Iranian animus against all the occupying forces, the advisers' failure to achieve significant progress, disappointment over the trickle of lend-lease goods, and constant delays with grain shipments. Nor had the United States been sufficiently active in opposing the Russian pressure tactics that many Iranians found threatening. In short, the United States had performed poorly thus far in its new third power role and Dreyfus wanted the State Department to recognize that reality.[21]

THE JERNEGAN MEMORANDUM

The gloomy news from Dreyfus might well have led the State Department to reconsider the direction of its Iranian policy. Certainly the advisory missions had fallen far short of what the British and Iranian governments had expected. Indeed, under the the circumstances imposed by the war and Iran's weakened condition, the United States could have realistically accomplished little of lasting value. At the same time, the State Department's efforts, though limited, clearly had aroused Soviet anxiety and met with resistance.

Frustration did not, however, shake the Near East Divison from its earlier notions about America's role in Iran, and in early 1943 those assumptions became the basis for a statement of the department's objectives for postwar Iran. That statement had rather modest beginnings. It did not come about as a response to some high-level request for a policy. Rather, it came in the form of an unsolicited memorandum prepared by thirty-one-year-old John Jernegan, recently assigned to the Near East Division as a desk officer. Before assuming his new duties, Jernegan had served as vice consul in Barcelona. As Wallce Murray became more wrapped up in his duties as political adviser, his assistant in the Near East Division, Paul Alling, brought Jernegan in to build up his severely undermanned staff. The new officer had never even been to the Near East. What little knowledge he possessed came from reading the *Arabian Nights* and T. E. Lawrence's *Seven Pillars of Wisdom*.

Within a few months at the Near East Division, Jernegan discovered that Iran demanded his full-time attention. He contacted a variety of missionaries, scholars, archaeologists, and any one else who might expand his scanty knowledge. By January 1943 he had spent almost half a year monitoring the growing cable traffic between Washington and Tehran. One winter afternoon when his office was surprisingly quiet, he had an opportunity to think more broadly about his work. No one had asked him to prepare a policy statement, but he believed that greater American involvement required a more formal outline. "I am going to write an idealistic document," he told his office mate that afternoon.[22]

The document that emerged bore the heavy imprint of Wallace Murray. In it Jernegan synthesized the unformulated assumptions that had thus far governed the growing American involvement in Iran. Its importance lay not so much in its analysis of the current situation as in its attempt to reorient American policy from wartime necessity to the postwar peace. To date the United States had concentrated on Iran's importance as a supply route and a source of petroleum as well as its strategic value in the context of global strategy. "I wonder," Jernegan asked rhetorically, "if we should not begin, privately, to base our response [to unstable conditions in Iran] on our winning the peace?"[23]

Knowing too little about Iran to propose effective prescriptions for internal problems, Jernegan concentrated most on Allied relations. The Anglo-Soviet rivalry struck him as the most formidable barrier to an independent and stable Iran. As the two powers vied for influence, they threatened Iranian sovereignty and the application of other Atlantic Charter principles. If history served as a guide, and Jernegan assumed it would, then the two powers were likely to continue their destructive rivalry after the war ended. Meanwhile the current occupation had so badly weakened the Iranian government that foreign powers had an open invitation for future intervention; Soviet policy had made Azerbaijan particularly vulnerable to a takeover. Caught in a cycle of mutually reinforced suspicions, the British and Russians could find in each other's actions a justification for a permanent occupation.

Jernegan, in recognizing that such a nightmare had inspired the Iranian government's initial appeals for American aid, proposed that the United States undertake what amounted to a New Deal for Iran, building public works projects, providing material aid, and protecting Iran from foreign exploitation. He argued that

> the United States alone is in a position to build up Iran to the point at which it will stand in need of neither British nor Russian assistance to maintain order in its own house. . . . We can so firmly establish disinterested American advisors in Iran that no peace conference could even consider a proposal to institute a Russian or British protectorate or to "recognize the predominance" of Russian or British interests.[24]

Such a policy hinged on Jernegan's assumption that the United States and its representatives were somehow "disinterested" and could therefore act impartially to help eliminate the great power rivalry over influence in Iran. Furthermore, Jernegan argued that by relieving its Anglo-Russian allies of a "constant source of friction," the United States would be performing a service of value far beyond what would be immediately realized by Iran itself. In an unabashed tribute to the idea of American "innocence," Jernegan went on to conclude that neither the Russians nor British "could suspect the United States of having imperialistic designs in a country so removed from us and where we could never hope to employ military force against any adjacent power." Such a remarkably naive idea would seem only the product of youthful idealism if it had not often appeared in various forms in the rhetoric of leading Americans including President Roosevelt and Secretary Hull.[25]

Jernegan recognized the need to balance his idealism with an appeal to American self-interest and stressed that the United States would realize tangible benefits from such an enlightened policy. Although he believed that the principal appeal of such a policy to most Americans would arise out of their sympathy "with anything savoring of assistance to the underdog," he also touched upon the general consensus that conditions of the modern world demanded that the United States play an active role in postwar international affairs, since it could not "be indifferent to the welfare of any part of the world, no matter how remote, because sooner or later it will affect our peace." Indeed, it was Jernegan who introduced the idea that later appealed so much to President Roosevelt, that Iran could serve as "a test case of the good faith of the United Nations." Through cooperative policies the Allies would demonstrate their ability to serve the interests of powers both great and small.

The goals set down in the Jernegan memorandum were diplomatic and political, not military. Proposing a program based on aid and oriented toward the postwar period, it would allow the State Department to establish the priorities of American policy. The State Department, not the War Department, would have the major voice in determining what Iran's needs were and what personnel and supplies should be sent there. The belief in American exceptionalism made it possible for Jernegan to assume that "disinterested" Americans could transcend the old practices of self-interested imperialism. But more important, Jernegan, like Murray, had identified the Soviet Union and its designs on Azerbaijan as the greatest threat to a lasting peace. Though he did not dwell on the fear of communist expansion, it emerged as a subtext of the general Russophobia that pervaded the State Department.

The reception of the memorandum far exceeded Jernegan's modest expectations. Wallace Murray adopted it almost as his own and sent it on to Secretary Hull, Assistant Secretaries Berle and Acheson, Under Secretary Sumner Welles, and postwar Planning Director Leo Pasvolsky, noting that "the attached memorandum is a summary of the thoughts of Near East and myself regarding the general bases and directions of our policy toward Iran. . . ."[26] Eventually the memorandum in summary form reached President Roosevelt, who gave its broad objectives his informal endorsement.

Even though he was in the best situation to evaluate the substance of Jernegan's recommendations, Louis Dreyfus did not receive a copy of it until a month after it had circulated through the State Department. In sending his reactions to the department, Dreyfus heartily endorsed the general thrust of Jernegan's ideas, but at the same time, without any evident intent to discredit the memorandum, he wrote what could have been read as a trenchant critique of it. There were, he observed, "obstacles in the way of our obtainment of our Iranian objectives." The Russians, through a "positive and aggressive policy," clearly intended to ensconce themselves in Iran. Corrupt and selfish Iranian politicians posed another problem; the U.S. advisers could not succeed without their cooperation. Dreyfus suspected the British too. They seemed to be giving the Americans sufficient rope to hang themselves, after which Britain could profit from the American failure. Besides, the British did not need the Americans in a disinterested role but as an additional buffer against Soviet expansion. And Dreyfus recognized that the Untied States might become the author of its own undoing if it sent incompetent advisers or provided those in Iran with inadequate support.[27]

An even graver weakness stemmed from the memorandum's uncritical acceptance of the assumptions of American exceptionalism. Could anyone realistically expect the United States to make a substantial commitment to Iran without a tangible stake in that nation? And as American interests grew, would not Iran then move into the kind of neocolonial system the United States maintained in Latin America? Any policy that proposed to eliminate Russian and British influence would realistically have to anticipate a far greater American presence. Iran would remain within some sphere of influence or balance of power system—the very mechanisms of political order that Jernegan, like Cordell Hull, had rejected as inherently unstable.

Only the notion that the United States could function in a "disinterested" role allowed Jernegan to escape the contradictions in his proposal. Yet nothing that the United States did between 1941 and 1943 in regard to Iran could be described as selfless or neutral. Each step taken to promote the war effort had, at least in part, promised to advance some immediate or potential American interest. The reduction of Russian and British influence would not only relieve foreign pressures on Iran, but also open the door to American commerce. The 1943 trade agreement was a step in that direction. Wallace Murray's overtures to the Presbyterian Mission Board had been an early effort to contain Soviet ambitions. Similar motives had influenced the decision to send advisory missions. At each step the State Department had identified an American interest or the danger posed by Anglo-Soviet ambitions as justification for greater involvement. Certainly self-interest and rivalry are a legitimate basis for a foreign policy. Unfortunately, in this case, they undermined the central assumption upon which Jernegan had based his argument that the United States could bring a new era to Iran and the Middle East.

Nor would the methods proposed for achieving these policy goals prove particularly fruitful. Americans have always overestimated the effectiveness of foreign advisers as instruments of policy, whether the advisers are missionaries, customs collectors, Point Four technicians, Peace Corps volunteers, or military missions. In this regard, Jernegan was no exception. The checkered record of colonial administrators or other western cultural emmissaries to the third world never limited his faith in what Americans might accomplish in Iran. Advisers to police agencies and armies may increase stability, but they seldom institute democratic reforms. Finding competent advisers was even more difficult in Iran's case than in many other areas. Few Americans knew anything about conditions there or elsewhere in the region. As a result, Jernegan's proposal rested on a shaky proposition. Advisers could symbolize American concern. They might even shore up some weak government agencies, but in such small numbers with limited resources they were unlikely to alter Iran in significant ways. The very conditions that made their presence seem so necessary also made their task impossible. By weakening the central government, the occupation had worsened political corruption, economic distress, political factionalism, and popular discontent. In order to address those problems while ensuring the uninterrupted movement of supplies, the advisers needed support from the occupying powers and a strong, stable central authority capable of implementing and enforcing policies.

The memorandum was also misguided, and perhaps even dangerously so, in its notion that the United States could assume a major position in Iran without aggravating the rivalry among the great powers. How would Americans in 1943 have reacted to a Russian oil concession in Mexico or a less threatening British mission to the Cuban Army? Should one be surprised that every initiative the Americans took in Iran aroused some sign of Soviet hostility? Nor did the British have any great desire to share the Middle Eastern stage with the United States. Only their weakness and fear of Soviet expansion had generated their interest in an increased role for the Americans. The end of hostilities would most certainly lead both the Russians and the British to a more jaundiced view of this new interloper in Iran.

Finally, Iranian leaders had given no evidence that they shared Jernegan's grand vision for their country. They had repeatedly made their support for the American advisers contingent on increases in American material aid. The presence of the

United States as a third power in Iran was not calculated to end big power rivalry, but simply to allow the Iranians to conduct a more autonomous foreign policy. And once the immediate threat of the occupation ended, American efforts at reform would more than likely seem an unwarranted intrusion on Iranian sovereignty, with Jernegan's new deal looking a lot like old-style imperialism to many Iranians. Nor could it even be assumed that the Iranians would necessarily benefit if the United States successfully eliminated foreign rivalries. In 1907, big power entente almost spelled disaster for Iranian independence. Jernegan had failed to realize that the Iranian government had little incentive to seek cooperation among the powers.[28]

Why then did the State Department adopt Jernegan's memorandum with so little discussion of its many problematic assumptions and potential shortcomings? In reality, Jernegan had added little to current American policy for Iran beyond shifting the focus from the war to the postwar era. Most of his assumptions were so widely shared that they generated little debate. Criticism would arise only when the Near East Division tried to enlist other agencies whose priorities conflicted with theirs. Jernegan himself later discounted the impact of the memorandum: "It is true that American policy did follow its general lines, but it might have done so without any memorandum." In short, Jernegan had imposed a framework on a policy that had previously grown piecemeal in response to wartime circumstances.[29]

To show how widespread Jernegan's views were within the American foreign policy apparatus, we can compare the Roosevelt administration's policy in Iran with its China policy. In China too the United States sought to reform a weak, inefficient, and corrupt government. At first the administration justified its aid to China as a contribution to the war effort. Eventually, China's internal chaos, like Iran's, threatened to undermine plans to win both the war and the peace. Big power rivalries had been even more destructive in China than in Iran. The United States sought to reduce foreign pressures by promoting a more stable, liberal-democratic government. It encouraged a broad program of economic and political reforms under the tutelage of American advisers. Their efforts, as in Iran, were concentrated on government finance and the military.[30]

Since China's problems dwarfed those of Iran, the comparison is far from exact. Still, Chinese leaders voiced many of the same complaints that Iran's leaders did. American advisers lacked the resources to take significant initiatives. As historian Warren Cohen has observed, "China received all the praise and some of the loyalty due an ally, but little of the substance." And Cohen's conclusion could have applied equally well to Iran: "Once again, the Roosevelt years demonstrated that American policy was designed to serve American interests without particular regard for China." That was a far cry from some conception of benevolent or enlightened "disinterestedness."[31]

In both China and Iran American policymakers assumed they could exercise a significant influence over the internal politics of these countries. That misjudgment would later haunt the China hands, for it made them vulnerable to the charge that they had "lost China." Differing circumstances, not a more successful policy, postponed a similar collapse in Iran. Iran had a somewhat stronger government facing a less effective opposition. Tribal insurrections did not amount to full-scale civil war. The Tudeh Party never had the strength or appeal of the Chinese communists. And the consequences of the occupation, no matter how disruptive they were, could not compare to Japan's devastating invasion of China. Still, the United States would fail in Iran, as it did in China, to mitigate conditions that would disrupt the peace. The failure to realize more tangible benefits from American involvement would leave Chinese and Iranian leaders constantly dissatisfied. Jernegan and others erred in believing that the United States had the will, the resources, and the capability to turn Iran or China into stable societies, much less western-style democracies. In short, they had too much faith in American exceptionalism. A more realistic policy would have understood that internal disorder and foreign rivalries were permanent conditions for the indefinite future.

In adopting the Jernegan memorandum the State Department made no new commitments. Rather, it acknowledged what had been implicit in each step of the increasing American involvement in Iran. The United States commitment to Iran would extend beyond the war. As a consequence of it, the State Department had two immediate tasks in 1943. First, it had to win wider acceptance for its policy assumptions among other government agencies as well as with the British, Iranian, and Soviet governments. Second, it had to create additional instruments of American policy while making existing instruments more effective. What the department had not yet acknowledged was the danger of staking future U.S. security on an area of the world in which American interests clashed with those of its wartime allies. Moreover, there was little reason to believe that the Jernegan memorandum contained a real blueprint for stability in Iran.

NOTES

1. Gaddis Smith, *American Diplomacy During the Second World War* (New York, 1965), pp. 13–15. See also James MacGregor Burns, *Roosevelt: The Soldier of Freedom* (New York, 1970), p. 187; and Robert Dallek, *Franklin D. Roosevelt and American Foreign Policy, 1932–1945* (New York, 1979), pp. 337–38. For a good discussion of negotiations over the Atlantic Charter, see Dallek, *Franklin D. Roosevelt and American Foreign Policy,* pp. 283–85. See also Herbert Feis, *Churchill-Roosevelt-Stalin* (Princeton, 1957), pp. 20–25 and 27–29. See Dallek, *Franklin D. Roosevelt and American Foreign Policy,* pp. 529–38 for a concise discussion of Roosevelt's foreign policy leadership. It is my own view that Roosevelt sometimes did not realize his limitations, particularly when he dealt with what are now known as third world areas. His role in American policy towards Iran, while never of great importance to him, may have had an unintended impact, as we shall see in chapter 4.

2. On the problem of isolationism, see Wayne Cole, *Roosevelt and the Isolationists, 1932–1945* (University of Nebraska, 1983), and the review by Arthur Schlesinger, Jr., "Desperate Times," *New York Review of Books,* 24 November 1983. On the idea of historical lessons, see Ernest R. May, *"Lessons" of the Past* (New York, 1973), especially chs. 1 and 2.

3. All these issues are discussed in greater detail in the preceding chapter. For another good source, see Bruce Kuniholm, *The Origins of the Cold War in the Near East* (Princeton, 1980) pp. 140–55.

4. On the bureaucratic infighting over foreign oil policy, see Michael B. Stoff, *Oil, War, and American Security* (New Haven, 1980), pp. 22–33. On American attitudes toward the Soviet Union, see Ralph Levering, *American Opinion and the Russian Alliance* (Chapel Hill, 1978).

5. See for example FR, 1942, 4, pp. 153, 165–66, 179, and 180–81.

6. Ibid., pp. 181, 202–3, 206, 214–217. Dreyfus must have found it frustrating that British tactics, whatever their motives, seemed to work. The Majles passed a bill addressing the currency shortage and the Iranian minister issued a declaration on food that Dreyfus and Bullard helped prepare.

7. Ibid., pp. 195–96.

8. Ibid., pp. 214–17.

9. Ibid., pp. 214–17.

10. FR, 1943, 4, p. 188 and pp. 320–25. See also Kuniholm, *The Origins of the Cold War in the Near East,* pp. 154–55.

11. FR, 1943, 4, p. 328.

12. Ibid., p. 328.

13. Gaddis Smith, *American Diplomacy During World War II,* p. 39.

14. FR, 1943, 4, pp. 633–35. For another episode of similar import involving the consul in

Tabriz, Bartol Kuniholm, and an assistant food adviser, Rex Vivian, see ibid., pp. 347–48. See also SD 891.24/405, 184, 3/31, 43, Hull to Ambassador in Moscow.

15. FR, 1943, 4, pp. 347–48 and 346. FO, 35096, E445/82/34, 2/16/43, Bullard to C. W. Baxter.

16. FR, 1943, 4, pp. 338–46.

17. Ibid., pp. 351–54.

18. Ibid., pp. 355–57.

19. Ibid., pp. 338–42.

20. Ibid., pp. 338–42.

21. SD 711.91/96, 529, 4/22/43, Dreyfus to Secretary of State.

22. Jernegan letter to author, 2/18/73. See also Kuniholm, *The Origins of the Cold War in the Near East,* pp. 156–57.

23. FR, 1943, 4, pp. 330–36 and especially 331–34, "American Policy in Iran," memorandum by John Jernegan, 1/23/43. This is the document that I refer to as the Jernegan memorandum.

24. Ibid., pp. 331–34.

25. See Wendell Willkie, *One World* (New York, 1943) and a good analysis in John Blum, *V Was For Victory* (New York, 1976), pp. 262–78 and on Henry Luce, pp. 284–85, for another example.

26. FR, 1943, 4, p. 330 and 330n.

27. Ibid., pp. 355–57.

28. On the purposes of Iran's appeal for American aid, see Rouhollah Ramazani, *Iran's Foreign Policy, 1941–1973* (Charlottesville, 1975), pp. 70–91.

29. Jernegan letter to author.

30. Dallek, pp. 330–31, 355–58, 387–88, and 486–88. I should emphasize that the differences between American aid to China and Iran are more significant than the similarities. Dallek's discussion of American China policy makes clear how much more complicated U.S. goals were for some of the following reasons: traditional American interest in China, China as an active war theater, the need for a counter to potential Soviet expansion in Asia, and the scale of Chinese problems.

31. Warren I. Cohen, *America's Responses to China* (New York, 1971), pp. 162–63.

4 *The Declaration on Iran*

In his memorandum, Jernegan had assumed that the State Department would be responsible for American policy in Iran, although in 1943 State Department control there was far from complete. Diverse individuals and agencies continued to operate at cross purposes in Iran. The advisers who were supposed to help secure the supply route received no cooperation from the Persian Gulf Command that operated it. The individual missions lacked any effective coordination. General Ridley sought to improve the army's morale, while finance adviser Millspaugh wanted to cut the military budget. Lend-lease administrators had supplies vital to Iran and other Middle Eastern countries, but limited authority to make them available. If the United States had a policy for Iran, no one, including Louis Dreyfus, knew what it was.

The muddle over American operations in the Middle East was an almost inevitable consequence of the rapid growth of American operations there. At the same time it reflected President Roosevelt's administrative style. Confused lines of authority at the operating level allowed the president to retain overall control. He arbitrated large policy questions when his subordinates clashed. By early 1943 he sensed that some clarification of responsibility was necessary to keep supplies moving efficiently to the Soviet Union. Rather than making uninformed decisions, he sent his personal emissary, Major General Patrick Hurley, to investigate American operations in the area and to encourage a "single team" concept among the proliferating civilian and military agencies.[1]

PATRICK HURLEY AND AMERICAN POLICY FOR IRAN

Throughout the war Patrick Hurley served Roosevelt as a roving ambassador and troubleshooter. Most of his missions took him far away from the United States to deal with issues low on the president's list of priorities. Though Hurley had served under Herbert Hoover as secretary of war, he had few qualifications as either a diplomat or a strategist. And Roosevelt undoubtedly called on Hurley, who had been associated with the conservative wing of the Republican party, as he did on such distinguished Republicans as Robert Lovett, Henry Stimson, and Navy Secretary Frank Knox, principally to give a bipartisan cast to his administration's foreign policy.

Despite his conservatism, Hurley shared FDR's admiration for Theodore Roosevelt and his progressivism, for in actuality Hurley had few organized political ideas. He treated broad generalities like those in the Atlantic Charter as if they were a precise blueprint for all foreign policy and allowed two deeply held prejudices to color much of his thinking. He abhorred communism and harbored Irish antipathy for all things British, particularly British imperialism. His fear of a red menace provoked him to urge the assault by the U.S. Army against the Bonus Army in 1932. By 1943, however, the Russians' heroic wartime defense had somewhat muted his strident anti-Soviet rhetoric.[2]

After meeting Hurley in China, correspondent Teddy White dismissed him as a "hustler" and an "ignoramus" on foreign affairs. His biographer, Russell Buhite, described him as a "careerist," one of those self-promoting people who make their way in public life by being useful to people in power. Born into the family of a poor coal miner, Hurley had a spotty education before coming to Washington, D.C., to study law. Although he returned to Oklahoma to make his fortune in land titles and oil rights, he was happiest near the corridors of power in Washington where he had contracted a chronic case of Potomac fever. As the owner of the Shoreham Hotel, he provided himself with a prestigious address. He paved his way to social status and enhanced his political influence when he married the daughter of Fleet Admiral Henry Wilson. In the 1930s as an attorney for oilman Harry Sinclair he played a crucial role in settling Sinclair's claim against the Mexican government after it expropriated American-owned oil fields. That experience gave him a background in the international oil industry that would prove valuable on his wartime trips to the Middle East.[3]

Hurley's fact-finding mission brought him to Iran for a short stay. While there, he developed a sympathy for the people and their struggle to stay out from under the control of the British and Russians. He did not then or later recognize Iran's appeal for American assistance as the application of a third power strategy. After conversations with the shah and a few Iranian officials as well as a variety of Americans, he concluded that Iran stood at the center of an explosive Anglo-Russian contest for power, with the British seeking to preserve their oil and trade monopolies and the Russians still aspiring to secure a warm-water port on the Persian Gulf. Hurley argued that "if the Germans were totally defeated . . . there would be open conflict in the Middle East between the forces of the United Nations." He thought that the Iranians had become so anglophobic that in the event of such a conflict they would side with the Russians and that, since many Iranians had come to view the Americans as instruments for shoring up waning British power, continued close association with British policies in Iran threatened to destroy American prestige in the country. In Hurley's opinion, nothing less was at stake than the realization of Atlantic Charter principles as the basis for peace in the region.[4]

Hurley discovered a level of confusion within the American policy apparatus that he thought contributed to the explosive situation. According to his analysis, lack of leadership at the top had left American civilian and military advisers uncertain whether "to support conquest and imperialism or the Atlantic Charter and Four Freedoms. . . ." Even though the Iranians saw the American advisers as tools of British imperialism, he thought that these advisers did not in fact even have a clear sense of "what should be their attitude in the conflict between Russia and Britain."[5]

The disarray Hurley observed among American agencies was no doubt real enough, and certainly he was correct in observing the potential for conflict among the Allies. But his proposal for an appropriate American response conflicted with the implications of his analysis. After harshly criticizing the British, he proposed a policy of benevolent Anglo-American interventionism around the Middle East, believing somehow that the two Anglo-Saxon powers could work together to establish "strong enlightened governments" in the region and end the danger of Anglo-Russian rivalry. "The achievement of the purposes of the Atlantic Charter . . . depends in great measure on the unity of the English-speaking people," he concluded. Hurley's contradictory stance toward the British may have stemmed in part from his recognition that the president did not share his anglophobia, and also from his belief that cooperation with the British best served American interests in the Middle East.[6]

Hurley did suggest several constructive steps to strengthen Iran's ties to the United States and Great Britain. Both powers, he urged, should raise their legations to embassies and appoint ambassadors who could cooperate with one another in promoting Anglo-American interests. To give Iran more standing at the peace conference, he thought the Iranian government should join the United Nations by declaring war on Germany. More important, he wanted the United States to give adequate assurances that the Atlantic Charter applied to Iran. That would substitute, he undoubtedly believed, for the formal treaty commitment Iran had sought and the State Department had declined to make. And like the "Open Door" notes, such assurances would serve notice that the United States opposed any intention other powers might have to carve Iran into spheres of influence. If American involvement had not in fact gone beyond these recommendations, the United States might have played the role Jernegan had prescribed. It would have set aside narrow American interests to achieve regional stability. Hurley, however, like Murray and Jernegan, saw those initiatives only as first steps toward a far greater American presence.[7]

Hurley's report provoked a critical response from Secretary of State Cordell Hull, who was undoubtedly more upset by such poaching on his department's turf than by anything Hurley had said. After all, none of the general's recommendations conflicted with current policy. There was, all the same, an important difference between the two men that reflected diverging approaches to American foreign policy. Hull wanted to view Iran in a global framework. He correctly sensed that the intensity of the Anglo-Soviet rivalry in local situations would depend largely on overall relations between the two powers. In true Wilsonian fashion, Hull thought that if the United States mediated general disagreements between its allies, the particulars of their conflict over Iran would take care of themselves. Hurley, like Jernegan, saw that in some ways Iran presented a special case. If the Allies could not compromise in Iran, they would not reach broader understandings.

An effective policy would have to bridge both of these points of view, but given the intractability of most Allied disputes over Iran, Americans were more inclined to focus their diplomacy on general than on particular issues. Hull dismissed the substance of Hurley's report. He recalled that the United States had already pressed its allies to give assurances to Iran, and that the Iranians for their part had shown no great desire to declare war on Germany. Hull did begrudgingly concede that the elevation of the legation to an embassy would be a constructive sign of American interest.[8]

As was often his response when subordinates fought, Roosevelt for the moment did nothing. At least as a result of Hurley's trip the president now knew that the United States had developed a substantial interest in Iran as it had in Saudi Arabia.

And both Hurley and Hull had told him that present Allied tensions over Iran posed a threat to the peace he hoped to achieve.[9]

GENERAL CONNOLLY AND AMERICAN AID

The struggle over the particulars of American policy waged between the War Department and the State Department struck Louis Dreyfus as increasingly inopportune as the political situation in Iran appeared to deteriorate. Indeed, many Allied observers saw Iran precariously balanced on the brink of chaos. Disappointment over the performance of the American advisory missions had led the Iranian press to unleash a campaign aimed especially at Arthur Millspaugh and those in the government who supported his mission. Dreyfus believed that more effective results from the advisory missions might ease the current unrest. But he could not persuade General Connolly that he should supply Ridley and Schwarzkopf with trucks, radios, boots, clothing, and the other basic supplies they desperately needed. Only with great reluctance had Connolly granted American diplomatic personnel access to commissary and mess facilities.[10]

By June 1943, Dreyfus was fed up. A rash of Iranian newspaper articles attacking the behavior of American soldiers gave him an opportunity to air his differences with Connolly. Dreyfus was not content simply to rebuke the PGC. He used the occasion to explain to Connolly the broad outlines of American policy that Jernegan had laid out in his memorandum. Connolly agreed only to instruct his troops to act as good will representatives of the United States as long as they were in Iran. Beyond that he would make no commitments. Thus the PGC channel for material assistance to Iran remained closed. Dreyfus poured out his frustrations to Secretary Hull. And while he waited for Washington's reaction to his complaint, he sent his new third secretary—John Jernegan—to appeal to Connolly.[11]

Jernegan was prepared to instruct the general about American diplomacy. Instead, Connolly offered him a penetrating critique of State Department policy and its assumptions. He assured Jernegan that though he wished to be cooperative, he found many of the proposed policies unsound. What real interest did the United States have in Iran, he asked. Without tangible interests, there was no substantial reason to carry out Jernegan's policies. The Iranian people had impressed Connolly as "so corrupt and demoralized that it would be next to impossible to do anything with them for many years." In particular he objected to assisting a repressive feudal regime that in no way shared American ideals nor effectively ruled in its own domain. The Russians, he believed, could undermine State Department policies whenever they wished. So complete was their sway over Azerbaijan, they could install a puppet government there at any time. Such a client could then declare its independence and petition for admission into the Soviet Union. That strategy would violate neither the Tripartite Treaty nor the Atlantic Charter. "Regardless of the method employed," Jernegan noted, "Connolly felt there was nothing the United States could do to prevent Soviet domination of Iran and he thought the Russians had definite ideas along this line."[12]

Even if Connolly was overly pessimistic, Jernegan and his superiors needed to address the substance of his criticisms. Why, indeed, should the United States become the champion of a nation whose political and social institutions contradicted the very reasons for which America had gone to war? How useful was American technology for a society in which most of its people lived in a premodern culture? And what price would the United States pay to contain the Soviet ambitions? Those questions would continue to haunt Iranian-American relations for the next thirty-five years.

Efforts to convert Connolly were largely misspent, because the general's views were also those of his superiors in the War Department. At that time, for example, the Office of War Information (OWI) had found itself similarly frustrated. Military brass had little patience with OWI and the Military Intelligence Service (MIS) had quickly shelved an OWI plan for propaganda in Iran. In doing so, MIS had used the same arguments Connolly had given Jernegan. The War Department still saw no need for a more active policy because the Allies already controlled the supply route. Even after State Department representatives had discussed their assumptions with top military brass, the War Department refused to circulate the Jernegan memorandum or to agree that its analysis had any relevance to the war effort.[13]

BRITISH POLICY TOWARD IRAN

Political unrest in Iran forced the British Foreign Office to review its policy. Sir Reader Bullard warned that "the Russians are acquiring, in comparison to ourselves, a popularity which albeit undeserved, must be taken into account as a very serious factor. . . ."[14] All the signs Bullard had seen pointed to a more aggressive Soviet policy. Having closed many consulates in the 1930s, the Soviets had now begun to reopen them. A wider diplomatic network would only enhance their capacity for disseminating propaganda and intrigue. So, too, would the lifting of Reza Shah's strict censorship laws. Bullard had learned from his sources that Russian occupation forces in Azerbaijan had disarmed Iranian security forces, weakened the central government's influence, and encouraged ethnic separatism. The Persians were just too weak to resist Russian demands or to offend their northern neighbor in any way.

Adrian Holman, Consular Officer of the British Legation, believed it was the sudden burst of American interest that had most unsettled Iran's relations with the big powers. "The presence of American advisors in various branches of Persian government, and the fact the American government means to stake out a claim in this country and stay with or without connivance, has sharpened still more Russian suspicions which the American government might find difficult to dissipate."[15] Holman speculated that at least some of the Russians' seemingly aggressive policies were a defensive response to their fear of facing a unified Anglo-American rival. To ensure future big power cooperation, the British would have to exercise more restraint.

Bullard made another observation that had eluded Hurley, Murray, and other architects of a containment policy in Iran. The Persians traditionally feared their predatory northern neighbor more than any other power. Thus, if the British now offered assistance while the Russians continued to threaten Iranian independence, the political winds would soon shift in Britain's favor. American diplomats, by contrast, were inclined to treat any Iranian overture to the Russians not as a defensive maneuver but as a realignment toward the Soviet orbit. Had they been more mindful of Iran's long efforts to remain independent through the application of a third power strategy, then perhaps they might have adopted the perspective of one Foreign Office wag who commented that "at worst the Persians are very indigestable to those who try to assimilate them, and this may be their strongest asset in resisting encroachment."[16]

Bullard reminded the Foreign Office how much their own efforts to contain the Soviet Union depended on a successful American policy. He went so far as to argue that "from the British point of view the Americans are, perhaps, the sole hope of Persia." To that Neville Butler of the Foreign Office replied "that the success of the present American advisors in Persia is probably our best hope for establishing the kind of Persia that suits our interests." Butler did not mean a Persia subservient to England or a nation whose weakness invited further imperial gains, as Hurley and other anglophobes assumed. Rather, Butler wished for an independent, prosperous, and contented nation. To that end, he concluded, the Foreign Office "had an obligation to do what we can" to make the advisory missions successful.[17]

When the discussion in the Foreign Office turned to possible new policies, Under Secretary Sir Alexander Cadogan had to admit that he had found "no heroic remedies." The war situation prevented the British even more than the Americans from diverting supplies from the Soviet Union to meet Iran's current needs. Cadogan thought only that in the future the Iranians' most pressing civilian requirements might receive a higher priority. In fact, all Cadogan could recommend was more effective propaganda. Any strategy beyond that to extend British administrative control, including any attempt to displace the American advisers, might provoke the Russians to tighten their grip on the north. The ensuing Anglo-Soviet standoff would produce a situation comparable to the 1907 partition. W. H. Young agreed that no other avenues were open: "After all, to Russian eyes our activities, and still more those of the Americans, can hardly fail to indicate an exaggerated interest in Persian affairs."[18]

Nothing that was said in the Foreign Office confirmed the American suspicions that the British harbored plans to extend their imperial hegemony. British diplomats were all too aware of their inability to sustain an effective defensive policy, much less an expansionist one, in Iran. At the same time they appreciated the limits that the war imposed on any plans to reform Iran. American advisers were far more important as political symbols than for any possible accomplishments. As things stood, any American presence, no matter what form it took, helped to contain possible Soviet expansion. Better to have an overly idealistic or misguided American policy than none at all. The British already seemed to sense that in the future the United States would become the senior partner in Iran, the Middle East, and in other areas once thought of as in their own sphere of influence.

A POLICY CONSENSUS EMERGES

By the fall of 1943 the State Department had attempted to pull together some of the disparate strands of its policy for Iran. Cordell Hull sought to enlist the president's support by summarizing for Roosevelt the broad outlines of the Jernegan memorandum. "I feel that State Department policy should be implemented more actively than heretofore," Hull argued. Such a step required the cooperation of interested agencies, especially the War Department and the PGC. Hull therefore requested the president's permission to have the Joint Chiefs of Staff extend Connolly's mission to include assistance for the advisory missions.[19]

The reference to supply operations brought the whole matter to the attention of Harry Hopkins. We should recall that Hopkins had played some role in the appointment of Connolly, a former WPA assistant, to head the PGC. Now Hopkins used his skill at mediation to alleviate some of the tension among the American agencies working in Iran. He told the Soviet Protocol Committee that it might be appropriate at this time to reevaluate supply operations with an eye to modifying Connolly's mission. His intention was primarily to promote cooperation among the American agencies rather than to force a reevaluation of policy.[20]

Hopkins had picked an appropriate moment, for over the past months the War Department had grown more sensitive to the consequences of political unrest in Iran. Half a year earlier, General Albert Wedemeyer had warned the Joint Chiefs that "a starving and dissident population will prey on our supply lines." That comment had fallen on deaf ears. Other top military men recognized that Wedemeyer, the head of the Policy and Strategy Group within the Operations and Planning Division, was both more politically conscious and more anti-Soviet than most generals. But as the Allies went on the offensive, the military became more sensitive to the geopolitical significance of the American presence in Iran.[21]

In October, the War Department heard from its own sources that the Russians and British had definite postwar ambitions. The military attaché in Tehran reported that the Russians might be planning to incorporate northern Iran into the Soviet Union. When he found British officers totally complacent about that possibility, he began to suspect the existence of a secret Anglo-Soviet protocol involving territorial adjustments. The Middle East Branch of Military Intelligence suggested that the ineptness of American policy not only aggravated tensions among the powers, but endangered what had now become a vital national interest in the region. "America is on trial in Iran," Military Intelligence told the Joint Chiefs:

> The eyes of all Middle Eastern countries are upon us. At a time when American oil reserves are dwindling and efforts are being made by the State Department to keep Ibn Saud friendly so that huge oil reserves in the Arabian peninsula may be exploited by us, it is folly to antagonize the people of the Middle East.[22]

Like Hurley, these intelligence officers believed that vacillation between supporting the British and the determination to aid Russia had obscured any overriding American strategy. Such confusion only encouraged both Russian and British ambitions. Should the Soviet Union exploit the current situation to absorb northern Iran, Great Britain might similarly extend its control over the south and central areas. American security interests would suffer. Not until the War and State Departments adopted "a unified policy based on military necessity and constructive statesmanship" would an effective American policy emerge.[23]

The similarity between this military intelligence analysis and the views expressed by Patrick Hurley was not coincidental. Behind the scenes, Hurley had continued to promote the team concept that Military Intelligence had recommended. His concern was not without a personal motive, for he had informed Henry Stimson of his desire to head all military and diplomatic operations in the Middle East. On 5 October 1943 he asked Assistant Secretary of State Adolph Berle for another special assignment to Iran. He proposed that he retain his military rank as a major general while working through the State Department to implement policy. "The President was unwilling to have him report directly to the War Department," he confided to Berle, "because everything he reported found its way into the papers."[24]

Two issues riled Hurley: British tactics, which he found "cruel and avaricious," and General Connolly, who struck him as so obsessed with his supply mission "that he had ceased to maintain other points of view." Hurley was outraged that the British could exploit starvation to extend their political control, then turn around and blame the Iranian government for the food shortage. Hurley's understanding of both issues was as always far from complete. Connolly was dutifully fulfilling the wishes of his superiors. And even though the British had withheld food deliveries, they did so to force the Iranian government to act, not to extend British influence.[25]

Once again, the direct-action Hurley had a simple solution to a complex problem. "He felt that a first-rate, two-fisted man, preferably in uniform, ought to go to Iran and sit on the situation," Berle noted. "Also, a man who could assure the cooperation of General Connolly or an appropriate replacement. . . ." Berle needed little subtlety of mind to figure out who Hurley had in mind. "I am perfectly clear that the Iranian situation is a terrible mess and that only a two-fisted, hard hitting man is likely to clear it up," he told Under Secretary Edward Stettinius. Wallace Murray agreed that since Dreyfus was sick and due for home leave, Hurley could act as chief of mission at least long enough to resolve the conflicts among the legation, PGC, and various other agencies.[26]

Berle soon approached Chief of Staff William Leahy about the whole problem of Iran and Hurley's appointment. To put the State Department's differences with Connolly in proper perspective, Berle emphasized the vital interests the United States had developed in Iran. "The long range results to American interests in the Middle East (among which may be noted the oil interests we have in Iraq and Arabia and our relations with Turkey) might become extremely complicated," he warned. Although Leahy held Dreyfus rather than Connolly responsible for the current mess, he was willing to cooperate. As a concession, he offered to find specialists at the Military Government School who might join the Millspaugh mission. And more important, he accepted the two-fisted general panacea, recommending that Roosevelt give the green light to Hurley's proposed assignment.[27]

All the strands of American policy now seemed to be coming together. The War Department had recognized Iran's geopolitical importance and the need for a greater level of U.S. commitment there. Three months later it granted Connolly the discretionary authority to assist the advisers. President Roosevelt also seemed to think that the argument for an effective policy accorded with his desire to promote independent governments in the Middle East and to keep the region open to American commerce. Still, in his normal oblique fashion, he indicated his support not so much by any direct statement as by approving Hurley's mission.[28]

To an historian, it seems remarkable that the process of increasing American involvement took place with so little understanding of circumstances in Iran, with such superficial knowledge of Middle East politics, and with no real analysis of the possible consequences. Jernegan, it may be recalled, had not yet been to the Middle East when he defined State Department policy there. Hurley's "expertise" derived from a trip of only a few weeks. The man with the greatest firsthand knowledge, Louis Dreyfus, was by this time almost totally discredited and would soon be posted to Iceland. Though more expert than the others, Wallace Murray had not been to Iran in over a decade.

It would not be much of an exaggeration to suggest that the involvement of the United States in Iran grew mainly because Americans were there. The justifications came later, although they remained consistent with the tradition of American expansion. The combination of Iran's appeal for assistance with the weakness of the once-dominant foreign powers created an opportunity; reform, idealism, and the chance to promote national security and acquire valuable resources provided motivations. Once the War Department lent at least modest support for the advisers, a method for promoting these interests seemed to exist. But equipped with opportunity, method, and motive, few policymakers thought much about how American actions might complicate future relations among the great powers beyond the borders of Iran.

THE DECLARATION ON IRAN

At the Moscow Foreign Ministers Conference in October 1943, Secretary of State Hull and Foreign Secretary Anthony Eden had made a futile attempt to iron out troublesome differences with the Russians on a range of issues, including tensions over Iran. Their determination to address the question of Iran during the conference was evident when they ordered John Jernegan and Sir Reader Bullard to join their delegations in Moscow. All the same, Iran received a low priority among the many topics on the agenda. Not until the last few days did the British succeed in raising the idea of a three-power declaration on Iran. By that means the Allies would recognize Iran as a member of the United Nations and promise some form of postwar assistance. As a UN member, Iran would become eligible to participate in the peace conference. No power could then easily force an ally into disadvantageous concessions or territorial adjustments. In that way, they believed, the declaration would serve as a barrier to Russian expansion. To ensure Hull's active support, Foreign Secretary Eden had agreed that the declaration should include a pledge to support the American advisers and to withdraw from Iran after the cessation of hostilities.[29]

Molotov killed the whole proposal. He claimed that he had promised the Iranian ambassador that the ministers would not discuss Iran. Only by the procedural device of creating a subcommittee had the British and Americans managed to keep discussions alive. Still, these talks foundered on Soviet intransigence. Russian members insisted that since the Allies had given adequate assurances, a new declaration might only arouse Iranian suspicions. Soviet diplomats had used exactly the same excuse two years earlier when Hull asked them for a public statement on Iran. With the talks stalemated, the three ministers agreed that any declaration would have to wait until Roosevelt, Churchill, and Stalin met at Tehran a month later. An air of cordiality, inspired by a series of broad understandings, obscured any uneasiness Hull and Eden might have felt from failing to make headway on Iran.[30]

Although the meeting of Roosevelt, Churchill, and Stalin in Tehran in late November 1943 provided an extraordinary opportunity to achieve a new framework for their relations with Iran, the Big Three faced a weighty agenda. What was the status of Overlord? What strategy would they follow to defeat Germany? How would they resolve the question of future Polish boundaries and the future Polish government? Would there be a postwar international organization to keep the peace? With so much of consequence at stake, Iran was not likely to occupy a prominent place on the agenda. On 28 November 1943 President Roosevelt held his long-awaited meeting with Premier Stalin. He had purposely chosen to see Stalin without Churchill present. The two touched on a broad range of matters that included Charles de Gaulle, China, Indochina, and India. In addition, an important matter that involved Iran did come up at one of their private meetings. At Cairo, Roosevelt had mentioned to Andrei Vishinsky, the Soviet delegate to the Allied advisory council for the Mediterranean, the idea of trusteeships for "immature" nations. At Tehran he proposed to Stalin that the Allies establish an international trusteeship to operate the Iranian State Railroad and to create a free port on the Persian Gulf. Roosevelt later recalled that "Stalin's comment was merely that it was an interesting idea and he offered no objection."[31]

But Roosevelt gave another account of this conversation to his personal friend John Houghteling. As Houghteling reconstructed the conversation for the State Department in 1945:

> Mr. Roosevelt stated that Marshall Stalin expressed interest in this proposal, and asked if it was a serious suggestion. When Mr. Roosevelt stated that it was so intended, Stalin excused himself and conferred briefly with Foreign Commissar Molotov. Upon his return Stalin stated that he was agreeable to the proposal.[32]

Thus, Houghteling's version suggests that Stalin and Roosevelt had reached a tentative agreement.

It is just as likely that Stalin left the room, not to talk with Molotov, but to catch his breath. The president had offered him, with no evident strings, a prize that had eluded the tsars for over a century—direct access to a warm-water Persian Gulf port. Furthermore, Roosevelt had made his gesture without consulting either the State Department or Churchill. In fact, it would be more than a year before the State Department learned that any such conversation had occurred. Churchill would most likely have been apoplectic had he learned that Roosevelt had casually undone a century of British effort to keep the Russians out of the Gulf.[33]

Roosevelt's casual disregard of Iranian sovereignty contradicted the spirit of the Allies' grand tribute to their hosts, the three-power Declaration on Iran. The Allied leaders' presence in Tehran created an unparalleled opportunity to discuss Iran's relations to these powers. Prime Minister Soheili indicated that his government would value a declaration of respect for Iranian sovereignty. Patrick Hurley managed the actual process of drafting and signing the Allied statement. His access to Roosevelt allowed him to keep Iran on the conference agenda whenever Soviet intransigence, the crush of other issues, or mere indifference threatened to shunt the matter aside.[34]

On 28 November, Hurley received permission from Roosevelt to discuss a three-power statement with Eden and Molotov. He had become a passionate advocate of a declaration because he believed that guarantees, backed by the United States, would become a formidable barrier to either communism or imperialism. John Jernegan had already helped him prepare a rough draft to present to the foreign ministers. Eden readily agreed that a declaration was desirable. To avoid the usual Soviet stonewalling they decided to have Soheili approach Molotov. That ploy got no results, since Molotov again refused to discuss the idea. Hurley now played his trump card. By asking Roosevelt to intercede with Stalin he won Soviet consent for a declaration.[35]

Averell Harriman recalled that Stalin never seemed to treat the declaration as a serious matter. The Big Three had been so casual about it that Harriman discovered at the last minute that they had never signed the document. He took the only English draft to Stalin and asked the premier whether he wanted a Russian text. Once his interpreter had translated the text verbally, Stalin said he approved. He asked Harriman to have Roosevelt sign before he affixed his own signature. After Churchill signed, Hurley took the text to the shah, who also signed. John Jernegan later recalled that neither the Russians nor the British had taken any initiative on the declaration, "although the British were favorably disposed from the beginning."[36]

In its most significant provision, the "Declaration of the Three Powers Regarding Iran" reaffirmed the Tripartite Treaty's earlier guarantees of Iran's independence, sovereignty, and territorial integrity. The Allies also recognized Iran's contributions to the war effort, promised within the limits of their present capabilities to give Iran economic assistance, and agreed that as a member of the United Nations Iran would receive consideration for her postwar economic problems. Hurley had failed, however, to extract a specific pledge of support for the American advisers, though the promise of economic assistance implied that some cooperation might be forthcoming.[37]

The Declaration on Iran might in some ways best be compared to John Hay's "Open Door" notes. It was essentially an agreement among the powers to refrain from carving up a nation in no position to protect itself. Since there was no mechanism for enforcing the declaration's self-denying provisions, its effectiveness hinged on whether the powers chose to respect its terms. The promise of economic aid was so provisional that it did not bind the parties to taking any concrete action. As previously mentioned, the Tripartite Treaty already obligated the British and Russians to the declaration's major provisions.

So why all the fuss about a document that was to a large extent redundant? For the British and Iranians, as for Hurley, the declaration had value above all because the United States had made a formal commitment to Iran. Having refused to sign the Tripartite Treaty, Roosevelt had now bound the United States to uphold its crucial provisions. In the future, the declaration would afford the United States a strong rationale for opposing Soviet actions in Iran. Without the declaration, such American intervention would have been more difficult to justify. The special recognition given Iran also boosted the prestige of the shah's shaky regime. Thus the declaration, though largely symbolic, did have some tangible significance.

It is more difficult to explain why Stalin suddenly consented to sign the declaration after Soviet diplomats had twice earlier thwarted similar initiatives. Louis Dreyfus suggested quite plausibly that Stalin merely wanted to make a friendly gesture toward Iran or was at least reluctant to offend the Iranians, especially after the British and Americans had openly supported the declaration. We should not overlook Stalin's success at the conference. He had wrung important concessions from his Allies on Overlord, the Baltic states, and Polish boundaries. Nor should we discount the real sense of good will the three Allied leaders must have felt after their meetings. Why should Stalin wish to intrude a sour note on the matter of a declaration that imposed no new obligations?[38]

More important, Stalin may not have wished to discourage Roosevelt's scheme to internationalize the Iranian railroad and port system. There can be no doubt that Stalin considered access to the Persian Gulf a major Soviet war aim, though not one he would risk antagonizing his allies to achieve. Molotov had pressed for just such a concession in his 1939 negotiations with Ribbentrop. Without extracting any sort of *quid pro quo,* Roosevelt seemed at least tacitly to have recognized the legitimacy of that Soviet aspiration. To refuse cooperation on the declaration might have led the president to reconsider his proposal.

We must conclude that the declaration had far more importance to Iranian, British, and American diplomats than to the three Allied leaders. For them, it was a parting gift to their Iranian hosts. It did seem to symbolize the hope that burned brightest at Tehran, that the Allies could find a formula for a lasting peace. But just as the Allied leaders' good will would begin to fade as soon as they left Tehran, so too would their pledge to cooperate in helping Iran. Military success had obscured for the moment the depth of the divisions among them. But as diplomatic issues assumed greater consequence, friction over issues like Poland's boundaries or Iran's oil could no longer be avoided.

ROOSEVELT AND IRAN

President Roosevelt quickly demonstrated that Iranian-American relations had a low priority for him. While in Tehran, he made little effort to treat the shah as a significant leader. By contrast he made a major effort to befriend Ibn Saud, the warrior monarch of Saudi Arabia, for whom he found time to spend a day talking and feasting on his return from Yalta. Of course, American companies controlled a Saudi oil concession that promised to cover the world's largest oil reserves. When the king admired Roosevelt's wheelchair, the President gave it to him as a gift, even though Ibn Saud's 6′6″ frame would not fit into it. Roosevelt had consulted the king on a wide range of issues, including Palestine.

As a visitor to Iran, however, Roosevelt spent only two hours in amiable conversation with the shah who had paid him a courtesy call. Flying into Iran, Roosevelt had noticed the bare slopes of the Zagros and Elbruz mountains. Turning on the famous Roosevelt charm, he talked of returning to Iran as a private citizen to supervise a reforestation program. The somewhat innocent young shah had concluded, as Roosevelt undoubtedly intended, that the president had a genuine sympathy for Iran and its people. Had he known Roosevelt better, he would have guessed that the reforestation idea more truly reflected the president's fondness for trees than his interest in Iran. And Roosevelt left Iran without ever paying a return visit to the shah. Cordell Hull, perhaps in part responding to the sting of being excluded from the conference, later chided the president for his carelessness by pointing out that "the chagrin of Iran is all the more poignant because Marshal Stalin took special pains to call upon the shah, with whom he remained in conference nearly two hours."[39]

Roosevelt did make one final gesture that indicated some concern for promoting closer Iranian-American relations. As he left for Cairo, he asked Patrick Hurley to formulate an American policy "which might be used as a pattern for our relations with all less favored nations." Roosevelt indicated that he wanted a proposal for stabilizing Iran and its economy. Did this then mean that the president was prepared to commit the United States to a special relationship with Iran, as the State Department had urged? That is, of course, one possible reading of his request to Hurley. But as anyone familiar with Roosevelt's style might suspect, he was just as likely simply looking for a harmless way to keep Hurley busy and to thank him for his efforts. After all, Roosevelt had already received a summary of the Jernegan memorandum sent by Secretary Hull the previous August. That does not mean that the president either read or remembered it. Nevertheless, if Iran had been a priority, he would have been well aware of the general direction of American policy.[40]

Hurley's report to Roosevelt offered nothing that was new. It echoed the Jernegan memorandum and in addition dispelled any illusion that the Declaration on Iran embodied a real consensus among the Allies. The general charged that the Russians and the British continued to undermine American efforts at nation-building. He focused his particular ire on the British distribution of American lend-lease supplies. Why should the British use American goods to promote their own imperial interests? In this issue, Hurley had raised a red herring. Perhaps, the British did operate the Middle East Supply Center with an eye to their own interests. Nonetheless, the Combined Chiefs had assigned them the responsibility for the Middle Eastern theater and, as the State department's lend-lease administrator Dean Acheson later observed, the United States did not have the necessary administrative personnel to take over from the British.[41]

Hurley was not totally without hope that American policy for Iran could promote postwar cooperation among the Allies. But to that end he had no new remedies. Rather, he urged the president to establish tighter American controls over supply operations and to upgrade existing American programs.

To Hurley's report Roosevelt gave a blessing both enthusiastic and empty. "I was rather thrilled with the idea of using Iran as an example of what we could do by an unselfish American policy," he told Secretary Hull in January 1944. That was almost his last significant comment on American policy toward Iran. He asked Hull to make an appropriate reply to Hurley. From then on Iranian policy remained, largely as it had before, in the hands of the State Department. Roosevelt undoubtedly did accept both Hurley's recommendations and the general thrust of the Jernegan memorandum as being consistent with statements he had made about American relations with underdeveloped nations. His attention to Iran, however, proved short-lived and his definition of an "unselfish approach" to U.S. policy was appropriately vague.[42]

Since Hurley had said so little that was new, his report should have sparked little controversy. Indeed, most State Department officials endorsed his recommendations. The reference to lend-lease operations brought a copy of the report across

Dean Acheson's desk. The eminently Anglican Acheson had little of style or substance in common with Hurley's frontier approach to diplomacy. The general's infatuation with pious generalities, his vitriolic anglophobia, and his simplistic solutions all offended Acheson, who as a conservative internationalist viewed the British role in the Middle East as vital to regional stability.[43]

At the end of the day, Acheson and his assistant, Eugene Rostow, sat down with a pitcher of Manhattans to discuss an appropriate reply to Hurley's report. Their shared irritation rose as the pitcher emptied. Rostow returned to his office where Acheson's pique and the Manhattans overcame his discretion. Borrowing a phrase from the often acerbic Clare Booth Luce, he dubbed Hurley's proposal an "innocent indulgence in messianic globaloney." In attacking the supply operations, Hurley had overlooked all the practical problems dogging effective lend-lease distribution. And advisers, Rostow reminded his colleagues, "were a classic device of imperialist penetration." Most important, Acheson and Rostow attacked the idea that the United States ought to displace the British from the Middle East. Such a move, they argued, might set off a chain of political disruptions that no one had yet anticipated.[44]

This broad critique from a highly placed official should have triggered a significant policy review within the State Department. Nothing of that sort occurred. Wallace Murray dismissed Acheson's comments as a "frivolous and unwarranted interference in political matters of primary concern to this office [Political Affairs]." Never once addressing the substance of Acheson's remarks, Murray simply concluded that the memorandum contradicted existing departmental policy. As in its dealings with General Connolly, the State Department chose to ignore those critics who challenged its operating assumptions.[45]

We must assume that State Department officials would have been more receptive had Connolly and Acheson gone beyond criticism to suggest an alternative course of action. Yet both had alerted the department to the dangers inherent in the idea of reforming Iran through advisers and of supplanting the Soviet Union and Great Britain as the dominant powers in Iranian affairs. Both critics had anticipated that as the advisers failed, they would weaken American influence, not strengthen it. Both understood that political circumstances, whether local or regional, did not favor the kind of sweeping changes Hurley and Jernegan envisioned.

The timing of Acheson's memorandum was almost as significant as its substance. Despite the continued rhetoric of reform and nation-building, American policy was already in transformation. Oil and national security interest had begun to supersede any idealistic reasons for America's involvement in Iran. Iranian criticism of the U.S. advisers indicated that the State Department would need to find more effective instruments for asserting American influence and support for Iran. Growing concern over Russian ambitions had led American diplomats to greater cooperation with their English counterparts. In short, by January 1944 there was almost nothing "disinterested" about American policy for Iran. The United States had become a power with a permanent stake in the geopolitical orientation of Iran and the entire Middle East.

NOTES

1. On Hurley's mission, see Richard Pfau, "The United States and Iran," pp. 146–47. This view of Roosevelt's administrative style and strategy is widely held. See, for example, William Leuchtenberg, *Franklin D. Roosevelt and the New Deal* (New York, 1963), pp. 328–29.

2. The major source on Hurley is Russell Buhite, *Patrick Hurley and World Affairs* (Ithaca, NY, 1973). See also Don Lohbeck, *Patrick J. Hurley* (Chicago, 1956), although the

author's bias and devotion to Hurley make this account almost worthless. Theodore White, *In Search of History* (New York, 1978), p. 198 seems to offer a more realistic, though hostile, view of Hurley's role. Bruce Kuniholm, *The Origins of the Cold War in the Near East,* pp. 165–71, credits Hurley with more influence than I see him exerting. Kuniholm is much taken with the comment the president made to his son Elliott, "I wish I had more men like Pat [Hurley] on whom I could depend. The men in the State Department, those career diplomats . . . half the time I can't tell whether to believe them or not." Elliott Roosevelt, *As He Saw It* (New York, 1946), p. 193. I suspect the comment was more reflective of FDR's attitude toward diplomats than a tribute to Hurley. Another view of Roosevelt's fondness for Hurley can be found in William Leahy, *I Was There* (New York, 1950), p. 227.

3. Buhite, *Patrick Hurley,* especially chs. 1–3. White, *In Search of History,* pp. 197–98.

4. FR, 1943, 4, p. 366, Hurley memorandum for President Roosevelt.

5. Ibid., pp. 368–70.

6. Ibid., pp. 368–69. Some of Hurley's confusion may have stemmed from his desire to flatter Roosevelt as well as to discuss policy. He placed great emphasis on the ability of charismatic leaders to influence change. He may have believed that, but I am sure he also made the point to soften his harsh view of the British, which he knew Roosevelt did not share.

7. Ibid., pp. 369–70.

8. President's Secretary Files (PSF): State Department, memorandum by Cordell Hull for the President, 5/22/43, Roosevelt Library, Hyde Park, NY.

9. To compare the growth of American interest in Iran with Saudi Arabia, see Aaron D. Miller, *Search for Security: Saudi Arabian Oil and American Foreign Policy, 1939–1949* (Chapel Hill, N.C., 1980), ch. 1–3.

10. Vail Motter, *The Persian Corridor and Aid to Russia,* p. 455. See also FR, 1943, 4, pp. 499–503.

11. Ibid., pp. 499–504.

12. Ibid., pp. 386–88, memorandum by Jernegan, 9/23/43. See also SD 891.20/249, 684, 9/21/43, memorandum by Jernegan, enclosure with Dreyfus to Hull which includes some parts deleted from the *FR*'s version.

13. MMRB, OPD, ME 381, 8/11/43. On the relationship between OWI and the military see Allan M. Winkler, *The Politics of Propaganda* (New Haven, 1978), especially ch. 4.

14. FO 35098, E2929/82/34, 170, 5/3/43, Bullard to Foreign Secretary Eden.

15. Ibid., p. 1, Holman memorandum.

16. Ibid., pp. 10–11. See also ibid., minute by W. H. Young, 5/25/43.

17. Ibid., see minute by Neville Butler, 6/10/43.

18. FO 35098, E3033/82/34, minute by Sir Alexander Cadogan, 5/25/43. Cadogan agreed with Sir Anthony Eden that it would be foolish to replace Bullard merely to placate his American critics. See also FO 35098, E2929/82/34, minute by W. H. Young.

19. FR, 1943, 4, p. 377, Hull to Roosevelt. See also Vail Motter, *The Persian Corridor,* p. 455.

20. Ibid., p. 389.

21. MMRB, OPD 210.684 (3–10–43), 4/15/43, Wedemeyer to Gen. J. Hull. On Wedemeyer's political sense, see Russell Weigley, *The American Way of War* (New York, 1973), pp. 332–33. On the political dimensions of military planning see Michael Sherry, *Preparing for the Next War* (New Haven, 1977), chs. 1–2.

22. MMRB (Suitland, Md.), OPD336 Russia, 148, MIA(Tehran) to MID-WDGS, 9/6/43.

23. MMRB, AG/SI, 3850 Iran, Chief—Middle East Branch of MI to Gen. Marshall, 10/19/43.

24. SD 123 Hurley, Patrick J./109 1/2, Memorandum by Berle, 10/5/43.

25. Ibid., and FR, 1943, 4, p. 392.

26. Ibid., pp. 392–93.

27. Ibid., pp. 393–94, Berle to Leahy, 10/15/43 and p. 396, memorandum by Berle, 10/20/43; p. 396, Stettinius to Roosevelt, p. 399. On the redefinition of Connolly's mission see Vail Motter, *The Persian Corridor,* p. 457.

28. On Roosevelt's attitude toward the U.S. role in the Middle East, see for example, FR, 1944, 5, pp. 1–2, FDR to James Landis (Director of Foreign Economic Administration in Cairo).

29. FO 35104, E7424/82/34, Holman to C. W. Baxter, 11/13/43; FO 35103, E6480/82/34,

Clark Kerr (Ambassador in Moscow) to FO, 1167; FR, 1943, 4, p. 400, George Allen to Hull, 11/4/43.

30. FR, 1943, 4, pp. 400–404; FO 35103, E6604/82/34, Clark Kerr to FO, 10/30/43.

31. For a good general discussion of planning for the conference and the major issues, see Dallek, *Franklin Roosevelt and American Foreign Policy,* pp. 418–41. See also Feis, *Churchill, Roosevelt, and Stalin,* pp. 240–87, for a detailed account, and Gaddis Smith, *American Diplomacy in World War II,* pp. 74–79 for a brief version. See also Winston Churchill, *Closing the Ring* (New York, 1962 ed.) for a readable participant account. On Iran, see FR, 1944, 5, p. 483, Roosevelt to Edward Stettinius, 12/8/44. I find it hard to credit Patrick Hurley for planting this idea in Roosevelt's mind (see Kuniholm, *Origins of the Cold War in the Near East,* pp. 166–67). Nor does it seem that Roosevelt remembered correctly when he said Churchill was present when the idea first came up. It is hard to believe the British would have acquiesced or allowed the matter to proceed without further extensive discussions. The matter seems to have come up first during one of the three private conversations Roosevelt had with Stalin, the most likely one being 29 November when Molotov was present, but Churchill was not. See J. M. Burns, *Soldier of Freedom,* pp. 406–7 and Feis, *Churchill, Roosevelt, and Stalin,* pp. 254–55. See also FR, *The Conferences at Cairo and Tehran,* pp. 483ff.

32. FR, 1945, 8, pp. 525–26 and p. 526n. See also FR, 1944, 4, p. 455.

33. For the discovery of this exchange, see FR, 1945, 8, pp. 523–26.

34. FR, 1943, *The Conferences at Cairo and Tehran,* pp. 648–49.

35. Ibid., pp. 648–49 and 890–91. Dreyfus and Jernegan filed separate accounts of the politics leading up to the declaration. They contain no significant discrepancies. See also the Herbert Feis papers, Library of Congress, Box 53, Notes on the Teheran Conference.

36. Harriman and Abel, *Special Envoy,* p. 265.

37. For the full text of the declaration, see FR, 1943, 4, pp. 413–14.

38. FR, 1943, *The Conferences at Cairo and Teheran,* p. 843. See also Keith Sainsbury, *The Turning Point, Roosevelt, Stalin, Churchill, and Chiang-Kai Shek, The Malta, Cairo, and Teheran Conferences* (London and New York, 1985).

39. For a good account of FDR's meeting with the Ibn Saud, see Miller, *Search for Security,* pp. xi–xii and ch. 5. On the reforestation proposal, see OF, 4678, Roosevelt Library, Roosevelt to Mrs. L. Stuyvesant Chandler, 1/12/44. PSF: Iran, Box 30, Hull to FDR, 12/13/43, Roosevelt Library. During his visit, Roosevelt did take time to visit the troops of the PGC.

40. FR, 1943, 4, p.420n; and Vail Motter, *The Persian Corridor,* pp. 444–46.

41. FR, 1943, 4, pp. 420–24, Hurley to FDR, 12/21/43.

42. Ibid., pp. 423–24. Vail Motter, *The Persian Corridor,* 445 and 445n.

43. For an example of the State Department's response to Hurley, see SD 123 Hurley, Patrick J./128 1/2, memorandum by H. B. Minor; 1/12/44. On Acheson and foreign policy, see Gaddis Smith, *Dean Acheson* (New York, 1972), ch. 1–2.

44. SD 891.00/1–2844, memorandum by Acheson, 1/28/44. Eugene Rostow provided me with the details of this situation and of several later encounters with Hurley. Interview, Nov. 1972.

45. SD 891.00/1–2844, note by Wallace Murray.

5 Oil

To understand how American interest in Iran shifted from a vague ideological concern for Iranian independence to a widely held preoccupation with Iran's relation to American national security we must turn our attention to oil. By late 1943 the Allies had organized a transnational economic system to sustain the war effort. Iran served as the final link through which Great Britain and the United States channeled the material resources of the west into the Soviet Union. Although each of the major powers realized that the wartime policies they had adopted for Iran had potential consequences for the postwar era, at first they had made the uninterrupted operation of the supply route their top priority. The Persian Gulf Service Command upgraded Iran's road, track,. and port facilities to meet the heavy demands imposed by the inter-Allied war economy. In the Declaration on Iran the Allied heads of state had acknowledged Iran's contribution to the war effort, no matter how unwitting or unwilling it had been. All the same, Iran had remained a decidedly secondary theater of the war. And ironically, as its importance as a supply route diminished after 1943, Iran figured ever more prominently in the Allies' long-range planning.

In considering Iran's significance for the United States, security officials of the War and State Departments began to argue for the perpetuation of the United States' wartime role there. As it had in the past, Iran's proximity to the Soviet Union and the major world trade routes figured in the calculation of American policy. But policymakers also understood that parts of Iran almost literally float on an underground sea of petroleum. Equally important, Iran's Persian Gulf coast overlooks some of the richest oilfields in the world. On the eve of World War II the Middle East accounted for just 5.5 percent of total world crude oil production. That figure belied the obvious potential of the region. In the ten years from 1929 to 1939 American oil companies alone had increased their stakes tenfold, from $10 million to almost $100 million. By 1943 British and American oilmen had no doubt that the center of the world petroleum reserves was shifting to the Persian Gulf basin. Harold Ickes, the head of the Interior Department and wartime petroleum administrator, had informed

Secretary of State Hull in the summer of 1943 that "the northeast region including Iran, Iraq, Kuwait, Saudi Arabia, Quatar, and the Trucial sheiks . . . will produce an overwhelming portion of the world's oil in the next twenty years."[1]

What was more, the war had created circumstances likely to alter the dynamics of the world oil industry. The executives of the Anglo-Iranian Oil Company (AIOC), for example, realized that the presence of Soviet and American forces in Iran might instigate a scramble for oil concessions. In that case, AIOC could lose its monopoly over Iranian oil. As a precaution, they sent Basil Jackson, a roving diplomat and troubleshooter, to Iran with a survey team to locate possible reserves outside the existing concession area. Jackson was almost stunned by what his team discovered. As Ickes soon learned, AIOC's tests indicated reserves so vast that they promised to dwarf even those of the United States. Most of the new oil lay outside AIOC's domain. The area within the Russian occupation zone showed the least promise. To the southeast in Baluchistan, however, lay possibly vast fields easily accessible for American or British development.[2]

World War II had emphasized what had become ever more obvious during the twentieth century: Ready access to petroleum was essential to survival in peace or war. Oil provides the energy that moves modern armed forces. Winston Churchill had realized the future strategic importance of secure reserves in 1914, when the British navy converted from coal to oil. To guarantee a steady supply, he acquired a majority interest for the Admiralty in the Anglo-Persian Oil Company (APOC). Royalties from the concession filled Treasury coffers, while the oil fueled the fleet. By 1943 Churchill's prescience had become conventional wisdom. Harold Ickes reminded his fellow Washington officials that "about 60 percent, or nearly two out of every three tons, of supplies sent to our expeditionary forces are oil."[3]

The quantities of fuel consumed by the war machine almost defy adequate description. A single armored battalion burned 17,000 gallons to move just 100 miles. The U.S. Fifth Fleet at the height of its operations consumed oil at the rate of 3.8 billion gallons per year. Herbert Feis, an economist and sometime adviser to both the State and War Departments, summed up a view that had become self-evident during the war, "Oil, enough oil within our certain grasp, seemed ardently necessary to greatness and independence in the twentieth century."[4] In short, the United States could not assume the mantle of world leadership unless its foreign policy met the nation's unslakeable thirst for oil.

For most of the twentieth century American oilmen and government officials worried about too much, rather than too little oil. Among the advanced industrial nations, the United States had the unique advantage of having sufficient reserves to fuel its own economy as well as those of Europe and Asia. American wells had the capacity during the war to provide United Nations forces with almost 80 percent of their needs. American oilmen developed overseas concessions largely because their proximity to foreign markets offered savings in royalties, transportation, and marketing. Only briefly had Americans faced the prospect of declining domestic capacity. World War I had imposed a heavy drain on domestic reserves. At that time, the 1920s American love affair with the automobile sustained a high demand for oil, while new discoveries lagged. That short-lived crisis inspired the first major efforts of American oil companies to establish a foothold in the Middle East.[5]

In the 1920s two concessions and two companies dominated Middle Eastern oil. APOC held exclusive control of the concession granted in Persia. In addition, Anglo-Persian shared with Royal Dutch-Shell the rich Mesopotamian concession, first organized as the Turkish Petroleum Company, but then renamed after the war the Iraq Petroleum Company (IPC). British domination made it impossible for American companies even to explore for oil in the Mesopotamian basin.[6]

Faced with the postwar energy scare, American oilmen demanded that the

State Department support their efforts to enter Iraq by enforcing the "Open Door" principle. In negotiations, they had a bargaining chip even more potent than pressure from Washington. While APOC and Royal Dutch-Shell had cornered a disproportionate share of Middle Eastern oil, Standard of New Jersey, Standard of New York (also known as Standard-Vacuum or Mobil), Texaco, and several other American companies supplied over 60 percent of the world's markets, including 50 percent of the oil imported into Great Britain. It took six years of Byzantine negotiations before the two Standard companies managed to open the door of IPC in 1928 for themselves, Gulf Oil, and a subsidiary of Standard of Indiana. (APOC, Royal Dutch-Shell, and Compagnie Française des Pétroles also received 23.75 percent shares, while Calouste Gulbenkian, an Armenian national who helped obtain the original concession, held on to 5 percent.) As oil economist John Blair observed, the partners operated IPC not to make profits, but to supply the operating companies with oil priced below current world levels. The marketing and refining branches of these companies then realized profits in a way that avoided tax liabilities to the British government.[7]

By the time the IPC consortium had been formed, the world oil picture had shifted from shortages to surpluses. The huge east Texas and Louisiana discoveries had left the American market awash in oil. The IPC partners looked for a cartel arrangement that would close the recently opened door to the Middle East. As a first step they adopted what was known as the "Red Line" agreement. The name refers to a line Calouste Gulbenkian drew with a red crayon to designate for the IPC partners what he recalled as the old Ottoman Empire. Gulbenkian's line encompassed Turkey, Iraq, Palestine, Saudi Arabia, and the Trucial sheikdoms, but significantly excluded Iran and Kuwait. Under the terms of agreement the partners reactivated a self-denying ordinance contained in the original Turkish Petroleum concession of 1914 that barred the members from independent operations in the Turkish concession area. All new fields would be operated through IPC, and since IPC had preference in exploring the area, any newcomers were effectively excluded.[8]

Controlling production and supplies was one problem; distributing those supplies through orderly markets while maintaining prices at profitable levels was yet another. In the late 1920s the major integrated oil companies (those who participated in all phases of the industry from exploration to drilling at the well through marketing at the pump), now known as the "Seven Sisters," found themselves caught between the cutthroat practices of wildcatters, domestic producers, and independent refiners on one side and the antitrust laws on the other. Under these conditions, they were virtually unable to eliminate crippling competition in the American market. The antitrust laws did, however, allow them to combine abroad so long as collaboration did not restrain domestic competition. The two major Standard companies of New Jersey (Exxon) and New York (Mobil), for example, conducted most of their Far Eastern operations through a jointly held though largely independent subsidiary, Stanvac.[9]

By 1928 chaos had engulfed world oil markets as ruinous competition drove prices and profits down. Few producers practiced even rudimentary conservation. That same year, just by "coincidence," Walter Teagle, chairman of SONJ, and Sir John Cadman, chairman of APOC, happened to meet for grouse shooting at the Scottish estate of Sir Henry Deterding, who was chairman of Royal Dutch-Shell. Inevitably the three men found time to talk about the current world oil situation. In what came to be known as the Achnacarry (the name of Deterding's estate) or "As-Is" agreement, they decided to eliminate what they viewed as excessive competition by dividing world markets among their companies.[10]

Such an attempt to cartelize the world oil industry proved easier to conceive of

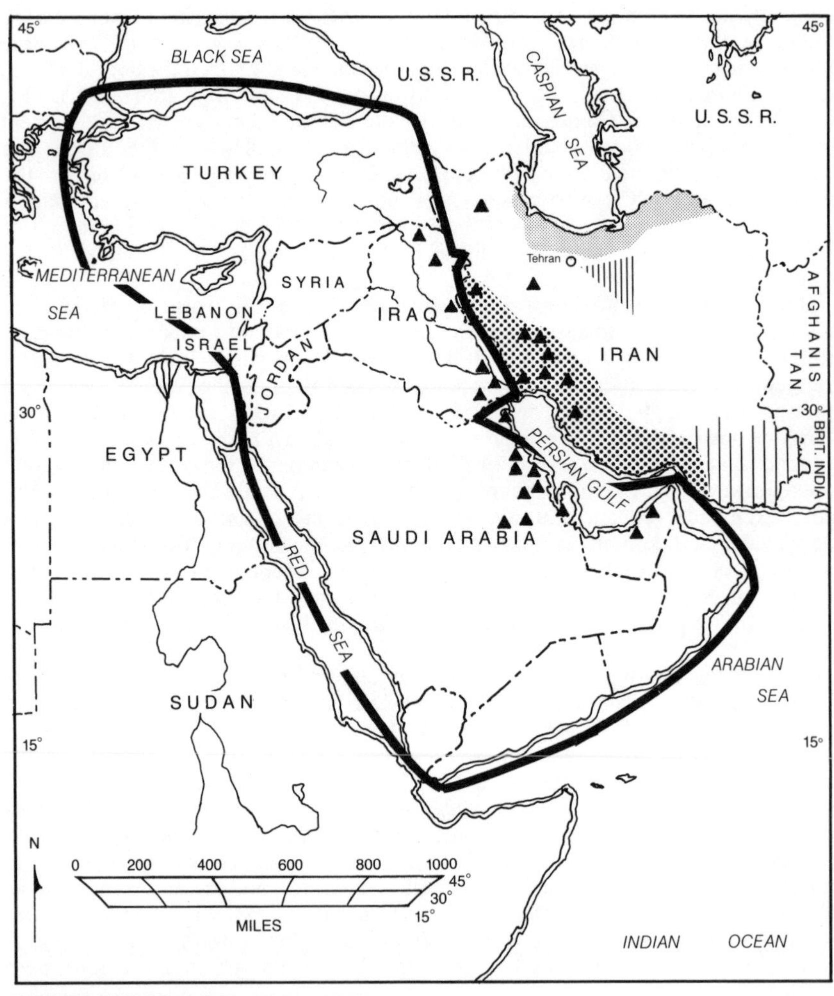

MIDDLE EAST OIL 1941–1953

- Old Khoshtaria Concession
- Kavir Khorian Petroleum Company
- Red Line Agreement Area
- Anglo-Iranian Oil Company
- Prospective Stanvac Concession Area
- ▲ Gulf Area Oil Fields

than to maintain. Some members of the IPC consortium like Gulf Oil wanted to find oil reserves they could develop and operate independently. And neither the "Red Line" nor "As-Is" agreements prevented newcomers such as Socal (Standard of California, now Chevron) from entering the concession area or IPC members from opening new fields in Iran or Kuwait where the "Red Line" did not apply. Nor could the majors prevent revenue-hungry producers like the Soviet Union from flooding world markets with cheap oil.

Three major finds of the 1930s undid the cartel efforts of the IPC partners. Twenty miles off the Persian Gulf coast of Saudi Arabia lies Bahrain, at that time a sheikdom under British control and within the Red Line area. In 1930, geologists for Eastern Gulf Oil, a Gulf Oil subsidiary, discovered that Bahrain had perfect structures for a major pool of oil. Gulf had a problem, however; it belonged to IPC and thus had to offer the concession to the consortium. With no desire to see another large field opened, IPC turned down the concession on the grounds that its prospects were poor. As a result, Gulf sold its option to Socal.

Before it could actually operate the concession, Socal had to skirt the barriers of British colonial restrictions. To that end it chartered a Canadian subsidiary, Bapco (Bahrain Petroleum Company), which in 1931 began drilling. Socal never doubted that IPC had purposely misrepresented Bahrain's potential. In October 1931, Bapco drillers struck oil in large commercial quantities. More important, Socal geologists recognized that the structures of Bahrain stretched across the bay to Saudi Arabia. Socal therefore opened negotiations with Ibn Saud, whose military and marital successes had united the tribes of the Arabian peninsula under the House of Saud.[11]

Frustration in Bahrain had left Gulf Oil hungering for a concession it could operate free from IPC's restrictions. One-hundred-twenty-five miles up the coast from Bahrain lay a star-shaped wedge of land Gulbenkian had left outside the red line he drew. This was Kuwait. In 1930 Gulf agents began negotiations with Sheik Ahmad, the ruler of this British protectorate. Just as Gulf was on the verge of success, the British government intervened to block the concession. Then APOC entered the bidding. Anglo-Persian had no more desire to find oil in Kuwait than IPC had had in Bahrain. As the company's agent later admitted, "we had to get the concession to protect our huge investment in Persia. For Kuwait is nearer markets and if competitors found oil there, the Persian business would have been undercut and ruined."[12] That comment gives an adequate sense of the importance the concession in Iran had for APOC and the British government.

For two years Gulf Oil and APOC fought to control Kuwait. The State Department entered the fray on Gulf's behalf by once again insisting that the British respect the "Open Door" concept. The department's vigor in this case may have had something to do with its representative to the Court of St. James—Andrew Mellon, Gulf Oil director and the major shareholder. In 1934 the rivals made peace at Sheik Ahmad's expense by creating the jointly held Kuwait Petroleum Company. Later Gulf discovered that the price of peace was much higher than it had anticipated. APOC retained the right to supply its share of Kuwait oil from its concessions in Iran or Iraq. Furthermore, the agreement prevented either partner from using Kuwaiti supplies to disrupt in any way the other's "trade or marketing position. . . ." Worse yet, when Anglo-Iranian crews began drilling in 1936 they chose a site with little prospect of yielding oil. Only two years later were Gulf Oil drillers able to go to the obvious place. There they hit one of the largest oil reservoirs anywhere in the world. Even then Anglo-Iranian showed no zest for commercial production. The concession languished until more propitious times after World War II.[13]

Only through devious business practices, British imperial clout, and the coming of war had AIOC prevented the production of Kuwaiti oil. It did not have the same success in Saudi Arabia. There Ibn Saud had more power and independence than the small sheikdoms under British protection. What was more, the prospective concessionaire, Socal, did not have to contend with IPC restrictions. In 1936 Socal joined forces with Texaco to market its oil in the Far East instead of relying on Socony-Vacuum. In one stroke it acquired markets for its oil from Bahrain and Saudi Arabia as well as diversifying the substantial financial risk that attended oil production in a climate of extreme political and economic uncertainty.

The Socal-Texaco ventures would not have upset the world marketing picture save for one problem. Had the partners produced oil in limited quantities, Texaco could have distributed most of it through its current market share. But three years after the first successful well (1938), Aramco (Arabian-American Oil Company, the Texaco-Socal subsidiary) had a potential capacity of 200,000 barrels per day with markets for just fifteen to twenty thousand barrels. To make matters worse, Ibn Saud was starved for revenues because his personal expenses were enormous and the war had curtailed production and limited his revenues from pilgrims traveling to Mecca. Aramco feared that failure to assuage the Saudi monarch with ample funds would open the door to a British rival.[14]

The onset of World War II brought something of a temporary lull to the Anglo-American rivalry for Middle East oil. Private corporations could not easily compete with the war machine for the scarce materials and transportation needed to continue the development of new fields. Fear of sabotage or Axis attack led the Allies to close a number of major wells. Such circumstances also help to explain why Standard Oil showed so little zeal in pursuing Iran's overtures in 1940. Relations with Saudi Arabia became most uncertain. Ibn Saud might well have cancelled the Aramco concession had the State Department not supported the company's plea to have the government make up part of his lost revenues from the United States Treasury. Partly in response to Aramco's pressure and partly out of anxiety about British intentions, President Roosevelt agreed in 1942 to take on some of the burden of Ibn Saud's expenses by making Saudi Arabia eligible for lend-lease aid.[15]

War may have limited opportunities to expand oil operations in the Middle East, but it did not mean that oilmen relaxed their vigilance. They knew that no matter what disruptions they now faced, the industry stood on the brink of a new era of power and prosperity. If anything, the international rivalry for oil concessions and markets promised to become more intense. To avoid destructive competition and to meet the exigencies of war, government officials in Washington and London began to explore the possibility of a bilateral petroleum agreement. That was a step the industry both supported and feared.[16]

FOREIGN OIL POLICY

World War II brought the federal government and the oil industry into an uneasy alliance. No executive department had ever been formally charged with responsibility for foreign oil policy. The Roosevelt administration created the Petroleum Administration for War (PAW), headed by Interior Secretary Harold Ickes, to coordinate all phases of wartime oil production and distribution. That had not, however, satisfactorily resolved the question of control between the private and public sector or among the various government bureaucracies that also wanted jurisdiction over oil.

The elaboration of a foreign oil policy and an apparatus to pursue it proved to be an enormously complicated matter. At home private landowners controlled subsoil rights, except on the public domain where the Interior Department exercised stewardship. Abroad, foreign governments usually retained control of their own oil. Since oil companies generally had to deal with government representatives, the State Department became the obvious agency to represent American interests. As a result, oilmen traditionally took their problems and solutions there. As we have seen, the State Department had several times used its channels to help open closed doors.

War abroad also meant war at home between Ickes and Secretary of State Hull. Both men sought control over foreign oil policy. Ever the bureaucratic imperialist, Ickes saw in his wartime role as petroleum administrator an opportunity to poach the State Department's responsibilities. He insisted that all oil policy, whether foreign or domestic, should be under a single authority, which meant, of course, Harold Ickes. Hull believed that by tradition and experience, his department could best coordinate the dealings between American oil companies and foreign governments.[17]

Roosevelt solved this conflict over executive authority as he so often did. He hedged his bets in such a way that ultimate control remained in his own hands. Ickes gained jurisdiction over production and both foreign and domestic supplies. But when political problems arose, the oil companies continued to use the offices of the State Department. If the question involved scarce materials to build facilities for producing or transporting oil, the War and Navy Departments, as well as Foreign Economic Administration (FEA or lend-lease) often had the deciding voice. And in the context of the war, the long-term requirements of the military and other national security questions began to shape thinking about the United States' stake in foreign oil reserves.[18]

In dividing authority within his administration, Roosevelt had addressed only one dimension of the problem. Whether ultimate determination of foreign oil policy would remain in the private sector or be shifted to the government remained uncertain. Despite Ickes' determination to make the government a senior partner in the oil business, private oilmen exercised a powerful influence over decisions affecting their interests. In many areas of the Middle East they had more contacts with local governments than did the State Department. The department had traditionally used its offices to promote private oil policy rather than treating foreign oil policy as an instrument of larger American purposes. Indeed, Ickes had found the relationship between the public and private sector too cosy to serve what he defined as the public interest.[19]

For all his rectitude, Ickes could not easily maintain a clear line between the public and private good. Many of the staff of the Petroleum Administration for War that he headed came perforce from the offices of the major oil companies. Their transformation into public servants was seldom complete. These new officials brought to Washington their knowledge of the industry and a residual sympathy for its special problems. Nor did the industry relax its efforts to protect itself from what it considered excessive government intervention. Oil executives formed an advisory body called the Petroleum Industry War Council that mirrored every facet of the public bureaucracy. The price of collaboration between the two groups came high. Ickes had to agree to set aside many of the antitrust restrictions that private oilmen, particularly the major integrated internationals, found too restrictive. As historian Michael Stoff concluded, "No decision escaped industry scrutiny. Local and national advisory committees gave oilmen, who were free from prosecution for many antitrust violations, a dominant voice in formulating and carrying out policy."[20]

There can be no doubt either that the presence of so many former industry officials in the wartime government bureaucracies further enhanced the industry's ability to shape public policy. During later investigations, Senator Owen Brewster of Maine accused the industry of "infiltrating" the government by "putting men from various oil companies into various positions in our State Department and into the oil picture where, at any rate, they would be fully informed regarding the evolution of our oil policy, and be able, perhaps, to exert a very considerable influence upon its evolution."[21] Such a simple conspiracy theory does not adequately describe the interaction between representatives of the private and public sectors. On the one hand there were officials like Ralph K. Davies from Socal, who while serving as deputy petroleum administrator, and with Ickes' approval, continued to draw his $49,600 salary from his former employer. Yet Davies became such a vigorous advocate of the public interest that Socal later dismissed him for his "uncompromising attitude toward the oil companies on behalf of the interests of the government." Oilmen who had business with the PAW generally avoided Ickes and Davies. They sought, instead, the offices of Davies' assistant, J. Terry Duce, who came to the government from Aramco. Before that Duce had been his company's most effective lobbyist with the State Department. Not so surprisingly, when debate over the government's efforts to acquire Saudi Arabian oil became most heated, Duce resigned to assume his former position.[22]

Two other quasi-public, quasi-private sector executives played key roles in shaping American oil policy for Iran: Patrick Hurley and Max Thornburg. As previously mentioned, Hurley had applied his legal talents to oil and gas leases before serving the government. He became a close friend of maverick oilman Harry Sinclair, from whom he received a retainer while he conducted freelance diplomacy for President Roosevelt. When Hurley first came to Iran in 1943, he and Sinclair undoubtedly had some inkling of its potential oil reserves. Sinclair had already tried in the 1920s to promote an Iranian oil concession. Soon after he returned from Iran, Hurley made casual inquiries at the State Department about the current status of Iranian concessions.[23]

For Hurley such initiatives never raised a question of impropriety. He believed unequivocally that only the entry of American private interests would allow Iran to escape the clutches of Anglo-Soviet imperialism, as a good dose of American free enterprise capitalism cured Iran's domestic economic ills. A greater American presence would also limit Russian and British opportunities. So Hurley saw himself as a go-between, someone who would inform the shah and Iranian officials of the advantages of granting concessions to Americans while at the same time urging entrepreneurs like Sinclair to apply for them. Since the benefits seemed in his mind to be mutual, Hurley did not see any conflict of interests in his actions.

Whereas Hurley acted publicly with almost simpleminded candor, Max Thornburg moved with catlike surefootedness behind the scenes. He had an uncanny knack for being on hand wherever the action was. From 1941 to 1943 Thornburg served in the State Department as petroleum adviser. So complete was Thornburg's loyalty to the major international oil companies that Senator Brewster later accused the industry of "planting" him in the Department. In fact, economic adviser Herbert Feis had recruited Thornburg because his experience with Bapco might strengthen the department in its bid to retain control over foreign oil policy. But unbeknownst to Feis, Thornburg continued to maintain both his ties to and his salary from Socal.[24]

Now it was not uncommon for executives from private industry to receive salaries from their former employers. The excruciatingly circumspect Ickes had ruled that people coming to his agency need not suffer financially for entering government service. What was unusual in Thornburg's case was that neither Feis nor Secretary Hull was aware of his continuing ties to Socal. Thornburg pursued his work at the State Department with singleminded devotion to the interests of the oil companies in general and Socal in particular. After the disclosure of these links forced his resignation, Thornburg managed to pop up regularly on the scene of crucial negotiations, sometimes in Washington, then in Iran or Saudi Arabia, or perhaps in South America.[25]

By late 1943 the Roosevelt administration had begun to formulate a foreign oil policy that recognized the extraordinary potential of the Middle East. The industry did not allow that process to go on unattended. It had the political resources to protect what it saw as its future interests. Those interests did require a more active role for the government in opening doors and keeping them open. But tradition and self-interest also dictated that the industry, not the government, would have the final say in defining the national interest whenever it involved the disposition of foreign oil concessions.

OIL AND SECURITY

In 1943 questions of foreign oil policy went far beyond the matter of jurisdiction between the public and private sectors. World War II demonstrated that it was almost impossible for industrial nations to conduct a successful war effort without access to the resources of third world nations. The Manhattan Project, for example, relied on the Belgian Congo as one crucial source of its uranium ore. As Herbert Feis had emphasized, oil had more strategic importance than any other single raw material. By 1943 it was clear that much of the world's oil lay not in the United States or the western hemisphere, but in the Middle East.

In Washington, a note of panic had crept into discussions of foreign oil policy. The heavy demands of war had turned chronic gluts into shortages. Commodore Andrew Carter of the Army-Navy Petroleum Board warned that the nation faced dire consequences:

> During the past year it has become more and more apparent that the known petroleum reserves within the continental limits of the United States, and indeed within the Western Hemisphere, are inadequate to meet over a period of years either the wartime needs of the United States or the needs of the civilian economy once normal conditions are established.[26]

Herbert Feis later recalled the same sense of anxiety among his government colleagues: "The United States—so the alarming conclusion traveled—was about to become dependent on other countries for oil; in that event American security, power, and freedom of action would be in peril." Ickes wondered publicly whether the United States would have the reserves to "oil another war."[27]

Among various officials and committees a consensus quickly formed that the United States must find a means to limit the drain on oil in the western hemisphere while promoting the greater use of reserves in the Middle East. One suggestion was for the government itself to enter the oil business, as had been proposed once before during the brief energy crisis of the early 1920s. Now, both the State Department's Committee on International Petroleum Policy and Harold Ickes' PAW recommended that the government establish the Petroleum Reserves Corporation (PRC) to secure the country's future oil needs by acquiring overseas concessions. Such a course of action had strong backing in the military departments. The Joint Chiefs' anxieties about oil had led Admiral William Leahy to urge that "prompt action be taken in connection with the acquisition of such reserves." Ickes had already sold Henry Stimson and Navy Secretary Frank Knox on the idea. Stimson recalled that after a cabinet meeting on 4 June 1943, "Frank Knox spoke to me about the United States getting hold of a big pool in Saudi Arabia which is owned by American corporations. . . ." The three men agreed that Ickes would approach the president about the matter. Indeed, Stimson thought their proposal had no opposition save on the question of "what method and what means to use in securing [reserves]."[28]

The question of means was far from incidental. With the feud between himself and Hull still raging, Ickes predictably assigned no role to either the secretary of state or his department. More important, Ickes and the Navy Department both envisioned direct government participation, including a "proprietary and managerial interest in foreign petroleum reserves." The State Department's planners had anticipated only that the government might purchase options on oil held by American corporations. In the end Roosevelt backed Ickes' scheme to charter the PRC and charge it to acquire Saudi oil by purchasing Aramco's stock.[29]

Such an aggressive government policy had several major drawbacks. Many local rulers who eagerly dealt with private oil companies were profoundly suspicious when a foreign government became involved. Officials in the industry and a few in the State Department feared that the PRC initiative might spur a tendency toward nationalization among local governments. And even if the U.S. government did purchase an oil company, that action would have little impact on the current crisis. It took as many as five years to bring newly found oil to world markets. Wartime shortages of men and materials further complicated that problem. In future wars, there was little guarantee that the United States could protect access to oil in an area as strategically vulnerable as the Middle East.[30]

More threatening was the possibility that the PRC's efforts would provoke a disastrous rivalry between British and American interests in the region. Stimson, for example, pleaded urgency not so much because he thought the oil would assist the war emergency, but because "these properties are likely to be picked up by the British unless we get hold of them." Most Americans still feared that the British would exploit the war effort to enhance their imperial position. In a thinly veiled attack on current British petroleum policy, Stimson observed that "at present it appears that though the United States controls only 48 percent of the world reserves, it is developing and exploiting some 60 percent of the amount developed in the world, a large part of which is being exported from the United States for the use of other nations who have not similarly exploited their own reserves."[31]

James Byrnes, the president's wartime industrial czar and the head of the Office of War Mobilization, was incensed by what he saw as a British strategy to exploit American resources rather than their own. He urged the president to demand from the British a one-third interest in Iran's oil fields as payment for oil shipped under lend-lease. The president had no desire to damage Anglo-American cooperation and therefore he shelved Byrne's proposal. Still, just the notion that the United States might seek part of England's most valuable foreign concession indicates the divisive potential that oil policy held for both war and peace. Harold Ickes made the point most directly: "Tell me the sort of agreement that the United States will reach with respect to the world's petroleum resources when the war is over, and I will undertake to analyze the durability of the peace that is to come."[32]

While Ickes and the PRC attempted to negotiate the purchase of an oil company, Secretary Hull launched an independent effort to secure agreement with the British over the role of governments and private oil companies in developing Middle Eastern oil. The British too had reasons to talk. The Anglo-Iranian Oil Company feared that ruinous postwar competition would frustrate its own plans to increase production in Iran. Worse yet was the prospect of the American government pouring its vast financial resources into the competition for Middle East reserves. Neither the British government nor its oilmen could hope to maintain England's position under such circumstances.

In December 1943 Hull issued an invitation to talk that ultimately led British and American diplomats to the bargaining table. Though ostensibly these were talks between governments, private oil interests in both countries monitored the proceedings at every stage. Both Hull and Ickes foresaw a bilateral pact as just one of a series of postwar agreements such as the Bretton Woods and Dumbarton Oaks agreements that would establish new instruments of international cooperation. Ickes hoped as well to promote behavior among private oil interests that would square with the public good. British officials were less burdened with such lofty aspirations. Cooperation might help sustain a status quo that favored British interests and, above all, help keep the United States government out of the competition for Middle East reserves.[33]

Oilmen had, of course, more tangible objectives. AIOC officials feared that the United States government would upset private arrangements like the "Red Line" and "As-Is" agreements. That step might increase the risk of ruinous overproduction and price competition, not to mention threatening the company's supremacy in the region. AIOC saw the talks leading to greater American participation within limits set by Anglo-American cartels. It was just those limits that led American oilmen to favor talks. Some revision of the "Red Line" agreement and of British colonial policy might allow them to escape their junior status. An oil agreement would certainly notify local governments and British competitors that American firms had strong backing in Washington. That was a message that the leaders of Iran were eager to hear.[34]

THE UNITED STATES AND IRANIAN OIL

The Iranian government had already been actively cultivating stronger ties with the United States. The occupation not only severed Iran's third power link to Germany, but it also created the prospect that the British and Russians might renew their partition scheme of 1907. From the Iranian perspective, the United States alone among the world powers had the capacity to help Iran sustain its independence. By 1943 the Iranians had received assurances that the Americans had no intention of seeing their country succumb to Anglo-Soviet imperial ambitions. The United States had promised, too, to extend material benefits through its advisers and lend-lease, although the actual results of these efforts had proven too paltry to satisfy either Iranian needs or expectations.

Iranian political leaders were too realistic to rest their country's future on American expressions of good intentions. And though part of the appeal of the United States as a third power lay in the apparent remoteness of its interests, Iranian leaders had learned in previous dealings with western powers that a political commitment had to have an economic or strategic basis. Over the past century various Iranian rulers had bartered valuable concessions to finance their excesses or to achieve foreign policy goals. Thus it is no surprise that in turning to the United States, Iran showed a willingness to secure new political ties with an oil concession. Wallace Murray had correctly identified political links as Iran's real objective in 1940 when it invited Standard Oil of New Jersey to negotiate a concession agreement.[35]

Diplomatic and material support were not the only benefits Iran might gain from the United States. Reza Shah had made it painfully evident in 1933 that he resented the terms of Iran's concession with AIOC. The British government earned more in taxes and dividends from its shares than Iran received in royalties. Nothing compelled AIOC to place Iran's interests before its own. So, for example, if market conditions dictated, Anglo-Iranian Oil Company might draw more heavily on its IPC fields, no matter how badly Iran might need additional revenues. An American concession would promise Iran an alternative source of funds as well as a possible lever with which to pry more favorable terms from AIOC.[36]

Even before the Americans became seriously involved in concession negotiations, the State Department and other interested agencies had discussed ground rules under which American businesses might enter into Iranian ventures. They learned in 1943 that a firm called American Metal and Ore had applied for Iranian mineral concessions and mining rights. Despite its name, American Metal was a London-based holding company in which Americans held only a minority interest. Patrick Hurley was so vexed when he learned of the company's ploy that he alerted Secretary of State Hull. Hurley insisted that the State Department scrutinize the background of "all persons and concerns" proposing to do business in Iran. Once again he demonstrated how much his economic and political agendas had become entwined: "Iran is now anxious for Americans to open business relations here, but this attitude toward the United States could be injured if we permitted shoestring promoters and exploiters to enter as the first Americans to arrive on the ground."[37] In short, Hurley was asking the department to act a little like the Securities and Exchange Commission by providing the Iranian government with relevant information about American companies who sought to enter its markets.

Hurley was not the only anglophobe provoked by American Metal's strategy. From his lend-lease office in Cairo, the Middle East Director, James Landis, warned that any further concentration of valuable concessions in British hands would undermine American efforts to promote Iranian independence. "In light of our interests in Iran and contributions to it," he recommended, "I would not like to see any concessions of any nature granted to the British without our consent."[38]

Few people in Washington assumed such an extreme position. Nevertheless, the State Department wanted Americans to appear as independent agents whenever possible, since the United States did not yet bear the stigma of British imperialism that had so provoked many Iranian nationalists. For that reason George Allen of the Near East Division argued that British interests should not dominate ostensibly American firms. So long as Americans held the majority position, the British could not exploit the United States' prestige to realize imperial goals. As a result of this consideration the State Department opposed the American Metal and Ore bid as well as any other such backdoor approach to Iran.[39]

In that action and in its support for an American oil concession the department crossed the line John Jernegan had drawn in his memorandum. American diplomats were not neutral when they opposed British or Russian initiatives to secure their own interests in Iran. And there was nothing disinterested about the quest for a concession, which was, at least in part, prompted by the desire to maintain adequate U.S. oil reserves. Even when concessions could be justified on strictly economic grounds, American officials saw a direct link between oil negotiations and questions of national security. So, soon after the Jernegan memorandum had circulated through policy channels, the United States and its corporate citizens embarked on a course that invalidated Jernegan's central assumption.

The concession talks began innocently enough. Indeed, the Iranian government, not private oilmen or American officials, made the first inquiries. The Iranians were not blind to the friction oil might cause among the Allies. The advocates of positive equilibrium believed that Iran's independence remained more secure when big power rivalries flourished. In February 1943 the Iranian commercial attaché in Washington contacted Standard Oil of New Jersey to learn if the company might be interested in an Iranian oil concession. At that time SONJ had every reason to look for new sources of Middle East crude. So did its sometime overseas partner—the Socony-Vacuum Company—with which it operated Stanvac. Though the two giants had among the largest world market shares, neither firm operated a significant Middle East concession. The minority positions they held in IPC satisfied the needs of neither firm and together they had grown more eager to break out of the restrictions of the Red Line.[40]

For Stanvac an Iranian concession had some attractive features. Iran stood outside the Red Line area and unlike Kuwait was not so much subject to British interference. And Iranian oil would allow the Stanvac partners to recoup some of the advantage Texaco and Socal had gained with their Bahrain and Saudi concessions or the advantage AIOC enjoyed through its Iranian monopoly and dominant role in IPC.

By June 1943 conversations between Stanvac and the Iranian Embassy in Washington had become sufficiently serious that the company turned to the State Department for advice. Above all, Stanvac wanted assurances that its desire to obtain a concession did not conflict with current American policy. Undoubtedly, too, Stanvac realized that by keeping the State Department informally involved it could use its diplomatic channels whenever politics complicated the negotiations. At this point the department offered no guidance, but officials did assure Stanvac's President, P. W. Parker, that they were eager to know the course the negotiations took.[41]

From the outset, talks between Stanvac and the Iranian government centered as much on politics as on oil. It was Iran's Prime Minister, Ali Soheili, who for political reasons revealed in October 1943 that concession talks were under way. Soheili believed that an enhanced American role would undercut the pro-British and pro-Russian opposition factions, while strengthening the influence of parliamentary groups who hoped to weaken the bonds between the shah and the army. Such political undercurrents had been evident during the talks in Washington between Stanvac and the Iranian Minister, Mohammad Shayesteh. Shayesteh had assured P. W. Parker "that it has long been the wish of his government and people to have American companies represented in the development of Iranian petroleum reserves," but that, as Parker explained, he could not ensure Stanvac's full cooperation until "he could be assured that our company had the full support of our government."[42]

What Shayesteh meant is not all together clear. He many only have wanted a guarantee that Stanvac was not, like American Metal and Ore, beholden to British interests. But more likely, Shayesteh and Parker were both after a commitment from the State Department that if the negotiations provoked British or Russian opposition, as had happened in the past, the two parties could expect active diplomatic support. The State Department was not then prepared to make either a specific or a hypothetical commitment. Beyond informing Parker that Stanvac could proceed with the department's blessings, Assistant Secretary A. A. Berle did not say what role, if any, the department might play.[43]

It was Louis Dreyfus who first recognized that the oil negotiations contradicted the idea of a disinterested American presence. Soheili had privately urged him to find American corporations that might wish to establish connections with Iran. Dreyfus preferred to concentrate on building American prestige without becoming embroiled in the business affairs of American corporations. He told Secretary Hull that any steps to promote an oil concession "would cause the British and Soviets to suspect that our attitude toward Iran is not entirely disinterested and thus weaken our general position."[44] Deeply engaged in his battle with Ickes over foreign oil policy, Hull could not readily advise Dreyfus just what his proper role should be.

Circumstances almost immediately transformed Dreyfus' dilemma from the abstract to the concrete. He discovered in November that Royal Dutch-Shell had dispatched two representatives to Iran to compete for the same concession in Baluchistan that Stanvac hoped to win. Could Iran become another Kuwait? Would the British government and private interests conspire to deprive Americans of a concession, not for the sake of developing new oil fields, but to preserve AIOC's hegemony? Certainly many Americans believed that would be the case.

Though Prime Minister Soheili did fear that the British intended to drive him out of office, he had no inclination to grant them further concessions. All the same, the Shell overture did provide him with a stick he could use to prod the Americans, since Stanvac had not yet dispatched representatives to Iran, and no direct talks could begin until they arrived. In the meantime, the two Shell agents could promote their cause. "Soheili states that the British representatives are pressing him to speed negotiations," Dreyfus warned, "and he does not believe he can delay much longer." As the Standard Oil agent, R. S. Stewart, headed to Tehran from Cairo with the authority to negotiate until agents came from the United States, Hull instructed Dreyfus to "make all appropriate assistance to Stewart and Standard-Vacuum representatives and express the hope that the negotiations will be kept open."[45] Business and politics had now mixed.

No matter how eagerly the Iranian government courted an American concessionaire, in the actual negotiations it proceeded with exquisite caution. After all, the Iranians could not afford to squander whatever political advantages they might gain from skillful bargaining. They seemed suspicious that Stanvac was bound by some secret contract to AIOC or to other British interests. The history of the Kuwait concession served as warning of how AIOC could deceive Middle East governments as well as its partners. Paul Alling assured Shayesteh that as far as the State Department knew, Stanvac had a genuine interest in developing a concession. He reminded the Iranian minister that the Standard Oil partners had major Near and Far Eastern markets for which Iran would be an advantageous source of crude oil. Besides, Stanvac had just despatched their agent, Thomas Draper, to Tehran with full authority to negotiate on the company's behalf. And without being explicit, Alling did promise that Stanvac had the backing of the United States government.[46]

Even though the oil negotiations proceeded slowly, Allied rivalries became more heated. The Soviet Embassy in Tehran, for example, made it clear that the Russians considered the negotiations a possible threat. And late in February of 1944 the State Department received a cable from Moscow, apropos of no current Soviet-American discussions, which asserted the Soviet Union's prior claim to any oil fields in northern Iran. Although Moscow had done exactly the same thing in 1940, the Soviet government once again felt the need to discourage any foreign interest from establishing a position too close to its borders. When approached by Chargé Richard Ford, officials at the Iranian Foreign Ministry denied that the Russian claim had any historic legitimacy. The Majles, after all, had never ratified the 1916 Khostaria concession before the Bolsheviks renounced it in 1918. Still, Foreign Minister Saed admitted that Iran had no wish to provoke the Soviet Union and therefore had no intention of granting any concessions in the northern occupation zone.[47]

The Russians were not the only ally made anxious by the prospect of a new American concession. Both Shell and the British Ministry of Fuel and Power greatly feared "American moves to secure fresh sources of oil in the Middle East." With the world oil picture in flux, British officials feared "our negotiating position generally will be impaired if they forestall us in this part of Persia."[48] Some British officials saw Stanvac as a Trojan Horse for the Petroleum Reserves Corporation. Once again they shuddered at the idea of their firms competing with the PRC, backed by the resources of the U.S. Treasury and Fort Knox.

The records indicate, too, that as far as the Foreign Office knew, Shell wanted oil, and not merely to obstruct the Americans or to preserve the AIOC monopoly. The Foreign Office believed that Shell had moved to head off another case of aggressive American competition, especially since insufficient initiative in the recent past had cost the British a position in many promising fields, like those of Saudi Arabia. Iran, they assumed, might become yet another area lost to the Americans unless Shell "kept up our end before the Americans get all there is left."[49]

The Iranian negotiations would not have caused the British so much discomfort had it not been for Secretary Hull's December invitation to the Foreign Office to talk about oil. Most of the possible American proposals, they worried, could only weaken the British position further. The Americans would probably ask for a relaxation of the kinds of colonial restrictions that had hampered Gulf Oil in both Bahrain and Kuwait. Or the Americans might have some new scheme to acquire British rather than American-controlled oil for the Petroleum Reserves Corporation. It was not so long past that James Byrnes had floated the notion of the United States government becoming a partner in AIOC. Similar talk had kept the diplomatic rumor mill flapping ever since. And in February Harold Ickes had suggested that the British might assign their half interest in Kuwait to the PRC.[50]

The Foreign Office had seen both Ickes' and Byrnes' proposals as trial balloons meant to test their future intentions. But even if Ickes had been no more than half serious, the British had become even more skeptical about the oil talks. After repeated urging from the Ministry of Fuel and Power, Churchill finally told his good friend Franklin Roosevelt that his countrymen were alarmed by aggressive American efforts to acquire new oil. Roosevelt at first ignored Churchill's obvious bid for reassurance. Then he tried to smooth the matter over. "I am having the oil question studied by the Department of State and my oil experts, but please do accept my assurances that we are not making sheep's eyes at your oil fields in Iran and Iraq."[51]

No amount of presidential glibness could soothe the tensions that oil rivalry had provoked. The Americans needed to have been more forthcoming about oil in Iran and the Middle East. As a step toward better Allied relations, for example, they might have proposed a moratorium on concession talks until the war ended. Or they might have sought to establish with the Russians and the British acceptable terms for future concessions in Iran. Such a move would have indicated that Roosevelt actually did want Iran to become a "test case" of what a disinterested Allied policy could achieve. Instead, American diplomats decided to continue along the present course, but paying a little more attention to allaying British and Russian concerns. Chargé Richard Ford made what must rank as one of the war's most naive assumptions "that with a careful and open handling of the question with both the British and Soviets, we might well be given a free hand, or at least a less competitive field than might otherwise be the case."[52]

In truth, Ford was not the only American thinking that way. Under Secretary of State Stettinius was then leading an American mission to London to iron out a range of Anglo-American differences. Members of the mission knew of the tempest brewing in the Iranian teapot. They warned that "this situation if allowed to drift without clarification, may create suspicions, especially on the part of the British and Russians as to American motives and may result in disastrous competition to the detriment of all parties concerned and of general Allied cooperation in Iran." That view at least appreciated the divisiveness of the oil competition. Surely knowing that, the mission members would have proposed postponing further efforts to win an Iranian concession. Not at all. Like Ford, they applied a little diplomatic balm to soothe the irritation. They told the British they had no reason for concern since "the negotiations being conducted are strictly commercial, the companies concerned neither sought nor obtained our diplomatic support or special privilege."[53]

How were the British or Russians supposed to swallow such a statement, which only in the most narrow or literal sense contained any truth? No American policymaker viewed the negotiations as "strictly commercial." Wallace Murray had long before identified Iran's political strategy in offering a concession. Many American officials had in turn sought concessions as private instruments through which the State Department could implement its policy of strengthening American ties to Iran while weakening British and Soviet influence. No one had been more outspoken on such matters than Murray himself, who not coincidentally happened to be one of the chief negotiators for the Stettinius mission. He knew also that the efforts to obtain a concession, though not a government initiative, had official blessings.

Nor could it honestly be said that Stanvac had neither asked for nor received official diplomatic support. Just two months before Hull had instructed the chargé to intercede on Stanvac's behalf. Soon after, the department arranged air travel priorities to speed Stanvac's representatives to Tehran. On other occasions, Patrick Hurley had used his access to the shah to improve the climate for American businesses. This is not to equate American efforts with the more direct interference being practiced by the Russians and British. Nor were the Americans behaving much differently in Iran than they behaved in other underdeveloped nations. The State Department was doing what it traditionally did for Americans abroad. Still, no matter how much Murray or Ford might deny or discount it, the United States government had become an interested party in negotiations with as much political as economic importance.[54]

As complicated as matters seemed in February 1944, they soon got worse. Over the next year the oil negotiations became entangled with at least four separate conflicts: political factionalism in Iran, competing American interests, the great power rivalries over foreign oil policy, and nascent Soviet-American cold war tensions. In Iran, many nationalists opposed the government's attempts to alienate more of its resources to foreigners. Along with the leftists, they attacked successive cabinets for conducting secret negotiations. Worse yet, from the State Department's perspective, Sinclair Oil Company decided it would join in the competition for a concession. That decision turned a two-party contest into a three-cornered one, and this rivalry between Americans offered Shell a potential advantage. The State Department, however, was almost powerless to intercede on the American side. Foreign oil policy was too much of a political football in Washington for a government agency to enter the contest on the side of a single private interest. That was not the worst of it. The Soviet Union began to give indications that it did not intend to sit idly by while its Anglo-American allies divided the spoils in neighboring Iran. By September of 1944 the Russians would join the chase for a concession. That meant Iran would become a test case, not of the Allies' good intentions, but of the cold war soon to come.

NOTES

1. These statistics are from Aaron Miller, *Search for Security,* pp. 8–31. The Ickes' quote is from SD 800.6363/1281, enclosures 1 and 2, Ickes to Hull, 8/13/43. I have relied on a variety of good histories of Middle Eastern oil to construct my account. Benjamin Schwadran, *The Middle East, Oil, and the Great Powers* (New York, 1954), especially pp. 301–32 is one of the good early histories. Stephen Longrigg's *Oil in the Middle East* (London, 1954) is another useful account. I have relied on John Blair, *The Control of Oil* (New York, 1976) to untangle

many of the interlocking arrangements that characterize the industry in the Middle East, as well as on Irvine Anderson, *ARAMCO, the United States, and Saudi Arabia* (Princeton, 1981). General readers will profit from and enjoy Leonard Mosley, *Power Play: Oil in the Middle East* (New York, 1973); Anthony Sampson, *The Seven Sisters: The Great Oil Companies and the World They Shaped* (New York, 1975); and Martin Melosi, *Coping With Abundance: Energy and Environment in Industrial America* (New York, 1985) for a comprehensive view of American energy policy. I cite Mosley frequently because he is accessible and draws on scholarly studies. For a general history of Iranian oil see L. P. Elwell-Sutton, *Persian Oil, A Study in Power Politics* (Westport, 1975).

2. SD 800.6363/1281, enclosure 2. See also Henry Longhurst, *Adventure in Oil: The Story of British Petroleum* (London, 1959). To clarify inevitable confusion, Anglo-Persian Oil Co. (APOC) became Anglo-Iranian Oil Co. (AIOC) in 1934 after Reza Shah changed the name of "Persia" to "Iran." It is now known as British Petroleum or BP, which established a major position in American markets by buying Standard Oil of Ohio (Sohio).

3. The Germans and Japanese both planned strategies before and during the war to secure access to petroleum. One of the Germans' most interesting tactics was gaining access to or control of key industrial materials through international cartels. Six major American corporations entered into such arrangements during the 1930s. Standard Oil of New Jersey (SONJ) or Exxon as it is now known, and I.G. Farben corporation had a series of patent pooling agreements covering synthetic gas and rubber. See Mark H. Lytle, "Thurman Arnold and the Wartime Cartels," unpublished ms., in the Papers of John M. Blum, Yale University Library (YUL), New Haven, Connecticut. See also Thurman Arnold, *Fair Fights and Foul* (New York, 1965), ch. 15. Robert A. Solo, "The Saga of Synthetic Rubber," *The Bulletin of Atomic Scientists* (April 1980), p. 32.

4. Harold Ickes, *Fightin' Oil* (New York, 1943), p. 9. The statistics on oil use are quoted in Michael B. Stoff, *Oil, War, and American Security,* p. 73. See also Herber Feis, *Seen From E.A.: Three International Episodes* (New York, 1947), pp. 95–97.

5. Blair, *The Control of Oil,* p. 32.

6. Mosley, *Power Play,* pp. 33–48.

7. Blair, *Control of Oil,* pp. 31–34; Mosley, *Power Play,* pp. 41–50.

8. Blair, *Control of Oil,* pp. 33–34; Mosley, *Power Play,* p. 67; Stoff, *Oil, War and American Security,* p. 93n.

9. See Irvine Anderson, *The Standard-Vacuum Oil Company and United States East Asian Policy, 1933–1941* (Princeton, 1975). The companies that comprise the "Seven Sisters" are AIOC (now BP), Standard of New Jersey (Exxon), Standard of New York (Mobil), Royal Dutch-Shell, Standard of California (Socal or more recently Chevron), Gulf, and Texaco.

10. Mosley, *Power Play,* p. 90; Blair, *Control of Oil,* pp. 54–56.

11. Mosley, *Power Play,* pp. 60–70. See also Miller, *Search for Security,* pp. 14–17.

12. Quoted in Mosley, *Power Play,* p. 80.

13. Ibid., pp. 77–88. See also Blair, *Control of Oil,* pp. 42–43.

14. Under the terms of its agreement with Texaco, the two companies created Caltex to operate the Bahrain concession. Socal acquired half of Texaco's markets east of Suez, while Texaco gained access to a more reliable source of crude. And since Socal had negotiated an agreement with Ibn Saud in 1933, Texaco became an equal partner in Casoc (California-Arabian Standard Oil Company) or as it is best known, Aramco, Arabian-American Oil Company. Initially, the British government did assume some of the burden of Ibn Saud's expenses. Miller, *Search for Security,* p. xii and note, pp. 19–21. Blair, *Control of Oil,* pp. 36–37. On the history of Aramco see Irvine Anderson, *ARAMCO, the United States, and Saudi Arabia.* To clarify any confusion, Casoc became Aramco officially in 1943. See also Stoff, *Oil, War, and American Security,* pp. 34–46.

15. Miller, *Search for Security,* pp. 32–54; Mosley, *Power Play,* pp. 137–49.

16. Anyone interested in foreign oil policy and specifically the aborted Anglo-American Oil Agreement would benefit from Michael Stoff, *Oil, War, and American Security.* He brings clarity to what were murky politics. I have drawn on his work in this and the next section.

17. Ibid., pp. 22–30.

18. Ibid., pp. 30–33.

19. Ibid., pp. 37–41; see also Miller, *Search for Security,* pp. 21–31.

20. Ibid., pp. 21–22.

21. *Congressional Record,* 80th Cong., 2nd sess., vol. 94, part 4, 4/28/48, pp. 4953 and 4937.

22. On Davies see also "R. K. Davies," memo not dated, Robert E. Sherwood Collection, Harry Hopkins Papers, Box 328, Oil Folder, FDRL; U.S. Senate, Special Committee Investigating the National Defense Program, *Hearings,* Part 41, *Petroleum Arrangements with Saudi Arabia,* 80th Cong., 2nd sess. (Washington, 1948), pp. 25207–25209. The structure of Ickes' staff is broken down in NA, Records of the Secretary of the Interior, RG 48, File 1–188: Petroleum Administration, Folder 2834. On Duce's resignation, see *New York Times,* 10/19/43. See also Miller, *Search for Security,* p. 36.

23. On Hurley, Sinclair, and Iran, see Russell Buhite, *Patrick J. Hurley and World Affairs,* pp. 130–32. See also SD 891.6363/800, 561, Dreyfus to Hull, 5/26/43. Dreyfus refers to a Hurley memorandum dated 4/21/43 that I was unable to find in the archives.

24. *Arabian Oil Hearings,* pp. 25262 and 25212–25213. See also Stoff, *Oil, War, and American Security,* pp. 28–32 and 64–70.

25. Stoff, *Oil, War, and American Security,* p. 65 and 65n.

26. NA, RG 334, File ANPB, 14/1–Foreign Petroleum Policy, Misc. Folder, Andrew F. Carter to Frank Knox, 1/17/44. Also in FR, 1944, V, pp. 17–20.

27. Feis, *Seen from E.A.,* pp. 95–99; Ickes, *Fightin' Oil,* p. 9. See also Stoff, pp. 72–74.

28. Stoff, *Oil, War, and American Security,* pp. 73–88. The consensus was elaborated in the report of Harley Notter's Post-War Advisory Committee in the State Department. They concluded by early 1944 that "American participation in the development of Middle Eastern oil is desirable because there will be greater assurance that the tempo of exploitation will be adequate in relation to the desired conservation of Western Hemisphere oil reserves. Furthermore, and of greater importance, United States policy should aim to secure this country, in the interest of security, a substantial and geographically diversified holding of foreign petroleum resources in the hands of United States nationals." SD, Harley Notter File, Box 17, PWC–33, 2/22/44. See also Henry L. Stimson, "Diaries," vol. 43, 4 June, 8 June and 11 June 1943, YUL. See also memorandum by General Boykin Wright, 11 June 1943, Stimson Correspondence, YUL.

29. Stoff, *Oil, War, and American Security,* pp. 77–80. See also FR, 1943, 4, pp. 925–30.

30. SD 800.6363/1243A, Hull to FDR, 6/14/43; SD 890F.6363/52, Feis to Hull, 7/3/43 and Hull to FDR, 7/6/43.

31. Stimson Diaries, vol. 45, 11/22/43 and Office of War Mobilization (OWM) notes, 9/20/43, Stimson Correspondence.

32. *Arabian Oil Hearings,* p. 25430, Byrnes to Roosevelt, 10/15/43; Stoff, *Oil, War, and American Security,* p. 151.

33. Ibid., pp. 89–20.

34. Ibid., pp. 118–120. See also Miller, *Search for Security,* pp. 83–84 and 99–107; Mosley, *Power Play,* pp. 151–55.

35. For a good general discussion of the development of this strategy, see Rouhollah Ramazani, *The Foreign Policy of Iran, 1500–1941,* pp. 277–300; and Ramazani, *Iran's Foreign Policy, 1941–1973,* pp. 17–19, 70–90.

36. Ramazani, *The Foreign Policy of Iran,* pp. 250–56. See also Mosley, *Power Play,* pp. 91–93.

37. FR, 1943, 4, Hurley Letter, 12/21/43, pp. 417–19.

38. SD, FW891.63/40, Landis to Winant, 1/1/44.

39. SD 891.63/40, Alling to Ford, 1/14/44. Paul Alling of the Near East Division urged the chargé in Tehran to bring the matter up with finance adviser Arthur Millspaugh. Millspaugh, he suggested, would certainly act in Iran's best interest. Alling also indicated that if Millspaugh liked the idea, the State Department would furnish his mission with a mining engineer. SD 891.63/47, memorandum by George Allen, 2/25/44.

40. Mosley, *Power Play,* pp. 156–67. Blair, *Control of Oil,* pp. 31–42. See also Sampson, *Seven Sisters,* pp. 38–42 and 119–24.

41. SD 891.6363/12–1144, Ambassador Tehran to Secretary of State, Embassy Enclosure 148, 12/11/44. For any historian trying to reconstruct the course of negotiations, this document is invaluable. It contains the embassy's chronology of the events that occurred during the long process. Hereafter, it will be cited as Emb. Encl. 148.

42. Abrahamian, *Iran Between Two Revolutions,* pp. 184–85. See also Ramazani, *Iran's Foreign Policy, 1941–1973,* pp. 92–93. SD 891.6363/808, Parker to State Department, 10/20/43.

43. SD 891.6363/808, Berle to Parker, 11/17/43.

44. FR, 1943, 4, p. 625, Dreyfus to Hull, 11/15/43 and p. 615, Hull to Dreyfus, 11/23/43.

45. For a good capsule description of Shell, see Sampson, *Seven Sisters,* pp. 13–16 and pp. 53–59. Shell did not have the same links to the British government as did AIOC. Its ownership was divided between Dutch and British interests. And like the Stanvac partners, Shell needed new sources of crude in order to realize its future market potential. See also FR, 1943, 4, p. 626 and on Soheili and the British pp. 339–40. Dreyfus thought the British wanted to replace Soheili with Seyyid-Zia-ed-Din, widely considered a political stooge. See also ibid., p. 627, Hull to Dreyfus, 12/20/43.

46. SD 891.6363/829, Alling memorandum, 2/18/44.

47. Emb. Encl. 148 and FR, 1944, 5, pp. 446–47, Ford to Secretary of State, 4/3/44.

48. FO 35128, E5037/545/34, N. M. Butler to Sir R. I. Campbell, October 1943.

49. FO 35128, E5037/545/34, Minute by R. W. Law, 9/23/43.

50. FDRL, OF 56, Fred Searles to Byrnes, 8/13/43, and Searles to Byrnes, 10/12/43; see also Byrnes to FDR, 10/15/43 reprinted in *Arabian Oil Hearings,* p. 25340. See also Stoff, *Oil, War, and American Security,* ch. 5.

51. FO W2206/34/76, 701, Halifax to FO, 2/11/44; FO W2717/34/76, 860, Halifax to FO, 2/20/44. FR, 1944, 3, pp. 100–101, Churchill to FDR, 2/20/44; FDRL, Map Room 604(2), Sec. 1, Oil Conference, 485, Roosevelt to Churchill, 3/3/44.

52. FR, 1944, 5, p. 445, Ford to Secretary of State, 3/9/44.

53. SD 740.0011/Stettinius/3–1944, Question 2, "Petroleum Concessions in Iran."

54. Emb. Encl. 148 reveals some of the State Department's steps taken on Stanvac's behalf.

6 *Oil and Cold War in Iran*

In 1946 a bitter Arthur Millspaugh wrote about the failure of his mission to Iran. Among the many factors that had hampered American efforts, he emphasized the shortsightedness of U.S. oil policy: "Oil occupied a prominent place among the [American] objectives in the Middle East, but in the Persia of 1944 this feature of our program proved more inflammatory than lubricating." It was not merely the conflict between the State Department's declaration of the United States' "disinterested" goals and the self-interested oil policy that dismayed Millspaugh. He objected even more to the decision to embark on such a controversial course "with no preliminary understanding with the Soviet Union and none of any particular value . . . with Great Britain."[1]

By the spring of 1944 oil policy could not be separated from the politics of the American advisers. The turmoil besetting the Soheili government involved both Allied competition for oil concessions and Millspaugh's reforms, which had provoked widespread opposition from a cross section of Iranians. Nor had there been economic or political benefits to vindicate the advisory program. The imminent fall of the cabinet jeopardized American hopes for a concession in the southern Iranian province of Baluchistan, since Soheili supported Stanvac.

The interplay of oil politics with Iran's internal factionalism was just one facet of the problem facing Americans in 1944. Harry Sinclair had announced that his company, too, wanted a concession in Iran. The large integrated companies had no desire to have small independents like Sinclair stake out a position in the Middle East. Yet that prospect was not as threatening as the evident desire of the federal government to enter the oil business through the Petroleum Reserves Corporation. Conservatives saw that move as a step down the road to socialism. Then there was the question of bilateral talks with the British. Anglo-American diplomats had not yet been able to agree on either a site or the topics for their forthcoming negotiations. One Iranian faction against another faction, independents against majors, the private versus the public sector, the British against the Americans—these were complications enough for American diplomats to manage. But a new problem arose when the Russians as well as the Americans and British sought to realize their long-term security interests through an Iranian oil concession. That effort brought the cold war to Iran.

AMERICAN RIVALS

In March Sinclair Oil Company surprised the State Department by announcing its intention to bid against Shell and Stanvac for the Baluchistan concession in southern Iran. Certainly no one associated with the negotiations welcomed this added complication. When Chargé Richard Ford learned that Sinclair's agent, Marcel Wagner, would open negotiations, he warned that rivalry threatened American prospects. The evidence indicates that the State Department preferred to have Stanvac represent American interests. Perhaps that was one legacy of the close ties between the department and the major international oil firms. Then, too, in the 1930s Mexican nationalization crisis, Sinclair had broken ranks with other American firms to reach a settlement with the Mexican government. Nationalization remained a bogeyman for oilmen in the Middle East. For that reason among others they had no desire to have a maverick like Sinclair enter their tight fraternity. Possibly the State Department believed that Stanvac had the necessary marketing and capital resources to develop an Iranian concession in ways more advantageous to the United States than others. But whatever their private motives, department officials publicly practiced a studied neutrality in the competition between Stanvac and Sinclair.[2]

On behalf of Sinclair, Marcel Wagner adopted a strategy that seemed designed largely to discredit Stanvac. The State Department had suggested that a joint bid might better serve these American rivals. Wagner rejected that idea because he thought Stanvac's ties with AIOC brought the American firm under a cloud of suspicion. Sinclair did not have a similar reason to foresake future operations in Iran to exploit oil from other sources. But that line of argument did not explain the advantages Iran might gain from awarding the concession to Sinclair.[3]

The Sinclair-Stanvac rivalry might not have posed such a threat had the Soheili government been more stable. The State Department would have been able to rely on the prime minister's good offices to protect the American position. But Soheili had never been particularly popular with the shah and with royalist factions. The British and their Iranian supporters had consistently tried to undermine him. And by seeking American assistance to build up the army, he had finally alienated the antiroyalist factions that had become the main pillar of his support. By March, the American legation recognized that Soheili's situation had become untenable. And when Soheili fell, the young shah could not handpick the next cabinet to see that it carried out the policies he favored.[4]

The shah's opponents had set their sights on a sweeping shift of power. The monarchy's power lay in the army from which Reza Shah had emerged as Iran's ruler. As a result, the old aristocrats, the mullahs, and other opponents of the Pahlevis had backed parliamentary actions to curb the army's size and function. Into this maelstrom stepped the bullheaded Arthur Millspaugh. He recognized the army as the major drain on Iran's overburdened budget. Sound finance dictated that the cost and size of the army be reduced. He therefore threw his support behind the antiroyalist factions who for quite different reasons favored the same policies.[5]

Millspaugh's assault on the army budget was just one more proposed reform that added new factions to the groups that opposed him. His unpopularity became so widespread that it dimmed any prospects for an American concession. Foreign Minister Mohammed Saed finally found it necessary to spell out his government's expectations in the most naked terms. As Ford reported, Saed "had personally been responsible for bringing Americans to Iran but . . . from the beginning he had felt that his country did not need their technical skills so much as for them to act as a cushion between British-Soviet conflicting interests."[6] So much for the American idea of nation-building.

The task of retrieving the situation for the Americans fell to the Petroleum Attaché for Iran and Iraq, Col. John Leavell. Having previously worked in the oil industry, Leavell understood full well the value of a concession in Iran—"as productive as the Anglo-Iranian concession and situated closer to future big markets." On the assumption that American access to Iranian oil was a top departmental priority, he sought to isolate Millspaugh from the negotiations. He urged the State Department to press Sinclair to avoid any delay: the sooner the negotiations were completed the less likely it was that the financial mission would alienate support for the Americans. An OSS agent learned that "a highly placed member of the Majles assured the Sinclair representative the concession in Baluchistan, if Sinclair would use his influence to have Millspaugh recalled." That comment more accurately reflected Millspaugh's unpopularity than Sinclair's prospects, for at no time did the Iranians give any other indication that he had much of a chance.[7]

Besides urging haste, Leavell proposed a plan that would eliminate Millspaugh's role in evaluating the concession bids. As a financial adviser with expertise in oil economics, Millspaugh could have been expected to tell the Iranians which bid best served their interests. Leavell persuaded the Iranian government to create a five-member panel to assume that responsibility. The only American on the committee was Rex Vivian, a member of the food advisory mission. That left the Iranians with four votes. Leavell reasoned that Iranian nationalists would be more receptive to a decision made largely by their own countrymen, who, he was certain, would choose Stanvac.[8]

Despite Leavell's successful intervention, the Sinclair-Stanvac rivalry continued to jeopardize American prospects. Wagner again refused terms under which the two sides would present a consolidated bid. On behalf of Sinclair, he demanded that his client maintain an equal financial stake as well as operating and management control. Stanvac would not and could not accept such terms. It would find itself once more a junior partner in a major concession. Besides, with the inside track, it could confidently expect to win without Sinclair. By 16 May both Stanvac and Shell had made firm offers, while Wagner would only promise that Sinclair would give more favorable terms than his rivals. Leavell charged that Sinclair was unfairly "asking for more favorable consideration." But what really irked the attaché were rumors that Sinclair and Stanvac had resorted to bribery, slander, and other dirty tricks to defeat each other. "This is the worst possible manner to have the negotiations proceed from the American viewpoint," Leavell fumed, since neither company might win the concession.[9]

Leavell had been operating, or so he asserted, on the assumption that this contest was more than the effort of a "commercial company to secure solely commercial rights without reference to the good of the nation." Thus he was stunned to learn that Secretary Hull refused to intervene between Stanvac and Sinclair. In fact, Hull ordered both Leavell and Ford to remain neutral. "It would be contrary to policy for the Department to insist either that one of the two companies withdraw or that the two companies present a combined bid." Leavell charged that he had been misled by the department's extraordinary attention to the negotiations. Had not the department encouraged the two companies to risk considerable money? And had it not given their representatives air travel priorities, despite the war situation? Well then, he had assumed that if the department followed such a course, particularly in a country with prospects "as uncertain as that of any country known to me, . . . [it] would protect [American companies] in the future."[10]

What then was the department's attitude toward a concession in Iran? Was it, as Leavell had assumed, a national priority? If so, why had Hull sent such confusing signals? Leavell had not really misjudged the department's commitment; he had simply become isolated from current oil politics in Washington. Harold Ickes had announced in February that the Petroleum Reserves Corporation was planning to build a pipeline across Saudi Arabia. Oil could flow from the Persian Gulf directly to a terminal on the Mediterranean. And by that stroke the government would gain access to Middle Eastern crude without the complications that might attend direct participation in a private company like Aramco.[11]

Only Cordell Hull among top Washington officials had shown any reluctance to embrace the pipeline project, because he steadfastly opposed any scheme that led to direct government involvement in the private sector. Furthermore, news of the pipeline project would most likely impede preparations for the Anglo-American oil talks while the British tried to measure this new threat to their Middle Eastern interests. Most conservatives criticized the plan as another White House attempt to socialize a major industry. Domestic and international producers, except those with a stake in the Persian Gulf, condemned the project, which they believed would destroy their position by flooding the country with cheap Arabian oil. So long as foreign oil policy provoked such controversy, Hull could not afford to intervene between Stanvac and Sinclair.[12]

Nor was the situation in Iran as desperate as Leavell thought. Americans often mistook the rapid rise and fall of cabinets there as a sign of terminal weakness. In reality the nationalism aroused by the occupation acted as a counterweight against factionalism. Often the shift in cabinets reflected the Iranian desire to deny foreign powers any grounds for further interference. If a cabinet seemed to gravitate too closely to the orbit of one foreign power, another cabinet, more accommodating to a rival power, might take its place. And no faction ever gained enough size or strength to destroy the power of the shah so long as he retained the backing of the army.[13] Mohammed Saed, who replaced Soheili, had shown himself as foreign minister to be friendly to both Britain and the Soviet Union. And like Soheili, he emerged as an enthusiastic proponent of an American concession.[14]

As one of his first acts in office, Saed informed Arthur Millspaugh that his government wished to hire foreign experts to help evaluate the oil bids. Millspaugh in turn alerted an American consulting firm, headed by Herbert Hoover, Jr. (the former president's son) and Arthur Curtice, who then applied for the position through the State Department. Their firm, United Engineering Corporation, had recently helped the Venezuelan government develop plans for its petroleum reserves and it had mediated a conflict with SONJ that had greatly increased Venezuela's royalties. The Iranian government gladly added Hoover and Curtice to the already extensive list of Americans providing technical assistance.[15]

The decision to hire two American oil advisers left little doubt that Stanvac would win the concession. "If an American company is selected by the Council [the body Leavell had worked to establish], I can almost assure Majles passage," Chargé Ford explained. "If a British company is selected, the concession will probably not be passed by the Majles and is likely to mean the fall of the present government."[16] Ford believed Sinclair had no prospect whatsoever unless Harry Sinclair or some equally well-connected representative came to Iran. Spurred on by Ford, Stanvac representative Thomas Draper urged the State Department to inform his company that the time had come to send a top official to close an agreement. How could Ford be so confident? Hoover and Curtice had leaked the decision to the embassy. Most likely Saed or some other officials had expected, and even encouraged, Hoover and Curtice to do so. At worst such a move might inspire Shell or Sinclair to offer more advantageous terms. And since the Iranian government was pursuing political as well as economic ends, the disclosure might well win support from Washington without Iran in fact having made any binding commitment. For that reason the Iranian government was actually in no hurry to make its decision.

Such circumstances created a fertile environment for friction among the Allies. Marcel Wagner charged the British with spreading vicious propaganda that after the war the United States would return to its isolationist ways and that Iranian politicians who had favored American companies would find themselves without foreign support. Wallace Murray assured Ford that the British were unlikely to have spread such divisive rumors. Still, Ford was suspicious. He had learned from the Shell representative, J. W. Boyle, that AIOC actively opposed his company's bid. Rather than believe Boyle, Ford assumed that the admission was only a ruse to lure the Americans "into a false sense of security," and that Shell wanted to block "any concession being granted in Iran which is probably the British objective."[17]

American oil representatives were little more trustful of their own countrymen. They charged that Rex Vivian, the American member of the Iranian oil committee, had given Boyle an advance copy of the contract written by Hoover and Curtice, the terms of which had already been leaked to the American Embassy. Just why Vivian should do such an unpatriotic thing they were not quite sure, but they assumed that venality had played a role. Hoover and Curtice did not escape the finger-pointing either. The oil representatives complained to an OSS agent that the two had written an unusually stiff contract that unfairly favored the Iranian government, particularly given the advantages AIOC enjoyed under the terms of its concession. And what then was Hoover and Curtice's motive? By serving the Iranian government in good faith they could "[angle] for the much bigger job of rewriting the Anglo-Iranian Company's contract. . . ."[18]

So preoccupied had all these parties become with their own rivalries that they ignored the signs that the negotiations might move in an unexpected direction. It was difficult enough for Iran to orchestrate events that affected the interests of reasonably friendly rivals. But what would happen if yet another party, one whose motives were impossible to determine, should suddenly enter the bidding? What if Iran did become a "test case" of the Allies' intentions? Could the three powers pass the test?

THE SOVIET OIL MISSION

The crisis began quietly enough. For almost a year the oil talks had been held privately between the oil companies and Iranian officials. Even leaks to the press in the spring of 1944 had caused little public comment. In August, antiwestern politicians began to attack the talks. The bazaars buzzed with rumors. Dr. Reza Radmanesh, a leading Majles spokesman for the communist Tudeh Party, charged that in hiring American petroleum advisers Saed had betrayed his country. In the midst of the commotion, Chargé Ford received a rare visit from Soviet Ambassador Maximov. After the necessary exchanges of pleasantries the conversation came around to oil concessions. Maximov indicated that he had heard that the Americans might have an eye on the northern area. Ford assured him that the Americans had restricted their bids to Baluchistan. To that Maximov replied "with respect to oil concessions in the southern area he was 'neutral' but when it came to Khorassan or other northern sections he was not neutral." Ford concluded that the Soviet Union had once again marked northern Iran off-limits to any other foreign power.[19]

On 6 September the real purpose of Maximov's unexpected visit became disconcertingly clear. The American Embassy learned that a high-priority Soviet oil mission would soon arrive in Tehran, headed by no less a figure than Vice Commissar of Foreign Affairs Sergei Kavtaradze. The Russians evidently meant to move with dispatch, for even before Kavtaradze presented his credentials in Tehran, the mission had sent a team of technicians exploring for oil in the north around Semnan.[20]

The responsibility for analyzing the Soviet gambit fell to the new U.S. Ambassador, Leland Morris, who like Louis Dreyfus was a career foreign service officer. Morris came to Iran in the spring of 1944 after Dreyfus had been reposted to Iceland. While Morris did have previous experience in the Middle East, he knew nothing about Iran or the current situation. His reports to the State Department show almost no grasp of either domestic or foreign politics. In commenting on the news that Russian technicians were exploring for oil, Morris confessed that he could explain neither the timing nor the objective of Kavtaradze's mission. That it might have something to do with the Anglo-American quest for a Baluchistan concession does not seem to have occurred to him, and he never made the connection.[21]

Though we can never be completely certain about Soviet motives, the scale and timing of Kavtaradze's demands left little doubt that the Russians sought at least to neutralize any advantage the Americans or British might have with a new concession by gaining one of their own. Possibly, too, the Soviets saw a concession as a way to secure a permanent position in northern Iran. They may even have had some need for the oil. Hoseyn Ala, the court minister and the shah's most trusted adviser, revealed on 2 October that the Russians had asked for exclusive rights over five years to explore for oil in a 200,000-square-kilometer area stretching across northern Iran from Azerbaijan to Khorasan. Five days later, Morris learned that while the Russians had offered no financial terms, they had talked about exploiting oil within five years.[22]

Such an extensive Russian concession would negate any advantage the Iranian government sought from granting one to the Americans. Everyone understood that the Soviet Union would run its oil operations with as many political agents as technicians. To make matters worse, Kavtaradze made it difficult for the Iranians to procrastinate because he insisted that they make a decision before he left and then announced he would be leaving soon. The Iranian government desperately sought some means to salvage a few political crumbs out of the mess Kavtaradze had made. Prime Minister Saed proposed to link the concession to one of his major goals—the withdrawal of Soviet occupation forces. He admitted to Morris that he was not optimistic that he could achieve such a *quid pro quo,* but thought "it was a good opportunity to show interest in this subject of prime concern." When the shah asked Saed to announce that Iran would weigh Soviet, American, and British bids at one time, he provoked Kavtaradze's wrath. Was not the vice commissar the representative of the Soviet government? And were not the American and British representatives merely the lowly agents of private corporations? For that reason, the Russian proposal should receive preferential treatment.[23]

Court Minister Ala, who favored the American bid, urged the shah to refrain from making any commitment until the cabinet could devise a new strategy. Ala personally favored three-power oil talks modeled on the current Anglo-American negotiations. While the powers talked, the pressure on Iran to act hastily might abate. That tactic was not without perils of a different sort. The failure to award a concession might jeopardize Iran's status in the Anglo-American negotiations. Hoover and Curtice had urged the Iranians to grant the southern concession "in order to increase all her production possibilities and thus secure the highest possible quotas from the conferees." In reality, quotas were not one of the goals of the oil talks, but Hoover and Curtice probably did not know that.[24]

Some nationalist factions suggested that Iran reject all the bids and establish its own development company to exploit oil in conjunction with a multinational consortium. Multinational participation in Iranian oil would have provided Iran with additional revenues and the Allies with additional oil, while giving no single power a discrete sphere of influence. Rival foreign interests would become intertwined in the same enterprise. Iranian participation in resource exploitation would have quieted nationalist fears and perhaps eased the factionalism that had accompanied the negotiations up to this point. A more stable and prosperous Iran might eventually have emerged, just as Jernegan and others had hoped. So why did the British and the Americans both reject this proposal without serious consideration?

For one thing, any form of national involvement, even the promotion of locals to high-level managerial or technical positions, was a practice the oil companies resisted. In part that was a consequence of the western notion that people like the Iranians had neither the intelligence nor the character to master the complexities of western technology and business affairs. Equally important, AIOC and the other giants did not want the locals to become sufficiently familiar with the oil business so that nationalization became practical. They were generally determined to maintain their control over the exploitation and marketing of oil wherever it was found. As a result, Morris did his loyal best to persuade the Iranians of the folly of the nationalists' proposal. He assured the State Department that it was "a weak bluff on paper," and told the Iranian finance minister "that nothing could be gained by this maneuver." He did not mention, however, that such a step might prove detrimental to the oil companies' short- and long-term interests.[25]

The idea of sharing a concession with the Soviets had about as much appeal as nationalization. At no time did Anglo-American diplomats ever discuss inviting Soviet participation in the oil talks, since they wanted a concession to tie Iran and its economy to the west. In addition, they maintained the charade that oil was a matter for private corporations, not public agencies, even though the British government controlled AIOC and the PRC was looking for a position in the Middle East. Three-power oil talks would give the British and American governments, not the oil companies, a deciding voice in the disposition of Iranian oil. Equally important, such a triumph for Iran would have encouraged nationalists around the world to reevaluate their dependence on the industrial powers.

Morris did understand that Iran had no easy way out of its present predicament unless the British and American governments in some way opposed the Soviets' demands. Sir Reader Bullard had persuaded him that this was yet another tactic to subvert Iranian sovereignty. Bullard dismissed Kavtaradze's approach as "unacceptable under international practice." If Kavtaradze succeeded in Iran, the Soviets might see a precedent for similar attempts to gain control over the resources of Bulgaria, Yugoslavia, and even Greece.[26]

Future spheres of influence were very much on the British diplomatic agenda in early October. Churchill had just flown to Moscow for bilateral talks with Stalin. Now that Soviet troops had entered the Balkans, the British prime minister had worked out with Stalin the cynical percentages arrangement by which they apportioned their postwar roles in Roumania, Hungary, Bulgaria, Yugoslavia, and Greece. There is no record, however, that either Stalin or Churchill made any reference to Iran. Nevertheless, both leaders now felt sufficiently confident about the war's successful conclusion to assert claims to various areas of geopolitical significance. Iran must have figured centrally in the calculations of both. President Roosevelt had remained publicly opposed to a postwar peace based on spheres of influence.

Privately, the president agreed with Churchill that it was necessary to come to some understanding about the Balkans. Nor did he express any great reservations, once Ambassador Harriman informed him of the substance of the talks between Churchill and Stalin. But faced with his toughest reelection campaign so far, Roosevelt urged his Allies to defer crucial decisions until after November.[27]

The president's unwillingness to have a flap with the Russians killed any immediate possibility of addressing the growing inter-Allied tension over Iran. Morris had proposed to the State Department that "either singly or conjointly with the British government" it inform Moscow that the United States was apprehensive about the current situation. But if other policy considerations precluded such a step, Morris recommended that the United States support a decision to cancel further negotiations for as long as six months or a year.[28]

That is what Saed did. On 8 October the prime minister stunned the foreign community when he announced that Iran would end oil negotiations until after the war. In private, Court Minister Ala explained to Morris that Kavtaradze had not only insisted on an oil concession, but also on exclusive mineral rights and the exclusion of all other foreigners from the area. As usual, he offered no financial terms. So outrageous were Kavtaradze's demands that the shah had ordered Saed to act.[29]

Just how big a gamble had the Iranians taken? On the one hand, they had no reason to believe Morris could persuade Washington to protect Iran from Soviet reprisals if they awarded Stanvac a concession without giving in to Soviet demands at the same time. In the past the Americans had seldom done more than invoke the Atlantic Charter or the Tehran Declaration. This time, Iran might need more substantial support. By contrast, the Soviet threat was tangible. The occupation troops constituted the most formidable danger Iran had faced in its modern history. On the other hand, the failure to award a concession might cost Iran substantial future oil revenues. That was a high price to pay for a return to the status quo ante oil talks.[30]

American oilmen refused to acknowledge that the Soviet pressure was a sufficient cause to deny them a concession. They preferred to blame their British rivals for this unsatisfactory turn of events. Since Saed's decision left AIOC's monopoly intact, AIOC or some other imperial agent must have sabotaged the negotiations, particularly when it had become certain that Shell would lose out to Stanvac. That is what Col. Leavell concluded: "The final outcome as concerns oil in Iran has been a complete victory for the British," because "they have unlimited amounts of oil developed . . . and any additional concession they might have received would have been of no practical value for years to come." Having observed that Shell's representative had been gloomy about his company's prospects, Herbert Hoover, Jr. did admit to Leavell "the possibility that the British might have put the Iranians up to calling off the entire negotiations, although he doubted that this had happened." In propounding this interpretation, the American oilmen seemed either unaware or unwilling to admit that the Iranians had followed a course recommended by Ambassador Morris. Indeed, the Iranian cabinet probably would not have acted so boldly without knowing in advance that the American Embassy agreed at least in principle with what they planned to do.[31]

In reality, many British officials saw benefits in a concession, whether Shell or Stanvac won it. AIOC's monopoly had become a target for Iranian nationalists and for the communist Tudeh Party. They had concluded that the existence of another concessionaire might deflect future hostility from them and reduce the likelihood that Iran would try to negotiate more favorable terms. One Foreign Office analyst described a concession for Shell as "providing us with a further much-needed source of sterling oil." As a consequence Bullard had received instructions to support the Shell representative. Other British officials thought an American concession might be even more desirable. Like the advisers, oil reserves in Iran might serve as a "counterweight to possible Russian ambitions in the area," and as "giving the United States a highly strategic entanglement." On that basis some British officials had reconciled themselves to Stanvac's likely victory. "If having gone in on the basis of fair play, the Persians grant a concession to the Americans, we shall have to take it. . . . We do not believe the Americans will be aggrieved if we win, and I think I can say that Shell will treat the matter the same way," one member of the Ministry of Fuel and Power remarked.[32]

That official had a stiffer upper lip than did Col. Leavell and the American oil representatives, for whom "fair play" was not part of their reckoning. But most important, the Soviet bid was so aggressive in its scope and timing that it constituted a far graver threat to Britain's long-term interests than did the prospect of the United States exploiting Iranian oil. For that reason, the British accepted Saed's decision.

THE SOVIET THREAT

The decision to cancel the oil negotiations did not relieve the Soviet pressure on Saed. At the peak of the crisis in October 1944, the Allied rivals conducted their diplomacy as if a cold war was already underway. The British and the Americans generally refused to accept that the Soviets could have any legitimate reason to demand an oil concession. They remained so wedded to the idea that the desire for hegemony in Iran and the Middle East had inspired the Kavtaradze mission that they seldom admitted that their own efforts to secure a new concession might explain Kavtaradze's presence. Quite possibly the Soviet Union did want a concession for its oil. The revenues earned might eventually have contributed to the enormous rebuilding task it faced after the war. And there were good reasons for the Soviets, like the Americans, to solidify their influence in Iran through the operation of an oil concession. The stability of neighboring states would have an obvious impact on the Soviet Union's postwar security. Yet the heavy-handed way in which the Soviets proceeded in Iran and in other border states did not give the British and the Americans much reason to trust their ally's good intentions. The Soviets exploited the occupation to seize advantages that Iran had little reason to concede, but even less capacity to refuse.

As early as September 1944, one month before Saed aborted the negotiations, Kavtaradze had indicated that the Soviet bid involved more than oil. Sir Reader Bullard learned that the vice commissar had stated "that Stalin was not satisfied with the present state of Soviet-Persian relations and said that on the reply to the Soviet application might depend the whole future economic relations between the two countries." When he heard that the negotiations had been halted, Kavtaradze warned that such a hostile act might have "unfortunate consequences." Ambassador Averell Harriman alerted the State Department to articles in *Pravda* and other publications that revealed the depth of "Soviet dissatisfaction with the Iranian government's decision."[33]

Kavtaradze's threat soon became substantive as the Russian Embassy staff openly insisted "that Saed must resign and the embassy will see to it that he does." On 16 October Soviet forces precipitated a food crisis in Tehran by halting grain shipments from the north. Then they disrupted internal transportation by allocating all railroad seats to Soviet personnel. In Tabriz, the capital of Azerbaijan, angry crowds protested Saed's decision. When Iranian police mobilized to control the crowds, Soviet troops disarmed them. And before Iranian army troops could muster, Soviet army units had isolated them in their barracks.[34]

The Soviets operated with a dagger as well as a club. Mindful of the exquisite protocol, the Soviet Embassy staff snubbed the shah's official party at a Soviet-Iranian exhibition soccer match. When Saed asked to have one particularly obnoxious official removed, the Soviet Embassy promoted him instead. Shocked to the point of outrage, Ambassador Morris castigated the Soviets' combination of insults and threats as "measures which smack of Hitlerean methods." In comparing the Soviets to the Nazis, Morris had adopted what would become a common cold war assumption that all dictators, whether fascist or communist, Russian or German, had the same appetite for world conquest. In that way, events in Iran quickly fell under the shadow of the Munich analogy. What might have been a limited, albeit threatening, Soviet response to a specific provocation was perceived by many officials in Washington and some in London as the first step in a Soviet global offensive.[35]

In October 1944 a report on Soviet activities in Iran crossed the desk of Charles Bohlen, a Soviet expert in the Division of East European Affairs. Bohlen warned his colleagues to consider the language with which the Soviets had attacked Saed's government. He specifically cited an article in *Trud* that accused the Iranians of "tolerating" acts of sabotage by "pro-fascist elements" against the supply route. "In fact," Bohlen argued, "this article has all the customary elements of a build-up in order to justify extreme Soviet pressure, if not action against the present Iranian government." He therefore concluded that the Soviets hoped "to force the resignation of Saed and the formation of a new government in Iran which would be prepared to continue negotiations for an oil concession."[36] To realize American objectives in the face of this Soviet offensive, the State Department needed to frame an appropriate policy.

The Iranians, meantime, struggled to ease Soviet pressures. The shah held a formal state dinner for the Soviet Embassy and its oil mission and pointedly left Saed off the guest list. Over toasts and caviar he assured his Russian guests that his government's action had implied no hostility toward the Soviet Union. At the same time he cultivated Morris' good offices by assuring the ambassador that he had no intention of buckling under "Russian efforts in the nature of economic or other sanctions." But then he reminded Morris that Iran could not follow such a course for long without active backing from Britain and the United States. If left to face Russian pressure alone, he might have to replace Saed under a pretext that appeared unrelated to the oil question.[37]

Sensing that more than Soviet threats might be needed to generate meaningful support from Washington or London, Saed tried to squeeze a bit more mileage out of the oil concession. After all, he had little else to bargain with. He assured Morris that his government would consider the American application as soon as it took up the concession matter again. Hoover and Curtice also informed the Stanvac representative that his company would get the bid when it was awarded. To J. W. Boyle, the Shell agent, Saed gave quite another impression. "Mr. Saed stated that he had always intended that the concession should be granted to British interests." That ploy was a bit too transparent, for as W. H. Young of the Foreign Office surmised, "it is at least possible that the Persian Prime Minister also assured the Americans that the concession would go to one of them."[38]

Even if Saed had taken them in, American and British diplomats were by now more concerned with the political contest the oil negotiations had triggered and with the danger that Soviet actions might disrupt the war effort. That left two plausible responses. On the one hand, both governments might encourage the Iranians to resist caving in to Russian demands, but only in the unlikely event that the Iranians had the gumption to sustain their current resolve and that the Russians did not hold their Allies responsible for Iran's decision. On the other hand, the two governments could work around the Iranians and protest directly to Moscow. Such a course risked straining the alliance or even jeopardizing the prospects for postwar cooperation.

British diplomats also had to consider how they could legitimately oppose the Russian bid for a concession as long as AIOC held its monopoly. And what if they continued the effort to expand British oil interests through Shell? Might that course of action not provoke a Russian reaction that would effectively eliminate Iran as a buffer state? Sir Reader Bullard argued that in pursuing all those goals current British policy sought the impossible. Something had to give. For example, "if His Majesty's Government consider it necessary to let the Russians have a free hand in this matter for the sake of advantages which it is hoped to gain elsewhere, let us at least do it with the realization that the life of Persia as an independent buffer for our protection will not be long."[39]

Bullard so feared the consequences of Soviet hegemony in northern Iran that he assumed the Russians would gain far more advantages from a concession in the north than Great Britain could possibly realize from whatever additional oil it acquired in the south. He had therefore encouraged the Iranians to cancel the negotiations—not to protect AIOC, as the Americans suspected, but to prevent the Russians from strengthening their position. "Since we want a concession badly, that would be something of a victory for the Russians," Bullard conceded, "but it would be better than our getting no oil and the Russians having a free hand in the north." Whether one believed that the Russians had actually won a victory, as he suggested, or had sustained a defeat, as Kavtaradze's outrage implied, depended on the motives for the Russian bid. If Kavtaradze had been sent to frustrate the British and American quest for Iranian oil, he had succeeded. If, however, he actually did want a concession, for whatever reasons, he had been thwarted.[40]

Some British officials still thought the oil was more valuable than any political objectives. F. A. Starling from the Ministry of Fuel and Power, for example, admitted "we are naturally concerned that any designs Russia might have in Persia should not adversely affect our established position there, or the possibility of getting the additional concession the Shell are negotiating." For that reason, he thought that the best outcome would be a concession for the Russians in the north and one for Shell in Baluchistan. But Starling was less concerned about new oil than about protecting AIOC's current position. Sir William Fraser, the dour Scotsman who headed AIOC after 1941, never ceased reminding the British government that "the concession itself is generally so favourable that it is worth . . . any sacrifice to prevent it being brought up for revision. . . ." Fraser calculated that Iranian-produced oil cost "about one half per ton of that produced in Iraq." Consequently, he and many other officials opposed any policy that might "bring the concession itself into question."[41]

Thus a near obsession with protecting AIOC often shackled Britain's freedom of maneuver. The Iranians could not help sensing that the British were often less than stalwart in their reaction to the concession crisis. When Iranian nationalists attacked the inequities involved in the British concession, pro-British factions could not make a strong case for the benefits Iran realized from this exploitative arrangement. Nationalist resentment became a graver peril to AIOC than Soviet aspirations in northern Iran. In that sense, efforts to preserve the concession actually brought it into question.

With the negotiations canceled, many officials in the Foreign Office began to doubt the wisdom of Bullard's hard-line strategy. W. H. Young did not believe Iran could hold out long against Russian pressure unless the British and the Americans established a position in the north. G. A. Warner assumed that the Persians did not have sufficient strength of character to resist for long. "In that case," he asked, "or in any case, is it not morally certain that the Persians will give way to the Russians the fact that Sir R. Bullard is inciting them to resist? Are we not, therefore, likely to get the worst of both or even more worlds if we pursue this course?"[42] In short, Britain might get no new oil, the Russians would be angered by British opposition, yet the Soviet Union would still have a stranglehold over northern Iran.

Such words of caution persuaded the Foreign Office to curtail Bullard's efforts to encourage Iranian resistance to Soviet demands:

> His Majesty's Government for their part do not wish to dispute the Persian government's decision to grant no further concession during the war, always on the assumption that this decision will be fairly and equally maintained. His Majesty's Government are not, however, prepared to advise the Persian government as to lengths which they should go to maintain their decision.[43]

Should circumstances arise that would require a more forceful response—a violation of the Tripartite Treaty, for example—the Foreign Office planned to deal directly with Moscow. But it warned Bullard not to reveal to the Iranian government that it had British diplomatic support. No one in London wanted to encourage the Persians to embark on a confrontation course that might unnecessarily damage Anglo-Soviet relations.

Above all, British diplomats understood that only if they coordinated their efforts with the United States could they sustain an effective policy. Great Britain, they sensed, was now the junior partner, even in areas like the Middle East where its position had once been dominant. Iranian leaders could not help but recognize that closer ties to the United States would better serve Iran's future interests than would continued links with Great Britain. Such calculations had given Stanvac an enormous advantage over Shell. They also reminded Iranian nationalists that the diplomatic benefits of the AIOC concession could no longer compensate for its political liabilities.

The oil crisis had come to embody in microcosm the very issues that framed Soviet-American confrontation in the cold war: disagreement over the spirit and letter of wartime agreements, over legitimate spheres of influence, over the relationship of the Soviet Union to its border states, over postwar international security arrangements, and over the future political orientation of third world or former colonial nations. Had the Allies desired to work out an understanding they might have established a framework in which to arbitrate even more divisive issues, like the postwar Polish settlement. But the existence of such a conflict in the middle of the war indicates that the Allies were not looking to compromise their differences. Indeed, they were seeking to establish Iran as a component of unilateral, in the British case bilateral, security spheres. As a consequence, this dispute festered for another year before erupting into a major postwar confrontation.

That is not to argue that the Americans at this time sought a confrontation or saw this conflict as inevitable. American officials drifted back and forth between the concern for the commitments made under the Tehran Declaration, the desire to acquire new oil reserves, the fear of Soviet expansion, and the effort to promote inter-Allied harmony. More often than not, these strands of American policy proved incompatible, if not downright contradictory. In reality the American commitment to Iran at this point was more rhetorical than real. Except in the Near East Division, no political constituency comparable to the China lobby or to Eastern European ethnic voters advocated a significant increase in American involvement there. It would take a much broader deterioration in Soviet-American relations to raise the American stake in Iran.

The lack of direction in American policy was evident in the State Department's tentative response to the crisis. One official claimed the available information was an inadequate basis for any policy decision. Ambassador Morris put no pressure on the department to respond more forcefully. As much as he found current events troubling, Morris did not want to provoke the Soviet Union. Only if the United States was prepared to back Iran fully would it be reasonable to encourage further Iranian resistance on the oil question. Morris did not advocate such a course because "that is something which might precipitate a very great divergence, if not a split, at the present time in Soviet-American relations."[44] Thus, when the Iranians came asking for support, he offered a sympathetic ear, but no commitments.

The line Morris took suited the political mood in Washington. President Roosevelt had no desire to have some flap with the Russians jeopardize his reelection bid. He had already trimmed American sails on the Polish question for fear that mounting antagonism to the Soviet Union might shake ethnic loyalty to the Democratic Party. Morris had advised Court Minister Ala not to expect any American approach to the Russians because of "the war and the imminence of elections," though Ala probably had difficulty comprehending the relevance of American electoral politics to his country's crisis. As the voters prepared to trek to the polls, Lord Halifax informed his government that the White House wanted to avoid "any jolts over Russia during the next few days."[45]

Yet even if both the Foreign Office and the State Department refrained from bearding the Russians over Iran, the crisis had helped to solidify the growing anti-Soviet consensus among British and American diplomats. The Foreign Office took heart that Soviet aggressiveness had made many Americans more receptive to concerted action. W. H. Young commented, "As a result of this we may hear rather less in the future about the naughtiness of 'ganging' against the Russians, to whom it is of course self-evident that British and American policy in Persia coincide and conflict with their own." The tension provoked by the oil crisis had worked the most significant change in Wallace Murray, chief architect of American policy for Iran. Only a few months earlier, when in London with the Stettinius mission, Murray had struck British officials as suspicious and unsympathetic. But as his anti-Soviet phobias increased, his anglophobia ebbed. "Wallace Murray is, as you know, preoccupied with the fear of Russian penetration of the Balkans and Middle East," Lord Halifax reminded his colleagues. Without wishing to overheat Murray's Soviet fears, Halifax at least hoped such concern would increase Murray's "desire . . . to cooperate with us on every issue." With classic wry understatement, W. H. Young remarked upon reading the note from Halifax, "It is a pity that it should require the stimulus of Russophobia to drive Wallace Murray to the conclusion that there is something to be said for us."[46]

British and American diplomats began discussing ways to relieve tensions without offending the Soviets or appearing to be responsible for Saed's policy. Murray preferred to put the issues into the context of the Tehran Declaration. Russian efforts to extract a concession under pressure clearly violated the spirit of the declaration. "If this statement were to be brushed aside as a scrap of paper, it would be a serious matter and a bad omen for future agreements with the Russians," he told Halifax. By invoking the agreement in this case, the British and Americans could preserve its integrity, Murray argued.[47]

Such an idea accorded neatly with the views of Foreign Secretary Anthony Eden. Like Murray, Eden thought that reference to the declaration would remind the Russians that while their allies conceded the Soviets' right to seek a concession, they also supported the Persians' right to refuse it. As a result, the British and American governments simultaneously sent notes to Moscow so mildly worded that they indicated little more than Anglo-American anxiety over the recent direction of Soviet policy. Both mentioned the hostility directed by the Soviet press against Saed, the British and American willingness to abide by Saed's decision, and the assurances the Allies had given in the Tehran Declaration.[48]

The Russians had coincidentally begun to relax their pressures on Saed's government. Tudeh Party leaders called off a demonstration scheduled for 2 November. When rumors of a coup d'état circulated, the Russian military commander in Tehran volunteered to help the Americans and British suppress any resulting violence. In the occupation zone, the Russians lifted their restrictions on the movement of Iranian army units and resumed grain shipments to Tehran. Saed was so encouraged by the improved atmosphere that he told Bullard he no longer intended to resign immediately.[49]

Both Murray and Sir Alexander Cadogan refused to admit to the Iranians that their governments had protested to Moscow. In fact Sir Reader Bullard had warned the British consulates that "it would be fatal if the Persians got to know this." The State Department and the Foreign Office had agreed, it seems, that the crisis had provided them with an effective lever with which to move Iran to set its house in order. If Iranian politicians knew they could count on their support no matter what they did, they would have less reason to attempt reforms. The British also worried that, secure in their knowledge of the notes to Moscow, the Iranians might provoke further confrontations with the Soviets rather than seeking an accommodation.[50]

News from Iran seemed to confirm a more conciliatory Soviet policy. Some officials in the State Department and Foreign Office assumed that their representations had led to the easing of tensions. Ambassador Morris, though he did not view the change as permanent, suggested "that American and British notes plus pro-Iranian publicity in London may have decided the Russians to back water." Morris' comment was an example of a common British and American belief that world opinion as expressed in the news media could alter Soviet behavior. Certainly, the Soviets were sensitive to criticism, but as their behavior in Poland demonstrated, they paid little attention to outside views, even those of Roosevelt and Churchill, which conflicted with their intentions.[51]

Wallace Murray concluded that the recent turn of events supported his idea that forceful diplomacy could contain the Soviet Union. He speculated to Lord Halifax that this episode "would be an object lesson to those who thought it was useless to try and exercise influence . . . and that there was nothing to be done but let position after position go by default." Halifax found Murray's conclusions most likely "premature or wide of the mark." He did not say so, however, because "it seemed undesirable to discourage his conclusions that to work closely with us is the only right policy for the United States."[52] Events soon showed that the Soviets had in no way abandoned their plan to wrest major political and economic concessions from Iran.

Neither Morris nor Murray believed that Iranian policies had affected the Soviets' behavior. More often than not American diplomats operated from the assumption that the actions of the big powers determined the outcome of events. The idea that a client state might act effectively on its own behalf did not often occur to them. Sir Reader Bullard at least recognized that "some credit must go to the Persian Prime Minister who refused to resign when many deputies and high officials wavered, and Radio Moscow accused him of wanting to use Persia as a base for fascist aggression against the Soviet Union. His tranquility made Russian blustering seem slightly ridiculous."[53] The United States by contrast would generally discount the political aspirations and skills of its third world allies, whom it treated as clients rather than as partners.

COLD WAR THEMES

During the brief lull in the oil crisis, American and British diplomats speculated about the significance of recent events in ways that suggested they were already preoccupied with cold war themes. Sir Reader Bullard, for example, having always viewed the Soviets as canny adversaries, found their clumsiness in this situation rather puzzling. "It is difficult to understand why the Soviet government embarked on their campaign for oil, if they did not intend to carry it out at all costs," he mused. "Its failure cannot help but damage their credit abroad, especially if all the details of their Hitler technique become known." Bullard was no less inclined than Morris or Murray to envoke the specter of "Red Fascism." And Bullard thought the fiasco might have occurred at the operative level rather than in policy planning. The self-important Ambassador Maximov might have misled Moscow about the prospects for a concession in order to dramatize his accomplishments. Still, he thought the Persians could learn from this Soviet diplomatic defeat that they could oppose the Russians without fatal consequences.[54]

The Foreign Office recognized that its note to Moscow could not have caused the shift in policy. Evidence of relaxing tensions had already appeared by 2 November, the day Ambassador Sir Archibald Clark-Kerr had delivered the British note in Moscow. All the same, the British continued to see the Iranian crisis as a propaganda battle. W. H. Young argued that the Soviets had tried to control the news from Iran, all of which passed through Allied censors. They had stopped all Iranian news releases, including Saed's statement on the negotiations. The British had parried that tactic by using their own channels to send the "truth" to the London press. Assuming that publicity had made the difference, Young, like Murray, thought that Iran and other similarly situated countries could resist the Soviet bullies successfully. He compared the Russian strategy to the *blitzkrieg*. Soviet officials tried to overwhelm their victims quickly. But if unexpected resistance arose, they might draw back in order to avoid being "shown up."[55]

The Americans in Iran believed that something more than oil had led to the attack on Saed. Ambassador Morris observed that in their overt hostility to the U.S. advisers the Russians had already indicated a profound suspicion of potential foreign influences in the northern zone. A. A. Curtice agreed that politics rather than oil had inspired the Soviet demand. He pointed out that the Russians had never objected to the British and American bids for a southern concession. Instead, they demanded extensive northern concessions to close the area off.[56]

That was precisely the conclusion of George Kennan, the chargé in Moscow who would soon emerge as a major architect of American cold war policies. Throughout the war he had found himself an isolated voice in the Moscow embassy much discomforted by Roosevelt's efforts at cooperation with the Soviet regime. Even more, he regretted the president's optimistic claims about the possibilities for postwar Soviet-American accommodations. That does not mean that Kennan's own thinking had achieved the clarity that it would find in later years. Frustration with what he saw as dangerous naiveté in Washington led him on occasion to overstate the military aspects of the Soviet threat to the west.[57]

In the fall of 1944 he concluded from recent commentaries in the Soviet press that "the basic motive of recent Russian actions in northern Iran is probably not the need for oil itself but the apprehension of potential foreign penetration in that area coupled with the concern for prestige that marks all Soviet policy these days." By establishing their own instruments of economic and political control, the Russians would eliminate opportunities for hostile powers in the region. Kennan ascribed the "old fashioned and unimaginative tactics employed," not to a Hitlerian style as others had charged, but to an "extensive preoccupation in Moscow today with the methods as well as the aims of Tsarist diplomacy." What then could the Allies expect from the Soviets in the near future? Kennan made the prescient prediction that the Russians might "drop the oil issue and the policy of intimidation for the time being and set about to undermine those individuals, particularly Saed, who are considered to have loaned themselves to this set of circumstances." Only when more favorable conditions existed could they be expected to revive the question of oil.[58]

The Soviet press and Soviet diplomats also introduced cold war themes into their explanation of the crisis. Many western observers have remarked that the Soviets are often faithful to the letter or the literal terms of their agreements, even when they violate their spirit. The Soviet press thus claimed that the Kavir Khurian concession of 1916 gave the Soviet Union a residual right to northern Iranian oil. We should remember that such an assertion was dubious at best. The Majles had never ratified the concession and then the Bolsheviks subsequently renounced all Russian concession rights in Persia. Only a tortured reading of the agreement could establish a renewed Soviet claim. Yet Kavtaradze at one point apparently told a group of Iranian deputies and editors that the Soviet Union "wanted oil in northern Persia . . . to protect Persia against Great Britain and the United States who after the war would follow imperialistic policies."[59] If the Soviet Union were to develop such resources, Iran would realize more substantial benefits.

British policy toward the AIOC concession made Kavtaradze's remarks somewhat credible. On many occasions the British had placed AIOC's interest ahead of those of Iran. But his statement also justified Saed's fear that the Russians wanted a concession for political reasons and that the "Soviets would use it as a cover for infiltration of the area by innumerable technicians." The speech also served as a textbook case of what Kennan had described as the "concern for prestige" that characterized recent Soviet foreign policy. The vice commissar reminded his audience (as if they needed any reminding) of the formidable power his nation wielded. To emphasize his point, he claimed that Churchill and Roosevelt always came running to Stalin whenever they needed anything.[60]

Though excusable as a bit of excessive nationalism, such a remark did not convey much concern for the preservation of inter-Allied harmony. And it cast a cynical light upon Stalin's refusal to travel far beyond his borders to meet his two major allies. What they had done as a sign of cooperation Kavtaradze used to demean them in the eyes of Middle Eastern leaders.

The Soviet press soon confirmed Kennan's prediction that Moscow would seek Saed's removal. On 4 November 1944 an article in *Izvestia* charged that in refusing the Soviet Union a concession, the Iranian ruling circle had rejected an offer of friendship. The Iran-Soviet treaty of 1921 bound the Iranians from turning former Russian concessions over to foreign nationals or their governments. The *Izvestia* article insisted that Iran had consistently violated that agreement that was vital to Soviet national security. The influence of Nazi agents operating freely in Iran was further evidence of the "vacillating" policies of the Saed government. Such an attitude towards "Hitlerite agents" evaded Iran's obligation under the 1942 Tripartite Treaty.[61]

The *Izvestia* article anticipated certain strategies of the Soviet Union's cold war in Iran. Each Russian initiative would have some purported legal basis in prior treaty agreements. It did not seem to matter that the invocations of one treaty might override obligations assumed under another. Nor did it trouble Soviet propagandists that their charges did not accurately fit the facts. The 1921 treaty referred specifically to the presence of "hostile" foreign elements in Iran. As of 1944, the British and Americans could hardly be said to conform to the language of the treaty. Saed had never been lax in pursuing suspected Nazi agents or in any way sympathetic to fascists. Both Bullard and Morris argued persuasively that no situation existed in Iran that violated the terms of the Tripartite Treaty.[62]

Izvestia also indicted Saed for a decision that it said was "caused by a malevolent attitude toward the Soviet Union." Instead of adopting an impartial posture, he had yielded to pressures from reactionary elements. As was generally true of such Soviet onslaughts, the argument had a grain of truth to it. Or, as the *Izvestia* article put it, "Why then [considering Britain's vast concession], should the Soviet Union's proposal concerning oil concessions in northern Iran meet with refusal, despite the fact that its conditions are profitable for Iran?"[63] The writer did not seem much bothered that, since Kavtaradze had actually offered no terms, Iran had no way to evaluate the economic potential of such an agreement. After once again chastising Saed for making deals with the British and Americans while turning a deaf ear to the Russians, *Izvestia* asserted that popular sentiment had so soured on the prime minister that he now had to resign.

Before reaching that conclusion, *Izvestia* made a reference in an obscure but pointed way to the presence of American troops in Iran without any treaty provisions. Yet Soviet officials knew full well that these troops were there exclusively to deliver lend-lease supplies, that the British were responsible for their presence, that British treaty agreements therefore provided a temporary framework for their presence, and that the Americans had made a reasonable, though futile, effort to come to terms directly with Iran. Incidentally, the Kremlin had recently awarded General Connolly and some of his staff medals for their heroic efforts in moving supplies. American diplomats worried that the remark anticipated some future Soviet demand on Iran for which either the presence of foreign troops or the lack of a proper treaty for them would in some way serve as justification.[64]

The sense that Allied diplomacy had effectively resolved the Iranian oil crisis had indeed proved premature. On 9 November 1944 Saed resigned, on the assumption that the Russians would then drop their demand for an immediate concession agreement and that Kavtaradze would leave. The Soviets had made such an offer on the condition that a "more trustworthy person" head the government. But Saed had misjudged Russian intentions. His departure did not immediately lead to improved Iran-Soviet relations. The Tudeh Party continued to stir popular discontent, the Russian press attacked Iran's government, and worse, from the Iranian perspective, Kavtaradze stayed on. A. A. Curtice voiced the widely held view that "the USSR will never give up her demands for oil in the north of Iran and will sooner or later force Iran to grant a concession."[65]

Oil had brought into the open conflicting Allied ambitions in Iran. Sir Claremont Skrine, a British diplomat who served during the war as a consul in Iran, later described oil concessions as the most crucial of many irritants leading to the cold war: "It was the vigorous American intervention, the financial, military, and gendarmerie missions, the apparent drive by the U.S. to capture the Persian market, and above all, the efforts of Standard-Vacuum and Shell to secure oil prospecting rights that changed the Russians in Persia from hot-war allies into cold war rivals."[66]

Skrine was just one of many British diplomats who remarked on the unusual level of American wartime involvement in Iranian affairs. Certainly the Soviets could not have remained indifferent to the emerging American presence in a sensitive border area of longstanding strategic importance. Yet neither the Soviets nor the Americans made any significant attempt to realize the cooperative spirit of the Tehran Declaration. Each side eyed the other warily as it tried to turn temporary wartime circumstances into long-term advantages. The oil concession rivalry became critical because it threatened to upset the fragile equilibrium among the great powers. AIOC's central role in Iranian political and economic life had made abundantly clear the many advantages a foreign power could realize from operating a concession there.

Above all, the oil crisis suggests that less direct American involvement in Iran might have had a restraining effect on both the British and Russians by depriving them of the means and the motivations for more active interventions. The American bid certainly had caused Shell to seek a concession. Possibly, too, it had inspired the Russians to send the Kavtaradze mission, though just as likely, it was only an excuse for the Soviets to demand advantages they would have sought in any case. There is no reason to assume that the Soviet Union would have left Iran alone if the United States had remained totally uninvolved. Stalin had indicated as early as 1939 that he had ambitions in the direction of the Persian Gulf. All the same, as Skrine and Arthur Millspaugh both argued, the decision to seek a concession during the war provoked an early Soviet-American confrontation.

Time would show that the United States could fulfill its oil needs from countries that raised fewer diplomatic issues than Iran. But the desire to contain Soviet and British imperialism as much as the need for oil had made the State Department receptive to an American bid on an Iranian concession. And as Skrine pointed out, the same desire had brought another irritant to big power relations in Iran, namely, the advisory missions.

NOTES

1. Arthur Millspaugh, *Americans in Persia,* p. 233.
2. FR, 1944, 5, p. 448n. For a more contemporary example of pressure against Sinclair as an independent, see Blair, *The Control of Oil,* pp. 84–85. On Sinclair and the 1920s scandals, see Burl Noggle, *Teapot Dome* (New York, 1963). On the Mexican expropriations, see Russell Buhite, *Patrick J. Hurley in World Affairs;* see also Clayton Koppes, "The Good Neighbor Policy and the Nationalization of Mexican Oil: A Reinterpretation," *Journal of American History,* 69 (June 1982): 62–81.
3. FR, 1944, 5, pp. 447–48, Hull to Ford, 4/4/44.
4. Abrahamian, *Iran Between Two Revolutions,* pp. 169–203, esp. pp. 181–82; Ramazani, *Iran's Foreign Policy, 1941–1973,* p. 97. Opponents of the monarchy had already reduced his influence over court patronage and the bureaucracy. As a condition of his succession to the throne, he had agreed to abide by the constitution and return to the Majles the power to select prime ministers and cabinets from its own ranks.
5. Ibid., pp. 183–84.
6. Arthur Millspaugh, *Americans in Persia,* pp. 114–15. FR, 1944, 5, p. 447, Ford to Secretary of State, 2/21/44.
7. FR, 1944, 5, p. 450, Leavell to Secretary of State, 6/16/44. See also SD 891.6363/7–1044, Leavell to Secretary of State. MMRB, OSS, Iran File, 86835, "Oil Concessions," 7/17/44. This document contradicts Gabriel Kolko's argument that Millspaugh served as an agent for American corporate imperialism. See Kolko, *The Politics of War* (New York, 1968), p. 299. He was by 1944 more of a liability than an asset.
8. FR, 1944, 5, p. 449, Leavell to Secretary of State, 5/16/44.
9. Ibid., p. 449.
10. Ibid., p. 451, Secretary of State to Ford, 6/27/44; SD 891.6363/7–2544, 531 (section 3), Ford to Secretary of State.

11. Stoff, *Oil, War, and American Security,* pp. 132–37.

12. Ibid., pp. 138–42.

13. For a discussion of internal Iranian politics, see Abrahamian, *Iran Between Two Revolutions* pp. 177–203, and for the connection between domestic and foreign policy, see Ramazani, *Iran's Foreign Policy,* pp. 88–90.

14. Abrahamian, *Iran Between Two Revolutions,* pp. 203–4. Saed had emerged in March 1944 as a compromise candidate. Having spent most of the past decade abroad as a diplomat, he had remained sufficiently independent of the court establishment to satisfy the antiroyalist factions. On several occasions in the past he had shown the young shah that he was personally loyal and trustworthy. Firuz Kazemzadeh, a leading historian of Persian and Russian diplomacy at Yale University, knew Saed personally while his own father served in the Moscow Embassy. He provided me with some of the background on Saed's ties to the shah.

15. Emb. Encl. 148; also SD 891.6363/845, A. H. Chapman (of United Engineering) to Petroleum Adviser, 3/3/44. On Venezuela, see Sampson, *The Seven Sisters,* p. 130.

16. SD 891.6363/7–2544, sec. 1 and 2, Ford to Secretary of State, 7/10/44. Several months later, with the decision still pending, Hoover and Curtice once again supplied the embassy with secret information. One of their tasks involved the preparation of a plan that anticipated future trends in the oil industry, including the possible impact of an Anglo-American oil agreement. When they finished, Hoover and Curtice supplied the embassy with a copy. Familiarity with the Iranian government's strategy might prove invaluable to any company entering into negotiations. Once again, Ford warned the department to treat this disclosure with utmost secrecy since "neither the British nor the Iranian governments are aware the Embassy has received a copy." He apparently did not think it relevant to mention the Russians at all. See also SD 891.6363/9–2744, Ford to Secretary of State, 9/27/44.

17. SD 891.6363/6–2244, Wagner to Murray, 6/22/44. For Murray's reply see SD FW891.6363/6–2244. For Ford's analysis see SD 891.6363/7–2544, 531, sec. 3, Ford to Secretary of State.

18. MMRB, OSS Iran File, 95847, "Iranian Oil Contracts," 10/6/44.

19. Nasrolleh Fatemi, *Oil Diplomacy: Powder Keg in Iran* (New York, 1954), p. 231. SD 891.6363/8–344, 1053, Ford to Secretary of State, 8/3/44.

20. Emb. Encl. 148.

21. FR, 1944, 5, pp. 452–53, Morris to Secretary of State, 9/21/44.

22. Ibid., pp. 453–54, Morris to Secretary of State, 10/2/44 and 10/7/44.

23. Ibid., pp. 453–54, Morris to Secretary of State, 9/22/44.

24. Ibid., 454–55; see also MMRB, OSS Iran File, C50317, 11/9/44; and SD 891.6363/9–2744, 48, enclosure, Ford to Secretary of State.

25. See Stoff, *Oil, War, and American Security,* pp. 74 and 77.

26. FR, 1944, 5, pp. 454–55, Morris to Secretary of State, 10/7/44.

27. See Averell Harriman and Elie Abel, *Special Envoy,* pp. 353–59; Feis, *Churchill, Roosevelt, Stalin,* pp. 449–53. See also Kuniholm, *Origins of the Cold War in the Near East,* pp. 195–96 and 196n. It seems to me a bit farfetched to attribute Soviet aggressiveness to the Churchill-Stalin meeting in Moscow. Both powers clearly had become preoccupied with postwar spheres of influence before the meeting took place. The Soviet Union had already initiated its oil concession strategy before Churchill announced his determination to go to Moscow. Nothing that we know about what Churchill and Stalin discussed would lead us to think that from that meeting Stalin would have had reason to assume he could be more assertive in acquiring a northern Iranian sphere. Indeed, Churchill's preoccupations with Greece, Yugoslavia, and Turkey should have warned Stalin that Iran was a more sensitive concern than before. See also Dallek, *Franklin D. Roosevelt and American Foreign Policy,* pp. 478–81.

28. FR, 1944, 5, pp. 454–55.

29. Ibid., p. 455, Morris to Secretary of State, 10/9/44.

30. On Hoover's attitude toward Iran and the oil talks, see MMRB, OSS Iran File, C50317, and enclosure with SD 891.6363/9–2744, both cited above in note 29.

31. SD 891.6363/10–1144, Memorandum "Herbert Hoover Jr. on the Oil Negotiations in Iran," 10/11/44. SD 891.6363/10–1644, A–561, Leavell to Secretary of State, 10/16/44. For a good picture of Shell Oil, see Sampson, *The Seven Sisters,* pp. 13–16, 53–59, and 70–77.

32. FO 40241, E6191/6058/34, minute by W. H. Young, 10/11/44. FO 35128, E573/545/34, minute by N. Butler, 10/14/44; also FO E6191/6058/34, F. A. Starling to Young, 10/11/44.

33. FO 40173, E6016/94/34, Bullard to FO, 10/1/44. FR, 1944, 5, p. 456, Morris to Secretary of State, 10/13/44. Ibid., p. 457, Harriman to Secretary of State, 10/17/44.

34. FR, 1944, 5, pp. 457–59, Morris to Secretary of State, 10/24/44; SD 891.00/11–444, 116, Consul in Tabriz to Morris.

35. FR, 1944, 5, p. 464, Morris to Secretary of State, 11/1/44. On the power of the Munich analogy, see Ernest May, *"Lessons" of the Past* (New York, 1973), especially pp. 19–36. On the relationship of rhetoric to policy, see Les Adler and Thomas Paterson, "Red Fascism," *American Historical Review* 85 (April 1970): 1046–64.

36. FR, 1944, 5, pp. 351–52, memorandum by Charles Bohlen, 10/24/44.

37. Ibid., p. 459, Morris to Secretary of State, 10/24/44, and p. 460, Morris to Secretary of State, 10/25/44.

38. Ibid., p. 459. See also FO 40173, E6743/94/34, conversation with J. W. Boyle, 10/25/44; FO 40241, E6383/6058/34, minute by W. H. Young, 10/31/44.

39. FO 40241, E6367/6048/34, 1049, Bullard to FO, 10/16/44. Most likely, Bullard was referring to Churchill's efforts at his Moscow meeting with Stalin to gain some leverage in the Balkans, Greece, and Turkey.

40. FO 40241, E6058/6058/34, 978, Bullard to FO, 10/2/44. Bullard understood that for compelling political reasons Iran would give the concession to Americans.

41. FO 40241, E6191/6058/34, Starling to R. M. A. Hankey, 3/2/44, and Starling to W. H. Young, 10/10/44. FO 35050, E982/1/34, memo of conversation between Sir A. Cadogan and Sir W. Fraser, 2/17/43. See also George Lenczowski, *Oil and State in the Middle East* (Ithaca, 1960), p. 76n. Lenczowski reports that between 1911 and 1951 Iran received a total of £113 million in royalties. By contrast, the British government received £250 million in taxes from AIOC and its subsidiaries. In addition the government received dividends from its stock and oil for the fleet. By 1950 the discrepancy was worse—Iran received £16 million while the British government's share was £50.5 million.

42. FO 40241, E6191/6058/34, Minute by G. A. Warner, 10/12/44.

43. FO 40241, E6262/6058/34, FO to Bullard, 672, 10/18/44.

44. SD 891.6363/10–1144, "Russian Petroleum Activities in Northern Iran," memorandum by Gay, 10/11/44. FR, 1944, 5, p. 465, Morris to Secretary of State, 11/1/44.

45. For British observation of FDR and the election see FO 40241, E6537/6058/34, 1092, Bullard to FO, 10/25/44; FO 40242, E6863/6058/34, 6005, Lord Halifax to FO, 11/7/44. See also Dallek, *Franklin D. Roosevelt and American Foreign Policy,* pp. 481–84; Feis, *Churchill, Roosevelt, and Stalin,* p. 451.

46. FO 40242, E6862/6058/34, Minute by W. H. Young, 11/8/44. FO 40242, E6863/6058/34, 6005, Halifax to FO, 11/7/44.

47. FO 40241, E6605/6058/34, 5809, Halifax to FO, 10/26/44.

48. FO 40241, E6515/6058/34, 9394, Eden to Halifax, 10/28/44; FR, 1944, 5, pp. 462–63, Stettinius to Kennan, 10/30/44; and ibid., p. 463, Kennan to Stettinius, 11/1/44.

49. Ibid., p. 466, Morris to Secretary of State, 11/3/44.

50. Ibid., p. 466, memorandum by Stettinius, 11/3/44; and ibid., p. 467, memorandum by Murray, 11/3/44. See also FO 40242, E6797/6058/34, minute by A. Cadogan, 11/3/44. The sudden shift in Soviet tactics did not cause the Iranians to ease their efforts to secure firmer American and British support. Dr. Daftary, the chargé in Washington, told acting Secretary of State Edward Stettinius that the distressing situation required the Americans to take a stand against the Russians. To Wallace Murray, Daftary added "that his government felt that they had no one else to turn to except the United States for help in this time of need. . . ." But as always the Iranians were playing their game of divide and conquer among the Allies. Their ambassador in London made almost an identical plea to the Foreign Office. In both instances the Iranians received the same reply. The Americans and British reiterated their determination to stand by the Tehran Declaration, but they also stressed that good relations with the Soviet Union remained a top priority. See also FO 40242, E7087/6058/34, 69, Bullard to British Consuls in Iran, 11/6/44.

51. FR, 1944, 5, p. 466, Morris to Secretary of State, 11/3/44.

52. FO 40242, E6868/6058/34, 6005, Halifax to FO, 11/7/44.

53. FO 40242, E6868/5054/34, 1156, Bullard to FO, 11/7/44.

54. Ibid., Bullard to FO, 11/7/44.

55. FO 40242, E6978/6058/34, minute by W. H. Young, 11/9/44.

56. SD 891.6363/11–1744, "Oil Negotiations in Iran," memorandum by H. B. Minor, 11/17/44.

57. For a brief discussion, see George Kennan, *The Nuclear Delusion* (New York, 1983), pp. 27–37; also his *Memoirs, 1925–1950,* chs. 7–11. And for a good analysis, see Gaddis, *Strategies of Containment,* pp. 3–53.

58. FR, 1944, 5, pp. 470–71, Kennan to Secretary of State, 11/7/44.

59. See, for example, SD FW891.6363/826, memorandum by H. B. Minor, 3/3/44. See also Ramazani, *The Foreign Policy of Iran, 1500–1941,* p. 133 and 133n., and p. 206 and 206n. FO 40241, E6673/6058/34, 1121, Bullard to FO, 10/31/44.

60. SD 891.6363/11–2244, 840, Morris to Secretary of State, 11/12/44. For an example of the problem of prestige, see MMRB, OSS Iran File, 115902, 2/13/44.

61. FO 40242, E6058/34, 5329, Soviet Monitor, 11/4/44.

62. On the 1921 treaty, see Ramazani, *The Foreign Policy of Iran, 1500–1941,* pp. 186–91 or J. C. Hurewitz, *Diplomacy in the Near and Middle East,* 2 vols. (Princeton, 1956), pp. 90–94.

63. *Izvestia,* 11/4/44.

64. On efforts to negotiate a treaty see FR, 1944, 5, pp. 351ff. On the medals to Connolly and staff, see Abel and Harriman, *Special Envoy,* p. 299.

65. MMRB, OSS Iran File, L50317, "Curtice on the Oil Situation," 11/29/44. FO, E7153/6058/34, 1283, Bullard to FO, 12/3/44. See also Abrahamian, *Iran Between Two Revolutions,* pp. 210–11.

66. Sir Claremont Skrine, *World War in Iran,* p. 227.

7 *The American Advisers in Iran*

In 1942 the State Department launched its advisory program for Iran in which advisers were to become the instruments of an American-sponsored "New Deal." The program encompassed five key missions, one each to the army, the Ministry of Finance, the gendarmerie, the urban police, and the Ministry of Food and Supply. Supporters of the missions argued that once the advisers had reformed key agencies, Iran would begin a transformation from an impoverished, semifeudal, traditional rural society into a progressive nation. Greater material prosperity would lead inevitably, as it had in the United States, to political stability. Iran would become at least in theory a sea of tranquility in one of the world's most chronically strife-torn regions. All of this would come about as a consequence of the new Iranian-American friendship, of which the advisers were to be the most tangible symbols as well as the major architects.

By 1944 few Iranian or American officials believed that these advisers offered any hope at all. As Arthur Millspaugh later concluded, "While the Department talked about a program, it actually had none. It had sent men to Persia without a plan and in accordance with no known principle of organization." The advisory missions were starved for resources, vilified in the Iranian press, and battered by political infighting both in Iran and the United States. So unsatisfactory were the relations between the missions and the Iranian government that many officials in Tehran publicly questioned the wisdom of maintaining close ties with the United States.[1]

But the State Department did not send the missions just to assist Iran. It had initially hoped that the "disinterested" American presence would ease traditional rivalries among the big powers. As Iran stabilized, the British, the Russians, or other foreign powers could not easily justify future interference there. By 1944, however, it had become clear that the advisers had aggravated the very rivalries they had been sent to quiet. Iran remained in turmoil and the Soviets showed evident hostility to the growing American presence. Plagued by Soviet suspicions, the vagaries of Iranian politics, and their own inability to achieve meaningful reform, most of the advisers looked forward to the day they would go home. Only two missions, the Ridley mission to the army and the Schwarzkopf mission to the gendarmerie, survived, not as agents of a "New Deal," but as instruments of an emerging containment policy.

THE ADVISORY PROGRAM

Millspaugh's criticism makes it reasonable to ask if the State Department had ever had any advisory "program" at all. The answer must be a qualified "yes." Most often the missions functioned autonomously, with Ridley scarcely concerned with Schwarzkopf's struggles, and Millspaugh proposing to cut the army budget as Ridley set out to improve army morale by strengthening supply operations and internal organization. Nor had the State Department ever created an administrative structure to coordinate the activities of the individual missions. All the same, the department saw the advisers collectively as instruments of its policy to support the war effort by assisting Iran. When the Iranians complained about the advisers or the Russians seemed to obstruct their initiatives, the department often sought to address the general diplomatic problem rather than the particular difficulties of individual missions.

There can be no question that the State Department had embarked on the advisory program with unrealistic expectations. The instrument it created—five understaffed and poorly supplied missions—was totally inadequate to the task the United States chose to take on in Iran, where strident factionalism, the venality of government officials and entrenched interests, the Soviet and British determination to extend their traditional influence, and the poverty and demoralization of the masses of largely landless peasants all acted to impede constructive political or economic change. None of the missions ever commanded supplies or resources adequate for even modest reforms. The number of Americans working for the Iranian government never exceeded seventy or eighty, and many of those were people unsuited for the work they had been sent to do. Few spoke the language or had even a passing familiarity with the culture or history of the nation they were supposed to transform. The harsh climate and the diseases endemic to the country drained the initiative from many energetic advisers.[2]

Worst of all from the advisers' point of view, even well-conceived programs could arouse opposition. If they were bold in their proposals, as Arthur Millspaugh often was, they were damned for destabilizing Iran's fragile political balance by threatening entrenched interests. But if they attempted no more than what was possible with a starvation budget and limited authority, as Ridley did, they were damned for disappointing Iran's expectations. Col. H. Norman Schwarzkopf struck a balance, stretching scanty resources to transform a bedraggled gendarmerie into a viable organization. But even then he had to contend with a host of interests opposed to any shift of police authority away from the army.

Awareness of some of these deep flaws in the program began to dawn shortly after the Tehran Conference. Before returning to the United States, Roosevelt's chief troubleshooter, Harry Hopkins, had asked Arthur Millspaugh for a report on American aid to Iran. Since Hopkins superintended aid to the Soviet Union and knew General Connolly, he was already aware of the discontent among the Americans in Iran. Nevertheless, what he learned came as a jolt. Millspaugh argued that the advisers could do nothing under the present terms of their missions unless they remained at least twenty more years. Hopkins asked the State Department to explain why Millspaugh seemed so discouraged.[3]

In his reply, Harold Minor of the Near East Division revealed that the State

Department did not share Millspaugh's view of the American role. Minor conceded that it might indeed take decades for the United States to achieve substantial results. But he feared that to impose an American presence of the kind Millspaugh advocated might result in "a kind of benevolent . . . imperialism which would be difficult to cut off because we would engage ourselves fully and officially to making our advisors succeed."[4] As a consequence, good reasons existed not to place either the prestige or the resources of the United States fully behind the advisers. At the same time he could not see the missions existing for the length of time necessary for them to realize their objectives, given the present American commitment. Even if Iranian officials did want the Americans as a buffer against the Russians and British, they would be "horrified" to think that Iran would be saddled with foreign advisers for the next two decades. The British had never indicated that they saw the missions lasting beyond the war. The Russians had never accepted them in the first place. Soviet officials might assume, then, that if the American advisers remained indefinitely, the Soviet Union could justifiably consolidate its present position in the north of Iran. As a result, Minor believed the United States should help Iran only so long as the Iranians continued to request assistance.

While Minor was obviously more concerned with broad diplomatic questions, Millspaugh and the other advisers were more preoccupied with the particulars of American assistance to Iran. They labored under the assumption that they were actually expected to achieve tangible results. Minor admitted that he saw the advisers in primarily a symbolic role. No one in Washington sought to rectify the confusion. Minor explained his position to Hopkins, but not to Millspaugh. Thus the advisers remained uncertain about the actual relationship of their missions to State Department policy for Iran.

They were not alone in their confusion. In February 1944 OSS agents informed Washington that the Iranians were "bewildered" by relations between the State Department and advisers. Officials in Tehran had the impression that the department selected the advisers, sent them to Iran, and then washed its hands of them. Yet the advisers, even those working directly for the Iranian government, maintained close contact with the embassy, which at times used its influence on their behalf.[5]

Sir Reader Bullard complained that the advisers had no cohesion among themselves. He saw Schwarzkopf concentrating solely on the gendarmerie without giving any indication he ever discussed his work with Ridley. Ridley, in turn, took a passive approach that seemed to please no one: nationalists found his presence obnoxious, antiroyalists saw him as a threat, and his supporters did not see enough progress to sustain their faith. While willing to concede that Millspaugh was devoted to his work, Bullard thought the finance adviser was so "perverse and uncompromising" that he had become his own worst enemy. And urban police adviser Stephen Timmerman was, in Bullard's eyes, simply an embarrassment. General Arthur Smith, who commanded British forces in the region, dismissed Timmerman as a "perfectly dreadful man. It is common talk by everyone that he is never sober, and his nose suggests the truth of this accusation."[6]

The OSS warned that such ineptitude played into Soviet hands: "The apparent clumsiness and lack of unified policy among the American group is leading an increasing number of thoughtful Iranians to believe they will have to look to the Soviet Union for aid."[7] Cold war fears began to shape the American view of the advisers. At the same time, a conceptual flaw clouded the OSS analysis. True, the Iranians did see the United States as a counterweight to the Soviet Union. It was also true that disappointment with the advisers had led them to question their growing ties to the United States. But the last thing that almost any Iranian wanted in 1944 was to increase Iran's obligation to the Soviet Union. Few among the most determined opponents of the monarchy would have allied themselves with the Soviet Union even to effect the shah's downfall. Continued vigilance against Russian imperialism remained a *sine qua non* for Iran's leaders, with the exception of the Tudeh Party. Ignoring that fact of Iranian political life, the State Department tended to regard the troubled advisory program as a problem of inter-Allied diplomacy rather than as an administrative problem.

That approach shaped the agenda of the Stettinius mission to London in the spring of 1944. The advisers and their troubles were one of a broad range of economic and political issues the mission hoped to discuss in order to promote greater inter-Allied cooperation. The British delegates evidently shared that concern, because they expressed their hope that the new ambassador, Leland Morris, might make an effort to pull the advisers together. Speaking on the Americans' behalf, Wallace Murray showed less interest in the advisers than in Russian hostility. "From an American point of view we are particularly anxious to secure Russian support for the work of Dr. Millspaugh and the American advisers to the Iranian government," he told the British.[8] A renewed promise to support the advisers would reaffirm the principles of the Tehran Declaration. To that end Murray also opened talks with Soviet representatives in London, who responded with several rounds of polite evasions. Soviet diplomats showed no desire to make a substantive commitment to either the advisers or the American presence in Iran. Chargé Richard Ford had reached a similar impasse when he opened parallel talks with Ambassador Maximov, who in a rare moment of whimsy remarked that "while he and Bullard were trying to save Iran, it would be up to Ford to save the advisors."[9]

When they are analyzed as a single policy instrument, the advisory missions stand as a conspicuous failure of American policy. They succeeded largely in aggravating American relations with the Iranians while their presence also contributed to the big power rivalries they were supposed to mute. The missions cannot, however, be treated only as a single unit, and to understand how and why they evolved as they did, it is useful to look briefly at the three most important ones.

THE RIDLEY MISSION

If longevity were the sole criterion, the American mission to the Iranian Army would have to be counted a great success. Military advisers worked with the army from 1942 until the 1978 Islamic Revolution drove virtually all Americans out of Iran. But in 1945, almost no one believed General Ridley and his assistants had accomplished much at all. The morale of the army remained low; its effectiveness for either defense or internal police functions was questionable; graft and corruption consumed the energies of most of the officer corps; and sympathy for Germany and fascism made the officers suspect among most internal political factions and the Allied diplomatic community. Even when Ridley improved supply and finance operations, British and Iranian critics laboring under unrealistic expectations discounted those accomplishments.[10]

Political controversy hampered the army mission from its inception. In Washington, the State and War Departments had never fully resolved their differences over the nature of the mission, its value to the war effort, or its relevance to overall American policy. Two issues had focused their dispute—General Ridley's official status and supplies for Iran. The Joint Chiefs of Staff had been unwilling at first to divert any equipment to the mission or to raise its supply priority. Only when Soviet ambitions began to alarm some military leaders, like General Albert Wedemeyer, had the War Department agreed to expand General Connolly's capacity to assist Ridley.[11]

Factional disputes within the Iranian government added to Ridley's burdens. From moment to moment it was not always clear who was actually running the army. Nominally under the authority of the minister of war, control often revolved among the shah, his chief of staff, or the prime minister. When given the choice of working under the shah or the minister of war, Ridley chose neither. Though he placed his office and staff within the War Ministry and was paid by the Iranian government, final authority for the mission remained with the United States War Department.[12]

Any person seeking to reform the Iranian Army would have had to delineate both its formal and its informal functions. Officially the army was charged with protecting Iran from foreign invaders and with suppressing the chronically contentious tribal and ethnic minorities like the Kurds and Qashqai. Recent history had shown that the army could perform neither task. It lacked the equipment, training, and experience to withstand any powerful invader like the British, the Russians, or the Germans. Only an alliance with one or more of the big powers had ever afforded Iran any measure of military security. And even after Reza Shah's long campaign to subdue the tribes, they remained largely autonomous and politically unpredictable. Most foreigners agreed that it was better to pay them tribute than to try to subdue them by force.[13]

Reza Shah's rise through the ranks dramatized some of the army's informal functions. The army provided ambitious young men who lacked family connections, formal education, or property some opportunity to gain position and fortune. By accepting a cross section of Iran's people, the army also socialized a significant element of the populace. For most illiterate Iranians, it was the one institution that offered them a rudimentary education. But a tradition of corruption and mismanagement limited opportunities in the army to only the most politically loyal, venal, and ruthless of its members. Most of the officer corps and ranks remained demoralized, badly trained, and poorly supplied. Wartime inflation reduced many to near penury. Both as a security force and as an agency for socialization, the army Ridley confronted stood largely disabled. It survived primarily as Iran's most powerful political faction.[14]

Ridley had readily perceived that he had neither the wherewithal nor the political resources to accomplish more than modest reforms. His primary task lay in the areas of supply and finance. When he arrived, those functions were dispersed among individual units. Local commanders made their own arrangements for equipment and salaries. With staffs bloated by surplus officers, the army suffered from an epidemic of graft and mismanagement. The lack of motorized transportation and a primitive communications system severely encumbered these forces, charged with the surveillance of a vast land area.

Unfortunately, Ridley had embarked on his mission with a near-fatal handicap. He arrived in Iran as an emissary bearing no gifts. The War Department had refused to grant him even a handful of crucial supplies that might have given him some of the leverage he needed to win the cooperation of entrenched interests. To overcome the inertia of the wallowing beast he had come to train, Ridley recommended a modest plan to reduce the army in size from over 100,000 to around ninety thousand men. More important, he wanted to eliminate all but the most able officers. That would allow a realistic restructuring of salaries to compensate for the ravages of inflation. And, finally, he suggested that a centralized system of supply and finance, served by a functioning motor transport network, would limit corruption, bolster morale, and allow for a more efficient use of scarce resources. On each of those fronts Ridley made only limited progress. Iranian officials and army officers resisted almost every proposal he made. Lend-lease restrictions, compounded by shipping bottlenecks, delayed the delivery of those few supplies Ridley had managed to wrangle from a reluctant War Department. Until General Connolly had his directive redefined in 1944, he refused to assemble trucks earmarked for the Iranian Army.[15]

As the Iranian government grew ever more disappointed with the trickle of supplies, it pressed to have the mission tripled in size. That was a shrewd tactic for, as experience shows, a larger mission generally commands more support and supplies. But the War Department insisted that worldwide manpower shortages made it impossible to enlarge the mission. Only State Department intercession on Ridley's behalf resulted in the addition of nine more men to his staff. Here was a classic example of incremental decision making that satisfied none of the parties involved.[16]

By May of 1944 Ridley thought he had done as much as he could. With scarce resources he had limited his work to establishing a centralized depot system and training the Iranians to run it. Beyond that he had reorganized the quartermaster corps, standardized procurement, and introduced accounting procedures. When the circumstances permitted, Ridley ran training schools for administration, engineering, medicine, supply, and finance. A factory had begun turning out shoes and clothing for the troops. And Ridley managed to have the entire army innoculated against typhus. Still, his efforts to end recruiting abuses, particularly those that allowed the well-to-do to avoid army service, could never overcome the army's entrenched practices. And though he did not share Millspaugh's determination to make draconian cuts in the army's size, he had been unable to effect even a modest decrease to about ninety thousand men.[17]

On 31 May Ridley recommended that when his current plans were completed, certainly by 1 November, the War Department should terminate his mission. "There exists no military necessity for this mission," Secretary of War Stimson informed the State Department. The State Department learned, however, that the shah wanted the mission continued indefinitely. The various interested parties kicked the matter around for half a year before the State and War Departments agreed to extend the mission for another five months, ending in March 1945. By that time the oil concession crisis had added a new complication. Secretary Stettinius warned Stimson that a decision to withdraw the mission at that point would have adverse political and psychological consequences. Even Ridley agreed that the departure of the mission then might leave a vacuum for another power to fill. "It is well known that the Russians would be glad to accommodate Iran in this respect," Ambassador Morris added.[18]

As in the past, politics rather than military necessity would determine the future of the army mission. Morris' comment demonstrated that the army mission had become a fixture of the forthcoming cold war, not the current conflict. Since Stettinius believed that "Iran is perhaps the most prominent area of the world where inter-Allied friction might arise," he asked Stimson to extend the army mission indefinitely as the shah had requested. He also urged the Joint Chiefs to grant Ridley a high priority on supplies. In that way the army could perform internal security functions once the Allied forces withdrew from Iran. The assumptions of the Jernegan memorandum, when blended in with the emerging cold war mentality, proved a potent brew. Having come to accept the State Department's concern, Ridley agreed that his mission should be continued, if State and War would coordinate their policies and if the Iranians accepted an open-ended agreement allowing him to cancel the mission with three months notice.[19]

Secretary Stimson not only authorized this extension, he asked the JCS to upgrade Ridley's supply status. The Joint Chiefs were more than willing to do so. By February 1945 they too had come to see Iran as a vital link in America's postwar security perimeter. They agreed that the supplies Ridley requested would contribute to world peace by making Iran more stable. Neither the end of the war nor the complaints of occasional congressional critics brought an end to the United States' mission to the Iranian Army. It remained a major instrument of American cold war politics and until 1979 a potent symbol of the Iranian-American alliance.[20]

THE TRIALS OF THE SCHWARZKOPF MISSION

Ridley's frustrations were trivial compared to the Jobian trials that Col. H. Norman Schwarzkopf faced. It was not just that he held a lower rank; the War Department also treated his mission to the gendarmerie or rural police force as junior to the army mission. Ridley at least received a few token supplies, no matter how reluctantly they were sent. Schwarzkopf at first got nothing. Acting Assistant Chief of Staff J. E. Hull thought that Schwarzkopf's supplies should come through lend-lease (FEA). Of course, the War Department, not FEA, controlled the equipment Schwarzkopf most needed. Upon his arrival he faced the bleak prospect of reorganizing a rural police force that lacked transportation or communications facilities.[21]

As low as the gendarmerie stood with the War Department, it commanded even less respect in Iran. As T. H. Vail Motter, the official historian of the PGC, observed, "The Gendarmerie had been the poor relation of the army, subsisting on the scraps from the budget table and unhonored."[22] While the army skimmed off the best recruits from an already dismal lot, the gendarmerie got the dregs. Illiteracy and opium addiction were rampant in the ranks. In addition, Schwarzkopf's Iranian superior, the minister of the interior, had far less prestige than the war minister. To make matters worse, in two years the post changed hands eleven times.

To those special difficulties should be added the standard list of adviser headaches. All Schwarzkopf's initiatives ran afoul of political machinations, both in Washington and Tehran. For example, he had to work one full year without a contract. And while the State Department and the Iranian government quibbled over details, the mission had no authority. Ministers generally ignored Schwarzkopf's recommendations, withheld vital information from him, and indulged in rumormongering that undermined Schwarzkopf's prestige any time his plans threatened their power or income. In the face of his Herculean task, Schwarzkopf had a staff of just eight officers and NCOs. The mission at its full strength never involved more than twenty men. With that skeleton force, Schwarzkopf was expected to vitalize a force of twenty-one thousand men that might well have been Iran's most corrupt and demoralized agency.[23]

Despite the many obstacles he faced, Schwarzkopf emerged as the most successful of the advisers. The embassy often praised him and his staff for combining vigor with a sense of tact and personal dignity. Schwarzkopf had managed within two months of his arrival to tour all the gendarmerie posts and produce a two-hundred-page reorganization plan. Two years later, he had overcome some of his many handicaps to establish schools to train NCOs, truck drivers, and motorcycle operators. Six more schools were in the planning stage. Somehow Schwarzkopf had managed to find an American radio engineer and then had scraped together enough equipment to install a rudimentary communications network. He even scavenged 150,000 yards of wool cloth that his tailors sewed into new uniforms. Thus outfitted, the gendarmerie marched proudly in review at the shah's birthday parade in November 1944. Participation in such a prestigious event commemorated the small miracle

Schwarzkopf had worked in upgrading the prestige and morale of his once bedraggled corps.[24]

Like Ridley, Schwarzkopf had early on discovered that the status of his mission was contingent on political factors outside his personal purview. The rise in the gendarmerie's fortunes came about as much from the determination of Anglo-American diplomats to guarantee Iran's internal security as it did from Schwarzkopf's efforts. The Military Intelligence branch of the War Department had concluded, in fact, that the gendarmerie rather than the army should become the target of American assistance. The reasons were eminently practical. An efficient gendarmerie would cost less, have a more immediate impact on rural security, and lend itself more readily to an upgrading program. Unlike the army, the gendarmerie posts were located outside urban centers. Assistance to the rural police would thus bring educational benefits to those areas where they were most urgently needed. More important, the gendarmerie could sooner reach a readiness level at which it could assist in policing the supply route. As one cynic observed, "Both the British and Russians as well as ourselves are anxious to avoid having Allied troops kill Iranians. Iranians do most of the pilfering. If the gendarmerie is efficient, the gendarmerie will kill the majority of thieving Iranians thus relieving international complications."[25]

Military Intelligence argued that the change of internal security operations from the army to the gendarmerie might have important long-term consequences:

> The United States War Department through its control of material essential to the development of both the army and gendarmerie can greatly aid or hinder the development of Iran. To develop the army at the expense of the gendarmerie is almost certain to increase the discouragement of the rural population in the probability of a bright future and push the country nearer the brink.[26]

Whatever its merits, that conception reflected an almost complete disregard for the realities of Iranian political life. It greatly exaggerated American capacity to influence Iran's internal affairs. And Military Intelligence did not seem to recognize the disruptive potential of its proposal. Rather than create stability, such a shift might have undermined the monarchy, exacerbated factionalism, driven the army to reassert its authority, or brought down whatever cabinet backed the gendarmerie. The established interests in Iran were opposed to any such sweeping change, especially one that would bring with it no material benefits.

The War Department had no desire to introduce such uncertainty into Iran. It recognized only that additional supplies for the gendarmerie might be a "good insurance investment," leading to the simplification of Iranian-American relations. That meant that by late 1943 Schwarzkopf had received the same supply priority as Ridley. General McNarney warned that this decision meant no cornucopia for either the gendarmerie or Iran: "No supplies will be provided unless they are clearly surplus and not needed for the war effort." Such begrudging support masked Schwarzkopf's small success. He had finally convinced at least a few people in Washington that his mission had some importance.[27]

Having assured himself a few supplies, Schwarzkopf embarked on the major step in his reorganization plan—the separation of the gendarmerie from the army. So long as both forces remained under army control, his would suffer from general neglect, which meant inadequate equipment, inferior personnel, and insufficient funds. Between Schwarzkopf and his goal of an autonomous gendarmerie stood the shah and the war minister who saw in this proposal the possible erosion of their authority. They rested their opposition on an old argument: the gendarmerie shared its responsibility for internal security with the army; it should therefore remain within the army.[28]

Schwarzkopf won out, but only on paper, for in Iran what one hand gave reluctantly the other eagerly snatched away. The Majles granted him executive authority, independent from the army, over promotions, discipline, and pensions. Then, parliamentary opponents rejected almost every recommendation he made for promotions based on merit. In addition, they blocked his requests for funds, new equipment, or qualified personnel. Schwarzkopf blamed his frustrations on the mindless arrogance of the "one hundred families" (what British diplomats dubbed "the Gang") who resisted even constructive change. Chargé Richard Ford thought that a status problem might have compounded Schwarzkopf's difficulties. Iranian generals and politicians did not like to defer to a mere colonel. Ford thus urged the War Department to promote Schwarzkopf to brigadier general. But even that simple bureaucratic maneuver took two years to execute. Schwarzkopf did not receive his new rank until the spring of 1946.[29]

Adversity did not daunt the gendarmerie mission. With remarkable resilience Schwarzkopf rebounded from the scuttling of his first reorganization plan by producing another. In the summer of 1944 he proposed to the minister of the interior that they dissolve the old gendarmerie to make way for an entirely new organization called the "Negahban." In that way Schwarzkopf hoped to attract young recruits who could receive proper training and pay. One feature of the plan dealt with the longstanding tension between tribal minorities and the Tehran government. Neither the army nor the gendarmerie had ever recruited among the tribes. Schwarzkopf believed that their inclusion in the security forces would eliminate a major source of tribal unrest.[30]

Whether he would actually have time to enact this plan was another matter, because the Iranian government had given no indication that it would renew his contract when it expired. The Russians continued to demonstrate their hostility to the mission by refusing to allow it into the northern zone. And the War Department had begun the process of terminating Ridley. Only the British seemed eager to have Schwarzkopf carry on. In fact, they even proposed that he assume authority over the urban police as well as the gendarmerie. With so little support, the State Department contemplated withdrawing the mission.[31]

Schwarzkopf shared that ambivalence. Having separated the gendarmerie from the army, organized training schools, and established supply priorities, he thought his mission had done all it could for the foreseeable future. If the State Department defined the American role in Iran as a short-term one, he favored the termination of the mission. But if the United States planned to carve out a long-term position in Iran, he thought the mission should embark on his new reorganization plan. That posed no problem for the State Department, for it had long before concluded that the United States was in Iran for the long run. In September of 1944 it agreed to extend Schwarzkopf's mission for one more year.[32]

Over the next year the entire cycle repeated itself. Schwarzkopf launched an ambitious plan to reform the gendarmerie. The minister of the interior authorized him to take the five key steps needed to establish the "Negahban," including the dissolution of the old organization, the issuing of an annual rather than a bimonthly budget, the establishment of courts-martial for gendarmes, their exemption from military service, and a revised promotion system. And no sooner did he have the authority he needed than his old opposition mobilized. The Majles defeated the enabling bill because many politicians feared the new organization would end their control over elections. Under the old system, they could bribe the officers who watched the voting places or intimidate voters to ensure that their candidate won. Incorruptible officers left too much to chance and the whims of the electorate. To overcome this opposition, Schwarzkopf threatened to end his mission unless, first, the Majles cooperated, and second, the War Department increased his supply allocations.[33]

But now it was the fall of 1945 and the circumstances Iran faced were not those of a year earlier. In particular, Russian interference with gendarmerie units in the northern zone had become more threatening. Schwarzkopf was still unable to send members of his mission into that area to train his forces. On many occasions, local Soviet commanders had refused to allow the gendarmerie to move or otherwise to perform their assigned duties. Faced with the possibility that the American presence would decline as Soviet pressures became more ominous, the Majles readily voted to give Schwarzkopf the powers he had requested. And the War Department, believing that current Soviet actions required an active American presence and an effective gendarmerie, granted Schwarzkopf his supply priority. The gendarmerie mission joined the army mission as an instrument of American cold war policies in the Middle East.[34]

MILLSPAUGH'S FAILURE IN IRAN

The State Department had at first assumed that long-term stability must rest on a viable economy, not on the military. Improving material circumstances would bring a measure of contentment to an otherwise restive population. Or so the rhetoric of the Jernegan memorandum went. However, no matter how much the Americans might talk about reform, or even sincerely desire it, they were willing to support almost any leadership that promised political stability, an inhospitable environment for communism, a measure of fiscal responsibility, and, above all, a favorable climate for American overseas interests. That often translated into close ties between Americans and reactionary elements in the Iranian military.

In that light it should come as no surprise that Arthur Millspaugh quickly became disillusioned with the State Department's commitment to reforming Iran. Millspaugh had gone to Iran assuming he had a mandate to undertake a small-scale economic and social revolution. Yet the Iranians had from the beginning held quite contrary expectations for his mission. They had not asked for a reformer, but for a statesman who could become their advocate in the highest American political circles. The Iranian government accepted Millspaugh because the nation's economic plight was desperate and the Americans had shown no inclination to send the kind of adviser they sought.

When Millspaugh reached Iran, its fragile economy had almost collapsed. Overseas trade had come to a virtual halt, foreign forces had overtaxed local resources, and Allied operation of the supply route had completely tied up the transportation system. Longstanding abuses made matters worse. The mismanagement of government finances had left the treasury on the brink of bankruptcy. Inflation had crippled the commercial classes and led to the hoarding of food supplies. The archaic administrative apparatus that managed Iran's economy was staggering under escalating demands.

Millspaugh arrived in Iran wearing the mantle of the conquering hero. Louis Dreyfus informed the State Department that "Dr. Millspaugh has come to understand in a comparatively short time the fundamental causes of Iran's financial and economic difficulties."[35] Within two months he had driven through the Majles a "Full Powers Bill" that seemed on the surface at least to give him near-dictatorial control over the economy. Not only did this bill give him the authority to regulate the collection, price, transportation, and distribution of grains, it gave him the right to administer the public domain and the recently ceded estates of Reza Shah. In addition, the Majles had granted him the power to set prices in the markets, to regulate the distribution of goods, and to direct the government's entire fiscal operations, including the preparation of the budget. The bill included provisions for a steeply progressive income tax, designed to redistribute the tax burden more equitably while curbing the worst ravages of inflation. In July 1943 Dreyfus described Millspaugh as "a power to be reckoned with," who had assumed control "over the entire financial and economic structure of Iran." What Dreyfus failed to see was that Millspaugh's impressive powers had not yet been seriously tested.[36]

It was clear early on that the mission had little solid political support. Opponents could frustrate reform simply by inaction. Many officials who were thought to be in Millspaugh's camp often did nothing to assist the mission. Paul Atkins, an economist on Millspaugh's staff, concluded soon after he arrived that "the Majles and much of the government administration would like us out of here and are trying to make things as uncomfortable as possible without being too conspicuous." Despite the opposition the mission met with in instituting its policies, the crux of its problem was, as Atkins perceived it, the lack of an administrative apparatus. Millspaugh simply did not have enough trained staff to impose his authority. So, for example, even though he supposedly controlled prices, he had no way to monitor what actually went on in the bazaars, and Iranian officials had no taste for enforcing unpopular price controls that would certainly provoke the wrath of the merchants. In appraising one new series of regulations, Atkins remarked, "they look quite imposing, but they carry no sanctions for their enforcement and Millspaugh has no power to establish sanctions."[37]

Millspaugh compounded the problem of an inadequate staff by assuming additional responsibilities. When food adviser Joseph Sheriden suddenly resigned in the spring of 1943, Millspaugh found himself in a quandary. Stable food prices were a prerequisite to the fight against inflation. The food adviser could assist in that effort by reducing hoarding and equalizing the distribution of commodities in short supply. Millspaugh decided to assume Sheriden's duties, even though he had no additional staff for the work. And Dreyfus was unable to ease the burden on the mission, because the State Department had ignored his urgent requests for additional personnel.[38]

Such adversity did not prevent Millspaugh from plunging ahead with plans for a comprehensive reform program. He was not at all fazed that its implementation would require sixty more people than were currently assigned to the mission. What did give him pause was the evidence of opposition to his program in the Majles. Many deputies complained about the extravagance of Millspaugh's plans. Yet rather than reformulate his proposal, he merely scaled down his request for additional staff.[39]

By August of 1943 a vociferous opposition had surfaced. A series of laws Millspaugh had proposed—a government monopoly of cereals, a steeply progressive income tax, and readjusted government salaries—had outraged almost all the entrenched interest groups in the country, such as "the Gang," war profiteers, merchants, Majles deputies, the newspapers, and the cabinet. His efforts to achieve economic stability had succeeded only in destroying what little political base he had had in Iran. He had done what no Iranian politician could have done—unify the factions. Prime Minister Soheili, after promising to back Millspaugh's program, remained ominously silent. The Majles not only refused to enact the enabling legislation Millspaugh had requested, but threatened to strip him of his authority over food.[40]

The finance adviser, as his staff had observed, was not someone readily given to compromise. Atkins, who had once described Millspaugh as "an old man—mentally as well as physically," found the director's manner abrasive and his attitudes doctrinaire. Opposition only stiffened his determination to maintain his authority. Millspaugh decided to force a showdown with "the classes of selfish privilege." Soon after the Majles failed to act on either his tax bill or his requests for staff, he announced that the mission would resign *en masse*. On 15 October 1943, despite Secretary Hull's objections, the finance mission carried out Millspaugh's threat. That left Prime Minister Soheili in the hot seat. As much as he might object to Millspaugh, he needed the mission as a tangible symbol of American support. While the Majles sought a compromise in secret session, he asked Millspaugh to reconsider.[41]

The British legation also used its influence to effect a reconciliation. Foreign Secretary Anthony Eden reminded the shah of an earlier promise to support the missions, and now asked him to keep his pledge. The shah's intercession apparently had the desired effect, for the Majles became more cooperative and in response Millspaugh withdrew his resignation and eliminated some of the controversial provisions of his income tax bill.[42]

That confrontation forced Dreyfus to recognize some of Millspaugh's more glaring weaknesses. On the one hand Dreyfus still believed that the mission had been unduly hampered by Iranian greed, corruption, and political sabotage. An unfortunate string of illnesses had also added to Millspaugh's difficulties. But those factors alone could not explain the severity of the recent controversy. On too many occasions Millspaugh had needlessly affronted Iranian sensibilities. No matter how laudable his ends, his means were too abrasive. Dreyfus had seen, too, how Millspaugh, who seldom consulted his aids on key decisions or involved them in the planning of major projects, rode roughshod over his staff: "In several instances the morale of the latter has been seriously affected by the failure of their chief of mission to seek their advice, or even inform them regarding important measures."[43] In that way Millspaugh added another complication to the many difficulties that plagued all the missions. Nevertheless, the evidence of Millspaugh's deficiencies did not then lead the State Department to reevaluate its commitment to him or its conception of the mission.

Having survived one crisis, Millspaugh soon became embroiled in another one that doomed his mission. In the spring of 1944 a political faction headed by the pro-British Seyyed Zia-ed-Din initiated a campaign to shift authority over the army from the shah to the Majles. Seyyed found a sympathetic supporter in Millspaugh, who "held to the belief that the army, in spite of some apparent reforms, constituted this wasteful government's most colossal extravagance."[44] Seemingly unaware of the hornets' nest he had uncovered, Millspaugh supported a Majles plan to restrict both the size and expense of the army. He even favored replacing the army with the gendarmerie because he thought that institution less likely to become an obstacle to democracy. In planning his budget, Millspaugh shifted funds from the army to programs for agricultural development and for increased social services.

Millspaugh had dug his own political grave. No matter how worthy his motives, no matter how beneficial his reforms might have proven to be in the long run, in the short run his strategy was a disaster. He had not even taken the precaution of assuring himself of the backing of the antiroyalists and the other factions who encouraged his plan. His position proved untenable. The press vilified him, a variety of Majles deputies showered him with verbal abuse, and throughout this ordeal, the shah and the cabinet remained pointedly aloof. The attacks did not abate until a year later, after Millspaugh had resigned and the State Department had terminated the mission.[45]

The foray he made against the army was not Millspaugh's only misstep. He had also promoted policies that threatened the delicate balance of Iran's relations with the Soviet Union. On reviewing the government's finances, he had discovered that Iran was obliged under a series of contracts to deliver munitions, grains, and piece goods to the Russians under highly unfavorable terms. The Soviet government frequently defaulted on these contracts or ignored making payments since there were no penalties. But if Iran failed to meet the impossible production and delivery schedules specified in the contracts, the Russians levied stiff fines against them, which the Iranians paid. The deeply anti-Soviet Millspaugh was determined to renegotiate these contracts for Iran's benefit. That was not something the Iranian government wanted, because, as Prime Minister Saed admitted, "the good relations with the Soviet Union were worth many times the million *tomans* such relations already cost Iran." But it was not just Millspaugh's blundering in this area of Iran's affairs that troubled Saed. He also criticized Millspaugh's "static mentality," his insistence on hiring high-priced Americans when qualified Iranians were available, the instability of his staff, and his failure to produce results. In stating his case Saed spoke for many influential Iranians.[46]

The unceasing flow of bad news, while it did not shake Hull's belief in Millspaugh's leadership, did finally force the secretary to suggest that the mission needed help. An administrative assistant might improve morale, relieve Millspaugh of the burdens of office routine, and strengthen the functioning of the mission. That suggestion came too late, for in May 1944 Ford predicted that the opposition would try to cripple Millspaugh. By June the Majles was debating a bill to cancel his economic powers. But just as the Majles had moved with all deliberate slowness in passing the legislation to help the mission, it now moved with great caution in driving Millspaugh out. This step would surely complicate Iran's relations with the British and Americans. Even though Bullard doubted Millspaugh's qualifications, British diplomats felt a proprietary obligation to the advisers. The intemperate abuse Millspaugh had suffered offended their sense of fair play while confirming their low regard for Iranian politicians.[47]

This time, when Millspaugh resigned, he did not ask his assistants to do so as well. For the moment, Saed refused to accept the resignation until he could persuade the Majles to allow the mission four months to show results. The ever politically naive Millspaugh assumed that he had won a major victory. In reality, Saed was waiting for a more propitious moment to dump him without offending the British and Americans. His government showed the same deference in this situation that it did in its onerous contracts with the Soviet Union. So long as the Foreign Office or the State Department showed any concern, the Iranians would look for a way to keep Millspaugh.[48]

By late 1944 the State Department had grown weary of the controversy surrounding Millspaugh's every move. When Averell Harriman made his fact-finding stop in Tehran, he recommended that Millspaugh be replaced. Ambassador Morris told the Iranians they could send Millspaugh home without offending the United States. The other members of his mission would have to decide for themselves whether to stay or leave. After attempting to serve in a reduced capacity, Millspaugh finally left Iran in February 1945. Some members of the mission made private arrangements with the Iranian government that allowed the gutted mission to survive. Under the new arrangement, the mission had two American directors who had no executive authority. Many of the remaining advisers had stayed on largely to collect their lucrative salaries.[49]

By late summer of 1945, Wallace Murray had been appointed ambassador, and he decided to make one last attempt to salvage the mission. Economic conditions were so desperate, he concluded, that Iran "unquestionably needs all the help it can get." The departure of the mission *en masse* might suggest that the government lacked American support. By September Murray had to admit that he too had failed. The mission had neither a coherent program nor any semblance of popular approval, and on 11 December 1945 it came to an end.[50]

THE ADVISERS AND THE COLD WAR

In many ways Millspaugh had become a convenient scapegoat for those Americans and Iranians who had contributed so much to the mission's failure. The State Department had refused from the outset to accept Iran's reasons for having invited the mission in the first place. As controversy raged over efforts to scale down the army with Millspaugh's support, Foreign Minister Saed had admitted with unusual candor "that his country did not need [the advisers'] technical skills so much as for them to act as a cushion between British-Soviet conflicting interests."[51] In short, Millspaugh, like all the advisers, was caught in a no-win situation. The State Department expected him to initiate reforms that would promote stability, but every program he proposed intensified the deep-rooted factionalism characteristic of Iran after the fall of Reza Shah. As Millspaugh sank into the mire of controversy, no one in Washington ever explained how American advisers could transform a society with a small middle class and an elite with no commitment to reform.

The army controversy demonstrated how substantive reform had run afoul of political rivalries. The Iranians preferred to attack Millspaugh rather than to adopt programs that might have left their national finances on a much sounder basis. The State Department could have and perhaps should have anticipated that without financial or material resources, the advisers had no way to induce the Iranian oligarchy to support reform. And throughout the war, the United States had no unilateral interests in Iran sufficient to justify an extensive aid program. Only as agents of the cold war would Americans play a major role in Iranian affairs.

The military missions survived largely because they helped to maintain Iran's political status quo. They made more effective those agencies through which the monarchy and many powerful political factions sustained their positions. The army and gendarmerie could between them suppress much of the ethnic and radical discontent that threatened Iran during the war. So even while Iranian politicians might oppose the more far-reaching of Ridley's and Schwarzkopf's reforms, they generally favored the continuation of these missions. The advisory program for Iran came to mirror the system the United States operated in Central America. U.S. assistance helped to sustain the ruling oligarchies, no matter how oppressive they might prove to be. Order, rather than reform, became the American goal. In that way the United States promoted an old rather than a new deal for Iran.[52]

When the war ended, the State Department persuaded President Truman to exempt the military missions from his directive to withdraw all American forces from Iran. While the State-War-Navy Committee drew up legislation placing the military missions on a more permanent footing, Representative Karl Mundt arrived in Iran to see for himself what role the missions served. Mundt feared that the presence of American military personnel, no matter how few in number, would allow the Russians an excuse to keep their troops in northern Iran. Although he was a fervent anticommunist, Mundt argued that the Russians had every right to be concerned. The presence of Americans in Iran could be no more tolerable to them than Russian advisers in Mexico would be to Americans. The analogy was a telling one, yet few Americans ever seemed to see how closely Iran's relationship to the Soviet Union paralleled Mexico's with the United States. Both larger powers had long histories of coveting their neighbors' territories. Both jealously guarded against any foreign presence along their southern borders. And both smaller nations had long feared the ambitions of their neighbors to the north.[53]

To Wallace Murray fell the task of persuading Mundt that the advisers should stay. He argued that they could play a vital role in preserving Iran from a Soviet threat. And by choosing to ignore all the signs of Soviet hostility, Murray could assert that at least technically the Soviet Union had never objected to the advisers. That rather specious argument did not convert Mundt. He made good his threat to attack the missions on the floor of Congress, but without much impact. In the fall of 1945 cold war fears had begun to override the fiscal conservatism and isolationism of many Congressmen, who passed the legislation making the military advisory missions a permanent feature of the Iranian-American alliance. They did so in order to support a new system of American national security and not in order to promote Jernegan's New Deal for Iran. So long as Iran opposed communism, its government, almost no matter what form it assumed, could count on American support.[54]

NOTES

1. Arthur Millspaugh, *Americans in Persia,* pp. 214–15.

2. MMRB, OSS R&A File, 2201, Appendix 2, OSS Report, "The Three Power Problem in Iran," 7/13/44. This report gives the numbers for the missions as of July 1944 as follows:

Millspaugh Mission	60	
Timmerman Mission	3	
Gendarmerie Mission	8	(officers)
Army (Ridley) Mission	20	(officers)
Agricultural Adviser	1	
Health Adviser	1	
Municipal Adviser for Tehran	3	
	96	total

The total of ninety-six does not accurately reflect the operating strength of the missions. The personnel figures for the Millspaugh mission fluctuated widely. One wag described the sixty-person mission as twenty in Iran, twenty on the way there, and twenty on the way home. Vail Motter, *The Persian Corridor,* p. 474n, states that at its maximum, though not its authorized strength, the Ridley mission had twenty-five officers and men; the gendarmerie mission had about twenty-two officers and enlisted men.

3. Millspaugh, *Americans in Persia,* p. 214.

4. SD 891.51A/1000, Memorandum by H. B. Minor, 2/15/44.

5. MMRB, OSS Iran File, 61429, 2/15/44.

6. FO, 40164, E1670/94/34, Bullard to FO, 3/14/44. See also FO, 40146, E1987/94/34, General Smith to CIGS, 5/16/44, for General Smith's condemnation of Timmerman. Other sources confirm his alcoholism and poor record as an adviser.

7. MMRB, OSS Iran File, 67797, 4/19/44. For a good summary of Iran's policy toward the Soviet Union, see Ramazani, *Iran's Foreign Policy, 1941–1973,* pp. 91–108.

8. FR, 1944, 5, p.324, memorandum by Foy Kohler, 4/13/44.

9. Ibid. p. 325, Ford to Secretary of State, 5/24/44.

10. Ibid., p. 328, Murray to Stettinius, 4/24/44. See also ibid., p.332, Hull to Ford, 4/30/44; ibid., p.337, Harriman to Sec. of State, 6/10/44; see also FO, 40172, E3850/94/34, 1506, Moscow to FO, 6/2/44; and on Maximov's comment, FR, 1944, 5, p.335, Ford to Sec. of State, 5/24/44.

11. Abrahamian, *Iran Between Two Revolutions,* pp. 177–78. See also FO, 40146, E1670/94/34, Bullard to FO, 3/14/44; MMRB, OSS Iran File, 61233, 3/6/44; and Millspaugh, *Americans in Persia,* pp. 114–15.

12. On the supply problem, see FR, 1943, 4, p. 510–11, Secretary of State to Dreyfus, 1/21/43. Ibid., p. 516, memorandum by LTC Chafee (WDGS), 3/13/43. See also MMRB, OPD

210.864(2–27–43), Asst. Chief of Staff to Gen, Brehon Sommerville (Chief of Staff ASF). The two departments also disagreed about how best to define Ridley's relationship to the Iranian government. The Iranians had originally proposed to appoint Ridley assistant minister of war. The State Department believed that from such a position within the government he could assist other advisers, act as a brake on British and Russian intrigues, identify dangerous pro-Axis factions, and generally enhance American prestige. Ridley and Dreyfus had both endorsed the idea. The War Department would have nothing to do with it. It simply was not army policy to have American officers serve as officials in a foreign government. But more than army rules was at issue. Had the War Department approved Ridley's mission or willingly looked to assume the obligations it involved, then a way would have been found to bend the rules.

13. Vail Motter, *The Persian Corridor,* pp. 169–73, 462.

14. Ibid., pp. 115–17 and 157. See also Abrahamian, *Iran Between Two Revolutions,* pp. 173–74.

15. Vail Motter, *The Persian Corridor,* pp. 465–66; Abrahamian, *Iran Between Two Revolutions,* pp. 204–6.

16. Vail Motter, *The Persian Corridor,* pp. 466–67.

17. Ibid., p. 466. On Iran's request for a larger mission, see FR, 1943, 4, p. 536, Iranian Legation to Department, 9/20/43, and ibid., pp. 398–99, memorandum by Murray, 10/22/43.

18. Vail Motter, *The Persian Corridor,* p. 467.

19. Ibid., p. 474. MMRB, OPD 210.684 Iran, Ridley to OPD, 5/31/44. Also OPD 210.684 Iran, Stimson to Hull, 6/23/44. See also Millspaugh, *Americans in Persia,* pp. 114–15. FR, 1944, 5, p. 427, Stettinius to Morris, 8/26/44; ibid., p. 433, Stettinius to Stimson, 10/25/44. SD 891.20 Mission/11–1444, 109, Morris to Secretary of State, 11/14/44.

20. FR, 1944, 5, p. 443, Stettinius to Stimson, 12/21/44. See also Vail Motter, *The Persian Corridor,* pp. 474–75; SD 891.20 Mission/12–1944, Morris to Sec. of State, 12/19/44; FR, 1944, 5, p. 444, Stimson to Stettinius, 12/27/44; MMRB, OPD 210.684 (5 Feb '45), note for the record, 2/9/45.

21. MMRB, OPD 210.684 Iran, J. E. Hull note for the record, 4/28/43; and OPD 210.684 Iran, J. E. Hull to CG-ASF, 8/26/43.

22. Vail Motter, *The Persian Corridor,* p. 462 and pp. 464–65.

23. Ibid., pp. 462–64, and 474n. FR, 1943, 4, pp. 513–15, Dreyfus to Sec. of State, 3/4/43.

24. Vail Motter, *The Persian Corridor,* pp. 468–70.

25. MMRB, AG/SI (Suitland, Md.) MID 370.093, Box 775, JICAME to MID, 10/14/43. MMRB, OPD400 Iran, note for the record, 10/30/43.

26. Ibid., JICAME to MID, 10/14/43.

27. MMRB, OPD 210.684 Iran, General McNarney to Col. Schwarzkopf, 10/12/43.

28. FR, 1944, 5, pp. 393–94, Ford to Secretary of State, 3/28/44.

29. MMRB, OSS Iran File, 61233, 3/6/44; SD 891.20 Mission/11, 899, enclosure 1, 3/28/44. See also Vail Motter, *The Persian Corridor,* pp. 478–80. Schwarzkopf also received a Distinguished Service Medal for his work in Iran.

30. SD 891.20 Mission/13, memo by Harold Minor, 5/11/44 and MMRB, OSS Iran File, 77044C, 5/23/44.

31. FR, 1944, 5, p. 418, Ford to Secretary of State, 7/1/44; ibid., p. 419, Hull to Ford, 7/4/44; ibid., pp. 421–22, Hull to Ford, 7/26/44; and ibid., p. 435, Stettinius to Morris, 11/29/44.

32. SD 891.105A/8–1444, 1075, Ford to Secretary of State, 8/19/44; FR, 1944, 5, p. 427, Sec. of State to Morris, 9/12/44.

33. FR. 1945, 8, pp. 529–31. See also SD 891.105A/5–1245, 292, Murray to Sec. of State, 5/12/45; SD 891.105A/5-2445, 344, Ford to Sec. of State, 5/24/45; SD 891.105A/6–545, Middle East to OPD (War Dept.), 6/5/45.

34. FR, 1945, 8, pp. 531–33.

35. Vail Motter, *The Persian Corridor,* pp. 163–64. See also FR, 1943, 4, pp. 517–18, Dreyfus to Sec. of State, 3/18/43.

36. Ibid., p. 522, Dreyfus to Sec. of State, 4/13/43; ibid., p. 526, Dreyfus to Sec. of State, 5/5/43; and SD 891.51/565, 540, Dreyfus to Sec. of State, 4/20/43. Ibid., p. 533, Dreyfus to Sec. of State, 7/4/43. Gabriel Kolko, *The Politics of War,* p. 299, cites that telegram of 4 July 1943 to support his case that the United States "was in fact directing much of Iran's affairs," and that Millspaugh was in Iran "to open Iranian riches to the United States." Readers of *Foreign Relations* will gain quite another impression merely by turning the page. Much of the subse-

quent correspondence about Millspaugh deals with his many disasters. See for example FR, 1943, 4, pp. 535–36, Dreyfus to Sec. of State, 8/29/43. I do not bring up this matter to engage in one of those footnote wars scholars seem to enjoy. Kolko's evident manipulation of sources undermines the credibility of an interpretation that has a great deal of substance.

37. Paul Atkins letter to Mrs. Atkins, 4/16/43. Paul Atkins Papers, Box 1, Yale University Library, New Haven, Connecticut. Hereafter cited as Atkins Papers. See also letters to Mrs. Atkins, 4/20/43 and 5/4/43, Atkins Papers, Box 1.

38. SD 711.91/96, 529, Dreyfus to Sec. of State, 4/22/43. See also FR, 1943, 4, p. 532, Dreyfus to Sec. of State, 6/29/43; and ibid., pp. 533–34, Dreyfus to Sec. of State, 7/19/43.

39. FR, 1943, 4, p. 534, Dreyfus to Sec. of State, 5/29/43.

40. Ibid., pp. 535–36, Dreyfus to Sec. of State, 8/29/43.

41. Ibid., pp. 536–55 and passim.

42. FO, 35077, E6519/82/34, memorandum from British Legation (Tehran) to FO, 10/17/43. FO, 35077, E6515/38/34, 1117, Bullard to FO, 10/26/43.

43. FR, 1943, 4, pp. 536–37, Dreyfus to Sec. of State, 9/22/43; ibid., pp. 337–39, Dreyfus to Sec. of State, 10/11/43.

44. Millspaugh, *Americans in Persia,* pp. 114–15; MMRB, OSS Iran File, 61233, 3/6/44.

45. Vail Motter, *The Persian Corridor,* pp. 467–68. See also SD 891.20 Missions/12–1444, memorandum of conversation with General Ridley, 12/14/44. Ridley told the department that the shah's dissatisfaction with Millspaugh was probably a result of his efforts to cut down the size of the army. See also Abrahamian, *Iran Between Two Revolutions,* pp. 208–9 and 212–13; Ramazani, *Iran's Foreign Policy, 1941–1973,* pp. 82–85.

46. Ibid., p. 82. See also FR, 1944, 5, pp. 391–92, Ford to Secretary of State, 2/21/44. The Iranians often made such complaints and while it is true the Americans and British seldom hired Iranians, it is not clear that Iranians had the necessary qualifications, as Saed claimed.

47. SD 891.51A/985, 69, Hull to Ford, 2/9/44; SD 891,51A/1014, 107, Acting Sec. of State to Ford, 2/25/44; SD 891.51A/1042, Ford to Sec. of State, 3/8/44; SD 891.51A/1030, Ford to Sec. of State, 2/11/44. See also FR, 1944, 5, pp. 424–25, Ford to Sec. of State, 8/12/44. Ibid., p. 413, Ford to Sec. of State, 6/25/44. FO, 40164, E3010/94/34, 501, Bullard to FO, 3/16/44; FO 40194, E3456/260/34, Bullard to Eden.

48. FR, 1944, 4, p. 419, Ford to Secretary of State, 7/3/44.

49. Ibid., pp. 436–40, Morris to Sec. of State, 12/1/44. SD 891.00/12–114, 4772, Harriman to Sec. of State, 12/11/44. FR, 1944, 5, pp. 440–44 passim. FR, 1945, 8, p. 538, Morris to Secretary of State, 1/8/45. Ibid., p. 543, Morris to Sec. of State, 2/3/45; see also ibid., pp. 548–50 and 550n. The Majles stripped him of his executive authority, which left only his title as financial adviser. That arrangement lasted just long enough for him to become embroiled in yet another political conflict. For months he had tried to oust Abol Ebtehaj from his position as head of the Iranian National Bank. Ebtehaj had long been Millspaugh's most outspoken critic. The Iranian Council of Ministers refused to remove Ebtehaj or to give Millspaugh the power to do so. That did it. Millspaugh once again threatened to leave Iran. He demanded that the State Department intervene on his behalf. When the department refused, he complained bitterly about its failure to support the advisers. Ambassador Morris finally decided Millspaugh had lost touch with reality. He informed the finance adviser that he no longer had the department's approval. With that final blow, Millspaugh went home.

50. Ibid., pp. 551–53, Morris to Secretary of State, 2/15/45; p. 556, Murray to Sec. of State, 8/10/45; and pp. 557–63. See also SD 891.51A/5–1145, Memorandum by Crane, 11/5/45.

51. FR, 1944, 5, pp. 390–92.

52. For one analysis of how American efforts at reform in Latin America have been transformed into a commitment to reactionary forces cooperative with American economic interests, see Walter LaFeber, *Inevitable Revolutions, The United States in Central America* (New York, 1983). I am struck by the parallels between the "American system" LaFeber describes in Latin America and American policy for Iran.

53. SD 891.20 Mission/10–945, Murray to Henderson, 10/9/45.

54. *Congressional Record,* 79th Cong., 1st sess., vol. 91, pt. 9, p. 11364, 12/3/45. See also Vail Motter, *The Persian Corridor,* pp. 476–80 and Ramazani, *Iran's Foreign Policy,* p. 159.

8 *Toward the Cold War*

After 1944 the State Department paid little more than lip service to the Jernegan memorandum's idea of nation-building in Iran. Instead, officials in the Near East Division sifted despatches for evidence that the Soviet Union would draw northern Iran into its orbit. Both the oil concession crisis and Soviet resistance to the U.S. advisers seemed to the Near East Division to presage future Soviet ambitions there, while the political activities of the Soviet occupation forces gave an ominous twist to Stalin's often-quoted observation on the liberation of Europe: "whoever occupies territory also imposes his own social system as far as his army can reach. It cannot be otherwise."[1]

Iran, of course, was not as sensitive an area for the Soviet Union as was Eastern Europe, but that would not necessarily prevent the Kremlin from using its troops in Iran to realize its postwar strategic objectives. Most Iranian, British, and American diplomats agreed with the observation George Kennan made in August 1944 that "the jealous and intolerant eye of the Kremlin can distinguish, in the end, only vassals and enemies; and the neighbors of Russia, if they do not wish to be one, must reconcile themselves to being the other."[2] The main objective of both British and American diplomats after the oil concession crisis was to see that Iran became neither.

From the point of view of Soviet leaders, Iran must have threatened to become an outpost for potentially hostile powers. The British and Americans could use their influence to weaken Iran's traditional ties to the Soviet Union, to promote anti-Soviet political factions, and to establish military and intelligence bases. In that light, defensive rather than expansionist concerns could explain the Soviet reaction both to the advisers and the oil concessions. But whether they were defensive or offensive, competing Allied interests invited a cold war confrontation over Iran.[3]

ALLIED FRICTION AND IRANIAN FACTIONALISM

The unsettled condition of Iran's internal politics was both a symptom and a cause of friction between the Soviet Union and the Anglo-American powers. Prime Minister

Saed's resignation in November 1944 inspired intense factional disputes in Iran. Saed's successor would have to silence a Babel of foreign and domestic voices making conflicting demands on the government. If the new prime minister wanted to appease the Russians, he would have to repress the conservative, pro-British factions and reverse Saed's oil policy. The British accepted the current status of the oil question, but they would not readily accept a cabinet that gave wide scope to leftists and nationalists hostile to their interests. The Americans would expect a cabinet sympathetic to the efforts of the advisory missions and neutral on the oil question. The antiroyalist factions still hoped to reduce the army's strength and its ties to the monarchy. The shah demanded a successor who like Saed was personally loyal, who would not wish to weaken the monarchy, and who would not needlessly antagonize the Allies.

The two most prominently mentioned candidates, Ahmad Qavam and Mohammed Mossadeq, fulfilled few of these conditions. During his previous tenure as prime minister, Qavam had worked to weaken the shah while improving his own ties with the Allies. Ambassador Bullard had no illusions about Qavam's affections for the British. Still he considered the old republican as the most able of the antiroyalist leaders. Other foreign observers assumed that with his large estates within the Soviet occupation zone, Qavam was peculiarly susceptible to Russian influence. The shah knew that Qavam harbored republican ambitions. The shah's hostility combined with the reservations among Anglo-American diplomats made Qavam an unacceptable choice at that time.[4]

Mossadeq was the leading candidate for the moderately antiroyalist "Individuals" Party, but he also had support from the Tudeh Party and from liberal factions, both of which were pro-Soviet and were strongest in the northern provinces. The two leftist parties encouraged Mossadeq's fervent nationalism and his opposition to western influences in general and to the American advisers in particular. It should thus be no surprise that the American Embassy viewed his candidacy with scant enthusiasm. Ambassador Morris described him to the State Department as "an independent elder statesman with a high reputation for patriotism and honesty. He appears to have the courage of his convictions, but is tactless and frequently garbles the facts of a given situation."[5] While Mossadeq did manage briefly to organize an unstable majority, he sensed that his tenure in office would be uncertain. Rather than sacrifice his Majles seat, he withdrew his candidacy.

Almost by default the position fell to Morteza Quli Bayat, the candidate of the National Union Party and a court favorite. Few prominent politicians in Iran were more royalist or conservative than he. His pledge to keep the Majles abreast of any further oil concession talks neutralized the opposition of the Liberals and the Individuals. Bayat even criticized his predecessors for conducting secret oil negotiations. But that was as far as he would go. He never attempted to reverse Saed's decision. He sought only to avoid any step that might provoke his major opponents, especially the Russians and leftists who harbored profound suspicions of his conservative and pro-British views. British diplomats saw his precarious balancing act as "typically Persian. The aim is to be so slippery and soft that the Russians will have nothing to bite on."[6]

The British predictably looked askance at Bayat's gestures toward the leftists. Sir Reader Bullard warned that such a policy made the Iranian government dangerously vulnerable to Russian interference. In reality, the strategy of accommodating neutrality had long served the Iranians in their dealings with the big powers. It denied the Soviets any substantial pretext for more forceful intervention. And it embodied an appreciation that Bayat could afford no actions that were likely to antagonize some substantial domestic or foreign interest.[7]

The Iranians had to exercise caution in their internal politics, because they had no indication that either Washington or London would give them substantial support in the face of continuing Soviet pressures. That is not to say that British and American diplomats were indifferent to Iran's predicament; rather they could not outline an effective course of action. Sir Archibald Clark Kerr, the British ambassador in Moscow, had begun to suggest in late November of 1944 that the Allies could give the Iranian government a much-needed boost by resolving some of their current differences. Both the State Department and the Foreign Office agreed. Yet by the time they had decided to approach Foreign Commissar Molotov, the information coming from Iran indicated that Russian pressures had abated. Clark Kerr now worried about backing Molotov into a corner. Such a move "might well result in the digging in of toes which now have the air of wanting to shift their ground."[8]

So what policy should the British adopt? Moscow's unpredictability in regard to its behavior clearly had left the Foreign Office in a quandary. Too strong a response might prompt further hostile actions. Too weak a posture might allow Molotov a chance to prevaricate in such a way that Soviet policy would remain unchanged. Thus Clark Kerr recommended a mildly worded note indicating to Molotov "that while we and the Americans have our eye on him and that while we are mindful of the joint guarantee of Persian integrity . . . we do not think he is."[9]

George Kennan, the American chargé in Moscow, shared Clark Kerr's determination to end Moscow's pressure on Iran. The two diplomats agreed that one way to do this was to make Iran the subject of future Big Three talks. Kennan explained to the State Department that he "could think of no action in Iran except possibly the intimation that this subject might or might not—depending on Soviet actions in the meantime—have to come up for discussion . . . at the next meeting of Marshal Stalin with the President and the Prime Minister. . . ."[10] Kennan did not believe that the present situation warranted placing Iran formally on the upcoming agenda, but like Clark Kerr he wanted to send the Russians a signal that their allies would hold them accountable for their actions in Iran.

When Clark Kerr did finally send Molotov a note, he omitted any reference to Big Three talks on Iran. He and Kennan had concluded that such discussions hinged on broader policy questions under consideration in Washington and London. Indeed, the most recent British War Cabinet meeting had weighed Persian and Russian policies against each other. Foreign Secretary Eden had warned his colleagues to expect a loud public outcry if Iran succumbed to Soviet pressures on an oil concession. As a result, the cabinet decided it was desirable to encourage current Iranian policy by informing the Iranian government that the Foreign Office had previously sent notes to Moscow in support of Iran. But Churchill balked at the idea of asking Stalin to designate Iran as a topic for future Big Three talks.[11]

The Roosevelt administration showed even greater uncertainty about how to respond. Despite the anti-Soviet views of the State Department and congressional conservatives, postwar cooperation with the Soviet Union remained a top priority of Roosevelt's foreign policy. The American public still had a favorable view of the Soviet alliance. Wallace Murray, therefore, must have understood that his call for a concerted Anglo-American response to current tensions in Iran would meet with resistance. At one department meeting Murray warned that "Russian disrespect for Iranian sovereignty is a serious threat to the British Empire and the present dispute, if allowed to continue, may have serious consequences."[12]

The task of presenting these views to President Roosevelt fell to acting Secretary of State Edward Stettinius. Few people in Washington placed much stock in the secretary's ideas about foreign policy. As historian Daniel Yergin quipped, "How seriously could others take a Secretary who seemed more concerned that messages to the President be typed on the State Department's special large-character typewriter than with the content of the messages. . . ?" Roosevelt probably picked Stettinius for just that reason. With "Big Brother Ed" at the helm at State, Roosevelt was even more firmly in charge of foreign policy than he was during Cordell Hull's tenure. In communicating Murray's concern, Stettinius only asked the president, "Do you approve backing up the British on this?"[13]

Roosevelt must have recognized that he had little understanding of the current situation in Iran. Certainly, he had no ready answers. Instead, he responded as he so often did in ambiguous situations; he stalled. To gain a clearer picture of the situation in Iran, he asked Ambassador Averell Harriman to stop in Tehran on his way back to Moscow. That choice cannot be attributed to circumstances alone. Roosevelt knew that Harriman would provide a report, not recommendations for a line of policy that as president he might find difficult to adopt. George Kennan once observed about the man he served under in Moscow that "he concentrated on what is indeed the central function of the diplomat: to serve as a sensitive, accurate, and intelligent channel of communications between one's own government and another one."[14]

That does not mean that Harriman did not hold definite views about the Soviet Union and its relations with its neighbors. He had long bridled under the string "of indignities and disagreeable incidents unrelated to political issues" to which the Soviets regularly subjected foreign diplomats. Nothing had done more to shake his hopes for postwar Soviet-American cooperation than Moscow's evident determination to snuff out any prospects of Polish independence. Just a few months before his mission to Tehran he had told Harry Hopkins, "Unless we take issue with the present policy there is every indication the Soviet Union will become a world bully wherever their interests are involved."[15] His apprehensions did not, however, lead him to argue, as George Kennan and others had, that more extreme steps like cutting off aid would force the Russians to cooperate more fully.

Sir Reader Bullard welcomed Harriman's visit as a sign that ineffective American diplomacy might finally end. Bullard had run out of patience with Leland Morris. He complained to the Foreign Office that "the fact that the State Department are so ill-informed about the situation here confirms my impression that the United States Ambassador, though honest, frank, and ready to help, is himself ill-informed as well as inert." Morris, as Bullard readily admitted, was not solely responsible for that state of affairs: "He complains of being left in the dark by the State Department, and I must admit I am sometimes better informed of their views through His Majesty's Embassy in Washington than he is direct."[16] Many American diplomats shared that view. George Kennan, for example, remarked that he sometimes learned more from Clark Kerr than he did directly from the State Department.

Such comments demonstrated that as of 1944 the United States did not have a foreign policy apparatus adequate to meet the responsibilities it had assumed during World War II. The problem was substantive as well as procedural. The Roosevelt administration often had more than one policy for a given country or region. As we have already seen, interagency disagreements often added a layer of confusion to policymaking. Trying to read the president's mind seldom yielded a clear sense of direction. So it was in this case in relation to Iran. Tensions simmered while the president looked for the reins in a situation that had little clarity and few possibilities for simple solutions.

By the time Harriman reached Tehran on 4 December 1944, the oil crisis had settled into an uneasy calm, and he used his brief stay to gather information. The shah soon learned that the arrival of an important American statesman did not translate into new commitments. When he pressed for increased material aid and diplomatic support, Harriman indicated only that the United States would stand by its Tehran Declaration pledges and keep the Soviet Union mindful of its treaty obligations. As their meeting ended, Harriman emphasized to the shah that Iran, not the United States, bore the primary responsibility for Soviet-Iranian relations.[17]

Harriman went from the Palace to the Russian Embassy compound, where he saw both Kavtaradze and Ambassador Maximov. The vice commissar remarked with feigned ingenuousness that "he was enjoying a vacation here that was doing him a lot of good." Perhaps, given the news he had to report to Stalin, he was speaking more truthfully than he intended. Maximov made no effort to conceal his outrage over the current status of the oil talks. He baldly confessed that he intended "to take aggressive measures to obtain Soviet objectives. . . ." What those measures might be, he did not say. Harriman sensed that Maximov had more than mineral rights and oil concessions on his agenda. His objectives might even include the overthrow of the present Iranian government. Maximov told him that since the Iranian government did not represent the people, the Soviet Embassy had an obligation to see that the popular will found political expression.[18]

Harriman concluded on the basis of his visit with Maximov and Kavtaradze that the shah had substantial reason to fear for the safety of his country. All the same he did not recommend any new policies for the United States. When he reached Moscow, he explained to Clark Kerr that his visit had not been intended to produce significant results, but only "as a minor hint to the Soviet government that he was keeping an eye on developments and as an opportunity to gain a better perspective on Soviet-Persian relations."[19]

British diplomats were startled that Harriman's visit produced such paltry results. For months they had urged Washington to see the dangers inherent in the Iranian situation. C. W. Baxter of the Foreign Office had warned Ambassador John Winant that Soviet oil policy, when viewed in combination with the opening of an embassy in Iraq, indicated that the Russians intended "to extend their influence throughout the Middle East." Wallace Murray, for one, had noticed the urgent tone that had surfaced in communications from the Foreign Office. He reminded his colleagues that "Sir Alexander Cadogan . . . is reported to have stated that while Great Britain will be prepared to give in to Russian demands to a very considerable extent in Eastern Europe and the Balkans, his government could not and would not yield in the vital area of Iran."[20]

The Foreign Office actively feared that the United States might desert them on Iran. Upon learning of Harriman's noncommittal response to the situation in Iran, R. M. Hankey remarked "that the Americans are not going to take a very firm line on this, in spite of their general anxieties." That observation led him to warn his colleagues to watch American attitudes closely: "We don't want them to rat on us or give us support so lukewarm as to show disagreement as they have done over Greece and Poland."[21] Hankey had not forgotten how the Americans had waffled on many issues in order to avoid controversy during the November elections. Nor did he have any illusions that the United States had the same stake in Iran as Great Britain did.

Because it had received no clear signals from the British and Americans, the Iranian government strove on its own to establish some autonomy in its dealing with the Russians. In the Majles, Mossadeq introduced a law that prevented any official from even discussing oil concessions with foreigners and the law made the Majles rather than the cabinet the arbiter of future oil policy. Mossadeq's maneuver had two important consequences. In effect, it ratified Saed's decision to postpone further oil negotiations until after the occupation ended, thus linking oil concessions to troop withdrawals, and it made the possibility of a secret deal that might betray Iran's national interest more remote.[22]

When Kavtaradze learned of the new law, he told Bayat that the Soviet government not only found it objectionable, but expected the Majles to amend it. Maximov even tried to persuade Ambassador Morris that the Soviet Union and the United States had been victimized by it, since the British already held a concession. In the meantime, Kavtaradze had decided to return to Moscow, but before leaving on 9 December he predicted that the Mossadeq law would damage Soviet-Iranian relations. And as if to underscore his presentiments, rumors flooded Tehran that Azerbaijan would soon declare its independence and apply for admission into the Soviet Union.[23]

Information about these mounting tensions persuaded President Roosevelt that he should raise the question of Iran with Stalin. The State Department, however, did not instruct Harriman to see the Marshal, as the president had asked, not because it opposed that step, but because it learned that while the mood in Tehran remained tense, Soviet authorities had taken no new actions that warranted any representations. An untimely approach to Stalin might only provoke him to take a harder line. The British Foreign Office also let matters slide until the middle of January 1945.[24]

President Roosevelt's sudden interest in Iranian affairs soon took an unexpected turn. At the Tehran Conference the president had proposed to Stalin a scheme for establishing an international trusteeship for the Trans-Iranian Railroad and for establishing a port on the Persian Gulf. At that time he had not mentioned the plan either to the State Department or to Churchill. Now, a full year later, the State Department learned about it for the first time when the president suggested that the plan he and Stalin had agreed upon might be profitably pursued. Roosevelt's bombshell caused a reaction that strained the conventions of bureaucratic blandness. Wallace Murray could barely conceal his shock. "Needless to say," he told his colleagues, "all of us and Mr. Bohlen are in complete agreement that it would be a great mistake to proceed along the lines suggested in the President's memorandum of December 8, 1944."[25] Murray feared that such an action would undermine the entire American diplomatic effort in Iran. Urged on by Murray, Secretary Stettinius sought a meeting with the president to persuade him to drop the idea.

Murray outlined his objections in the strongest terms. As if to avoid any appearance of the traditional, knee-jerk negativism associated with the State Department, he conceded that the trusteeship plan had positive features. It embodied the president's lofty idealism, it offered potential benefits to both Iran and the Soviet Union, and it might forestall future Soviet aggression. But none of those prospects struck Murray as substantial. Above all, he could see no way the United States could make such a plan palatable to the Iranians, who cherished both their sovereignty and the national railroad system that symbolized their hopes for modernization.

The British, he anticipated, would be just as strenuous in opposing the plan. They were no more likely to tolerate a Russian presence on the Persian Gulf now than they had been for the past century. What possible benefit could they realize from a Soviet naval threat to the British Empire's vital lines of communication in the region? Why would they welcome another major rival for economic hegemony? Murray pointed out that these were not merely the arguments of British imperialists, but also of those planners in the War Department who saw the continued strength of the British in the Middle East as vital to American postwar security. And to deliver the *coup de grace* he concluded, "The foregoing considerations might possibly be brushed aside, if there was any reason for confidence that the Soviets would participate in an international trusteeship on the high principles that the President has in mind."[26] For Murray, at least, the cold war in the Middle East was already underway. He did not share Roosevelt's conviction that the United States could reach useful accommodations with the Soviet Union. To him, the plan offered the Russians a road to a warm-water port and world conquest.

When Stettinius finally managed to see the president on 30 December 1944, Roosevelt indicated that he was not actively concerned about the idea at the moment, but that he thought it merited some further study. Even that proved too much for the department to accept. Officials there feared Roosevelt's penchant for turning an apparent whim into policy. Determined to kill the scheme once and for all, Acting Secretary Joseph Grew presented the State Department's objections as bluntly as possible. The plan, as Roosevelt conceived it, was simply unacceptable to the British and to the Iranians. "No matter how drawn up or proposed the plan would appear to Iran, and doubtless to the world, as a thinly disguised cover for power politics and old world imperialism," Grew insisted.[27] Although Roosevelt indicated that he wished to consider the matter further, the message had undoubtedly sunk in. He never again mentioned the idea of a trusteeship for Iran's railroad and port.

Since nothing came of the scheme, it is tempting to dismiss it as another of Roosevelt's trial balloons. Three considerations suggest that it requires more scrutiny. First, we must recall that Roosevelt claimed that he had actually proposed the scheme to Stalin and that the Soviet premier had accepted it in principle. That alone must have prepared Stalin to believe that the Americans had a tolerant attitude toward the extension of Soviet influence in Iran. In this way, Roosevelt had acknowledged the legitimacy of the Soviet Union's quest for security in the region.

One can certainly argue that the trusteeship plan to some degree encouraged the Soviet Union to press Iran for political, economic, and, if events had allowed, territorial concessions. Thus growing American opposition to Soviet initiatives during the last year of the war must have struck Stalin as a potentially ominous reversal of policy, and, perhaps, had led him to believe that he had been deceived, or possibly that the capitalists were revealing their true intentions, now that they no longer needed his support. Whatever Stalin concluded, there is every reason to believe that Roosevelt's gesture at Tehran complicated big power rivalries over Iran.

Equally significant was the timing of Roosevelt's attempt to revive his proposal. The president and his advisers were already preparing for the meeting at Yalta. Many of the discussions there would bear on the disposition of territory and political influence in the postwar world. Despite the Atlantic Charter and plans for an international security organization, Roosevelt was obviously willing to barter the territory and sovereignty of a nation like Iran in order to guarantee postwar big power cooperation. In doing so, Roosevelt acted with as much realism as cynicism. What he offered to give away he was in no position to protect. Neither the British nor the Americans could have prevented the Soviet Union from seizing the Iranian railroad, if Stalin had chosen to do so. The same realities prevented Churchill and Roosevelt from winning substantial concessions on Poland. Besides, the creation of an Iranian trade route might help to integrate the Soviet economy into the western system. And Roosevelt had never given any indication that he believed the United States had a substantial stake in Iran. Still, Roosevelt's casual disregard for Iranian sovereignty suggests that his commitment to a Wilsonian peace was more rhetorical than real.[28]

Finally, the revival of the trusteeship plan demonstrated once again the superficiality of Roosevelt's approach to Iranian-American relations. The president apparently regarded the Tehran Declaration as little more than a sop to Patrick Hurley and an innocuous gesture to improve the American image in the Middle East. He clearly did not share the concerns of the State Department and of the British that

Stalin intended to swallow Iran, which had for Roosevelt little of the importance he accorded to Saudi Arabia. He made far more of an effort to woo Ibn Saud than Reza Shah Pahlevi. Most likely, he believed that a concession to Stalin on what was to him a peripheral matter would help establish the basis for a lasting peace.

IRAN AND YALTA

By January of 1945 Prime Minister Churchill had concluded that Roosevelt did not adequately appreciate the potential problem Iran posed for the Big Three. He suggested that Iran should be on the agenda at Yalta. To dramatize his point, Churchill borrowed a phrase from one of Roosevelt's own comments on Iran: "This may be something of a test case. Persia is a country where we, yourselves, and the Russians are all involved. . . ." He included with this appeal a copy of a note from Moscow in which the Russians had spelled out their position on oil concessions. Indeed, it was the receipt of that note that triggered Churchill's approach to Roosevelt.[29]

The State Department had received a similar note in which Soviet Ambassador Gromyko described the Russian oil bid as an effort to benefit Iran and to promote friendly relations. Having at first led the Russians to expect a positive reaction, Saed had fallen under the sway of anti-Soviet reactionaries who persuaded him to deny the Russian bid. The Soviet press had expressed the official view that Saed was hostile to the Soviet Union and disloyal to Iran. Gromyko's government could no longer "overlook the unsympathetic attitude taken by the Americans with regard to Irano-Soviet negotiations regarding the oil concession." Nor could the Soviet government accept British and American suggestions that its actions constituted interference in Iran's internal affairs. Instead, Gromyko reiterated Kavtaradze's demand that the new petroleum law had to be rescinded or revised.[30]

After receiving the Russian and British notes, the State Department urged the president to discuss the Iranian question at Yalta, but without advance notice, which "would give the matter undue importance." The department agreed with Churchill that Iran constituted a "test case" with important implications for the postwar peace plans discussed at Dumbarton Oaks. Secretary Stettinius told the president that "Russia's continued and avowed dissatisfaction with the law arouses apprehensions which should be quieted."[31] Gromyko's note left no doubt that the Soviet government was aware of American and British concerns.

The Yalta conference disappointed American and British hopes for an understanding about Iran. Neither Churchill nor Roosevelt found an opportunity to discuss political tensions or oil concessions there. That forced Anthony Eden to assume the responsibility for raising those issues. Eden, in the hope of forestalling any move to divide Iran into spheres of influence, had proposed to Stettinius at the earlier conference at Malta that they push for the withdrawal of Allied troops as soon as the Persian corridor supply route was no longer needed. Stettinius readily agreed that it would be advantageous to remove the occupation forces as soon as possible. In broaching the matter during his talks with Stettinius and Molotov, Eden tied further negotiations on oil directly into his proposal for troop withdrawals. The Allies, he recommended, could publicly state their willingness to forego concession talks until after their troops had left Iran. Molotov refused to discuss these matters. He claimed that since the British had not previously raised the issue, he would have to give it lengthy study. In fact, all Molotov would say is that even though he did not understand why Iran had rejected the Soviet Union's concession bid, he was willing to let that matter drop.[32]

Even with support from Stettinius, Eden could not budge the obdurate Molotov. Several more frustrating rounds of talks left Stettinius eager to put Iran aside. But Eden was not prepared to give in so readily and with Churchill's blessing he approached Stalin directly. At the first mention of Iran, the marshal laughed. "You should never talk to Molotov about Iran," he remarked amiably. "Didn't you realize he had a resounding diplomatic defeat there? He is very sore with Iran." Did Stalin share his foreign commissar's chagrin? If so, he gave no direct indication of it beyond subjecting Molotov to that bit of humiliation. But Stalin could stonewall as well as his taciturn commissar. After Eden had explained his proposal for a joint troop withdrawal, Stalin said he would consider the idea. That was the last Eden heard of the matter, and Stalin never replied.[33]

As a result, the Yalta conference ended without any resolution of Allied controversies over Iran. No matter how large or how insignificant the topic was, Molotov thwarted each attempt to reach some understanding of it. Had he given any thought to the British proposal on troop withdrawals? No, he had nothing to add to his earlier statement. What did he think about a joint communiqué on Iran? Such a statement was inadvisable. Could the Allies simply state that they had discussed Iranian problems? Molotov objected to that idea too. Could they at least reaffirm the Tehran Declaration? No, he would not agree to that either. Thus the conference ended with a protocol of the meetings that failed to satisfy even the most minimal hopes of the Iranians, British, and Americans. "Mr. Eden, Mr. Stettinius, and Mr. Molotov exchanged views on the situation in Iran. It was agreed that this matter should be pursued through the diplomatic channel."[34]

THE TROOP WITHDRAWAL QUESTION

The failure of the Yalta conference would reverberate throughout the coming months. Events soon showed that Allied troop withdrawals would become another source of Big Three tensions over Iran. In January 1945 Russian occupation forces became involved in a labor dispute in the northern Caspian province of Mazanderan. According to reports from Col. Schwarzkopf, local gendarmes had clashed with striking workers from a government-operated textile mill. Russian troops then entered the plant, arrested the gendarmerie commander, and disarmed his troops. In response to that and to similar incidents, the OSS predicted that the Russians would block any attempt by the Iranian government or the American advisers to operate in the northern zone. Problems could be expected from the Kurds as well. "To keep the Kurds dissatisfied is a fundamental Russian policy," the OSS concluded. They might have added that it never took much effort to stir up Kurdish discontent.[35]

The State Department did not intervene in the Mazanderan incident, although the department was hardly uninterested. It supported Iran's protest and Acting Secretary Grew reminded Ambassador Morris that the Tripartite Treaty recognized Iran's right to maintain its internal security. Grew thought the Iranian government should persist, albeit in a "friendly and forthright manner," to advise the Soviet government of its need to move troops. But each time the Iranian government dispatched troops to a trouble spot, they ran into Soviet opposition. The Russians even refused to allow new troops to enter their zone. And no matter how loudly the Iranian government protested each instance of obstruction, the Soviets persisted in blocking all Iranian troop movements.[36]

The Iranians did not again raise the troop withdrawal question until the United Nations conference convened in May 1945. At the San Francisco meeting, Foreign Secretary Eden assured the Iranian representative that if the Russians proved cooperative, Britain would initiate a plan for step-by-step withdrawal. The Iranian government then sent notes to the Big Three requesting that the powers observe the

Tripartite Treaty. Iranian Foreign Minister Sephabodi assured the State Department that he had included the United States only to avoid inviting a Russian or British complaint that his action was prejudicial. Now, as in the past, the Russians ignored Iran's request.[37]

The British and Americans began to recognize that it was one thing to talk about immediate withdrawal, quite another to carry it out. A variety of political and economic circumstances complicated the removal of American and British forces from Iran. The British, for example, believed that they had to maintain a substantial garrison there to guard the Abadan refinery, a vital source of aviation fuel for the Pacific War. The Iranians themselves had asked the Americans to retain some railroad units to train local replacements. The State Department argued that a sudden evacuation would waste quantities of surplus equipment. The Joint Chiefs had already assigned one thousand troops to guard fixed installations until they could be dismantled. Other units were to stay on to operate the Abadan airfield. All those complications aside, the War Department simply did not have the necessary transportation to bring large numbers of troops home at once.[38]

Nonetheless the British and Americans did begin to evacuate Iran. The British decision to terminate supply operations as of 1 July 1945 made possible a gradual reduction of its forces. That policy however did not move the Soviets. As of June 1945 they had not indicated that any Russian troops would leave Iran in the near future. Even a Foreign Office request that the Russians agree to withdraw "*pari passu* and in stages before the final treaty date" had no evident impact on Soviet policy. Wallace Murray, who had recently become American ambassador to Iran, predicted that only the complete withdrawal of British and American forces would have an effect on the Russians. If anything, the signs from Iran indicated that the Soviet Union intended to establish a permanent position there. The Russians certainly made no attempt to allay American and British fears about their troops. A July editorial in *Pravda* calling for drastic internal reforms in Iran and criticizing the presence of reactionary forces in the Iranian government struck the Americans as a pretext for future Soviet interference.[39]

Matters became further complicated with the collapse of Prime Minister Bayat's cabinet and the appointment of the pro-British, royalist, and intensely reactionary Mohsen Sadr. As prime minister, Morteza Bayat had steadily alienated his conservative, prowestern supporters when he sought to oust Arthur Millspaugh. To reestablish parliamentary support, he made repeated overtures to leftists and pro-Soviet groups. In several instances he had appointed moderates to replace militant anticommunists. But a series of labor and electoral reforms eventually split his own National Union Party. Without a solid base, he could not withstand the constant attacks from his conservative critics. By late spring his cabinet had fallen. For six weeks various political factions struggled to find a suitable replacement.[40]

The choice of Mohsen Sadr, an ex-mulla, must have struck Moscow as a deliberate provocation. He quickly confirmed the Soviet's worst fears by appointing a cabinet that was both staunchly royalist and pro-British. His opponents on the left and center were so outraged that they boycotted the Majles for three months. Their absence prevented Sadr from winning a vote of confidence. At the same time his policies justified Soviet charges that Iran's government had fallen into the hands of reactionaries. *Pravda,* for example, had claimed that an Iranian Army awaited the departure of Soviet forces in order to seize power and establish a new dictatorship. In fact, Sadr's appointment of the aggressively anglophile General Hassan Arfa to head the general staff almost justified the charge. Arfa armed anti-Tudeh tribal minorities and eliminated leftist officers from the army. Wallace Murray told the State Department that he thought Sadr might have plans to abolish the Tudeh.

Russian diplomats were so hostile to Sadr that they refused to deal with him or his foreign minister.[41]

WASHINGTON IN TRANSITION

Iran was but one of a host of unsettled issues that faced Harry Truman after Franklin Roosevelt's death in April 1945. Historians have long debated whether or not Truman faithfully carried out his predecessor's policies, especially in relation to the Soviet Union. Since it was not at all clear what Roosevelt's policies were for Iran, it is particularly difficult to determine what impact Truman's succession to the presidency had on the direction of American policy there. Truman did quickly become far more concerned about Soviet pressures on Iran than Roosevelt had ever been. But comments Roosevelt made shortly before his death indicate that he planned to take a "tougher" line with Stalin; what that would have meant in Iran is impossible to say. We do know, at least, that Truman lacked Roosevelt's capacity for subtlety and evasion and that the new president's preference for a tough, active posture may have accelerated the pace at which Iran became a focal point of Soviet-American tensions.[42]

Perhaps more consequential than any deviation in policy between Truman and Roosevelt was the shift in how and by whom policy was made. Whereas Roosevelt had ignored many of the State Department's recommendations, Truman leaned heavily on the secretaries and undersecretaries, especially Joseph Grew and Dean Acheson. At first, he also relied heavily on Averell Harriman, Admiral William Leahy, and Secretary of War Henry Stimson to guide him into an office he had never been groomed to hold. None of those advisers had ever shared Roosevelt's and Hopkins's confidence that the United States and Soviet Union might establish a community of interests in the postwar world. Their views ranged from Harriman's belief that firmness might yield cooperation on some issues to Leahy's certainty that Roosevelt's decisions at Yalta had guaranteed Soviet domination of Europe and the inevitability of another world war.[43]

When Truman became president, Soviet-American relations were troubled and deteriorating, and during the first weeks he sat in the Oval Office, his advisers had a great opportunity to unburden themselves of concerns that Roosevelt had generally ignored or discounted. The arch-anticommunist Leahy prepared papers on Poland and on German troop surrenders in northern Italy. In them he emphasized the insulting tone Stalin had recently adopted. Harriman flew all the way from Moscow to warn Truman about the crisis he saw brewing in Eastern Europe. Arriving in Washington just ahead of Foreign Commissar Molotov, Harriman told the president that without a "vigilant, firm policy," the Soviet Union might overrun Europe. Harriman was by no means alone in his recommendation for greater firmness; most of Truman's advisers warned that without an immediate display of toughness both from him and from the United States, the war would still be won, but the peace would certainly be lost.[44]

Henry Stimson was one of the few people in Washington willing to concede that the Soviet Union's actions along its borders might be aimed at security, not conquest. That did not mean that Stimson proposed to give Stalin a free hand. Still, he had come to believe that the United States had to show signs of trust if the Americans expected the Soviet leader to trust them. And as an overseer of the Manhattan Project, Stimson understood more than most other advisers that the atomic age had introduced new uncertainties into postwar diplomacy.[45]

The situation in Iran suggested that Stimson's views of Soviet motivations and his proposal to pursue limited accommodations with the Soviets might have been the more credible. Certainly the British and the Americans had reason to believe that the activities of Soviet troops and political sympathizers indicated that Stalin might try to incorporate some of the northern provinces of Iran into the Soviet Union. But as the political ascension of Prime Minister Sadr demonstrated, Stalin had similar causes for alarm in that the British still maintained a powerful influence in Iran and would now have the additional support of the United States, with its greatly enhanced presence in the Persian Gulf region. The Soviets had certainly not forgotten that after World War I Persia became a staging area for their enemies. Iran could again become an Achilles heel, unless the Soviet Union could neutralize Anglo-American power.

Those potential fears did not much enter into the reckoning of those in the State Department who sought to establish Iran as a front-line barrier against postwar Soviet expansion. Circumstances allowed them ample opportunities to air their views. Truman eagerly sought the counsel of State Department undersecretaries like Grew and Acheson, who, since the secretaries were so often away at conferences, assumed major responsibilities for daily operations. Grew and Acheson in turn invited input from the geographic offices and from department experts like Wallace Murray before making policy recommendations to the president. The increased efficiency with which the department responded added to its growing influence.[46]

Secretary Stettinius had recognized that without internal reform the State Department could not now recapture its key role in foreign affairs. He had devoted his administrative talents to reorganizing, expanding, and improving the major geographic offices. As part of the reorganization, Stettinius had appointed Wallace Murray to head the expanded Office of Near Eastern and African Affairs (NEA). The greater American interest in that region had led to a rapid growth in the size of NEA and its functions. By 1945 it had a staff of over fifty people, compared to seven just four years earlier. Of all the countries under NEA's purview, Iran had always been one of Murray's great loves and most pressing concerns. As Stettinius began to share some of Murray's apprehensions about Soviet pressures in Iran, he came to see the need for a more able ambassador there. Appointing Murray to the post, he had found someone eager to alert Washington to every Soviet move.[47]

The man who replaced Murray as head of NEA was, if anything, more zealously anti-Soviet than he was. Loy Henderson had occupied himself with Soviet-American relations for much of his career. Early contacts with the revolutionary Soviet state had persuaded him that the Bolsheviks threatened the peace and stability of the world. Such prejudices led him to play a formative role in organizing the State Department's Soviet Service. A combination of strong convictions and deep personal loyalties made him a dominant figure in the group that included George Kennan, Charles Bohlen, and Elbridge Durbrow. This group held the undying conviction that diplomacy with the Soviet Union could be carried out only on the narrowest of grounds. Henderson's tour in Moscow during the 1930s had further entrenched his deep distrust of the Soviet government. He railed against those figures in the Roosevelt administration who seemed to him dangerously naive about the possibilities of Soviet-American cooperation. Substantial rumors suggested that he had been transferred out of the Eastern European Office in 1943 because of his hostility to the Soviet Union. His transfer landed him first in Iraq as ambassador before he returned to Washington to replace Murray as head of NEA.[48]

By 1945 NEA offered Henderson one of the most effective posts in the government from which to organize opposition to what he saw as postwar Soviet goals. When he became director, both Iran and Turkey were being pressured to make a variety of economic, political, and territorial concessions to the Soviets. In contrast to Eastern Europe, however, these were states in relation to which the United States had more capacity to affect the course of events. Since Henderson, like Murray, believed that the United States had vital national interests at stake throughout the eastern Mediterranean, he too advocated a more assertive American policy to bolster the flagging British position and to create effective barriers against Soviet expansion. Working together, Murray and Henderson would determine that Iran had far higher priority for the Truman administration than it had had for Franklin Roosevelt.

POTSDAM AND THE END OF THE WAR

The Potsdam Conference in July 1945 made all too clear the difficult task the new administration faced in enforcing the terms of either the Tripartite Treaty or the Tehran Declaration. Potsdam was not only the longest of the wartime conferences—two-and-one-half weeks—it was also the least productive. No substantial accords were reached on the most aggravating issue, Poland, nor on the most consequential topic that might have been discussed, the postwar international control of atomic energy. Soviet intransigence had scuttled any agreement on Poland. American determination to maintain a nuclear monopoly left atomic diplomacy as the unacknowledged specter haunting the conference. By the time Truman left Potsdam, he would be more convinced than ever of the need to halt Soviet expansion outside of Eastern Europe.[49]

As at Yalta, the British delegates took the initiative in discussions on Iran. Only the question of troop withdrawals was on the conference agenda. In private British and American delegates agreed that they were willing to talk about Middle Eastern oil concessions and about Soviet access to the Persian Gulf, but only if the Russians raised those issues. The British memorandum on Iran proposed the complete withdrawal of all foreign troops in three stages: (1) immediately from Tehran, (2) from the remainder of Iran except for the British garrison at Abadan and Russian forces in either the northeast or northwest zone, and (3) from those last areas.[50]

In his reply, Stalin insisted on a technically correct reading of the wartime treaties, rather than recognizing the spirit in which they were intended. Thus he asserted that the date for ending the occupation would be determined by the surrender of Japan, not Germany. That would give Russian occupation forces that much longer to influence internal Iranian politics. Stalin did at least make one token gesture when he agreed to carry out step one of the British proposal, the withdrawal of troops from Tehran. To a certain extent, Truman rather than Stalin had blunted the effect of the British initiative. He explained that the United States could not necessarily follow the suggested timetable. Although it was willing to remove its troops, it had quantities of supplies to protect. Stalin then forestalled any further discussions by declaring that he would have nothing more to say until he could study the matter further.[51]

The Soviets thus repeated the performance they gave at Yalta. Stalin did at least offer Truman and Prime Minister Clement Atlee a small glimmer of hope when he promised "that no action will be taken by us against Iran." But such a vaguely worded promise could only mean further trouble. It bound Stalin to practically nothing, yet gave the Americans and British reason to see the Soviet leader as that much more unprincipled each time Soviet occupation forces interfered in Iran's internal affairs. The mood at Potsdam and afterward was too frigid for such empty assurances not to have had an adverse effect on Allied relations. The delegates could only agree "that Allied troops should be withdrawn immediately from Tehran, and that further stages of the withdrawal of troops from Iran should be considered at the meeting of the Council of Foreign Ministers to be held in London in September 1945."[52] The Iranian government understood that the Allies' failure to deal seriously with troop withdrawals boded ill for the future.

Shortly after the Potsdam conference the war ended, and with victory came a need to reformulate American policy for Iran. In wartime, Congress might be willing to fund American troops delivering vital materials or it might extend aid to a country whose internal stability was strategically vital. But it was unlikely to continue to aid a country like Iran that had no significant constituency outside of the State Department and to a lesser degree the War Department and several international oil companies. Victory would also inevitably alter the Allies' thinking about their future interests in Iran.

To Loy Henderson fell the initial task of formulating some rationale for postwar American-Iranian relations. Henderson assumed that "the formulation of American policy toward Iran . . . will be governed in the future, as at present, primarily by the requirements of international security." As Jernegan and Murray had before him, he identified Soviet-British-American rivalries as the major obstacle to postwar security and to Allied solidarity. To meet that danger, he proposed two rather incongruous policies. On the one hand he proposed that the United States shift its assistance programs from unilateral to multilateral channels, operated by the Russians and British as well. The United States would also have to use its offices to reduce the factionalism and separatism that weakened the government's authority.[53]

Henderson recognized all the same that for a policy to be initiated and supported it had first and foremost to be rooted in national self-interest. There were tangible benefits for the United States in commerce, aviation rights, and of course oil in Iran, but the continued instability of the Iranian government along with the opposition of the British and the Soviets could prevent Americans from enjoying any of those opportunities. Private firms would be unwilling to risk capital in a country threatened from within and without. What then could the United States do to protect its interests? Henderson had some practical suggestions. The Allies could end their censorship, relinquish their control over Iran's internal communications, and evacuate their troops. These steps would help sustain Iranian sovereignty, and if that sovereignty came under threat from a third power, the United States should support Iran. Although Henderson referred vaguely to expansionist nations that might seek to exploit Iran's weakness, he obviously meant the Soviet Union, which he assumed had a "desire for access to the Persian Gulf." From that position Soviet hegemony would be virtually assured.[54]

Could the United States stabilize Iran so that it could become an effective barrier to Soviet expansion? The allure of new opportunities to promote both commercial and security interests seems to have blinded Henderson to the possible consequences that might flow from American efforts to tap resources that had once been exclusively within a Russian or British sphere of interest. Were Iranian oil, air rights, and commerce worth the increased danger of big power conflict? And what would it mean in the long run for the United States to rely on markets and resources that it could not adequately protect from either rival foreign powers or internal dissidents, whether from the left or the right?

State Department advocates of a *de facto* Iranian-American alliance never seriously considered the hidden dangers of such an alliance. Nor did they give much thought to the problems of projecting American influence in a region whose culture, history, and politics were virtually incomprehensible to all but a handful of Americans. It is true that by 1945 NEA included more Middle East experts. Harold Minor, George V. Allen, Gordon Merriam, and Edwin Wright all had wide personal or professional exposure to the region. The oil companies had also acquired far more sophistication in their understanding of the dynamics of the area. That did not mean, however, that the United States was equipped by experience or by commitment to solve the problems of Iran or the Middle East. Rather the United States had embarked on a major extension of the Monroe Doctrine in an area that would soon supersede the Balkans as the world's most explosive powderkeg.[55]

It is unfortunate that Henderson did not consider Henry Stimson's perspective on Soviet-American relations. Stimson had always let the realities of geopolitical power and spheres of influence shape his view of a stable international order. During the war he had grown increasingly discouraged by Ambassador Averell Harriman's insistence that Stalin had ambitions to extend the traditional Soviet sphere. He had mentioned those concerns to Anthony Eden when the two met in Washington in April 1945. After that talk Stimson had confided in his diary that "the one thing I could hang onto with any degree of hopefulness was the fact that Russia and the United States had always gotten along for a hundred and fifty years with Russia friendly and helpful. Our respective orbits do not clash geographically and I think on the whole we can probably keep out clashes in the future."[56]

Henderson's definition of American policy for Iran threatened the "one thing" Stimson had clung to. As long as Americans considered Iran in their sphere of interests, Soviet and American geographic orbits did clash. Walter Lippman had recently made the same observation. If the United States reached out for an ally in Roumania or Iran, that would be the same as the Russians reaching out for Mexico. Such a move would signal the coming of a troubled peace. Our later experiences with Cuba and more recently in Central America have made that point painfully clear. The Soviet influence in the Western hemisphere has never approximated the role Americans once played in Iran, yet several generations of American policymakers have expressed a blend of outrage and hysteria at what they view as a lurking communist menace in the Western Hemisphere. Both Iran and Cuba have become geopolitical arenas in which a miscalculation by either superpower poses a real danger of nuclear disaster. Was the American interest in Iran ever sufficient to warrant such a risk? Henderson never asked; he was concentrating instead on Soviet ambitions that he assumed would be the major problem of the postwar world.[57]

Henderson's approach to Iran was just one indication of the narrow ways in which many Americans defined both internationalism and national interest. A similarly narrow perspective influenced the decision in October 1945 to retain the U.S. military missions in Iran. No one in the State Department seemed to doubt that the missions should continue. The Iranian government had given the necessary assurances that it would cooperate to avoid a repetition of past conflicts. As a result, Secretary of State James Byrnes assured Secretary of War Robert Patterson that State had carefully weighed the advantages of continuing both military missions. "This favorable situation will, however, be subject to reassessment by this government, with the view to the withdrawal of the missions in the event their presence no longer serves American national interest," Byrnes told Patterson.[58]

Gone was any trace of the idealistic notion of helping Iran to help itself. Gone, too, was the idea that Iran constituted some form of "test case" for the Allies. The United States would assist Iran only insofar as that aid promoted the goals Americans had defined for themselves. Just how much did that idea differ from the motives that led the Soviet Union to interfere in Iran's internal affairs? Certainly, there was a categorical difference between American missions invited by the Iranian government and the obtrusive meddling of uninvited Soviet occupation forces. The United States never threatened Iranian sovereignty nor did it violate the letter or spirit of the Allies' wartime agreements. Still, each power pursued policies that played upon the insecurities of the other. It was impossible for both powers to achieve what each separately sought—a friendly government that would serve its interests in the region. And the American presence after the war had almost the same consequence as did Soviet pressures on the Iranian government. Both policies virtually guaranteed that Iran would become a center of cold war rivalry. The first Soviet-American showdown over Iran was not long in coming.

NOTES

1. Quoted in John Lewis Gaddis, *Russia, the Soviet Union, and the United States* (New York, 1978), p. 172. See also Milovan Djilas, *Conversations with Stalin* (New York, 1962), p. 114.
2. George Kennan, *Memoirs: 1925–1950* (Boston, 1967), p. 209.
3. Almost all historians acknowledge that judgments about Soviet views must be speculative or deductive. We simply do not have the evidence needed to reach substantive conclusions. For one good summary of Stalin's approach to postwar issues, see Adam Ulam, *The Rivals* (New York, 1971), pp. 3–27.
4. FO, 40188, E6908/189/34, 1168, Bullard to FO, 11/9/44. See also Abrahamian, *Iran Between Two Revolutions*, pp. 181–84.
5. Abrahamian, *Iran Between Two Revolutions*, pp. 199–212. See also SD 891.6363/11-544, 818, Morris to Sec. of State, 11/5/44. And FO 40188, E7093/189/34, Bullard to FO, 11/17/44.
6. Ibid., p. 212. See also FO, 40242, E7207/6058/34, 1241, minute by W H. Young, 11/25/44.
7. FO, 40242, E7207/6058/34, 1241, Bullard to FO, 11/25/44.
8. FO, 40242, E7115/6058/34, 3442, Sir A. Clark Kerr to FO, 11/18/44.
9. Ibid., Clark Kerr to FO, 11/18/44.
10. FR, 1944, 5, pp. 274–75, Kennan to Secretary of State, 11/20 and 11/22/44.
11. Public Records Ofice, London, CAB 65/48, Secretary's Standard File, 152nd. conclusion, 11/21/44.
12. SD 891.6363/11–2044, Murray to Stettinius, 11/20/44. Anyone familiar with Murray's former anglophobia must have been startled to hear him defend the British Empire. On the state of American public opinion toward the Soviet Union, see Ralph B. Levering, *American Opinion and the Russian Alliance, 1939–1945* (Chapel Hill, N.C., 1976), ch. 7.
13. PSF: Hon. Edward Stettinius, FDRL, President's worksheet, 11/21/44. See also Daniel Yergin, *Shattered Peace*, pp. 77–78.
14. Kennan, *Memoirs, 1925–1950*, p. 233.
15. Elie Abel and Averell Harriman, *Special Envoy*, pp. 328–29 and 344–45; Gaddis, *Russia, the Soviet Union, and the United States*, p. 163.
16. FO, 40242, E7244/6058/34, 1256, Bullard to FO, 11/25/44.
17. FR, 1944, 5, pp. 353–55, Harriman to Secretary of State, 12/11/44.
18. Ibid., pp. 354–55.
19. FO, 40243, E7838/6058/34, 3786, Clark Kerr to FO, 12/21/44.
20. FO, 40243, E/6058/34, Eden minute for Churchill, 11/29/44; FR, 1944, 5, p. 352, Winant to Secretary of State, 11/28/44; SD 891.6363/12–744, 10827, Winant to Secretary of State, 12/7/44; and also SD 891.6363/12–844, Murray memo for Stettinius, 12/8/44.
21. FO, 40243, E7838/6058/34, minute by R. M. Hankey to 3786, 12/29/44. On the Polish and Greek problems, see Dallek, *Franklin D. Roosevelt and Foreign Policy*, pp. 503–15.
22. Ramazani, *Iran's Foreign Policy*, pp. 231–32. FR, 1944, 5, p. 479, Morris to Secretary of State, 12/3/44. Morris noted that the law had teeth, since it carried with it a three- to eight-year jail term. See also ibid., pp. 479–80, Morris to Secretary of State, 12/5/44.
23. FR, 1944, 5. p. 481, Morris to Secretary of State, 12/6/44. On the rumors circulating in Iran, see FO, 40189, E7805/189/34, 20, Bullard to Consuls, 12/15/44.
24. FR, 1944, 5, p. 483, FDR to Stettinius, 12/8/44. Ibid., p. 483, Morris to Sec. of State, 12/8/44; and ibid., p. 485, Stettinius to FDR, 12/18/44.
25. Ibid., p. 483, FDR to Stettinius, 12/8/44. See also ibid., pp. 525–26, and p. 526n. for

further comment on the president's trusteeship proposal. Ibid., p. 484, Murray to Stettinius, 12/11/44; and p. 485, Stettinius to FDR, 12/18/44.

26. Ibid., pp. 485–86, Murray to Secretary of State, 12/19/44.

27. FR, 1945, 8, pp. 523–24, Stettinius to Murray, 1/2/45; pp. 524–25, Grew to FDR, 1/11/45; and p. 524n.

28. Yergin, *Shattered Peace*, pp. 42–63. Yergin offers a shrewd assessment of Roosevelt's balancing between Wilsonian rhetoric in his public addresses and his balance of power accommodations in his approach to Soviet-American relations.

29. FR, 1945, *The Conferences at Malta and Yalta*, pp. 336–37, Churchill to Roosevelt, 1/15/45.

30. Ibid., pp. 334–36, Gromyko to Secretary of State, 12/28/44.

31. Ibid., pp. 338–39, Stettinius to FDR, 1/17/45. Filing notations indicate that Roosevelt did not read Stettinius' note until after he returned from Yalta. Had he read it earlier, it is doubtful he would have given Iran a higher priority. His agenda for the conference included such pressing matters as a pledge from Stalin to enter the Pacific war, an improved understanding on the postwar government for Poland, a policy for liberated Europe, and agreements on Germany. Ibid., p. 338n. On the Yalta agenda, see Dallek, *Franklin Roosevelt and American Foreign Policy*, pp. 506–8.

32. FR, 1945, *Malta and Yalta*, pp. 342–43, "Briefing Book Paper," memorandum concerning Iran, 1/6/45. Edward Stettinius, *Roosevelt and the Russians* (Garden City, NY, 1959), pp. 65–66, and FO, 40177, E1114/94/34, memorandum, 2/17/45. Several historians have debated the context in which the United States entered into discussions about Iran at Yalta. See, for example, Kuniholm, *The Origins of the Cold War in the Near East*, p. 214 and 214n, and Diane Shaver Clemens, *Yalta* (New York, 1970), pp. 245–46. The essence of their argument concerns whether or not American policy toward Iran involved a double standard. Kuniholm rejects Clemens's idea that the United States dominated Iran economically or that it had established a virtual protectorate there, an idea Clemens undoubtedly derived from Kolko. In that I must agree with Kuniholm. Clemens's discussion is too simplistic and formulaic. It describes American policy according to a revisionist equation without a close look at actual circumstances. But Clemens, like Kolko, had a better sense of the consequences of the new American role in Iran than Kuniholm would acknowledge. The State Department was trying to impose what in essence was a double standard—a policy under which the expansion of American interests would reduce Soviet influence. The differences were far more than "perceptual," as Kuniholm suggests. The State Department was attempting like the British to establish a security perimeter that would block Soviet expansion toward the Persian Gulf—the one-time British "lake" soon to become an arena for massive American economic penetration and a vital regional security center. See also FR, 1945, *Malta and Yalta*, pp. 738–40, Meeting of Foreign Ministers, 2/8/45.

33. Ibid., p. 877, Meeting of Foreign Ministers, 2/10/45; Anthony Eden, *The Reckoning: The Memoirs of Anthony Eden*, 2 vols. (Boston, 1965), 2: 595–96.

34. FR, 1945, *Malta and Yalta*, pp. 819–20 and 877, and p. 982, Protocol of Proceedings, 2/11/45.

35. FR, 1945, 8, p. 360, Morris to Secretary of State, 1/4/45. See also MMRB, OSS Iran File, L51795, 1/5/45. The parallel in reporting between Schwarzkopf and the OSS sources offers circumstantial support to the Mosley claim that Schwarzkopf did establish the CIA network for Iran.

36. FR, 1945, 8, pp. 363–64, Grew to Morris, 1/4/45; ibid., pp. 365–67.

37. Ibid., pp. 369–70, memorandum by U. S. Delegate to UNO, 5/10/45; ibid., p. 370, Morris to Secretary of State, 5/10/45; ibid., p. 371, Ward to Secretary of State, 5/21/45.

38. Ibid., pp. 372–77. See also Vail Motter, *The Persian Corridor*, ch. 19.

39. FR, 1945, 8, pp. 377–78, British Embassy to SD, 6/3/45; ibid., pp. 380–81, memorandum by H. B. Minor, 6/18/45. Ibid., p. 387n., Murray to Sec. of State, 7/14/45; ibid., p. 388, Murray to Sec.of State, 7/16/45; see also *New York Times*, 7/10/45.

40. Abrahamian, *Iran Between Two Revolutions*, pp. 213–15.

41. Ibid., pp. 215–17. See also FR, 1945, 8, p. 388 and p. 417, both Murray to Sec. of State.

42. On Roosevelt's changing attitudes, see Gaddis, *Russia, the Soviet Union,and the United States*, p. 167; Dallek, *Franklin Roosevelt and American Foreign Policy*, pp. 521–28;

Yergin, *Shattered Peace,* pp. 42–68; and Walter LeFeber, *America, Russia, and the Cold War,* 4th ed. (New York, 1980), pp. 13–17.

43. Gaddis, *Russia, the Soviet Union, and the United States,* pp. 169ff.; Yergin, *Shattered Peace,* pp. 69–80. See also John Lewis Gaddis, *The United States and the Origins of the Cold War* (New York, 1972), pp. 206–15.

44. Yergin, *Shattered Peace,* pp. 74–77. See also Harriman and Abel, *Special Envoy,* pp. 447–62.

45. Stimson Diaries, 4/16/45, 4/26/45, and 5/10/45. See also Yergin, *Shattered Peace,* pp. 80–82; Martin Sherwin, *A World Destroyed* (New York, 1975), pp.160–64; and E. E. Morison, *Turmoil and Tradition* (New York, 1964), pp. 529–33.

46. On the reorganization, see Kuniholm, *Origins of the Cold War in the Near East,* pp. 234–37; and Yergin, *Shattered Peace,* pp. 77–78.

47. Most of this information came from an interview with Eugene Rostow, who admitted that his own relations with Murray were not always without friction.

48. Yergin, *Shattered Peace,* pp. 29–42. Interview with Loy Henderson, 2/72; and Kuniholm, *Origins of the Cold War in the Near East,* pp. 237–45. I cannot claim to share Kuniholm's sense that Henderson had a constructive influence on American policy. His anti-Soviet attitudes helped shape the inflexible assumptions that undergirded the emerging cold war consensus. Henderson was too much of an ideologue to seek some basis for Soviet-American accommodation. On the rumor about his transfer from the Eastern European desk to Iraq, see James Forrestal Papers, Princeton University Library, Office of CNO to Captain Smedberg, 2/26/46. Henderson himself acknowledges that his attitudes probably had accounted in part for his transfer. See also Yergin, *Shattered Peace,* p. 39.

49. John Lewis Gaddis, *The United States and the Origins of the Cold War,* pp. 236–54; Sherwin, *A World Destroyed,* pp. 221–28.

50. FR, 1945, Conference at Potsdam, 1:191, Staff Committee Paper, 6/22/45; ibid., p. 159, Grew to Truman, 5/30/45; ibid., 2:1391–92, 1330, Proposal by British Delegation, 7/21/45.

51. Ibid., 1:309, Seventh Plenary Meeting, 7/23/45.

52. Ibid., p. 310, Seventh Plenary Meeting, 7/23/45; ibid., 2:1496, Protocol of Proceedings, 8/1/45. On the Iranian reaction, see FR, 1945, 8, p. 389, Murray to Sec. of State, 8/3/45; and ibid., p. 390, memorandum by H. B. Minor, 8/7/45.

53. FR, 1945, 8, pp. 393–99, memorandum by Henderson, 8/23/45.

54. Ibid., pp. 393–400.

55. Loy Henderson, "Foreign Policies: Their Formulation and Enforcement," Department of State, *Bulletin,* vol. 15, 9/29/46. See also Kuniholm, *The Origins of the Cold War in the Near East,* pp. 241–44. Kuniholm seems to suggest that greater familiarity with the Near East produced better policy. I believe that many of these men wore ideological and cultural blinders. Policy may have been based on less superficial ideas, but it is not clear that many of these individuals understood Iran in any depth.

56. Stimson Diaries, v. 51, 4/16/45. See also Morison, *Turmoil and Tradition,* pp. 508–34; Yergin, *Shattered Peace* pp. 80–82. For Lippman's analysis, see Walter Lippman, *U.S. War Aims* (Boston, 1944) pp. 136–37.

57. On the problem of Central America, see LaFeber, *Inevitable Revolutions,* pp. 110ff.

58. FR, 1945, 8, pp. 534–36, Byrnes to Patterson, 10/17/45.

9 Cold War Crisis in Iran

In the confusion that followed World War II, American policymakers debated whether it was best to seek cooperation or confrontation with the Russians. The legacy of Franklin Roosevelt's efforts to build bridges of cooperation warred with the State Department's conviction that the Soviets could not be trusted. Caught in the middle were President Truman and his politically facile Secretary of State James Byrnes. At different times they tried both approaches. But neither way seemed to resolve any of the disagreements that threatened to disrupt the peace. Not surprisingly the most troublesome issues involved the areas that bordered the Soviet Union. The Balkan states, Poland, Manchuria, Japan, Turkey, Korea, and Iran all provoked angry disputes between the Soviets and their increasingly hostile Anglo-American allies.

Gradually a consensus emerged that would harden into an American cold war ideology. By the spring of 1946 American policymakers had concluded that toughness was the only language the Soviets understood. So too they determined that it did not pay to seek meaningful accommodations with them. The Russians proved intractable on almost every issue, while the swelling fever of domestic anticommunist and anti-Soviet politics narrowed the grounds on which the Truman administration found it safe to negotiate. Compromise became stigmatized as appeasement. To most American observers the Soviet Union seemed bent on conquest on a global scale. Only determined American opposition could save "free world" institutions from the communist menace. That lesson would be clearly spelled out for the Truman administration in the Soviet-American confrontation over Iran.[1]

No one could argue persuasively that the cold war began over Iran. Still, Iran did have a special importance in the postwar rivalry between the Soviet Union and the United States. Events there from the fall of 1945 through the spring of 1946 entrenched the suspicions of those Americans who feared that the Soviet Union had embarked on a plan of world domination. In addition, the United States did not confront a *fait accompli* in Iran, as it did in most of Eastern Europe, and American policymakers came to believe that in this case they had learned strategies for successfully containing what they saw as Stalin's expansionist ambitions.[2]

In many ways Iran was a special case among occupied countries at the end of the war. It had remained neutral early in the war and then had supported the Allied cause. The Tehran Declaration acknowledged the Iranians' contribution to the war effort. As a result, the Soviet Union's pressures on Iran for territorial, political, or economic concessions seemed a particularly indefensible violation of wartime agreements. Iran became for American policymakers a clear-cut case spelling out their most profound grievances against the Soviet communist regime. What is most striking about American policy after 1945 is that assumptions adopted in this transitional period changed little, even when events did not bear out predictions about Soviet ambitions in Iran. As the Soviet Union's influence steadily weakened, American cold war rhetoric hardened.

The timing of the crisis over Iran gave events there a special importance to American policymakers. They were able to apply concepts such as the domino theory that became standard tools of cold war analysis. If Iran toppled, they assumed that the entire Middle East would fall into Soviet hands, followed by India and the Southeast Asian subcontinent. And the behavior of the Tudeh Party and other leftist factions seemed proof that subversion would be an instrument of Soviet conquest. Ethnic separatism would add to the demoralization of the government as its subservience to the Kremlin grew. In response, the Americans, like the British before them, came to see an independent and stable Iran as a vital barrier to Soviet conquest of American geopolitcal resources in the Middle East. Thus the *de facto* Iranian-American alliance became a key link in the containment perimeter the United States sought to establish around the Soviet Union. American "defense in depth" would begin on the Soviet-Iranian border.[3]

In the fall of 1945 the Russians had two major instruments with which to pressure Iran—their occupation forces and dissident ethnic groups in the provinces under their control. For the Iranians such big power threats had long been a fact of political life, but the danger they faced from the Soviet Union in 1945 was greater than ever before. To secure their independence and territorial integrity they had to end Soviet interference in the occupation zone and arrange for the withdrawal of Soviet troops. The British did not promise to abet the Iranians greatly in obtaining these ends. In fact many Iranian leaders feared that the British would be content to reinstate a sphere-of-influence agreement comparable to that of 1907. In reality the British were as determined as the Americans to see the Russians out of Iran. Weakness, not imperial ambitions, prevented them from playing a more effective role. Still, the sometimes singleminded determination to maintain the AIOC concession undermined the British position in Iran. Nationalists viewed the British presence with the same jaundiced eye they cast on the Soviets.[4]

THE EVE OF CRISIS

As World War II came to a close, American policymakers offered three explanations for Soviet pressures on Iran. The most widely held theory assumed that Stalin wished to fulfill the tsar's ambition to have a warm-water port on the Persian Gulf. Patrick Hurley had embraced that idea and so apparently had Franklin Roosevelt when he proposed the trusteeship for the Trans-Iranian railroad. In that light his scheme might be defended as an attempt to ward off a more agressive Soviet effort to achieve that goal. George Kennan's observation in November 1944 that the Russians seemed preoccupied with the goals of tsarist diplomacy was consistent with the warm-water port idea.[5]

Some members of the State Department believed the Russians primarily sought oil. Charles Raynor, who succeeded Max Thornburg as petroleum adviser, thought that the Soviet Union faced a severe postwar oil shortage. Northern Iranian oil fields with close proximity to established transportation facilities at Baku could remedy the shortfall. Continued Russian pressures to reopen concession negotiations supported Raynor's view, even though most British, Iranian, and American observers remained convinced that any concession would be a front for political operations. During the fall of 1945 Ambassador Murray reported that despite the Iranian decision to postpone concession talks until after the occupation ended, the Soviets were drilling exploratory wells in their zone.[6]

Still other Americans linked Soviet behavior to a preoccupation with national security. Wallace Murray commented that "the ultimate Russian objectives may include access to the Persian Gulf and penetration into other regions of the Near East, but present aims are probably limited to the maintenance of a buffer zone in Iran as protection against attack from the south." During the war the Director of Military Intelligence had similarly concluded that the Soviets sought a *cordon sanitaire* and political control in the south. That idea, too, was consistent with Kennan's view of the Russian obsession with traditional tsarist ambitions.[7]

Policymakers often used concepts like "inevitable," "unlimited," or inexorable" to describe Stalin's expansionist ambitions, but the three assumed Soviet goals in Iran—a warm-water port, oil, and national security—were finite in scope. If Stalin sought any or all of those objectives, some room for negotiation still existed. Even Loy Henderson conceded that the Soviet Union had the right to seek an oil concession so long as it did not infringe upon Iran's sovereignty. And he agreed that many of the complaints made by ethnic separatists had substance beyond the apparent effort of the Soviets to stir discontent.[8]

The problem in the fall of 1945 perhaps lay principally in the reality that, in contrast to 1943 when Jernegan wrote his memorandum, the Allies now had more causes for conflict than for cooperation. Each Soviet goal threatened some actual or potential Anglo-American interest. A situation that fulfilled Stalin's definition of national security would most likely exclude his former allies from the region. His kind of "friendly" government in Tehran would undoubtedly seek to cancel or amend existing concession agreements. The Soviet Navy operating in the Persian Gulf would undermine the value of Western strategic oil reserves.

Conversely the American determination to develop commercial relations, aviation rights, and above all oil concessions would establish a dangerous foreign rival on Stalin's Transcaucasian doorstep. Facilities for commercial aviation could easily become bases for strategic bombers. Greater trade with the United States would strengthen political allegiances as well. And the flow of Persian Gulf oil to the west could only enhance American economic and military superiority. Great Britain was too committed to the United States, its imperialism too much on the wane, and its economy too weakened by the war to give the Soviets and Americans a common rival, as Germany once had. Even the discontent of Iranian ethnic minorities could threaten the Soviets. If unchecked by a Russian presence, it might easily spill over into the restive minorities that populated the border Soviet republics. No factor existed to ease the friction over Iran that had increased steadily since the oil concession crisis of 1944. As difficult as these relations were, they promised only to become worse.

In September 1945 the questions of troop withdrawals and Soviet interference in Azerbaijan divided the Allies. Since the Yalta conference, the two sides had been unable to agree on the terms or timetable for removing their occupation forces. That problem added to the discomfort Anglo-American diplomats felt over the exercise of Soviet influence in Azerbaijan. Throughout the war they had anticipated some Soviet attempt to detach Azerbaijan in order to create an autonomous state within a diminished Iran or to incorporate it into the Soviet Union. The continued presence of Soviet troops there increased the likelihood that, at the very least, Azeri separatism would flourish.

The Azeris harbored substantial grievances against the Tehran government. Reza Khan's efforts to centralize authority had diminished Azerbaijan's economic and political strength. The requirement that schools use Farsi rather than the Turkic Azeri dialect came to symbolize provincial alienation. The demise of Reza Shah created an opportunity for ethnic and tribal factions to assert their autonomy. Under the occupation, the Soviets were able to infiltrate and manipulate these provincial movements. Besides the Azeris, the traditionally discontented Kurds promised to threaten the unity of the Iranian state.[9]

News of the creation of the Democratic Party of Azerbaijan confirmed the fears of both Iranian leaders and Anglo-American diplomats. Ja'far Pishevari, who organized the Democrats, had long been associated with communism, the Soviet Union, and the Tudeh Party. A Turkish-speaking Azeri, Pishevari had been born in Tabriz before moving to Russian Azerbaijan in 1905 at the age of twelve. After World War I he had played a leading role in organizing Iran's first communist party group and he served in the government of the short-lived Soviet Socialist Republic of Gilan (1919–1920). When the movement collapsed, he fled to the Soviet Union. Time served in Reza Shah's prisons further embittered him against the Tehran government. Upon his release, he once again became active as a publisher and a member of the Tudeh Party.

In 1943 Pishevari was one of five Tudeh Party representatives from the north elected to the fourteenth Majles. When the Majles refused to accept their credentials, Pishevari returned to Tabriz, where by September 1945 he had established his Democratic Party. American observers incorrectly assumed that the new party and Tudeh were indistinguishable, when in reality the two groups had significant differences. Western-educated, Farsi-speaking, Marxist intellectuals dominated the Tudeh Party. Azeri patriots, like Pishevari, whose Bolshevik views had roots in the politics of the Caucasus region, led the new regional party. To emphasize their revolutionary intent, they had purposely adopted the name of their 1920 party.[10]

The Democrats stressed their own unique national identity and their profound grievances against the ruling political cliques. In announcing his party, Pishevari issued three major demands: Azeri would be the official language in schools and government offices; tax revenues would be used for regional development; and regional assemblies would be established as the constitution required. The almost simultaneous announcement by the newly formed Democratic Party of Kurdistan, espousing parallel goals and demands, underscored the seriousness of the Azerbaijan movement. And Moscow's hand seemed all too evident behind the scenes. George Kennan informed the State Department that the new parties had received wide coverage in the Soviet press. Wallace Murray indicated that the Russians had also revived their oil concession bid. Iran might soon lose two major provinces.[11]

Russian threats forced the Iranians to behave in a way one British diplomat described as "slippery and soft." When Azeri dissidents provoked incidents requiring some response from government forces, the Soviet commanders would not allow the gendarmes to perform their duties. Col. Schwarzkopf suggested that Prime Minister Sadr order their removal, since he did not want the evidence of their impotence to undermine his reform efforts. Sadr rejected the proposal. His government had no intention of yielding "supinely" to the Russians, he insisted. On the other hand, he would not resist the Russians in any way. The prime minister either chose to ignore the fact or actually did not realize that Soviet hostility to him and his cabinet was the most serious obstacle to improved Irano-Soviet relations. Instead, as it had since 1942, the Iranian government urged the United States to press for the earliest possible withdrawal of Soviet troops and to oppose any aggression. To ensure the best possible communications with Washington, the shah sent his most trusted adviser, Court Minister Hoseyn Ala, as ambassador.[12]

The London Foreign Ministers Conference proved to be one more in a string of frustrating encounters over Iran. A week before the meeting Iran's foreign minister had reminded the three powers that he had as yet received no reply to a note requesting the Allies to establish a final date for evacuating their troops. In response, Britain's new Foreign Secretary, Ernest Bevin, asked Molotov to confirm that the first phase would be completed by 15 December and by 2 March 1946 the Russians would leave Azerbaijan; at the same time the British would move out of the Abadan area. Molotov saw no need to discuss these troop withdrawals since the terms had been established under the 1942 Tripartite Treaty. To that Bevin replied that he was pleased that 2 March was agreeable. Molotov repeated his view that the matter was covered by prior treaty, but then added, "I would like you to keep in mind that the Soviet government attach exceptional importance to obligations undertaken." At that point the three men removed the question of troop withdrawal from their agenda.[13]

Had or had not Molotov actually committed the Soviet Union to a final date? Bevin and Byrnes seemed to think that he had. And in the past the Soviets had followed the letter of their formal agreements quite literally. Problems arose more frequently about "understandings" than about treaties. Molotov, as it turns out, had an ace up his sleeve that the Soviets would later play. They had always argued that two separate treaties governed their relations with Iran—the 1942 Tripartite Treaty and the 1921 treaty negotiated by Theodore Rothstein. Molotov and other Soviet officials would claim that article 6 of the 1921 treaty gave the Soviet Union the right to have troops in Iran, whereas the evidence demonstrated that the article applied to cases involving potential armed aggression. Byrnes and Bevin did not believe that such a threat existed in 1945. Yet as if to underscore Molotov's good intentions, Ambassador Maximov announced the end of Soviet censorship and the final evacuation of forces from Tehran.[14]

Nothing that happened in London or Tehran eased Loy Henderson's pessimism about Iran's future. He had no doubt that the Soviets planned to fan Azeri separatist discontent in order to annex the province and to spread Soviet influence throughout Iran. The United States, Henderson realized, had almost no means to counter such a Russian move. All the efforts during the war had failed to furnish the State Department with adequate instruments to affect the course of events. His only remedy was to remove all American troops immediately, even if that entailed a substantial loss of property. Once American troops had gone, the United States could press the British and the Russians to follow suit. Acting Secretary of State Dean Acheson recognized the weakness that Henderson's proposal revealed. "I agree [that the troops should be withdrawn]," Acheson said, "but don't see where it gets us."[15]

The example of Eastern Europe aggravated the State Department's anxieties over Iran. Wallace Murray drew a parallel between the situation he observed in Tehran and the recent experience of Rumania. Sooner or later the Russians would impose a government similar to the Groza regime. With that accomplished, they could realize what Murray assumed was their actual goal—a Persian Gulf port. The ambassador did not deny that British meddling had also added to Iran's factionalism. But the positive attitude toward Great Britain he had acquired a year earlier led him to excuse British interference as "defensive." By contrast he treated Soviet intervention as offensive, believing that only in the short run would the Russians be content to build their influence in the north and maintain Iran as a buffer state. Eventually they would pull the entire country into their orbit as they had done in most of Eastern Europe.[16]

Murray worried especially about Iran, because the creation of the Democratic Party of Azerbaijan lent itself so readily to Soviet purposes. Should the Tehran government ban the Tudeh Party, the Democrats could replace them. Their regional appeal would also abet the Russians' attempts to weaken the central government and to engineer the secession of key northern provinces. No matter how much the leaders of both parties might proclaim their Iranian roots, Murray had no doubt that pro-Soviet puppets and communist flunkeys were in control. The venality of the Iranian ruling class only made matters worse. Iran's leaders had neither the will nor desire to attack the "deplorable" social, political, and economic conditions that fostered discontent.[17]

From Moscow, George Kennan supported Murray's conviction that the Soviet threat to Iran was not an isolated case nor merely Moscow's attempt to secure a volatile border area:

> Azerbaijan party appears to conform to the nationality pattern previously observed in Bessarabia, Ruthenia, and Eastern Poland and currently evident with respect to Sinkiang and Turkish Armenia. As in other areas, Soviet fissionist technique seems based on racial affinities transcending the Soviet border.[18]

Kennan argued that by adopting that approach, the Soviets could claim to respect the Iranian government's authority, while simultaneously working to establish an autonomous provincial state.

By the time he sent that message Kennan had formed the views that he would elaborate soon after in his well-known "Long Telegram" of February 1946 and the "Mr. X" article he published one year later in *Foreign Affairs*. None of those views were new. As Daniel Yergin has persuasively argued, most of Kennan's ideas from 1945 were based on the Riga Axioms. It was timing and circumstance that gave Kennan's ideas so much impact in late 1945 and after. The events of the fall of 1945 seemed to discredit those who still thought accommodation with the Soviets remained a possibility. Kennan wove a string of Soviet initiatives into a comprehensive pattern of expansion. He confirmed for ardent anticommunists their belief that Soviet ambitions had no bounds. The Soviet leaders had launched a "patient but deadly struggle for total destruction of rival power, never in compacts and compromises with it." Kennan wanted Americans to see that in places like Azerbaijan the United States was essentially at war. Victory in Iran or elsewhere would not placate the "traditional and instinctive Russian sense of insecurity." Soviet leaders would not view their power as secure until the United States and its system had been destroyed.[19]

Kennan's analysis implied that negotiations with the Russians must give way to political resolve undergirded by military strength. But events in Iran would show that Kennan and those who applied his ideas had exaggerated the scope of the Soviet threat. As historian Firuz Kazemzadeh observed, "The Soviet Union had as its ultimate goal a Persian government controlled from Moscow, but has never been prepared for major political sacrifices, let alone war, in pursuit of this goal."[20]

Kazemzadeh's appraisal is the more persuasive, because it recognizes, as Kennan later came to argue, that the Soviet leaders were political realists, not fanatic, pathological ideologues. Kennan correctly saw that the Soviet strategy in Azerbaijan was evident elsewhere. And there seems no doubt that the Soviets wanted to bring at least parts of Iran into their orbit. All the same Kennan did not so clearly explain at the time his underlying belief that economic and political measures could contain the immediate Soviet threat.

The Iranian situation suggests too that by late 1945 a new American doctrine of national security explained in part the fear of Soviet intentions. Wallace Murray, for example, did not advocate American opposition to Soviet initiatives in Iran merely in order to contain Russian or communist expansion. Murray believed that Great Britain and the United States had vital interests to protect. The British faced a threat to their Iranian oil fields, to their lines of communication within the empire, and to India. The United States had a less tangible but no less significant stake in commerce with Iran and in airline routes. Soviet domination would exclude the United States. Worse yet, Soviet control over Iran or its government would preclude an American oil concession there, while endangering rich American fields in Kuwait, Bahrain, and Saudi Arabia. Thus Murray defined a system of "defense in depth" that extended the American security perimeter into the Middle East. American expansion would not only decrease the Soviet defensive arena, but it would afford the United States access to commercial and natural resources upon which its future security might come to depend.[21]

Most Washington policymakers were less certain about Soviet goals than Kennan and Murray. With counsel divided, the State Department had at hand no effective means to counteract Soviet pressures on Iran. Loy Henderson once again pushed for the immediate completion of the American troop withdrawal. He feared that any delay might expose the British and Americans to charges that they, too, were violating Iran's sovereignty. Murray, like Acheson, saw that step as a futile gesture. Only if the United States was "prepared to make a real fight with the Russians to get them out of Iran quickly," would immediate withdrawal have any impact, he argued. Since the United States did not appear ready for such a bold step, he saw no reason to waste surplus American property.[22]

President Truman finally ended the debate with an order for the immediate evacuation of all remaining American forces. The British also removed their troops, though with grave reservations about Soviet willingness to respect the 2 March date. They did not believe the Russians had even fulfilled their promise to evacuate Tehran. Still, they wanted to preserve the Anglo-American unity that promised to be the most effective barrier to Soviet expansion into Iran.[23]

CRISIS IN AZERBAIJAN

On 19 November the State Department learned that the Democrats of Azerbaijan had made good their threat to seize power. According to rumors, Russian troops had distributed arms to the rebel forces. Armed uprisings swept the province. When local gendarmes sought to put down the rebels, Soviet troops forced them back to their barracks. Rebels had seized all main routes into Azerbaijan and cut communications. A 1,500-man force sent by the shah to put down the rebellion was intercepted at Qazvin by Russian troops, who threatened to fire if the Iranians did not halt. Any attempt to move farther would constitute an attack on the Soviet Union, the Russian commander announced.[24]

News sources soon indicated that the rebels had gained almost complete control of Azerbaijan. On 23 November Pishevari's Democratic Party announced its goals—cultural and political autonomy within the Iranian state. The Democrats would elect their own regional "National Congress" and establish an administrative apparatus. They assured the world of their peaceful intent, but left no doubt they would resort to force if threatened by Tehran. Wallace Murray's efforts to appraise the situation were stymied on two fronts. He could not arrange passes to send members of his staff into the north, and he could not obtain information from the Soviet Embassy, where the recall of Ambassador Maximov had left no one of consequence in charge. Nevertheless, Murray informed Washington that the Iranian government's charges of Soviet interference were undoubtedly correct.[25]

News of the Azerbaijan rebellion sent a war scare across the United States. Until 19 November few Americans had heard of Azerbaijan, much less assumed that the United States had any vital interests at stake there. Editorial writer Joseph Alsop was one of many writers who sounded an alarm. His kinship with Franklin Roosevelt and close ties to the political establishment gave his views special importance. Alsop feared that Americans did not appreciate the gravity of the crisis they now faced. "It is difficult here in this country to lie awake nights worrying about a bleak and distant nation with a backward population and a frowzily corrupt government," he told his readers. "Yet it must be recorded that official American observers interpret the Iranian crisis in a manner that is downright spine chilling."[26]

Alsop then proceeded to construct for the uninitiated the sort of domino theory that would become a central feature of American cold war thinking: At a minimum the Russians planned to seize control of the Iranian government. That would allow them to withdraw the AIOC concession and thereby deliver a crippling blow to the weak British economy. Once they had secured a foothold on the Persian Gulf, the Russians would exert pressure on Iran's neighbors. British prestige throughout the Middle and Far Eastern colonial areas would have suffered a mortal blow. Alsop essentially repeated scenarios drawn up by Murray and Henderson.[27]

In a second editorial Alsop extended his warning: If the Russians were successful in Azerbaijan, "the United Nations will be done to death at the moment of birth." Russian domination of Iran and Turkey would kill any hope for cooperation among the Big Three in making the United Nations viable. Its demise would destroy any remnant of Roosevelt's plans for a stable peace.[28]

As the Iranian crisis developed, a second cold war theme emerged. Patrick Hurley had never lost his determination to shape American policy for Iran. He was equally determined to revenge himself against all the striped-pants career diplomats who he believed had thwarted his ambitions to become both ambassador to Iran and commander of American forces in the Middle East. His dramatic resignation as ambassador to China in the fall of 1945 brought him back to the United States in time to grab headlines. He now charged publicly that subversives in the State Department had blocked his appointment.[29]

Hurley had little doubt who the "traitors" were. Eugene Rostow's earlier description of Hurley's proposals on Iran as "messianic globaloney" still rankled. Thus he concluded that Rostow and his superior, Dean Acheson, had set about subverting the policies that he and Roosevelt had adopted for Iran. On his way to China, he had stopped in Tehran, where after only a few hours visit he became convinced that treachery in the State Department had destroyed the effectiveness of American policy.[30]

Hurley's spectacular claims about subversives in the State Department were a symptom of the red-baiting mania that was soon sweeping the United States. The ambassador typified the arch-anticommunist who lived in a world of conspiratorial demons. Nevertheless, his charges led to hearings before the Senate Foreign Relations Committee, where he lashed out at those he saw as enemies. After one session, he even tried to assault Rostow, before startled bystanders restrained him. Though the idea might surprise those familiar with Rostow's reputation since the Vietnam War, he personified for conservatives the "fellow travelers" whose influence over American foreign policy had given Stalin a green light on his crusade for world conquest.[31]

Hurley had no specific evidence of any wrongdoing. To substantiate his charges that American policy for Iran had been undermined, he read excerpts from the Atlantic Charter and the Tehran Declaration. It was its style more than its content that made his attack significant. Critics of the Truman administration's foreign policy would often adopt both his tactics—broad, unsubstantiated charges levelled against enemies real or imagined—and his rhetoric—that communist sympathizers and subversives had undue influence on policy. This performance anticipated by several years the assault on the "China hands." Such attacks would eventually inhibit the department's ability to attract qualified people and to function as an effective policymaking organization.[32]

CONTAINING THE CRISIS

The State Department had its attention focused on the crisis in Azerbaijan, not on Hurley. The Russian-supported uprising signaled the failure of American efforts to prevent Iran from becoming a postwar trouble spot. Mismanagement of the current situation could lead, many in the department feared, to World War III. Now the United States had to find policies that would contain the Soviet Union, preserve Iran's independence, save the United Nations from a premature demise, and maintain American influence and prestige in the region and the world.

Once Wallace Murray had confirmed the role played by Soviet forces in recent events, Averell Harriman on 24 November delivered an American note protesting these Soviet actions as violations of the Tehran Declaration and the United Nations charter. Within the spirit of the declaration, the Soviets were obliged to withdraw their troops, the State Department asserted. Since the United States planned to have virtually all of its forces out of Iran by 1 January 1946, the department saw no reason why the British and the Russians could not do likewise. The note also reminded Molotov of the obligations that the Big Three had assumed as members of the United Nations Security Council. What were Iran and other small nations to think if the leaders in the new world organization failed to meet their obligations?[33]

Molotov's reply indicated that the Soviet Union had no desire to resolve the crisis, only to employ a smokescreen of legalisms while its Azerbaijani clients consolidated their recent gains. As always, Molotov stressed that the Soviet Union would follow the letter of its agreements. The Tehran Declaration had said nothing about the size of Soviet forces or the duration of their stay in Iran, he reminded the State Department. Then he played his ace: Those matters were covered not only under the Tripartite Treaty, but also under the Soviet-Iranian Treaty of 1921. Under its terms, Molotov could justify, at least to Soviet satisfaction, an indefinite period of occupation. He concluded that recent events had given his government cause not to remove its troops by 1 January, as the State Department urged.[34]

The Russian threat forced the British to confront the reality of their economic and military weakness. The United States would act as the senior partner in defining policy during the crisis. At the same time the British would do nothing that jeopardized the AIOC concession. "The rights which the British hold in Iran through its majority ownership in Anglo-Iranian Oil Company are the largest single element in the global British oil position and perhaps Britain's greatest single external asset," State Department Petroleum Adviser John Loftus wrote.[35] The British found themselves in a dilemma. Like the Americans, they wished to contain Soviet expansion. They too had protested the action of Soviet troops in the Azerbaijan uprising. But their own imperial position prevented them from adopting a forceful posture. The nationalist outpouring against Soviet actions in the north could just as easily turn against AIOC. Some American and Iranian officials saw British policy as so passive that they anticipated some attempt to revive the sphere-of-influence arrangement from 1907. Undoubtedly some British diplomats considered that the only way to preserve their interests in Iran. Sir Reader Bullard, for example, had so little confidence in the capacity of Iran's government that he did encourage the idea of provincial autonomy. Such a policy would give more power to pro-British authorities in the areas of AIOC's operations.

Great Britain did what it could to force the Soviets to evacuate Iran, but that was precious little. Bullard tried unsuccessfully to persuade Iranian officials to institute reforms and to hold provincial elections in the hope that such modest steps might at least eliminate the pretexts for the current Russian interference. By December, London had withdrawn all but five thousand of its own troops. And the British Foreign Office returned to tactics it had found effective during the crisis in the fall of 1944. Hopeful as always about the deterrent effect of world opinion, the British Embassy in Tehran presented Iran's case to both the local and international press. In an effort to allow the Soviets a graceful way to back down, Ambassador Clark Kerr's office suggested to the Soviet Foreign Office that perhaps the commander of Soviet forces had exceeded his authority. Certainly, Moscow would not wish to see its forces similarly involved in future violations of Iranian sovereignty. To maintain a unified Anglo-American posture, the British persuaded the State Department to send a comparable note attributing Soviet actions to the excess zeal of local officials. If the Russians wanted to save face, they could, as the State Department and Foreign Office hoped they would, blame recent events on their man in Tabriz. Because such a step would have been a tacit admission of guilt, Soviet officials denied that any interference had taken place. The British, having invited the Soviets to join their invasion of Iran four years earlier, now found that they could not force them to leave.[36]

For the Iranians, the traditional tactic of playing the big powers off against each other had largely misfired. Still, that was the strategy Iranians knew best for deflecting the ambitions of rival powers. So once again the Iranian government resorted to a series of accommodations to protect its sovereignty. When the British or Americans suggested making concessions to the rebels, the Iranians readily agreed, though in fact they never recognized the legitimacy of the Democratic Party regime and in practice would do nothing. At the same time Iran constantly besought the British and American governments for some tangible indications of support. Any move the Russians made was immediately communicated to London and Washington.

That did not mean that Iran had turned its back on the Soviet Union. Even before the Azeri rebellion, the Iranians had formed a new cabinet to ease Soviet complaints about the reactionary Sadr, without unduly alarming conservative and pro-British factions. As Sadr's successor they chose Ibrahim Hakimi, a veteran of the constitutional revolution and a native of Azerbaijan. Hakimi inspired little enthusiasm in domestic circles, but neither did he provoke much alarm. Ambassador Bullard had once dismissed him as a "deaf, inexperienced, harmless nonentity." Whatever Bullard's reservations, Hakimi suited the need for a compromise candidate who would offend none of the powers.[37]

Hakimi, like most of his predecessors, tried to be "soft" toward the Soviets, that is, to take no steps that they might seize as an excuse for further interference. In addition he appointed three pro-Soviet northerners to cabinet posts, while excluding pro-British southerners. As the governor-general of Azerbaijan he selected former Prime Minister Bayat. And as an additional friendly gesture to the Soviet Union, he appointed Ahmed Qavam to a newly formed council of senior advisers. He even sought an invitation to Moscow to open talks on Azerbaijan and the troop withdrawals. Such a tilt to the left and north could have destroyed Hakimi's domestic base, if he had not included six royalist ministers in his cabinet and launched a campaign to repress the Tudeh Party. At times he spoke of outlawing it altogether. And he would never agree to negotiate with either the Azeri or Kurdish rebel governments, much less acknowledge the legitimacy of their claims. His attempts to placate the Soviet Union proved futile, nonetheless, because the Russians indicated they would negotiate only with Qavam.[38]

By December the Azeri Democrats had secured almost complete control over the province. They had proceeded with such speed that little actual violence resulted. That in turn made some of the Iranian government's charges appear exaggerated. The Soviet Union even admitted that it had stopped the Iranian security forces, but excused such actions as an effort to ward off threats to its occupation forces. As always the Soviet explanation seemed a bit farfetched. The occupation forces that numbered between thirty thousand (Molotov's figure) and seventy-five thousand (the American estimate) had little to fear from the Iranian Army.[39]

Although it was beleaguered, the Iranian government devised a strategy that retrieved some of its initiative. Soon after the rebel uprising, the Hakimi government requested a seat for Iran on the United Nations Security Council so it could better plead its case. The seat went to Egypt, not to Iran, but that disappointment did not prevent the Iranians from using the United Nations to publicize their grievances. Ambassador Hoseyn Ala reminded the State Department that Soviet actions in northern Iran posed a threat to the "prestige and effectiveness" of the new organization. And as the foreign ministers met in Moscow during a typically harsh Russian December, the Iranian government informed them that it intended to file a formal complaint with the Security Council.[40]

The Iranians demonstrated a shrewd grasp of diplomatic strategy when they identified their cause with the future success of the United Nations. The Americans had not always given Iran stalwart support; big power relations generally took precedence. In its appeal the Iranian government acted against the advice of the United States and in the face of strong opposition from the British and Russian governments. But knowing that the United States could not tolerate Soviet actions in Iran that might destroy the United Nations, Iran forced the powers to address its case. Although many historians have treated the crisis solely as a big power confrontation, the Iranians took many initiatives that shaped its ultimate outcome.

IRAN AND THE MOSCOW FOREIGN MINISTERS CONFERENCE

The Iranian crisis troubled the Truman administration as Secretary of State James Byrnes set off to meet Molotov and Ernest Bevin in Moscow. For Byrnes, the conference offered an opportunity to put his personal stamp on American foreign policy. He was determined to be the great peacemaker, the man whose leadership would untangle the knot of issues that had divided the World War II allies. Above all, he sought an agreement that would bring the Soviet Union into a UN atomic energy commission. Civil war in China, peace treaties for the Balkan states, turmoil in Greece, and an Allied government for Japan were among the other issues besides Iran that the three ministers had to face.

Unfavorable omens bedeviled Byrnes's trip. By virtually ignoring Bevin in the planning for the meeting, he had needlessly antagonized the British delegation. His domestic critics feared that the "cocky and unreliable Irishman" would fatally compromise the American monopoly of the atom bomb. George Kennan thought the secretary was so desperate to reach an agreement that the Russians would extract a heavy price for what would be a "superficial success." Before Byrnes reached Moscow, his critics had persuaded Truman to narrow the grounds on which he would allow Byrnes to negotiate. Even the weather seemed to conspire against the secretary. Between Berlin and Moscow the pilot of his plane lost his way in a blinding snowstorm.[41]

The conference began almost as badly. Molotov preempted Byrnes' vision of atomic diplomacy by insisting that the subject of international controls be placed at the bottom of their agenda. He preferred to talk about American troops in China and British intervention in Greece. Over the next months it became apparent that Greece along with Indonesia, where the British were also involved in civil conflict, would serve as the Soviet counter to charges of its interference in Iran. "So you want to talk about Iran," Molotov or another Soviet diplomat might say. "Then what are the British doing in Indonesia and Greece?" Such pressure soured Foreign Secretary Bevin who had come to Moscow convinced that the Russians "were attempting to undermine the British position in the Middle East."[42]

Resolution of the Iranian crisis was one of his highest priorities at the conference. Three times in Moscow Byrnes or Bevin tried to broach the question of Soviet troops in Iran. Three times they failed to make headway. Molotov and Stalin were no more accommodating at home than they had been at Yalta, Potsdam, or London. Rather than side openly with the British, as Acheson and Henderson had urged, Byrnes tried to mediate a rivalry in which the United States was now an interested party. At his initiative during the opening session the foreign ministers agreed to drop the troop withdrawal question and to talk about Iran only informally. While that may have spared them endless wrangling, it also spelled future trouble. Many of Byrnes's critics feared that his penchant for compromise was really akin to appeasement. Unless he could achieve an agreement through private negotiations, the continued presence of Soviet troops in Iran would haunt him on his return to the United States.[43]

Byrnes clearly understood that Iran might upset his ambitions to secure the peace. For that reason he told Stalin during their first private meeting on 19 December that Soviet actions had created a concern among Americans that the Tehran pledge was in danger of being broken. Aware that Iran intended to place its case before the United Nations, he warned Stalin that if Iran did so, the United States "would feel obliged to support Iran's right to be heard." It would be difficult for the Soviet Union to convince world opinion that a fifteen-hundred man Iranian contingent somehow threatened a Soviet force of thirty thousand.[44]

Stalin at first reiterated statements that Molotov had made in response to earlier American and British notes. The Tripartite Treaty gave the Soviet Union the right to maintain troops in Iran. Stalin, however, gave 15 March, not 2 March, as the treaty deadline. That discrepancy may have had some bearing on later events, for the British and Americans observed the early date; the Soviets did not. Stalin also invoked the Soviet Union's rights under the 1921 treaty and characterized Iran's present government as hostile to his country. Withdrawal, he told Byrnes, "would depend on the conduct of the Iranian government." But Stalin then introduced a new issue. The proximity of the Baku oil fields to the Iranian border created "a special problem" because of the danger of sabotage. Agents might cross the border to set them afire. So until the Soviet Union had more confidence in the attitude of the Iranian government, it had to safeguard the oil fields. Once the 1942 Tripartite Treaty expired, Stalin said he would review the situation to see if withdrawal was possible. He reminded Byrnes that small powers like Iran sometimes sowed discord among the major powers. Then as Byrnes was leaving Stalin repeated his comment that the Soviet Union had no territorial ambitions in Iran. He would withdraw his troops as soon as he felt secure about the Baku oil fields.[45]

Soon after Byrnes left Stalin, Foreign Secretary Bevin had a go at the Soviet premier. Far more than Byrnes, Bevin feared the consequences of Soviet intentions in Iran. Did the Soviet Union really expect an attack from Iran, Bevin asked. No, it was sabotage that concerned him, Stalin replied. Then he repeated the remark he had made to Byrnes—the Soviet Union had no claim against Iran.[46]

Talks with Stalin had left Byrnes skeptical. Like Murray and Henderson, he began to adopt a worst-case view of Soviet intentions in Iran. The possibility that Stalin would observe the Tehran Declaration struck him as increasingly remote. At a second meeting with the marshal on 23 December he tried once again to emphasize American concerns. The United States had no desire to oppose the Soviet Union at the very first meeting of the United Nations. But if the Iranians carried out their threat to file a complaint, the United States would support them. Byrnes thus encouraged Stalin to adopt a policy that would not force Iran to appeal to the Security Council.[47]

As an alternative, Foreign Secretary Bevin introduced a plan for a three-power commission, which Byrnes favored. The commission could "advise and assist the Iranian government in reestablishing satisfactory relations with the provinces. . . ." The three-power body could also seek some means to accelerate the withdrawal of Russian and British troops. When Stalin made no firm commitment to the Bevin proposal, Byrnes pressed him for some promise that the Soviet Union would take no action in Iran that would divide the powers. To that Stalin replied, that "no one had any need to blush if the question was raised in the Assembly. All [that] was needed was that the Iranian government should carry out its obligations and cease to be hostile to the Soviet Union." No argument Byrnes could muster changed Stalin's position. He left the meeting persuaded that the United States and Soviet Union faced a showdown over Iran.[48]

Was the Iranian hostility about which Stalin complained "either a fantasy or a tactic similar to that used throughout Eastern Europe," as Bruce Kuniholm has charged? Almost all English and American diplomats and historians have dismissed Stalin's remarks as "absurd" (Byrnes), not worth serious consideration (Wallace Murray), or "unconvincing" (Kuniholm). At first glance, it does seem almost impossible to accept Stalin's comments about his fear of sabotage as anything but preposterous. How could Iran seriously threaten its powerful neighbor? In what way could a 1,500-man security force endanger a 30,000-man army? All the same, Stalin may have had fears about his regime's authority that he dared not reveal to Byrnes or Bevin. Evidence exists that civil war went on in the Ukraine and in a few dissident pockets of the Soviet Union until 1947. Azeri nationalism could easily have spread along ethnic lines into the Baku region. Moreover, the Iranian government in its use of American advisers, its requests for aid and diplomatic support, and its offers of an oil concession had indicated its intention to align itself with the United States after the war. Factions hostile to the Soviet Union played a major role in Iran's politics. Even if the specific claim about sabotage was "patently absurd," as Wallace Murray charged, Stalin may have had other more genuine security concerns in the Caucasus region.[49]

In Iran, as in Poland and much of Eastern Europe, Stalin sought to establish

Soviet security interests through aggressive means, which forced many western statesmen to assume the worst about his future intentions. Still, their conclusion that the Soviet Union had embarked on world conquest greatly exaggerated the situation. As Adam Ulam has argued, Stalin was too much the realist to resort to "fantasy" or military-political adventurism. What then did he really want? Ulam has suggested "that he wanted for the Soviet Union what any self-respecting state would demand in her new position, a sphere of interest of her own, some rewards for her sacrifices and victories." Among those rewards he undoubtedly included an Iranian oil concession and a government friendly to the Soviet Union. He probably had no intention of driving the British and Americans out of the Middle East. As a committed Marxist he could assume that the contradictions of capitalist imperialism and rising third world nationalism would some day solve that problem for him.[50]

Christmas day brought Byrnes an unexpected surprise. Molotov indicated that the Soviet government would accept Bevin's proposal for a tripartite commission. In return Bevin accepted all the amendments that Molotov proposed, save for one, a compromise on the final evacuation date. Bevin believed the date was fixed by the treaty of 1942. If Byrnes thought that he would go home with an agreement on Iran, his hopes were soon crushed. The next day Molotov repeated his performance from earlier conferences by refusing to discuss Iran further. Byrnes and Bevin could not convince him to talk even informally. Iran had been stricken from their agenda, Molotov insisted, and he had nothing more to say. As Bevin and Molotov locked horns, Byrnes suggested that discussion of Bulgaria and Iran be deferred until the UN meeting in London. The final protocol of the conference made no reference to Iran.[51]

Byrnes left Moscow convinced that the foreign ministers had resolved every major issue on their agenda except for Iran. That exception offered his critics an inviting target. "Why was nothing settled about Russia's activities in Iran. . . ?" some congressmen asked. The *New York Times* observed that the protocol contained an "ominous silence" on Iran. Such criticisms stung. Byrnes could dismiss some as personal, but the anti-Soviet bloc had become so strident "that they would regard any agreement with Russia on any subject as appeasement."[52]

Not all of the criticism stemmed from partisanship, however. Harry Truman had come to share Henderson's view that the Soviets were on the march in the Middle East. As a result, he was especially troubled by the lack of an agreement on Iran. He was also miffed that the secretary of state had announced the results of the conference over the radio without informing him first. At a meeting aboard his yacht the *Williamsburg,* Truman vented his wrath on Byrnes. Six days later, on 5 January 1946, he read his secretary of state a handwritten letter in which he expressed his resentment of the high-handed way the Soviets were treating Iran. The time had come to face the Russians with "an iron fist and strong language." "I think that we ought to protest with all the vigor of which we are capable against the Russian program in Iran," Truman remembered telling Byrnes.[53]

The crucial question is not, as Truman and Byrnes seemed to think, whether this exchange ever took place, but whether Byrnes was guilty of appeasement, as his critics charged. Let us put the question another way. What more might Byrnes have done to resolve the Iranian crisis? The threat of force or retaliation would have been inappropriate. The Truman administration had not yet totally written off the possibility that the United States and the Soviet Union might reach some useful accommodations. In 1946 few Americans would have understood, much less supported, a military confrontation over Iran. Nor would atomic diplomacy have achieved more for Byrnes. His efforts to lean on the bomb at Moscow had emphasized its defects as a negotiating tool. Economic assistance had been equally ineffective as a bargaining chip. The Soviets had not been sufficiently desperate for such aid to make substantial geopolitical concessions for it.[54]

More important, as much as the Iranian crisis confirmed many Americans' worst fears about the Soviet Union, Iran was not the place or the issue over which the Truman administration was prepared to force a showdown. Circumstances, more than geopolitical strategy, had given American policymakers their investment in the crisis. The Azerbaijan uprising had occurred as they began to ask publicly just what Stalin wanted. As a result, the crisis seemed to prove that the Soviet hands in the State Department had been right all along; the Soviet Union had embarked on a campaign for world conquest. Whether or not that analysis was correct, the Iranian crisis allowed Kennan, Henderson, Murray, and others to discredit Byrnes and the idea of reaching accommodations with the Soviets in favor of a policy of containment.[55]

There is no doubt that Byrnes stepped on a political landmine at Moscow. The increasingly surly mood in Washington seemed to demand some display of toughness. Iran seemed as good a place as any to show the Russians that the United States would not allow them to gobble up their neighbors. But Byrnes had been more concerned with foreign than domestic politics in Moscow. He pursued the only practical course available to him by emphasizing to Stalin that the United States would hold him accountable for the provisions of the Tehran Declaration. Molotov and Stalin in turn had repeatedly promised that the Soviet Union would honor its pledges. Furthermore, while the evidence from Iran indicated a heavy Soviet participation in the uprising, both Murray and Henderson had admitted that the Azeris and Kurds had substantial grievances.

When Byrnes went to Moscow, he did not have much leverage with which to force the Soviet Union to leave Iran. He and Bevin had accepted 2 March as the formal treaty deadline. Unless their governments decided to deliver some ultimatum, they would have to wait until then to see if Stalin would keep his word. And as much as Truman might fume at his secretary of state, he had no better alternative. What more could he accomplish by protesting "with all the vigor of which we are capable against the Russian program in Iran?" Stalin already knew that the British and Americans opposed the provisional governments in Azerbaijan and Kurdistan. Thus neither the British nor the Americans had an effective means to resolve the Iranian crisis at the Moscow Foreign Ministers Conference. Byrnes had done as much as he could with the political resources at hand. It was the Iranian government that found a way to effect a resolution to the crisis. To keep its case before the court of world opinion, Iran appealed to the United Nations.

NOTES

1. John Lewis Gaddis, *The United States and the Origins of the Cold War* (New York, 1972), ch. 9. Daniel Yergin, *Shattered Peace*, pp. 137–256 is another historian who has traced the evolution of American postwar policy. For a close analysis of the shift toward a hard line in one key figure in the Truman administration, see Robert Messer, *The End of an Alliance: James F. Byrnes, Roosevelt, Truman and the Origins of the Cold War* (Chapel Hill, 1982), 137–200.

2. Bruce Kuniholm, *The Origins of the Cold War in the Near East*, pp. 303–4.

3. On the concept of defense in depth, see Leffler, "The American Conception of National Security and the Beginnings of the Cold War," *American Historical Review* 89, 2 (April 1984): 346–88.

4. For an analysis of Iranian foreign policy in this period, see Ramazani, *Iran's Foreign Policy, 1941–1973*, pp. 109–24. On the self-defeating British oil policy, see Anthony Sampson, *The Seven Sisters*, pp. 135–41.

5. On the railroad matter, see chapter 8 above and FR, 1945, 8, pp. 523–26. For Kennan's view, see FR, 1944, 4, pp. 470–71. For Hurley's view, see Russell Buhite, *Patrick Hurley and World Affairs,* and FR, 1943, 4, pp. 417–19.

6. SD 891.6363/12–1145, Memorandum by Raynor and Loftus, "Oil Concessions and the Problem in Iran"; on the evidence of exploratory drilling in the northern zone, see SD 891.6363/10–3145, 136, Murray to Sec. of State; also 891.6363/11–1545, 146; 891.6363/11–2645, 163, and 891.6363/12–1045, 184, all Murray to Sec. of State.

7. FR, 1945, 8, p. 418, Murray to Secretary of State, 9/25/45. See also MMRB (Suitland, Md.), AG/SI, 463.8 Iran, box 233, Chamberlain to Chief of Staff, (undated).

8. FR, 1945, 8, pp. 398–99, memorandum by Henderson, 8/25/45. Historian Roger Louis has shown that the British were similarly divided in explaining the sources of Soviet conduct. See Louis, *The British Empire in the Middle East,* pp. 55–64.

9. For a good summary of the relationship between the Soviet Union and ethnic and tribal discontent, see Ramazani, *Iran's Foreign Policy,* pp. 110–14.

10. On Pishevari and the Democratic Party, see Abrahamian, *Iran Between Two Revolutions,* pp. 198 and 217–18 and Ramazani, *Iran's Foreign Policy,* pp. 111–14.

11. FR, 1945, 8, p. 407, Kennan to Secretary of State, 9/14/45 and ibid., p. 412, Murray to Sec. of State, 9/18/45. Not surprisingly, the question of an American concession had also come up in August. The State Department had discussed that possibility with both Seaboard Oil Co. and Standard-Vacuum, but had decided that they should await a more propitious moment before entering into negotiations.

12. Ibid., p. 407, Shahanshah of Iran to President Truman, 9/10/45, and ibid., p. 409, Murray to Sec. of State, 9/15/45.

13. Ibid., pp. 402–3, and 408–9, Murray to Sec. of State. Roger Louis has shown that the British suffered from the same weakness; Louis, *British Empire in the Middle East,* pp. 64–67. See also ibid., pp. 413–15; see also James F. Byrnes, *Speaking Frankly* (New York, 1947), pp. 91–109; and Harriman and Abel, *Special Envoy,* pp. 506–9.

14. FR, 1945, 8, pp. 413–15; and ibid., pp. 415–16, Murray to Secretary of State, 9/21/45. On the 1921 treaty and its meaning, see Ramazani, *The Foreign Policy of Iran, 1500–1941,* pp. 186–91.

15. FR, 1945, 8, p. 410, memorandum by Henderson, 9/17/45; and ibid., p. 410n. for Acheson's response.

16. Ibid., pp. 413–16.

17. Ibid., pp. 417–18, Murray to Secretary of State, 9/24/45 and 9/25/45. On the Tudeh Party, see Abrahamian, *Iran Between Two Revolutions,* pp. 281–418. See also Zabih, *The Communist Movement in Iran,* pp. 71–122.

18. FR, 1945, 8, p. 424, Kennan to Secretary of State, 10/1/45.

19. For the text of the "Long Telegram," see FR, 1946, 6, pp. 696–709, Kennan to Sec. of State. See also Kennan, *Memoirs,* pp. 290–95, for his comments. Yergin, *Shattered Peace,* pp. 167–71, presents an able analysis of Kennan's argument and its shortcomings. I agree particularly that the idea of Soviet goals as "open-ended" took little account of the Soviets' postwar weakness and the realism that Soviet leaders showed in most of their dealings with the west.

20. Kazemzadeh, "The Soviet Union and Iran Since World War II," (unpublished paper given to author, 1972), pp. 1–2. For an interesting analysis of Kennan's views and the debate over the meaning of the "Long Telegram" and "Mr. X" article, see John Lewis Gaddis, "Containment: A Reassessment," *Foreign Affairs Quarterly* 55, 4 (July 1977): 873–87. Gaddis seeks to dissociate Kennan from a view of containment that Walter Lippmann described as a "strategic monstrosity." Did Kennan after all see containment largely in military terms and as an open-ended commitment to stop communist expansion anywhere? If one looks at Kennan's telegrams from the late war period, many of them stress the need for military strength as a way to gain concessions from the Soviets. Kennan may have seen containment as requiring a flexible use of various diplomatic, economic, and political instruments as well as military ones. Still, many of these telegrams emphasize the danger of appearing to be militarily weak or lacking the resolve to use the forces at hand. Kennan played into the hands of men like James Forrestal who lacked his subtlety of mind and understanding and who used Kennan's warnings to justify an aggressive American policy that stressed military preparedness. See also John Lewis Gaddis, *Strategies of Containment* (New York, 1982), ch. 2.

21. FR, 1945, 8, p. 419, Murray to Secretary of State, 9/25/45.

22. Ibid., pp. 423–24, Henderson to Murray, 9/24/45; ibid., p. 427, Murray to Henderson, 10/16/45.

23. Ibid., p. 428, Chargé, London, to Secretary of State, 10/18/45.

24. Ibid., pp. 431–39. For an eyewitness account of the uprising, see also Robert Rossow, "The Battle of Azerbaijan, 1946," *The Middle East Journal* 10 (Spring 1956): 17–32.

25. FR, 1945, 8, pp. 439–43, Murray to Secretary of State, 11/25/45; see also ibid., p. 455.

26. To gain a better sense of what the American public knew about the crisis and about Iran in general, I surveyed a cross section of newspapers with a range of regional and political points of view. U.S. opinion in general paralleled the views of the State Department. The papers included the *Chicago Tribune, Christian Science Monitor, Dallas Morning News, The Daily Worker, Los Angeles Times, New York Times, Salt Lake City Tribune, Saint Louis Post-Dispatch, San Francisco Chronicle, Wall Street Journal,* and *Washington Post*. In addition I looked at four popular weekly news journals—*The Nation, Newsweek, The New Republic,* and *Time*. Alsop's comments are from a *Washington Post* editorial, 11/18/45. That Alsop picked up on the Azerbaijan story so soon indicates that he had followed it before the crisis broke.

27. Joseph Alsop, editorial, *Washington Post,* 11/18/45. To better appreciate the resonance of Alsop's views within official circles, it is interesting to compare his column with a report from the American Embassy filed by Harold Minor. Minor wrote on December 11, ". . . the Russians are up to well planned and unscrupulous aggression with a short range objective of gaining ascendancy over a semi-autonomous northern Iran and influence over a central Iranian government, looking to one or more long range objectives such as encirclement of Turkey, oil concessions, access to the Persian Gulf, penetration of the Near East, a safety zone for their southern frontier, and out right Communistic imperialism." SD 891.00/12–1145, H. B. Minor to Loy Henderson.

28. Joseph Alsop, editorial, *Washington Post,* 11/25/45.

29. On Hurley's desire for an appointment to the Middle East, see Stimson Diaries, v. 47, 7/27/44.

30. On Hurley's reaction during his trip through Tehran, see SD 711.93/3–645, Hurley to Roosevelt, 9/7/45. See also *New York Times,* 12/7 and 12/8/45.

31. Eugene Rostow described this episode in an interview in 1972. Rostow's recollection was consistent with the coverage in the *New York Times.* His subsequent book on the oil industry, *A National Policy for the Oil Industry* (New Haven, 1947), provoked fury among conservative Yale trustees who demanded his ouster from the faculty. For some representative comments on subversion in the State Department, see editorials in *Chicago Tribune,* 11/29/45 and 3/17/46; *Los Angeles Times,* 3/16/46; *Salt Lake City Tribune,* 4/1/46. Senator Arthur Vandenberg made similar charges in his famous Senate speech of February 27, 1946. See *Congressional Record,* 2/27/46, pp. 1692–95.

32. *New York Times,* 12/7/45, article by W. H. Lawrence. A good short account of this episode and State Department reactions to it is in Yergin, *Shattered Peace,* pp. 154–55.

33. FR, 1945, 8, pp. 448–55. That note followed equally urgent communications from both the British and Iranian governments.

34. Ibid., pp. 468–69.

35. SD 891.6363/3–2846, "British Oil Position in Iran," memorandum by Petroleum Adviser Loftus. See also SD 761.91/1–847, Gallman (London) to Sec. of State, 1/8/47, for Britain's later willingness to accept a Soviet concession. See also Roger Louis, *The British Empire in the Middle East,* pp. 54–73. FR, 1945, 8, p. 475, Murray to Sec. of State, 12/4/45, and Abrahamian, *Iran Between Two Revolutions,* pp. 221–22.

36. FR, 1945, 8, p. 487, Harriman to Secretary of State, 12/10/45; and ibid., p. 497, Murray to Secretary of State, 12/15/45. On the British use of publicity, see SD 891.00/11–2645, Murray to Secretary of State. FR, 1945, 8, p. 448, Byrnes to Harriman, 11/23/45; ibid., p. 457, Harriman to Byrnes, 11/26/45; and ibid., p. 468, Harriman to Byrnes, 11/30/45.

37. On Hakimi, see Abrahamian, *Iran Between Two Revolutions,* pp. 214–15.

38. Ibid., pp. 509–10, Murray to Secretary of State, 12/22/45; and FR, 1946, 7, p. 291, Murray to Secretary of State, 1/1/46. For an incisive analysis upon which this account draws heavily, see Abrahamian, *Iran Between Two Revolutions,* pp. 220–21. See also Ramazani, *Iran's Foreign Policy, 1941–1973,* pp. 110–126 for a summary of Iran's problems in dealing with the Soviet Union.

39. For background on the situation in northern Iran, see SD 891.00/11–2645, 232, Ebling (in Tabriz) to Secretary of State; as well as two other messages from Ebling, SD 891.00/12–245, 235, and SD 891.00/12–2145, 240. See also SD 761.91/1–146, memorandum of conversation with the Iranian Ambassador and Secretary of State. On the question of troop strength, see FR, 1945, 8, pp. 481–82, Murray to Sec. of State, 12/6/45.

40. FR, 1945, 8, pp. 462–63, Iranian Ambassador to Secretary of State, 11/28/45; ibid., p. 500, memorandum by Henderson, 12/17/45; and ibid., p. 513, memorandum by George V. Allen, 12/26/45.

41. One of the best perspectives on Moscow is offered by Gregg Herken, *The Winning Weapon* (New York, 1981), pp. 69–94. Herken more than anyone has given us a picture of how the bomb affected Byrnes's approach to diplomacy. For Byrnes's own account, see Byrnes, *Speaking Frankly,* pp. 110–122. See also Yergin, *Shattered Peace,* pp. 147–51. For Kennan's criticism, see Kennan, *Memoirs, 1925–1950,* p. 286–88. See also Bohlen, *Witness to History,* pp. 248–49.

42. Bevin, quoted in Yergin, *Shattered Peace,* p. 148. See also Herken, *The Winning Weapon,* pp. 77–78, and Gaddis, *The United States and the Origins of the Cold War,* pp. 285–90. Kuniholm offers a good summary of the discussion of both Iran and Turkey at Moscow: Kuniholm, *Origins of the Cold War in the Near East,* pp. 282–91.

43. For Murray's and Acheson's views, see FR, 1945, 8, pp. 510–13.

44. Byrnes, *Speaking Frankly,* pp. 118–19. See also FR, 1945, 2, pp. 684–85. On troop strength, see FR, 1945, 8, pp. 481–82.

45. Byrnes, *Speaking Frankly,* p. 119; FR, 1945, 2, pp. 684–87.

46. FR, 1945, 2, pp. 688–90.

47. Byrnes, *Speaking Frankly,* p. 120.

48. Ibid., p. 120. See also FR, 1945, 2, pp. 750–52, and Bohlen, *Witness to History,* p. 250.

49. Byrnes, *Speaking Frankly,* p. 119; FR, 1945, 8, 510–11; Kuniholm, *Origins of the Cold War in the Near East,* p. 286. On conditions in the Soviet Union, see Alexander Werth, *Russia at War* (New York, 1965) and *Russia: The Post-War Years* (New York, 1971).

50. Kuniholm, *Origins of the Cold War in the Near East,* p. 288. Adam Ulam, *Stalin* (New York, 1973), pp. 640–42.

51. Byrnes, *Speaking Frankly,* pp. 120–21. FR, 1945, 2, p. 805.

52. For a reaction to popular criticism, see Walter Lippmann, "Mr. Byrnes and His Critics," editorial, *Washington Post,* 1/3/46. For samples of the criticism, see *New York Times,* 12/28 and 12/30/45. On Byrnes's response, see Byrnes, *Speaking Frankly,* p. 122.

53. Harry S. Truman, *Memoirs: Year of Decision* (Signet Ed., New York, 1965), pp. 604–6. Byrnes, *Speaking Frankly,* p. 122 and pp. 237–39. Historians have doubts as to whether Truman ever dressed Byrnes down as he claims. Byrnes himself denied that the two had any substantial disagreement over Iran or his handling of the conference. It seems equally likely that with ten years having elapsed before Truman wrote his *Memoirs* he recalled his feelings more clearly than his actions. At the time he may have been more angry with Byrnes than he was with Stalin and the Soviet Union. Soviet-American cold war hostilities were far more clear-cut in 1955 than they had been in January 1946. For a more sympathetic treatment of Byrnes and a thorough analysis of the Byrnes-Truman contretemps, see Messer, *The End of an Alliance: James F. Byrnes, Roosevelt, Truman and the Origins of the Cold War,* pp. 156–80. Bruce Kuniholm has also done a good analysis of this exchange and the controversy over it. See Kuniholm, *Origins of the Cold War in the Near East,* pp. 294–99 and 298n. Also Herken, *The Winning Weapon,* pp. 88–90.

54. On atomic diplomacy at Moscow, see Herken, *The Winning Weapon,* pp. 77–88. The difficulty Byrnes faced in creating diplomatic leverage is nicely captured in John Lewis Gaddis, *Strategies of Containment,* pp. 16–18.

55. For a good overview of the evolution of containment policy, see Gaddis, *Strategies of Containment,* pp. 3–88.

10 The Iranian Crisis and the United Nations

Failure to resolve the Iranian crisis in Moscow shifted attention to the opening meeting of the United Nations Security Council in London. Neither Stalin's reassurances on Iran nor Ernest Bevin's plan for a tripartite commission adequately addressed the Iranian government's objections to the actions of Soviet troops in Azerbaijan and Kurdistan. By January of 1946, the State Department realized that Iran would bring its case to the Security Council. What was less clear was whether the fledgling organization could survive its first case, especially one that involved conflict with a permanent member.

THE IRANIAN CASE

Shortly after the Moscow Conference, Ambassador Bullard had persuaded Prime Minister Hakimi to refrain from placing Iran's complaint on the upcoming Security Council agenda. He explained to Ambassador Wallace Murray that such an appeal would foreclose any possibility that the Soviets would accept Bevin's commission plan and that launching an appeal before the United Nations had organized its procedures might undermine its long-term effectiveness. The likelihood that British activities in Greece and Indonesia would make them vulnerable to similar charges of interference may have also led the British to oppose Hakimi's strategy.[1]

Bullard's pressure on Hakimi aroused Murray's old suspicions of British imperialism. Murray speculated that the British might have concluded that northern Iran was lost and had therefore decided to consolidate their own sphere in the south. The State Department had no desire to see the revival of the old Anglo-Russian entente system that might well exclude American influence. Nor did the department wish to see a precedent established that would prevent small powers from having recourse to the Security Council. Murray thus gave Hakimi assurances that he had American support for an appeal to the United Nations.[2]

On 19 January 1946 the Iranian delegate to the United Nations, Hasan Taqizadih, delivered Iran's complaint against the Soviet Union's interference in Iran's internal affairs. Taqizadih also described his government's frustrated attempts to negotiate a settlement, but did not refer to Iran's main concern, the Russian refusal to evacuate its troops. The Soviet Union, he understood, would deflect that issue with a legalistic reading of the 1942 Tripartite Treaty. In later communications to the Security Council, Taqizadih did indicate Iran's desire to have Soviet troops withdrawn. And as the Iranians had anticipated, the Russians refused to acknowledge the substance of their complaint. Rather than answer the Iranians, the Soviet delegate, Andrei Vishinsky, complained that British military forces were suppressing nationalist uprisings in Indonesia and Greece.[3]

The State Department had learned that in these situations the Russians were likely to stonewall. On the other hand, American diplomats did not want, any more than the British, a confrontation that would cripple the United Nations at birth. Thus Secretary Byrnes instructed the American delegate Edward Stettinius to follow a procedural strategy. The United States asked both the Security Council and the General Assembly to take up Iran's case immediately. Byrnes did not so much care whether either body successfully addressed Iran's complaint as long as the opening session established Iran's right to be heard and the United Nations' prerogative in such a case involving a small power and a permanent member of the Security Council. Once the delegates had agreed on those two points, the State Department was more than willing to have the Soviet Union and Iran move ahead through bilateral negotiations. The Security Council could then serve as a watchdog over the negotiations, in effect assuming the position the United States had assumed in World War II.[4]

Discussions of Iran's complaint at the London meeting of the Security Council never moved far beyond procedural issues. For each charge Taqizadih made, Vishinsky countered with a Russian version of the facts. Often the delegates exchanged insults and accusations. On several occasions Bevin and Vishinsky went head-to-head in a war of words. But when Bevin charged at one meeting that the Soviet Union had violated the Tripartite Treaty, Vishinsky insisted that the discussion be restricted to procedural issues. That posture left the delegates at an impasse. Not until 30 January did the Security Council find a way out. Since the Soviet Union and Iran had indicated their willingness to negotiate directly, the council directed the two parties to proceed through bilateral talks. To placate Vishinsky, the other delegates agreed that Iran's complaint would not remain formally on the council agenda. But both Bevin and Stettinius insisted that the council be kept abreast of the negotiations and that it retain the right to ask for further information.[5]

Stettinius suggested to Secretary Byrnes that this outcome was satisfactory from the American viewpoint. The Security Council had addressed Iran's complaint and negotiations, he now believed, could lead to a settlement consistent with the principles of the United Nations charter. That assessment must have been based on appearances alone, for the Security Council had in actuality accomplished very little. In establishing procedures, it had moved Iran no closer to a solution than it was before the discussions began. Iran would enter the negotiations with few indications that the British and Americans would offer more than rhetorical support. What is more, Vishinski had demonstrated that the Security Council could be rendered virtually impotent, if a permanent member chose to frustrate its efforts. The bitterness of much of the debate indicated how badly the alliance spirit had eroded over the past months. The United Nations had done nothing to deflect the Soviet Union and the United States from their cold war confrontation.[6]

The Iranians had brought their complaint to the United Nations principally to ensure that the Soviets would have to operate in the light of world opinion. More than likely, they never assumed that the Security Council would solve the problem of Soviet interference or arrange a troop withdrawal. And as Bevin's plan for a tripartite commission struck many nationalists as an excuse for the big powers to arrange some division of Iran, they had been aware all along that just one alternative—direct negotiations with Moscow—could lead to a satisfactory solution. For Moscow to agree to talk, Hakimi had to resign. Once again Iran would reorient its internal politics in order to meet a foreign threat. Hakimi greatly facilitated his own downfall by alienating both his domestic supporters and the British and Soviet Embassies. As the fiery nationalist Mohammad Mossadeq declared to the Majles, "We have no choice but to replace Hakimi with a premier who will be welcomed in Moscow." That man was waiting in the wings—Ahmed Qavam.[7]

Qavam must rank as one of the most elusive figures in Iran's political history. For some, he was among the shrewdest of statesmen, a leader who guided Iran through several perilous eras while maintaining its independence. For others, he was a creature of circumstance, reacting from situation to situation with no overriding plan, surviving, by playing contending forces off against each other. The shah generally mistrusted him as a proponent of republicanism. The British and Americans feared that he had pro-Soviet leanings. The Tudeh Party and other factions alternately embraced and vilified him. Ervand Abrahamian probably best captured this enigmatic figure as a politician of the Rooseveltian stripe—a "realist who recognized politics as the art of the possible. . . ."[8]

The very qualifications that commended Qavam as premier in January 1946, especially his open door to Moscow, tended to disturb many American observers. The sour mood of anticommunist hysteria had already begun to burden American public opinion and foreign policy with a "black hat"/"white hat" mentality. Those who showed any willingness to negotiate with Moscow were seen at best as appeasers and at worst as traitors. Foreign statesmen who sought accommodation with the Soviet Union were by definition enemies of the United States. Editorial writer Drew Pearson demonstrated how crudely the formula could be applied when he dismissed Qavam as "a virtual Russian puppet." Raw economic determinism explained, for Pearson, Qavam's pro-Soviet tilt. "The Russians have permitted [Qavam] to get away with all sorts of economic concessions in North Iran under the protection of Red Army troops. As a result, Qavam is one of the wealthiest men in the Near East," Pearson told his readers.[9] He did not acknowledge, and most likely did not know, that as the son of Qajar nobility Qavam had inherited vast estates in northern Iran. He had had in addition the good economic sense to marry another wealthy aristocrat. The Russians had contributed to Qavam's financial well-being only by leaving his assets alone.

More knowledgeable observers held Qavam in higher regard. Wallace Murray thought Qavam was the appropriate choice to lead Iran out of the quagmire. Harold Minor described Qavam as "not a leftist, nor an idealist, nor a Russian tool, but rather an elder statesman and member of the traditional ruling, landed, entrenched class."[10] Minor had little patience with the self-serving politics he associated with Iran's ruling elite. Still, he believed Qavam was a good choice, who, through expediency rather than a pro-Soviet bias, might accept closer ties with Russia.

As much as Qavam might have been responding to the politics of the moment, three objectives directed his course: the eventual dissolution of the Pahlevi monarchy, the promotion of elite interests, and the preservation of Iran's independence from foreign power domination. His longstanding commitment to the constitutional revolution drove him to oppose the monarchy. To that end he sought to divorce the shah from the military by placing the army under civilian control. He was not, however, in any sense a social or political revolutionary. Opposition to the shah was one of his goals, but Qavam otherwise preferred to preserve the prerogatives of

Iran's elite classes. In foreign policy, Qavam belonged to the "positive equilibrium" school. That group sought to achieve balance among the rival powers, playing the Russians against the British while calling on the United States when the balance swung too far in any direction. Such a position put Qavam at odds with Mossadeq and other nationalist proponents of the emerging doctrine of "negative equilibrium" or effecting a minimal foreign influence in Iran's internal affairs.[11]

Even before Qavam assumed the premiership, he had initiated four lines of policy. First, he instructed Hasan Taqizadih to press Iran's case before the Security Council. Qavam understood that American support would depend on such a course and assured Wallace Murray that no Iranian politician would dare to drop the appeal. Second, Qavam reversed Hakimi's policy on the Azerbaijan government by organizing a mission to meet with the rebel leaders. Third, he made overtures to the leftist factions by removing from office some of the most objectionable rightists, like the pro-British army chief, General Hassan Arfa. That step also served as a friendly sign to Moscow. Finally, on 18 February he left for Moscow to head an Iranian negotiating team.[12]

Although bilateral Soviet-Iranian talks had begun, the Iranian crisis continued to trouble Soviet-American relations. Soviet harrassment of American diplomats in Iran fueled American suspicions of Russian motives. Neither American diplomats nor newsmen were allowed travel permits to enter the Soviet zone. The embassy in Tehran depended largely on the consulate in Tabriz for information. To ensure a more effective gathering of information, the State Department had replaced the ineffectual Samuel Ebling with Robert Rossow, who not coincidentally had served briefly in the OSS. Rossow would distinguish himself by his resourcefulness in monitoring Soviet troop movements.[13]

In the past, when the Soviets had been hostile to an observant American consul, they had forced the State Department to reassign Bartol Kuniholm, Ebling's predecessor. The Soviets now similarly tried to discredit Rossow. After he held a brief meeting with the rebels, the Soviet press announced that he had publicly acclaimed Pishevari's government. The State Department feared that the Iranians might subsequently construe Rossow's presence in Tabriz as "sympathy and support for the rebels," and in that light they thought it might be better to reassign him. Wallace Murray recognized the move against Rossow as a replay of the Kuniholm case. The Russians wanted to deny the Americans any reliable information. In deference to Murray, the State Department allowed Rossow to stay on in Tabriz.[14]

Had the Iranian crisis been an isolated event within otherwise amicable big power relations, it would not have sparked so much concern. But by February 1946 Soviet relations with Great Britain and the United States had become openly bitter. In a speech on 9 February Stalin described what he saw as a hostile ring of capitalist nations encircling the Soviet Union. To protect his nation from that threat, he announced a new five-year plan emphasizing the production of arms and munitions. *Time* magazine called the speech "the most warlike pronouncement uttered by any top-rank statesman since V–J day." From Moscow George Kennan observed that Soviet leaders in their public comments made no references to international cooperation.[15]

American leaders waded in with outbursts of their own. Republican spokesmen had begun to make Soviet relations a partisan issue. John Foster Dulles and Senator Arthur Vandenberg openly criticized Secretary of State Byrnes for what they saw as his failure to "assume moral leadership." More threatening to Byrnes was their criticism of his willingness to appease the Russians. President Truman had also been pushing Byrnes to adopt a tougher posture. In response to these pressures, the secretary issued what might be construed as his own declaration of cold war. On

28 February in a speech to the Overseas Press Club he sharply criticized Soviet actions, without making any direct references to the crisis in Iran. This speech introduced Byrnes's new policy of "patience with firmness."[16]

Like many policymakers in Washington, Byrnes had been much affected by George Kennan's analysis of Soviet behavior in his "Long Telegram." In essence Kennan legitimized the hostility many American leaders had come to feel toward the Soviet Union. He offered compelling reasons why the United States should shift its efforts from seeking negotiated accommodations to exerting counterforce against "the steady advance of Russian nationalism. . . ." Kennan argued that the Soviets would seek constructive solutions "only when Communist power is dominant." As a paranoid revolutionary rather than a statesman of realpolitik, Stalin was sensitive only to the "logic of force," not the "logic of reason."[17]

Historians have long recognized the extraordinary reception Kennan's telegram received. As John Lewis Gaddis has pointed out, policymakers were able to extrapolate from Kennan's analysis a new framework for Soviet-American relations to replace the old policy of *quid pro quo.* Most crucial were the ideas that Soviet ambitions were limitless, that they required the destruction of the American way of life, and that diplomacy could succeed only when it was supported by military force and firm resolve. Kennan's analysis confirmed Wallace Murray's contention that American support for an independent Iran was necessary to contain the Soviet Union.[18]

On 6 March 1946 Winston Churchill said publicly what many American policymakers had concluded in private. In a speech at Westminster College in Fulton, Missouri, Churchill introduced the phrase "Iron Curtain" into popular usage. Much that Churchill said echoed Kennan's analysis. International communism posed "a growing challenge and peril to Christian civilization." The Russians did not seek war so much as "the indefinite expansion of their power and doctrine."[19] It was only in his conclusion that Churchill departed sharply from current administration thinking. He proposed an Anglo-American military alliance to counter the Soviet threat. As much as they might agree with Churchill, members of the Truman administration felt compelled to distance themselves from his conclusions, which for the moment had moved too far ahead of popular opinion.

THE IRANIAN CASE: ROUND TWO

If British and American leaders wanted their worst fears about Soviet intentions confirmed, they had only to look to Iran, where the Russians seemed bent on employing the same script they had used in Eastern Europe. Nothing that occurred in February indicated that the Soviets would respect the 2 March deadline. In fact, all signs pointed to an indefinite period of occupation. Pishevari informed Robert Rossow that as of 11 February Soviet forces had begun signing six-month contracts for the purchase of local supplies.[20]

Rebel demonstrations and periodic popular unrest provided the Soviets with a flimsy pretext to stay on, and Qavam in Moscow gave no indications that he had made any progress in his negotiations. Both Stalin and Molotov had emphasized that an oil concession would be a prerequisite for troop withdrawals and that they viewed Iran's continuing refusal to grant it as hostile to the Soviet Union. As always they hid behind the tortured legalities of the 1942 and 1921 treaties. But now the bottom line was all too clear. Molotov stated in late February that Soviet troops would evacuate only certain areas of Iran by 2 March and he expected Qavam to accept the continued presence of these troops for an indefinite period of time. Furthermore, he demanded recognition of Azerbaijan autonomy and the formation of a joint-stock oil company in which the Soviet Union would hold a majority interest.

Qavam could not agree to any of these conditions. To accept Azerbaijani autonomy or a permanent occupation would be political suicide. Mossadeq's 1944 legislation made it illegal for any Iranian to negotiate on oil concessions with a foreign power while troops occupied Iran. Thus Qavam insisted on linking an oil agreement to troop withdrawals, which meant he could do nothing before 2 March to achieve such an agreement. To make matters worse, Stalin and Molotov had said for the first time that they would not honor the deadline.[21]

American and British diplomats learned about the negotiations only after Qavam returned to Tehran in early March. That made their outrage even more intense when, as the 2 March deadline passed, Soviet troops remained in full occupation. In Moscow Qavam formally protested the violation of existing treaties. In the Majles, Mossadeq denounced the Soviet action to "an unusual outburst of applause and excitment." The Soviet press announced that the troops would remain in certain districts of northern Iran "pending examination of the situation." From Robert Rossow in Tabriz came even more shocking news. Not only had the Russians refused to withdraw their troops, but they seemed to be reinforcing them. Rossow reported heavy movements around Tabriz and columns moving in the direction of the Iraqi and Turkish borders. Several days later large-scale armor reinforcements reached Tabriz, along with a story that General Ivan Bagramian, a combat veteran with a "spectacular record," had assumed command. Rossow concluded that the Soviets had launched "a full-scale combat deployment."[22]

President Truman would later recall that he had actually threatened to use force against the Soviet troop movements. No one involved in the crisis remembers any such threat. The American response was in reality quite restrained. When news from Tehran confirmed that the Soviets had violated the 1942 treaty, Ambassador Ala asked the State Department to protest immediately. Secretary Byrnes declined to do so until the department could be assured that no one in the Iranian government had actually asked the Russians to remain. By 5 March it was clear that the Soviets had acted unilaterally. George Kennan had learned from Qavam that, having failed in his talks with Molotov and Stalin, he would return home. That satisfied Secretary Byrnes. Through Kennan he sent a stiffly worded note that asked for the prompt withdrawal of Soviet forces. Byrnes cited American obligations as a member of the United Nations and as a signatory of the Tehran Declaration to justify the protest. In violating its wartime agreements, the Soviet Union had created a threat to world peace, Byrnes charged.[23]

Early State Department analysis of the crisis reveals how neatly it fit into the emerging cold war consensus. For example, the Ambassador to Turkey, Edwin Wilson, suggested that the Soviets in Iran were using surrogates to bring pressure on Iraq and on Turkey as well. An autonomous Kurdish state would be an indirect way to encourage separatism among the Iraqi and Turkish Kurds. Rather than risk a direct military involvement, they could use the Armenian and Kurdish fronts to encircle Turkey in anticipation of possible future interventions. Rossow had even reported rumors of a Kurdish plan for military operations that would allow them to gain control over Turkish Kurdistan.[24]

Wallace Murray, like Joseph Alsop, thought a domino theory best conveyed the danger of the crisis. After Iran's independence was gone, a Soviet-dominated government would certainly cancel the AIOC concession. The Russians could then block any British attempt to reclaim the lost concession and could assume it for themselves. With their foothold on the Persian Gulf secured, the Soviets could then turn their attention to Bahrain and Kuwait, where Iran had historic claims. By supporting those claims, the Soviets would then be able to orchestrate the termination of American oil concessions in these places. From that position of strength, they could pressure Ibn Saud to terminate the Aramco concession. Once Aramco was lost, IPC's days in Iraq were numbered.

Murray understood that people who did not appreciate the Soviet menace might find his scenario a bit fantastic. Nevertheless, he was convinced that the Russians had already provided ample proof "of their insatiable appetite for territorial and economic acquisitions." The prize at hand was sufficiently important to drive the Russians on. They would simultaneously cripple Great Britain, and gain control of the world's richest oil fields. Soviet troops would certainly arrive to protect such valuable resources. In carrying out this plan, the Russians had an advantage beside their armed presence in Iran. Since they had made no commitment to Zionism, they could pose as the international defender of Arab rights.[25]

Several aspects of Murray's analysis are worth further consideration. Too often our focus on the substance of diplomatic correspondence distracts us from its language. Murray would not be the last to compare the Soviet state to a monster, a disease, or some kind of mindless force. Like Kennan, he imagined the Soviets as irrational—driven not just by national security concerns or the rational calculation of interests, but by an "insatiable appetite" of the kind that drove Adolph Hitler. In that way, Murray's thinking evoked the themes of "red fascism" that shaped so much American analysis of Soviet behavior. Murray also exaggerated the ability of the Soviets to appeal to traditional Islamic cultures. Because American support for an independent Jewish homeland would make the United States unpopular among the Arabs, he assumed that the Soviets would benefit, almost regardless of their own actions. So to combat Soviet influence, the United States should not support Zionism, no matter what the merits of the Jewish cause. But in posing the problem in this way, Murray forgot the great degree to which Middle Eastern people feared Russian expansion and, even more, how alien they found Marxist atheism. Anger at American actions did not make Soviet imperialism or communism any more attractive. As a result of these gaps in his understanding, Murray's preoccupation with the cold war only muddled his thinking about an effective American policy for the Middle East.[26]

The Iranian crisis provided George Kennan with an opportunity to apply the analysis of the "Long Telegram" to a specific set of events. Kennan had been unable to substantiate a rumor reported by Murray that the Soviets had ordered a general mobilization in the Caucasus-Baku region. This lack of confirmation did not strike him as significant: "Rigidity of administrative control, fantastic permanent security precautions and vastness of territory and manpower make it possible for Soviet government to conduct military operations on limited border sections (as was the case in first Finnish war) with little or no visible repercussions on the life of the country as a whole." More to the point, Kennan did not doubt that "Soviet armed forces are there to win Soviet objectives by intimidation if possible, by force if necessary."[27] As Kennan saw it, American and British military weakness held the key to Soviet calculations, especially since the Russians did not in any way share the great hopes many people in England and the United States held for the United Nations. Before the United Nations could act, the Soviet Union would consolidate its gains in northern Iran.

Like Murray, Kennan saw the possibility of a domino effect originating in Iran. The Russian press had made pointed comments about British and American weaknesses. Kennan thus concluded that "if Professor Tarle [a writer for *Izvestia*] can continue to point with glee to the military weakness and political disunity of Britain and America, then Iran will not be the end of the story."[28] That meant that Soviet ambitions went beyond the immediate pressure for an oil concession and an autonomous Azerbaijan.

There are several reasons for dwelling on these analyses of events in Iran. They demonstrate the pessimism that existed within the foreign policy bureaucracy about the future of Soviet-American relations. They also demonstrate that the consensus on Soviet ambitions that informed later national security planning was largely formed by early 1946. But even more important, the dire predictions that people like Kennan and Murray made about Soviet plans for Iran and the Middle East proved to be wrong. If the Soviets did have some plan to control the Middle East, they showed remarkably little resolve in carrying it out. Of course, American diplomats could easily argue that by pushing for a firmer American policy, they had prevented the Russians from realizing their ambitions in that region. Most likely, American opposition did make Stalin hesitate to force Iran into making major political and economic concessions. Yet the evidence that diplomatic pressure could alter Soviet policymaking did not lead Murray or other policymakers to modify their thinking about Soviet ambitions. As Soviet influence in the region dwindled, American policymakers continued to see almost every disruption, every sign of discontent, as evidence of the unfolding of a Soviet plan for world domination. American successes only confirmed the need to strengthen the United States' security perimeter. As Melvin Leffler has argued, policymakers seldom subjected their ideas to any real analysis or allowed contradictory evidence to upset their assumptions.[29]

A ROUND FOR JAMES BYRNES

With Soviet forces indefinitely ensconced in northern Iran, the State Department laid plans for a diplomatic showdown. For months Secretary Byrnes had chafed at the criticism of his policies. Now the Russians had presented him with an unprecedented opportunity to demonstrate his new tougher posture and to silence his domestic critics. No one could legitimately deny that the Soviet Union had violated a wartime agreement. Molotov had not even deigned to answer the American protest note. The NEA staff persuaded Byrnes that Soviet troop movements were tantamount to an invasion. Showing the relish with which he awaited the confrontation at the United Nations, he smacked his fist into his palm and said, "Now we'll give it to them with both barrels."[30]

Not everyone shared Byrnes's determination to face the Russians down. Charles Bohlen pointed out that legally and militarily the United States was on shaky ground. Since it had not signed the 1942 treaty, it had no formal right to enforce the treaty provisions. Any military threat would most likely strike the Soviets as an empty bluff, because the United States no longer had sufficient forces to conduct effective military operations in the Middle East. That led Assistant Secretary Acheson to recommend a limited response to "leave a graceful way out," if the Russians wished to avoid any further escalation of the crisis. As a result of this consideration Kennan was instructed to deliver a second American note as an indication that the Americans had a close eye on the Iranian situation. The note asked for an explanation of the movement of Soviet troops. Once again, the Soviet Foreign Office maintained a stony silence.[31]

Byrnes' desire to play savior to Iran was bedeviled by Prime Minister Qavam, who would not pursue a consistent policy. On his return from Moscow, Qavam found himself besieged on several fronts. He managed to postpone a confrontation on domestic issues by allowing the Fourteenth Majles session to end without presenting his cabinet. He could then rule until new elections were held. When that might be, no one could guess. This parliamentary limbo also meant that no faction could overturn Mossadeq's concession law. If the Soviets wanted to obtain an oil concession under a legal guise, they would have to withdraw their troops.[32]

The foreign crisis presented Qavam with an even more ticklish problem. The adoption of a cold war mentality had led the great powers to demand that the Iranian government take sides. If Qavam drifted too far in either direction, the powers might seek to secure their current positions by dividing Iran in the same manner as Germany or Korea. The Americans and the British told Qavam that Iran's only hope for a satisfactory resolution lay in a quick appeal to the Security Council. The Soviet chargé informed Qavam that his country would treat such an appeal as a hostile act that would have "unfortunate results for Iran." In the face of such conflicting pressures, who could blame Qavam for the equivocal way he kept his promise to be "steadfast in prosecuting Iran's case before the Security Council?"[33]

Somehow, Qavam did manage to steer through the political minefields. On 18 March he made good his pledge to send Iran's complaint to the secretary general of the United Nations. At the same time Qavam assured a press conference that Iran meant to show no unkindness to the Soviet Union. Just three days later, Qavam made a compensatory gesture to his Soviet neighbors. Rumors flew about Tehran that an Iranian-Soviet oil deal was imminent. The director of the National Bank hinted that the deal would lead to Soviet troop withdrawals. Wallace Murray had learned that the agreement involved a joint-stock company in which the Soviets would hold a 51 percent interest.[34]

Qavam took special pains to justify that step to the Americans. He asked Murray what he thought about the exchange of an oil concession for an agreement on troop withdrawals, and when Murray equivocated, he pointed out that even if the Security Council actually censored the Soviet Union, the Russians would most likely "vent their wrath on Iran and himself." Besides, he believed that the AIOC concession made a similar arrangement with the Soviet Union long overdue. Qavam assured Murray that troop withdrawal would be an absolute precondition for any concession agreement. In keeping with the diplomacy of "positive equilibrium," the Iranians sought to balance any increased Soviet influence with a comparable gesture to the United States, so Qavam indicated that a Russian concession would lead to a deal in Baluchistan for American interests.[35]

American and British diplomats seldom had much confidence in Iranian politicians and Murray was no exception. He refused to let Qavam know exactly what he would recommend to the State Department or how he personally viewed the prime minister's predicament. In reality, he found Qavam's arguments convincing. Murray also opposed any solution that left the Soviet troops in Iran or the Russians hungering for revenge. Besides, he thought that a Soviet oil concession was inevitable and might actually improve Iranian-Soviet relations. "We cannot after all provide Iran with an insurance policy against all dangers," Murray reminded his colleagues. At least this settlement would limit Russian gains, while giving both the United States and the United Nations a "partial victory."[36]

The timing of the leaks about the oil concession suggests that Qavam had already made the deal in Moscow. As soon as Qavam left in February on his mission, Murray had received hints that there were new opportunities for Standard-Vacuum, as if Qavam hoped to offset the deal he knew he must make. He then had to wait until circumstances permitted him to announce the new joint-stock company without provoking a backlash, either from the British or the Americans or the fiery Mossadeq. Murray's reaction proved the wisdom of that strategy. By late March a concession seemed a modest price for Iran's independence. Conversely, the indication that bilateral negotiations had reached a settlement undercut Iran's complaint to the Security Council. In that way Qavam could keep faith with the British and

Americans without unduly antagonizing the Russians. That was diplomatic juggling at its best.[37]

If the Soviets thought they had made a deal with Qavam in Moscow, they undoubtedly resented his insistence on presenting Iran's complaint to the Security Council. For them it was a needless embarrassment before the world community. For Qavam, however, it was a necessary way to keep the adversaries balanced. The British and Americans had insisted that he press Iran's case in the United Nations. Without their support, Iran had no real leverage against the Soviets. Andrei Gromyko, the Soviet delegate to the Security Council, had asked for a delay from 25 March until 10 April, because his country had not expected Iran's complaint and was therefore not prepared to discuss it. Besides, Gromyko insisted, negotiations were still underway.[38]

The Soviet response was monotonously predictable. Russian delegates had adopted the same posture at every preceding international meeting. That does not mean, however, that Iran's complaint did not take the Russians by surprise, especially after they had warned Qavam against it. And as soon as Hoseyn Ala, Iran's representative to the United Nations, filed the complaint, they pressured Qavam to withdraw it. The prime minister announced that he favored a delay and rebuked Ala for opposing him. Murray then urged Qavam to follow Ala's course and with that, Qavam again reversed himself.[39]

The British meanwhile frustrated a Soviet effort to shift discussion to the Paris foreign ministers meeting, where undoubtedly they would have found a way to stifle any negotiations. Foreign Minister Ernest Bevin warned that if the Security Council did not face the Iranian question squarely, the United Nations would be dangerously weakened. President Truman ended speculation about American intentions. He told a press conference that the United States would insist on a hearing for Iran. Here was the toughness toward the Russians that many administration critics had found lacking.[40]

The Russians now stole the American thunder. As Byrnes eagerly awaited the UN showdown, Tass announced that the evacuation of Russian troops had begun on 24 March. Withdrawal would be completed within five to six weeks, "if nothing unforeseen should take place." Whether Tass meant complications with the oil deal or political disruptions in Iran was never clear. Indeed, the phrase left the door wide open for the Russians to reverse course on almost any pretext. On the evening of 25 March the new Soviet Ambassador to Iran, Ivan Sadchikov, delivered three notes that contained the bill for the removal of Russian troops. The first note repeated the essence of the Tass anouncement, including the ominous caveat, "if nothing unforeseen should take place." The second note contained the terms for the joint Iranian-Soviet oil company, the same terms Murray had learned about earlier. In the third note, the Soviets volunteered to intercede in the Azerbaijan negotiations.[41]

Qavam received the notes with mixed feelings. While he was obviously pleased that the Russians would withdraw, he objected to the implicit qualifications contained in the conditions. In addition, he hoped for better terms on the oil concession. As for Azerbaijan, Qavam had no desire for Russian assistance there. He preferred to negotiate directly with Pishevari.[42]

The Tass announcement should have brought an end to the crisis on terms all the parties could abide. But public events often have a dramatic reality of their own. The British and the Americans demanded their pound of Russian flesh, and Secretary Byrnes in particular had seized on the crisis to promote his own political agenda. He had widely proclaimed his determination to lead the American delegation at the first meeting of the United Nations in the United States. By embarrassing the Russians there, he could shore up his political base in Washington. In addition, the Iranian case had raised some ticklish procedural questions that promised to have a significant impact on the future effectiveness of the United Nations. Could the Soviet Union, for example, prevent the Security Council from hearing Iran's case, and at the same time unilaterally force the Iranian government to make concessions? Truman and Byrnes wanted to assure the world that the United Nations could fulfill its responsibilities.[43]

It should come as no surprise, then, that the Security Council meeting generated considerable acrimony. Andrei Gromyko was determined to keep the Iranian case off the agenda; Byrnes was equally resolved to have it heard. Gromyko told the first session that Iran and the Soviet Union had reached an agreement and since Russian troops were withdrawing, he saw no need to have further discussions. Secretary Byrnes replied that the Iranian government had neither acknowledged the agreement nor withdrawn its appeal. As long as a threat to the peace existed, Iran should have a right to address the council. Gromyko rejected Byrnes's argument. The Russians, he declared, would not discuss any substantive aspects of the case. In fact, Gromyko warned that they would refuse to attend meetings where the case was being considered. Despite his objection, the council voted nine to two against his proposal for a delay. Tempers by now were badly frayed and the council was deadlocked. The French delegate recommended that a three-member subcommittee weigh the various proposals and report back to the council. With that, the first stormy session adjourned.[44]

The American position hinged on the condition that Iran and the Soviet Union had not actually reached an agreement. If they had already done so, Byrnes's hard line would seem merely an effort to embarrass the Russians, not to protect Iran or world peace. The secretary thus instructed Murray to find out the status of the negotiations between Iran and the Soviet Union. Qavam assured Murray that while the two sides were talking, no formal understanding had yet been achieved. The prime minister insisted, undoubtedly to please the United States, that Iran would not drop its case until the Russians had evacuated. With that assurance, Byrnes confidently opposed Gromyko's efforts to delay discussions. The Soviet delegate angrily chided Byrnes and denied that Ala had acted under instruction from his government in bringing Iran's case to the council. Byrnes stood fast. He believed that the council would become useless if it denied Iran the opportunity to be heard. Gromyko would not yield at all. Once again, he asked the council to postpone further discussion. This time, when the council voted against him, Gromyko marched out. [45]

Gromyko's departure from the council sent shock waves through the American public. Newspapers across the country charged that the Russians had proven unwilling to work within the bounds or the spirit of the United Nations. George Gallup discovered that 77 percent of American voters "decried" the Russian tactics. A *Washington Post* editorial expressed the common feeling that the Russians wanted to stall until "the last breath of independence had been squeezed out of Iran." Most of the newspapers did not actually believe that the Russians intended to leave the United Nations.[46]

Indeed, a resolution of the crisis was at hand. On 29 March, in Gromyko's absence, Byrnes had successfully proposed a council resolution calling on Iran and the Soviet Union to report on the status of their negotiations. On 3 April the council convened to hear letters from Gromyko and Ala. Gromyko again insisted that as of 24 March an agreement had existed under which the withdrawal of Soviet troops was unconnected to other matters. Ala presented quite another view. He charged that Soviet interference continued as before, that no positive understanding had been achieved, and that troop withdrawal was conditional on an oil concession and on autonomy for Azerbaijan. When Byrnes asked how the Security Council should proceed, Ala asserted that the Soviets must make their evacuation unconditional and must promise to have their troops out by 6 May. Under those conditions, Iran would not pursue its case, so long as it remained formally on the agenda.[47]

Fearing these comments would undermine the agreement he was about to reach, Qavam repudiated Ala's statement. That did not stop Byrnes from pressing the case. Proceeding on the basis of Ala's proposal, he moved that the Security Council postpone further discussions until 6 May. In so doing, he assumed that the Soviet Union would remove its troops regardless of the state of negotiations. Since the case would technically remain on the council agenda, it could be revived should any new circumstances interrupt the withdrawal. When the council adopted his proposal by a nine to zero vote (Poland abstaining), Byrnes had his victory. He returned to Washington with the praise of other council delegates who applauded his role in the debates.[48]

Just as Byrnes completed his triumphant mission to the United Nations, Qavam struck an agreement with Ambassador Sadchikov. Under its terms, the Russians would withdraw unconditionally over a five- to six-week period. In addition, they recognized Azerbaijan as an internal Iranian problem to be settled by direct negotiations between the rebels and the Iranian government. There was a price, of course, even though it was technically not linked to withdrawal. The Soviet government would receive a twenty-five-year oil concession. During that time it would own 51 percent of the development company. For the following twenty-five years, ownership of the concession would be shared on a fifty-fifty basis. Qavam in turn promised to submit the oil agreement to the Majles within seven months.[49]

The war clouds that had so suddenly rolled in now dissipated, and Byrnes reaped the rewards of his showdown strategy. James Reston in a *New York Times* column praised the secretary for having acted "without fear of provocation" to "stand behind the principles of the [UN] Charter." The *Washington Post* suggested that Byrnes had thwarted the Soviets' attempt to bind the United Nations to the purposes of Soviet ambition. Some former critics like "Polyzoides" in the *Los Angeles Times* now applauded Byrnes's toughness, which "more than anything else, has saved, even temporarily, a serious explosive situation." A few of Byrnes's critics, however, remained unconvinced. The *San Francisco Chronicle* complained that "Secretary Byrnes seems to mistake a pose with a chip on his shoulder for forthright firmness with the Russians." But what "forthright firmness" meant in practice, the *Chronicle* did not say.[50]

During the course of the crisis, the newspapers played a major role in introducing the public to the administration's cold war assumptions. Editorials frequently harped on the scope of the Soviet Union's expansionist goals as well as on the threat to American security. A. C. Tainton-Pothberg in the *Washington Post,* for example, described the Russians as compulsive bargain-hunters playing "cheap diplomacy" for a "breath-taking empire." Writers like Joseph Alsop and Bernard Nover in the *Washington Post* and C. L. Sulzberger in the *New York Times* defined America's interest in the crisis in the same terms used by defense planners. Oil, civil air rights, water transit, and the geopolitical balance of the Middle East were all at stake. These editorial writers all urged toughness to contain the Soviet Union. Alsop suggested that American sword-rattling had at least for the moment upset the Russian timetable for gaining control of the Middle East. Bernard Nover was not so sure. He warned that the Russians had merely changed tactics once they had concluded that "there were other ways of skinning the Iranian cat besides the direct and brutal methods which Russia has thus far sought to employ." Clearly the newspapers had joined in the requiem for the idea of postwar big power cooperation.[51]

Most observers of the crisis believed the outcome had vindicated American faith in the United Nations. Senator Tom Connolly of Texas, the bombastic head of the Foreign Relations Committee, declaimed that "to my mind, what has happened is the augury of the continuing usefulness of the United Nations through such experience." The *Los Angeles Times* thought that firmness with the Russians at the United Nations had also inhibited their designs on Turkey, Iraq, and the Middle East. "The Russian work was too coarse," the *Times* remarked. "The United States cannot stop the Russians from playing, but it may have stopped her from playing too rough."[52]

As in 1944, success in an Iranian crisis would prove transitory. The United Nations certainly had provided a forum in which to expose Soviet actions to international attention. American efforts most likely had advanced the date for the withdrawal of Soviet troops from Iran. But the larger issues dividing the Soviets and the Americans over Iran remained unresolved. The Soviets would complain about the evidence of American hostility, while the Americans anticipated renewed Soviet attempts to penetrate the Middle East. Neither side had shown any inclination to compromise what it saw as its long-term security interests in favor of international cooperation, in or out of the United Nations.[53]

THE HANGOVER

The end of the crisis did not mean the end of Iran's case before the Security Council. It remained something of a political football until it too passed out of the spotlight. Upon his return to the council, Gromyko insisted that the case should be formally removed from the agenda. Everyone knew an Iranian-Soviet agreement had been reached. Soviet troops were leaving Iran. Those circumstances made it illegal to defer discussion until 6 May, he insisted. Although Hoseyn Ala wanted the question to remain on the agenda, the Soviets circumvented his efforts to have it kept by extracting a promise from the prime minister that he would ask the council to drop the case.[54]

Ala once again attempted to defy Qavam. He told the council that while an agreement did appear to exist, the Iranian government did not think it could dictate the Security Council's actions. Yet another note instructed Ala to withdraw Iran's complaint. On that basis Gromyko pressed for the withdrawal of the case. When Stettinius resisted, a week of procedural wrangling followed. Even though the issues at stake often seemed to be narrow legalisms, the debates were often bitter. Finally, the council voted to retain the question, even after Gromyko had insisted that his government would not participate in any further substantive discussions.[55]

The Iranian case occasionally generated new excitement. Ala ruffled the council on 20 May when he announced that he could not confirm that Russian troops had actually left Iran. His government had no control over Azerbaijan, where Soviet interference continued as before. Qavam, however, led the council to believe that Ala had spoken on his own authority; Soviet troops had in fact evacuated. Ala's action so outraged leftist groups in Iran that they demanded his immediate recall. The United States now intervened on Ala's behalf. After all, his actions at the United Nations had greatly facilitated Byrnes's effort to confront the Soviets. Byrnes told Qavam that a decision either to recall his ambassador or to repudiate him would hamstring the council's efforts to deal with Iran's case. By acquiescing in the

American request, Qavam not only made a positive gesture to the United States, but also one to the shah, who counted Ala among his most trusted advisers.[56]

The rift between Ala and Qavam left the Security Council in a quandary. After a desultory discussion it adjourned further discussions for the indefinite future. Then on 4 June, having heard nothing more from the Iranian delegate, the council delayed further debate. Although the complaint technically remained on the agenda, it was never again discussed. The Iranian case had become history. Had the United Nations survived its first test? On one level it had acted successfully; Iran's complaint had been heard and the Soviet Union had seemed to respond to the pressure to reach a settlement that satisfied world opinion. On other levels, the significance of the case was much harder to determine. The United Nations could not be effective when a major power was party to a dispute. The Soviets had shown that they could block or at least disrupt any proceedings they opposed. Nor had the United Nations been altogether neutral in this instance. The Security Council had largely sided with the United States. That was in large part a reflection of the strength of Iran's appeal and the weakness of the Soviet position. But the case also seemed to justify Soviet fears that the United Nations would function as an instrument of the western powers in general, and of the United States in particular.[57]

On many occasions Soviet leaders expressed their resentment of the way the United States had handled this crisis. On 4 April, Walter Bedell Smith, formerly General Eisenhower's assistant and newly appointed ambassador to the Soviet Union, held a late night interview with Stalin. The two men talked at length about the crisis in Iran. Stalin emphasized his bitterness at efforts to deny the Soviet Union an oil concession and at the role the United States had played at the United Nations. At the Paris foreign ministers meeting three weeks later, Molotov told Byrnes with what amounted to ironic understatement that the American attitudes in the Security Council "had not been those of a friend." Charles Bohlen, acting as an interpreter and adviser to Byrnes, deduced that "the observations of Molotov and Vishinski again reveal the Soviet thesis that the relations between the great powers were more important than strict observance of the [UN] Charter. . . ." A month later Ambassador Sadchikov made a similar point to George Allen. In refusing to comply with the Soviet Union's request to defer Iran's case, the United States had shown a discourtesy that the Soviets would never have committed. They could not comprehend what had motivated the Americans.[58]

In the spring of 1946 any sign of Soviet discomfort could only have persuaded American policymakers that they were on the right course. Firmness in the Iranian crisis had prevented the Soviets from successfully duplicating their strategy in Rumania. That tough stance had also established the United Nations as an effective instrument of international relations. Stalwart support from the British demonstrated the wisdom of Churchill's call for an Anglo-American partnership. And despite Qavam's equivocating, the United States had established in its alliance with Iran a barrier to Soviet expansion into the Middle East. Those were among the lessons American policymakers drew from their success in the Iranian crisis of 1945–46.

In reality American foreign policy had entered into an era of increasingly rigid thinking. The cold war consensus formed in this period locked policymakers into assumptions that would in the future severely restrict their options. Even as the Russians drew back from their aggressive moves toward the Persian Gulf, the United States tried to expand its own strength in the region. Worst-case scenarios informed American policymaking. Most Americans assumed that Stalin was just biding his time before renewing his quest to dominate the Middle East. The idea that the Soviet

Union might have some legitimate security concerns in the region no longer mediated the American interpretation of events.

During the crisis it also became clearer how the determination to maintain a cold war consensus could silence debate over foreign policy. In March the Russian press had given heavy play to statements by Senators Pepper, Kilgore, Taylor, and Mitchell criticizing the administration's growing truculence toward the Soviet Union. All these men would suffer subsequent widespread abuse from anticommunist witch hunters. George Kennan, however, worried that the Russians would misconstrue their remarks as evidence that powerful domestic factions might oppose current policy. If that led the Russians to underestimate American resolve, they might "advance into positions from which they cannot withdraw and which we cannot accept." Kennan, of course, was largely concerned with keeping diplomacy in the hands of the professionals and out of the hands of well-meaning amateurs and political partisans. In less responsible hands, similar arguments would soon be used to equate criticism or disagreement, sometimes even objectivity, with treason. Some of the State Department's best people would see their careers destroyed by the zealots of cold war orthodoxy.[59]

Not until the 1950s and the Mossadeq oil nationalization crisis would Iran again figure so centrally in the formulation of American policy. That does not mean, however, that American diplomats ignored Iran. Many issues that arose during the 1945 crisis remained unresolved. Would Pishevari's separatist government establish Azerbaijani autonomy? And what would be the consequences of the establishment of the Iranian-Soviet oil company? Would the Majles approve it? Would it establish sufficient Soviet influence to drag Iran into Moscow's orbit? Would the Russians find other ways to undermine the government in Tehran? What level of American assistance was needed to maintain Iran as a barrier to Soviet expansion? And finally, how would Iranian oil figure in the postwar development of the international petroleum industry? Those issues would constitute the agenda of Iranian-American affairs for the next five years.

NOTES

1. FR, 1946, 7, pp. 294–95, Murray to Secretary of State, 1/4/46. See also SD 791.00/1-546, Stettinius to Secretary of State.

2. FR, 1946, 7, pp. 299–301, Murray to Secretary of State, 1/10/46. Ibid., pp. 293–94, Memorandum by Acheson, 1/3/46.

3. For the United Nations documentation, see *United Nations Security Council Journal,* 1st year, Series 1, Meeting 1–42, 1/17/46–1/26/46, pp. 13–73 (hereafter cited as UNJ). Since the relevant materials are readily located in these pages, I will not make further individual citations. Notes will indicate other related sources. On Iran's strategy for the UN, see Ramazani, *Iran's Foreign Policy,* pp. 127–28. See also FR, 1946, 7, pp. 306–7 and 306n., Stettinius to Secretary of State, 1/22/46.

4. Ibid., pp. 289–90, memorandum by Harry Howard, 12/27/45. See also ibid., pp. 290–308 and passim, for the working out of the American position. See also ibid., p. 309, memorandum by Stevenson, 1/24/46.

5. UNJ, pp. 70–83. The *New York Times* offers extensive coverage of these events during this period. FR, 1946, 7, pp. 309–11, Head of Soviet Delegation to the President of the Security Council, 1/24/46. Ibid., pp. 314–15, Stettinius to Secretary of State, 1/26/46.

6. Ibid., pp. 325–26 and 326n., Stettinius to Byrnes.

7. Ibid., p. 305–6, Murray to Secretary of State, 1/21/46. Mossadeq quoted in Abrahamian, *Iran Between Two Revolutions,* p. 222.

8. Abrahamian, *Iran Between Two Revolutions,* pp. 225–26.

9. Abrahamian, *Iran Between Two Revolutions,* p. 226. Editorial by Drew Pearson, *San Francisco Chronicle,* 3/30/46 (the editorial was widely syndicated.)

10. SD 891.00/1–1646, 74, Murray to Secretary of State. See also SD 891.00/1–1646, memorandum by Harold Minor. FR, 1946, 7, p. 331, Murray to Secretary of State, 2/8/46.

11. Abrahamian, *Iran Between Two Revolutions,* pp. 226–27.

12. SD 891.00/1–2546, 117, Murray to Secretary of State. FR, 1946, 7, pp. 331n. and 334n.

13. On Rossow and the consulate, see Kuniholm, *The Origins of the Cold War in the Near East,* p. 318.

14. FR, 1946, 7, p. 302–3, Murray to Secretary of State, 1/14/46; and ibid., pp. 301–2, 302n. and 303n.

15. *New York Times,* 2/10/46. See also Yergin, *Shattered Peace,* pp. 166–67. See also Kuniholm, *Origins of the Cold War in the Near East,* p. 310 for the State Department reaction. FR, 1946, 7, pp. 690–96.

16. Byrnes, *Speaking Frankly,* pp. 254–56. Yergin, *Shattered Peace,* pp. 185–87. See Department of State, *Bulletin,* 14, 3/10/46, pp. 355–58.

17. For Kennan's telegram, see FR, 1946, 7, pp. 696–709. See also Kennan, *Memoirs,* pp. 308–11 for his discussion of the telegram.

18. For two able but conflicting analyses of Kennan, see John Lewis Gaddis, *Strategies of Containment,* pp. 19–24 and Yergin, *Shattered Peace,* pp. 167–71. It must be clear that my own views correspond most closely to Yergin's. I have always believed that Kennan exaggerated his arguments, partly in frustration, partly to maximize their impact. In the hands of less knowledgeable or sophisticated politicians, those ideas became dangerously simplistic and a barrier to reducing Soviet-American tensions.

19. Yergin, *Shattered Peace,* pp. 176–77. *New York Times,* 3/7/46.

20. FR, 1946, 7, pp. 332–33, Rossow to Secretary of State, 2/11/46. Rossow later published some of his recollections of the Azerbaijan crisis. See Robert Rossow, "The Battle of Azerbaijan, 1946," *Middle East Journal,* 10 (Winter 1956): 17–32.

21. On Qavam's visit to the Soviet Union, see Ramazani, *Iran's Foreign Policy,* pp. 135–36. See also SD, OSS/I&R Reports, 4619, v. 7, 2, pp. 12–16.

22. *New York Times,* 3/3/46. For Qavam's protest, see UNJ, pp. 65–66. FR, 1946, 7, pp. 335–37. See also Ramazani, *Iran's Foreign Policy,* p. 137, and FR, 1946, 7, pp. 340–44, Rossow to Secretary of State.

23. Many historians have examined Truman's claim that he threatened to use force. (Truman, *Memoirs,* 2:605; *New York Times,* 8/25/57). Several have done extensive digging. See, for example, Kuniholm, *Origins of the Cold War in the Near East,* pp. 320–21n.; Ramazani, *Iran's Foreign Policy,* pp. 138–39; Richard Pfau, "Containment in Iran, 1946: The Shift to an Active Policy," *Diplomatic History* 1 (Fall 1977): 360–61. Similarly, I discussed this matter in an interview with Charles Bohlen (January 1972). He confirmed what other sources indicated—that Truman's memory had tricked him. There is, however, some evidence that Truman and his advisers at least considered the use of force. Historian John Blum of Yale University told me that before leaving the navy in 1946 he recalled a meeting among the navy chiefs. They had considered the problem of using force in the Persian Gulf area and had told the president or the Joint Chiefs that any such attempt would be a logistical nightmare. The Soviet Union would have the advantage of theater air superiority and short internal lines of supply. Perhaps Truman had remembered some of this more hypothetical discussion. It still constituted no direct threat of force. See also FR, 1946, 7, editorial note, pp. 346–48. On the actual American response, see FR, 1946, 7, p. 334, Ala to Secretary of State, 3/5/46; ibid., pp. 337–39, Kennan to Secretary of State, 3/4/46; ibid., pp. 340–42, Byrnes to Kennan, 3/5/46. Roger Louis has pointed out that the British had hoped to beat the drum of the Atlantic Charter in order to embarrass the Soviets. The Americans had by now adopted that strategy as their own. Louis, *The British Empire in the Middle East, 1945–1951,* pp. 66–69.

24. SD 891.00/3–1146, 300, Wilson (Ankara) to Secretary of State.

25. SD 891.24591/3–1146, 312, Murray to Secretary of State.

26. For one interesting analysis of American cold war metaphors used to describe Soviet behavior, see Nagai Yonosuke, "The Roots of Cold War Doctrine: The Esoteric and the Exoteric," in Iriyae and Yonosuke, eds., *The Origins of the Cold War in Asia* (Tokyo/New York, 1977), pp. 19–26. For connections to recent American policy for Central America, see Walter LaFeber, *Inevitable Revolutions,* pp. 219ff.

27. SD 891.24591/3–1346, 788, Kennan to Secretary of State. One can profitably contrast

this telegram with the analysis of Kennan's views offered by John Lewis Gaddis, "Containment: A Reassessment," *Foreign Affairs Quarterly* 55, 4 (July 1977): 873–87. Gaddis seeks to dissociate Kennan's views from those that Walter Lippmann labeled "a strategic monstrosity." Many of Kennan's cables from this period stress military strength as a key ingredient for American policy. It is not so surprising then that many of his colleagues read military force as crucial for a successful containment policy.

28. SD 891.24591/3–1346.

29. For one good example of that kind of thinking, see MMRB, A Report to the National Security Council, NSC–7, "The Position of the United States with Respect to Soviet-Directed World Communism," 3/30/48, pp. 1–13. See also Leffler, "The American Concept of National Security," pp. 366–67.

30. FR, 1946, 7, editorial note, pp. 346–48. See also ibid., pp. 345–46 and 346n.

31. Ibid., 348–49. See also Kuniholm, *Origins of the Cold War in the Near East,* pp. 320–23 for an excellent reconstruction of the background of this episode and the note to Moscow.

32. For a good analysis of Qavam's political strategy, see Abrahamian, *Iran Between Two Revolutions,* pp. 222–29.

33. FR, 1946, 7, p. 344, Kennan to Secretary of State, 3/6/46; ibid., pp. 349–50, memorandum by George Allen, 3/11/46; ibid., p. 354, Murray to Secretary of State, 3/14/46; and ibid., p. 357, Murray to Secretary of State.

34. Ibid., p. 365. See also ibid., pp. 369–71, Murray to Secretary of State, 3/22/46.

35. Ibid., pp. 369–75. See also FO 371/45487/E7835, Bullard to Baxter, Oct. 1, 1945. Bullard was highly amused by Murray's indignation when the Iranians showed "ingratitude—to *him,* who for so many years had defended them. . . ."

36. Ibid., p. 375, Murray to Secretary of State, 387, 3/23/46.

37. Two major studies of Iran come to somewhat similar conclusions. See Abrahamian, *Iran Between Two Revolutions,* p. 223; Ramazani, *Iran's Foreign Policy,* pp. 139–40.

38. FR, 1946, 7, p. 366, Gromykó to Secretary General of the Security Council, 3/19/46. See also UNJ, p. 353.

39. FR, 1946, 7, pp. 376–78, Murray to Secretary of State.

40. Ibid., pp. 368–69, British FO to British Embassy (Washington), 3/21/46. Ibid., p. 372, Byrnes to Murray, 3/22/46. See also *New York Times,* 3/23/46.

41. FR, 1946, 7, p. 379, Kennan to Secretary of State. Ibid., pp. 379–81, Murray to Secretary of State, 3/25/46.

42. Ibid., pp. 379–81.

43. On Byrnes's attitude, for example, see Thomas Campbell and George Herring, eds., *The Diaries of Edward R. Stettinius, Jr.* (New York, 1975), pp. 448–49. See also Messer, *The End of an Alliance,* pp. 195–200.

44. For the official minutes of this Security Council meeting, see UNJ, pp. 366–468. *New York Times,* 3/26/46; FR, 1946, 7, pp. 381–85, 389. Only the Polish delegate voted with the Russians on the motion for delay.

45. FR, 1946, 7, p. 385–87, Murray to Secretary of State, 3/27/46. *New York Times,* 3/27 and 3/28/49. UNJ, pp. 411–20.

46. As mentioned earlier, this evaluation is based on the reading of ten major daily papers representing a range of opinions, regional diversity, and major chains. See in particular the *New York Times,* 3/30 and 4/4/46; *Washington Post,* 3/29 and 3/31/46. Even the caterer at the UN was polled, explaining that the Russians had not left because of Iran, but because the shipment of vodka was late. ("We're sure everything will be straightened out," he added hopefully, "and there will be demand for the stuff.")

47. *New York Times,* 4/3/46. FR, 1946, 7, p. 403; UNJ, pp. 453–54.

48. FR, 1946, 7, pp. 407–9. *New York Times,* 4/4/ and 4/5/46.

49. FR, 1946, 7, pp. 405–7, Murray to Secretary of State, 4/4/46. *New York Times,* 4/6 and 4/7/46.

50. For an example of the war scare provoked by the crisis, see Drew Pearson, *San Francisco Chronicle,* 3/15/46. Pearson claimed that Pentagon officials had discussed the possibility of war. That information does in some way confirm John Blum's recollection. See also *Chicago Tribune,* 3/26/46. For editorial responses, see, for example, *New York Times,* 4/15/46; *Los Angeles Times,* 3/26/46; *Washington Post,* 4/6/46; and *San Francisco Chronicle,* 3/27/46.

51. *New York Times,* sec. 4, 4/7/46 and 4/5/46; *Los Angeles Times,* 4/18/46; *Washington Post,* editorials, 1/18, 3/27, 3/29, 3/31, 4/4, and 4/17/46.

52. Connolly quoted in *New York Times,* 4/5/46. *Washington Post,* 3/29/46; and *Los Angeles Times,* 4/18/46.

53. On Byrnes's thinking, see FR, 1946, 7, pp. 441–42, memorandum by Bohlen.

54. FR 1946, 7, pp. 410–11, Stettinius to Secretary of State, 4/8/46 and ibid., pp. 415–17. See also UNJ, pp. 489–91.

55. *New York Times,* April 8–15, 1946. See also FR, 1946, 7, pp. 420–37 for American analysis of the UN proceedings. The Iranian case still managed to grab occasional headlines. On May 6 the council turned to Ala and Gromyko for reports. True to his word, the Soviet delegate was absent. Ala acknowledged that the Soviets had evacuated most of northern Iran. His government did not, however, have adequate information about Azerbaijan. The ambiguity of Ala's report and the Soviet absence led Stettinius to propose that further proceedings be delayed until May 20. Ibid., pp. 450–51, Stettinius to Secretary of State, 5/6/46; ibid., pp. 456–57, Stettinius to Secretary of State, 5/8/46. See also SD 891.00/5–1146, Chargé Tehran to Secretary of State; and SD 891.00/5–1446, 5116, Harriman (London) to Secretary of State.

56. FR, 1946, 7, pp. 477–78, Byrnes to Allen, 5/22/46; ibid., pp. 480–82, Allen to Byrnes, 5/25/46.

57. Ibid., Stettinius to Byrnes, 5/22/46, and editorial note, pp. 493–94.

58. FR, 1946, 6, pp. 732–36, Smith to Secretary of State, 4/5/46. FR, 1946, 7, pp. 441–42, memorandum by Bohlen, 4/28/46. See also SD 891.00/5–2146, 17, Allen to Secretary of State.

59. SD 861.24591/3–2246, 905, Kennan to Secretary of State.

11 The Iranian-American Alliance and the Cold War

The withdrawal of Russian troops alleviated the most direct threat to Iran. It did not, however, spell an end to Iran's troubles with its northern neighbor. The Iranian crisis was actually a drama with three acts, with act one opening in the Security Council and ending with the departure of Soviet troops. The Soviet Union had in essence traded one instrument of its wartime Iranian policy—Red Army forces—for a less direct, but more workable postwar instrument—an oil concession. The agreement Moscow demanded as a *quid pro quo* for troop withdrawal covered much the same area that Soviet forces had once occupied. Such an arrangement clearly had as much to do with politics as with the probable location of oil.

Act two hinged on Qavam's efforts to negotiate with the separatist governments of Pishevari and Qazi Mohammed. As long as they maintained their autonomy, Iran's sovereignty was compromised and its future independence in doubt. Through the rebels the Soviet Union could pressure the Iranian government to adopt a friendly posture. At the same time, Tehran could not expect a successful reconciliation with the dissident provinces unless it addressed some of their legitimate grievances. But to focus on the autonomy movements would be to forget what the crisis was about in the first place—oil. The final act in this drama involved Soviet efforts to win Majles approval for the concession they had wrested from Qavam in act one. Whatever the Soviets wanted in Iran, whether a Persian Gulf port, strategic territories, political influence, economic advantage, or some combination of these factors, an oil concession remained for three years their primary demand on Iran.

A possibility exists that the Soviets actually wanted a concession to produce oil. Soviet officials, like their American and English counterparts, must have recognized the enormous strategic and economic potential of Middle Eastern oil. That oil could do more than serve domestic Soviet markets. It could earn substantial foreign currency that would ease the costs of the massive reconstruction task that faced the Soviet Union. Soviet diplomats knew full well how much the English government benefited from AIOC revenues. Why then would the Soviet Union not wish to assume an oil position in Iran, when it was clear that the development of Middle Eastern oil would reshape the postwar international economy?

In 1946 few American or British diplomats believed that the Soviet Union could have economic rather than political or strategic ambitions in Iran. Evidence that the Soviets had dispatched drilling teams and sunk exploratory wells did not alter the dominant view. The pressure for a concession appeared to parallel Soviet demands on Turkey for bases and for control of the Straits, and the role of the Communists in the civil war in Greece. Most Americans accepted the argument of Sir Reader Bullard that the Soviets had all the oil they needed. Iranian oil would serve them primarily as an economic lever with which they could disrupt international markets and enhance their strategic position vis-à-vis the United States and Britain.[1]

By the summer of 1946 the Truman administration had concluded that Russian aspirations in the direction of the Persian Gulf, if fulfilled, "would have a disastrous effect not only on American interests in the area, but on our general position vis-à-vis the Soviet Union. . . ."[2] As the administration moved toward the Truman Doctrine and a redefinition of American security interests in the eastern Mediterranean, it became determined to deny the Soviet Union the two instruments it might use to extend its influence over Iran—the oil concession and the separatist governments. Not coincidentally, success in that effort would eliminate the chief threat to growing American hegemony over Middle Eastern oil. What role private corporations and private agencies would play in postwar oil policy remained an open political question. But on one point virtually all policymakers agreed: National security required continued American development of Middle Eastern oil. Serious rivalry from either the Russians or the British was unacceptable.

AMERICAN STRATEGY AND THE REUNIFICATION OF IRAN

The American determination to keep Iran out of the Soviet orbit raised a fundamental dilemma. While the Truman administration considered that country of increased importance to security interests in the region, the American presence there had declined as a consequence of postwar demobilization. By contrast, the British, who had lost much of their political influence in the region, retained a greater economic role in Iran than they had had even before the war. As AIOC expanded its operations, Iran's dependence on its oil revenues would increase correspondingly. Hence the increasingly anglophobic nationalist factions sought more tangible signs that the United States would provide Iran with effective support, particularly against the Soviet threat. Most often, when they asked for material assistance and firm strategic commitments, the State Department offered advice on internal affairs, reaffirmed the Tehran Declaration, or invoked the principles of the United Nations charter. Prime Minister Qavam had little reason to assume that the United States would come to Iran's aid if Soviet pressures escalated.[3]

The task of sustaining American influence in the face of a declining presence fell to George Allen, who on 11 May 1946 replaced Wallace Murray as ambassador. Increased American involvement in the Middle East during the war had created a small group of informed diplomats, of whom Allen was one of the most able. He had spent the last several years in the Near East Division under the tutelage of Loy Henderson. Not surprisingly, he shared his chief's major assumptions about the danger Soviet ambitions posed to American security interests in the Middle East. Henderson showed his confidence in him by assigning Allen to brief Secretary Byrnes during the March Security Council meeting. Byrnes had so appreciated his manner and energy that Allen emerged as a natural choice to head the embassy in Tehran.[4]

Both the British and American ambassadors generally assumed that it was their function to advise the Iranians on how to run their affairs. Allen had to decide quickly what to make of Qavam and the prime minister's often impenetrable political strategies. Murray had come to accept Qavam's concessions to the left or the Soviets as necessary parts of his political juggling act. At first Allen was inclined to adopt his predecessor's tolerant view, but when Qavam arrested prominent pro-British figures, removed the ban on Tudeh Party meetings, included Tudeh members in his government, and proposed extensive concessions to the Azeri and Kurdish dissidents, Allen decided he must deflect Qavam from his leftist course. Cold war assumptions had narrowed the options of any Iranian who wanted to rule with American backing.[5]

The relative weakness of the American presence in Iran made Allen particularly sensitive to the mounting leftist attacks on the gendarmerie mission headed by Col. H. Norman Schwarzkopf. The ambassador feared that in attempting to appease the Soviet Union Qavam might compromise the mission. Should Soviet sympathizers drive it out, the United States would lose one more vestige of its wartime role. Equally important, the gendarmerie had the responsibility for supervising the election of the Fifteenth Majles, which would vote on the proposed Iranian-Soviet oil company. Allen warned the State Department that "discontinuance of the mission would be a serious step along the road to complete Soviet domination of Iran. . . ." The gendarmerie had by now become an instrument of cold war containment politics designed "to prevent one more country from falling into Moscow's orbit."[6] Allen's appeal persuaded the State Department to arrange with the Iranian government to renew the mission for another two years. The War Department, after three years of inaction, finally promoted Schwarzkopf to brigadier general.

Qavam wooed the left, not out of any pro-Soviet leanings, but from a determination to build a ruling coalition. In 1946 the Tudeh Party and Democratic Party of Azerbaijan were the only organizations in Iran that in any contemporary sense constituted political parties. Qavam wanted to form a party of his own through which he could realize his program to reduce the power of the monarchy, to institute significant reforms, and to bring Azerbaijan and Kurdistan back under Tehran's control. To achieve those goals, he created his own Democrat Party, so named to remind Iranians of the old constitutional Democrats, and the name intentionally confused the party's relationship to its Azerbaijan rivals. The new Democrats attracted a spectrum of reformers, nationalists, northern anti-British aristocrats, and noncommunist radicals. Though Qavam allowed the Tudeh Party to retain its three cabinet posts, he frustrated any communist attempt to seize control of his party.[7]

While he was forming his new party, Qavam postponed elections until September, when he hoped to have enough support to control the Fifteenth Majles. Allen, however, was not persuaded that Qavam sought only to outflank the Tudeh Party and Pishevari; the leftward drift Qavam was following struck him as another phase in a program of Soviet penetration. Allen was convinced that the Democrat Party and its propaganda paralleled Soviet tactics elsewhere. His analysis demonstrated how cold war assumptions colored American policy. In proposing to reform Iran's land system and its national security forces, Qavam pursued policies he had favored since the days of the constitutional revolution. But because Allen viewed such policies as concessions to the left, he lost faith in Qavam. As has been traditional with cold war policies, American diplomats prefer the status quo, no matter how unjust it is, to leftist reforms. Allen thus supported the shah and others who similarly mistrusted the prime minister. In that way he restricted Qavam's ability to advance programs that might have contributed to the long-term stability that Americans sought. The United States had also moved toward becoming the mainstay of a monarchy that had little popular support.[8]

By August, Qavam's maneuverings had achieved mixed results. The Qashqai and other conservative southern tribal groups thought he had sold out to the Tudeh Party. Those suspicions were enhanced when his government supported the demands of the workers during communist-inspired strikes against AIOC, and when he retained the Tudeh Party members in his reorganized cabinet. The shah, who always feared strong prime ministers, viewed him with profound mistrust. And even though he had attracted numerous factions into his Democrat Party, Qavam could not reach an understanding with Pishevari and the Azeri Democrats. Negotiations had foundered almost immediately when, among his many demands, Pishevari insisted that his officers be retained in the Iranian Army at their much-inflated present ranks. The shah could never swallow such a condition, because his authority, no matter how uncertain it was, rested heavily on the loyalty of the officer corps. The Azeri officers would owe their allegiance to Pishevari and possibly to the Tudeh Party. Once Qavam terminated the negotiations, relations between Tehran and Tabriz deteriorated even more.[9]

Qavam was caught in a foreign as well as a domestic crossfire. In September 1946 the Soviet ambassador reminded him that the deadline for elections he had agreed to in March was now fast approaching. The Soviet-Iranian oil agreement could not go into effect until elections were held. In response, Qavam claimed that he could not call elections until the situation in Azerbaijan was resolved. The two Soviet instruments thus conflicted: To gain the oil concession, the Soviets might have to allow Tehran its authority in Azerbaijan. At the same time that he was fencing with Soviet Ambassador Sadchikov, Qavam had to placate George Allen. So he indicated to the American that he would be firm with the rebels even if he had to resort to force. But Radio Moscow threatened Soviet intervention if the Iranian Army took action against the rebels.[10]

In the face of those pressures, both Qavam and the shah asked Allen to translate his vague references to the United Nations and American support into concrete terms. At one point Qavam suggested that "prompt military action" in response to a Soviet intervention was what he had in mind. As always, the Iranians indicated a willingness to pay in oil. They hinted on several occasions that they would offer an oil concession to American firms. Allen could do little more than repeat his assurances that Iran could rely on the United Nations. Mistrust of Qavam and his intentions made the State Department reluctant to spell out in precise terms what the American commitment might mean. Chastened by the 1944 crisis, the department had already decided to divorce oil concessions from current American policy to avoid any implication that American support for Iran was contingent on its own self-interest rather than based on principle. Besides, for reasons that will soon be made clear, American firms were not much interested in an Iranian concession at this time.[11]

That is not to say that Washington was not greatly concerned about the course of events in Iran or was unwilling to respond forcefully. In the fall of 1946 the Truman administration was in the process of reformulating the American role in the Middle East. Loy Henderson argued strenuously that Soviet designs on Iran necessitated a greater show of American support, and not only because of the Azeri problem and the Soviet oil concession. Allen had informed him of a possible Soviet-Iranian agreement granting the Soviets exclusive air transportation rights in northern Iran. With civilian air transport playing a crucial role in postwar American strategic thinking, Henderson grew alarmed. In October he stated that "Iran has been progressively passing under the domination of the Soviet Union. This trend of events is incompatible with the United States' interests."[12]

Henderson was most fearful that Qavam was, or might become, a Soviet puppet. The prime minister had recently acceded to Soviet demands that he call elections. That could mean a favorable decision on both air rights and the oil concession was imminent. Henderson warned "that unless we show by concrete acts that we are seriously interested in carrying out our various assurances to Iran, the Iranian government and people will eventually become so discouraged that they will no longer be able to resist Soviet pressure."[13] He had in mind either an Export-Import Bank loan or favorable action on Iran's request for military assistance.

Henderson was no lone voice crying in the wilderness. His assumptions operated throughout the national security bureaucracy. That became obvious when the State-War-Navy Coordinating Committee, the precursor to the National Security Council, asked the Joint Chiefs of Staff to evaluate Iran's strategic importance to the United States. In response, the military chiefs applied many of the assumptions of U.S. Latin American policy to the Middle East. "Iran is an area of major strategic interest to the United States," they replied. As a consequence, they argued that "United States policy towards Iran is to prevent civil disturbances which might invite intervention by powerful neighbors and which might endanger American economic interests in the Persian Gulf area."[14] Most likely Iraq and Afghanistan were not the "powerful neighbors" the Joint Chiefs had in mind.

Oil was the basis for the Joint Chiefs' conclusions, but not Iran's oil. American policymakers did not covet Iranian oil, though they would have welcomed a concession for an American firm and they appreciated the importance of the AIOC concession to Britain's economy. In 1946 as in 1944, broad strategic considerations weighed far more heavily on their thinking than narrow economic ones. Iran held the key to defending the sources of oil in the Middle East under American control, the Joint Chiefs observed. If the United States lost its access to oil in Iraq or Saudi Arabia, it might have to fight an oil-starved war. It was equally crucial to the cold war balance of power to deny the Soviets the oil in these fields. Should the Soviets maintain a sphere in northern Iran or continue to provoke the Kurds, they could move at any time against British and American oil fields in the region. Worse yet, the Soviet Union might imperil American security by seizing control of all Iran. Such a conclusion bolstered the Near East Division's case for a greater show of American support there.[15]

By this time a series of events had conspired to bring about a momentous change in Qavam's strategy. Between 17 and 19 October he dissolved his cabinet, sent his leftist spokesman Muzzafar Firuz to Moscow as ambassador, freed a number of rightist opponents like Hassan Arfa, forced Tudeh Party sympathizers out of government posts, appointed anticommunists to govern key provinces, and dropped some of his more radical reform programs. In forming his new cabinet, Qavam eliminated all three Tudeh Party members, while keeping for himself two key positions—minister of the interior with control over the gendarmerie, and minister of foreign affairs. What had brought about this sudden break with the Tudeh Party that so clearly favored American and British interests?[16]

One crucial factor was the revolt of the southern tribes spearheaded by the Qashqais. As conservative Muslims, the Qashqais feared the growing communist influence on the national government. Very possibly their unrest had been spurred on by British consular officials. They demanded for their tribes and provinces the same autonomy that Pishevari had insisted on for Azerbaijan. As support for the movement spread among Arabs and conservative Muslims, tribal leaders pressed Qavam to dismiss the Tudeh Party, to repress the communist labor unions in the oil fields, and to give the southern provinces greater representation in his new cabinet. Qavam's action against the Tudeh obviously met the major demands of the southern dissidents. It similarly placated conservative army officers who were unhappy with recent concessions to the left. And since Qavam often found himself hamstrung by the Tudeh's oppositioin to his policy initiatives, he gained more freedom of maneuver by getting rid of them.[17]

George Allen and the new British Ambassador, John Le Rougetel, had also worked to move Qavam rightward. Le Rougetel assumed his post with the usual British disdain for Iranian politicians. He soon became so critical of Qavam's leftward drift that he sought to use his embassy's resources to encourage rightist and pro-British factions. As the two ambassadors conspired to affect Qavam's political course, Allen received information about treachery in Qavam's cabinet. It seems that one of the Tudeh Party members was conspiring with the Soviet Embassy to arrange the air transport agreement the Soviet Union sought in northern Iran. When Allen confronted the prime minister with this information, Qavam gave no indication that he would take any action. For several days Allen wondered what more he should do. He had no authority to interfere in what was clearly a domestic political matter, but he realized that no one in Washington had enough grasp of the situation to guide his actions.

Urged on by Le Rougetel and Robert Rossow, his political officer, Allen decided without formal approval to go directly to the shah with his story of Tudeh betrayal and Soviet intrigue. To the distressed monarch, he recounted the unsatisfactory outcome of his meeting with Qavam. What, the shah wondered aloud, should he do? Having come this far, Allen went on to propose a scenario that would force Qavam to reform his cabinet, to resign, or to face arrest. The shah agreed to play the role Allen outlined for him. By that time, however, Qavam had already seen the necessity of a move to the right. Allen's intercession may have done little more than confirm for Qavam the wisdom of a political realignment. But these actions on Allen's part also revealed the depth of the American determination to limit Soviet influence in Iran. In addition, Allen showed that the United States preferred to work with the shah and the monarchy rather than with the more representative, but less reliable, parliamentary factions. Cold War politics did not nourish democratic government in Iran.[18]

Some members of the State Department thought that by placing the embassy in the middle of a domestic struggle Allen had exposed the United States to damaging criticism from the Soviet Union. Henderson staunchly defended his protégé, who, he believed, had faced a dangerous situation without much guidance from Washington. And now that Qavam had broken with the Tudeh Party, Henderson was more determined than ever to commit U.S. economic and military resources to Iran. Eventually, the State Department would endorse Henderson's recommendations. And on 28 October Secretary Byrnes authorized the sale of $10 million in arms to Iran. But that still left Allen for the moment without any precise definition of the American commitment there. Qavam particularly wished to know what the United States would do if he moved against Azerbaijan and the Soviet Union renewed its interference. So with Qavam beleaguered by Russian threats and Tudeh demonstrations, Allen could only invoke the agencies of world opinion, the United Nations, and the principles of American foreign policy.[19]

News that the United States would send arms apparently emboldened the shah and Qavam to resolve the situation in Azerbaijan and Kurdistan. In early November, Qavam announced that the long-awaited elections for the Fifteenth Majles would begin on 7 December though in Iranian fashion they would take months to complete. Several weeks later he indicated that security forces would not only supervise the elections in provinces under Tehran's control, but in Azerbaijan as well. That brought an ominous rumbling from the Soviet ambassador and threats from Radio Moscow. Allen, however, assured the Iranians that the decision to send troops to

Azerbaijan was a proper one. And when Qavam asked whether the State Department would support his decision to apprise the Security Council of the Soviet threats, the answer from Washington was unequivocal: Qavam should inform the UN and that is what the prime minister immediately did.[20]

Qavam was now prepared to move, In late November the army occupied Azeri-speaking Zanjan on Azerbaijan's border. On 8 December patrols crossed the border. They made their first contact with Azeri forces the next day. The army then proceeded almost without opposition toward Tabriz. Nowhere did Pishevari's promise to fight to the death lead to significant armed resistance. By 12 December armed mobs had driven Pishevari's forces from Tabriz. The deposed prime minister fled once more across the border into the Soviet Union. Cheering crowds lined the streets to welcome the Iranian army forces as they moved into Tabriz. By 13 December Tehran had reasserted its authority over Azerbaijan. And when the Kurdish Republic of Mahabad fell soon after, one more threat to Iran's independence had been eliminated. The Azeri commitment to Iranian nationalism ran deeper than the allure of autonomy, compromised by heavy Soviet interference.[21]

Where then were the Soviet Army columns? Where were the Tudeh and communist mobs? Where were the economic sanctions? Despite all the worst-case scenarios, the Soviet Union did not take any action against Iran; in this instance, the assumptions of the cold war consensus had proven wrong. Why had the Soviets deserted governments that would have potentially established a wedge for them into the Middle East? Their inaction is even more puzzling because it undermined the credibility of their threats against Qavam and the Tehran government. There is probably no single or simple explanation. Twenty-five years earlier the fledgling Bolshevik government had similarly sacrificed Iranian communists in return for the 1921 friendship treaty with Iran. Most likely, too, Moscow had come to view Pishevari as a liability and his cause as no longer worth defending. Why take risks on behalf of an ineffectual puppet? Nor should we discount the impact of signals from Washington that the United States took a hostile view of what it saw as a coordinated Soviet drive on Greece, Turkey, and Iran. In that light we should recall Firuz Kazemzadeh's observation that the Soviet Union would never risk war to achieve its goals in Iran. Furthermore, the Soviets were still engaged in asserting their control over eastern Europe. The ravages of the war had left them too weak to face possible armed resistance along two fronts.

There is one more probable factor behind this inaction on the part of the Soviets. The fall of Pishevari cleared the way for elections and elections made possible a decision on the oil concession, to which the Soviet government had always given top priority. And even with the loss of two major policy instruments—Red Army forces and the Azeri Democrats—Moscow still had its Tudeh Party supporters and the prospect of an oil agreement. Final approval was far from certain, for the United States had indicated that it opposed any Soviet plan to exploit Iran through its oil.

THE POLITICS OF OIL

In late 1946, as in 1940 and 1944, oil became the focal point of big power tensions in Iran. The Soviet concession was just one of several factors that might determine the relationship of Iranian oil to international politics. Britain's declining influence, coupled with rising Iranian nationalism, spelled a troubled future for the AIOC concession. The Iranian government on several occasions indicated a determination to revise the concession on more favorable terms. AIOC in turn pursued narrowly self-interested policies that doomed its once-impregnable monopoly over Iranian oil. And then there was the prospect of a new American concession. The Iranian government continued to dangle its untapped fields as a bait for increased economic, military, and diplomatic assistance from the United States.

Simple economic determinism would produce a neat equation. Of all the overseas resources that the United States might exploit, none had greater economic importance than Middle Eastern oil. Iran had the second largest oil reserves in the region. By 1954 American firms held a 40 percent interest in the former AIOC concession. Given that in 1953 the United States contrived to overthrow the government of Mohammed Mossadeq that had nationalized the AIOC concession, it might seem that the United States had all along sought a dominant role for American oil companies in the development and marketing of Iranian oil. While a number of historians have argued just such a case, the reality is a bit more complicated.[22]

The postwar years brought an oil surplus rather than a shortage to the international oil industry. The capacity of Saudi Arabia to produce in large volume created the greatest danger to orderly markets and stable prices. The special favor of the American government had allowed the Saudis to resume full production by 1944 and to embark on programs to increase their refining and shipping capacities. By contrast, Kuwait did not produce oil in quantity until 1947, while Iran and Iraq did not expand their oil production until even later. As historian Michael Stoff has shown, postwar oil deals had a new flavor. In the prewar years, companies had most often sought to acquire promising concessions. But for two years after the war "no new concessions were opened; instead, old ones became more and more entwined as the great international firms began to place their own interests in order. An enormous consolidation of enterprise occured."[23]

Two clouds hung over the oil companies—the proposed Anglo-American oil agreement and the 1927 Red Line agreement. By 1946 American oil executives had come to see both as liabilities. The efforts of the government to enter the oil business through the Petroleum Reserves Corporation had greatly disturbed private interests. Industry leaders feared that continued government assistance or oversight as a result of an oil agreement would increase the danger of government regulation or ownership. Independent domestic producers anticipated that the Anglo-American pact would create international cartels that could flood American markets with cheap foreign oil. And if the federal government regulated foreign oil, how long would it take before it extended its reach to domestic oil as well? By late 1946, the oil pact was dead. Private oil companies would find their own mechanisms for ensuring security and order.[24]

The Red Line agreement proved burdensome in another way. By 1946 production from Saudi wells was more than one hundred times greater than prewar levels. The Aramco partners, Texaco and Socal, did not have sufficient worldwide outlets for so much oil. Yet Ibn Saud's appetite for revenues forced them to produce more oil than the market required. Failure to maintain the flow of money might lead the king to alter the concession or to invite in other companies. At the same time, neither of the Stanvac partners, Standard Oil of New Jersey and Mobil, had added appreciably to their supplies of crude. An assault by Aramco on their markets could prove disastrous, since Arabian oil was far cheaper than crude oil from their Latin American fields. The Aramco partners needed markets and capital; the Stanvac partners needed oil: marriage seemed like the perfect solution. But before they reached the altar, another marriage had to be dissolved. As long as the Stanvac partners belonged to the IPC consortium, they were bound to AIOC and the Red Line agreement. Saudi Arabia stood within the Red Line's restrictive clauses. Until a way could be found to protect AIOC's position in Iran and Iraq, the British were not likely to give the lovely couple their blessing. The State Department generally looked with favor on this private matchmaking.[25]

In the presence of oil surpluses, the State Department and private oil interests could exercise restraint toward Iranian oil. In fact, by 1946 the competitive disadvantage created by Saudi oil production temporarily eliminated almost all American interest in an Iranian concession. The State Department chose to respect the restrictions imposed by Mossadeq's 1944 oil law, especially since American policymakers saw Iran not as a new source of Middle East oil but as a buffer to protect far more vital fields in Iraq and Saudi Arabia. If Americans received a concession, the United States could not effectively oppose Soviet demands on Iran. A Russian concession would seem an unavoidable *quid pro quo* for an American one.

When Iran's case came before the Security Council in January 1946, the Iranian government had privately indicated its eagerness to grant a concession to American interests. Wallace Murray had urged the department to pass that information on to the oil companies in utmost secrecy. As Secretary of State Byrnes stated, "We have been at great pains to make clear that our action in the Security Council re Iran was based on principle untainted by motives involving oil. . . ." The State Department asked the companies not to send representatives so long as Iran's case was before the Security Council and the 1944 law remained in effect. As a consequence Byrnes was outraged to learn that the ubiquitous Max Thornburg had shown up in Tehran as a representative for several oil companies. He warned the embassy that Thornburg's presence could do untold damage. Byrnes left no doubt that current policy should take precedence over any private deals. "Please inform Thornburg of our views," he ordered, "and tell him we would appreciate it if he would cooperate with our long-term policy with regard to Iran by leaving the country at once without discussing Iran's oil problems."[26]

One reason for the State Department's disenchantment with the Anglo-American oil agreement was its implications for Iran. British negotiators insisted that the pact should include a provision obligating the signatories to "support" each other's existing concession rights. Twice the American delegates had insisted on removing this condition. If it were to be applied to Iran, it might force the United States to defend the terms of the AIOC concession. How would the United States then oppose Soviet demands for similar terms that would impair Iran's sovereignty? As one department analyst observed, "in the Anglo-Iranian *de facto* position there is found everything objectionable that might be anticipated in an exclusive monopolistic concession for Russia in northern Iran."[27] Here again, we see that political considerations weighed more heavily than economic ones in shaping the American position on Iranian oil.

The same was true for the Iranians, who understood the political importance of their oil far more than its economic value. In fact, a weak grasp of the international industry would hamper all their plans to use oil as a political instrument. In particular they failed to see how rapid expansion in Kuwait and Saudi Arabia limited foreign dependence on Iran's vast reserves. Though Iran's two major goals for oil policy both anticipated the nationalist assault on AIOC, their immediate purpose was to limit the impact of the Soviet concession. The Iranian petroleum attaché in Washington once more sought the advice of oil consultants Herbert Hoover Jr. and A.A. Curtice, who had played a central role in the 1944 concession negotiations and had assisted Venezuela in reaching far more favorable contract terms than Iran with the oil companies. The Iranian government now envisioned the formation of an oil consortium, modeled somewhat along the lines of IPC, to exploit the Baluchistan concession previously sought by Stanvac, Sinclair, and Shell. The Iranians proposed to exclude AIOC, but to include Shell, a Stanvac/Sinclair combine, and Iranian and Russian government corporations. Responsibility for operating the concession would fall exclusively to the Americans. In that way the Iranians could satisfy Soviet demands, while denying them use of the concession as a political base. As we have just seen, however, the Middle East oil situation at that time made such a proposal unattractive. More important, American oil companies had not yet accepted the idea of local governments participating in the exploitation of their own oil. As a result, no American firms showed an interest.[28]

Though it was unable to attract the interest of American oil companies, the Iranian government did not cease in its efforts to undermine the AIOC concession without opening the door too wide to the Soviet Union. This time Iranian representatives suggested that the United Nations might establish a commission to investigate existing international concession agreements. It might even be possible to have an international corporation develop all of Iran's oil. Given the vast extent of American overseas oil holdings, such a proposal must have landed in the State Department with the dullest of thuds. The department hid behind the Anglo-American oil agreement that would soon be buried. A spokesman explained that because the pending oil pact bound the United States to respect existing concessions and legally acquired rights, the department could not support any proposal to place AIOC's holdings under a UN-sponsored corporation. He might just as well have admitted that the United States would never encourage Iran to take any step that endangered American overseas oil interests.[29]

A new Anglo-American oil agreement demonstrated how diplomatic oil companies could be when their interests were at stake. Archival records show that the State Department was not formally consulted and was as much surprised as the Iranians were by what the oil companies arranged. We have already seen that four major American companies were eager to see the Red Line agreement abrogated. As the dominant partner in IPC, AIOC promised to be a major stumbling block. Its markets for Iranian and Iraqi oil might soon be awash with oil supplied from Saudi Arabia. So in return for AIOC's cooperation in ending the Red Line agreement, the new Aramco partners agreed to a twenty-year contract with AIOC to purchase 134 million tons of petroleum from Iran and/or Kuwait, where AIOC held a 50 percent share with Gulf. The contract also committed the partners in principle to build a pipeline to deliver Persian Gulf oil to a Mediterranean port. The Red Line agreement was soon as dead as the Anglo-American oil agreement.[30]

The State Department had every reason to be distressed by its exclusion from these private arrangements that had so much bearing on strategic American interests. Through the new Aramco partnership, the United States had now become closely associated in Iran with the unpopular AIOC. The Soviet Union had gained a potential new justification for its oil demands. In this way the oil companies behaved as if they and their interests, not the United States government and its interests, controlled foreign oil policy. This is not to imply that the State Department saw the two as incompatible. The department had long seen the Red Line agreement as a violation of the Open Door principle and was glad to see it ended. The contracts also helped to guarantee that Middle Eastern oil would ease the drain on Western Hemisphere sources. Orderly marketing and production of Middle East oil would produce additional benefits.[31]

To George Allen fell the task of selling the new oil deal to the Iranian government. Allen argued that the arrangement benefited American interests in Iran, since "it will provide a large western outlet for Iranian oil and consequently contribute to the stability of Iran for which we are working." He understood that the Iranians might find some aspects of the arrangement distasteful and for that reason he recommended that the pipeline company have an American rather than a British headquarters. As was its habit, AIOC had acted with little regard for Iran's stake in the disposition of its oil. When the shah complained to Allen that his government had never been consulted, the ambassador hid behind the legal nicety that a private deal did not require consultation with any government. He assured the shah that the contract would "create a material American interest on Iranian soil."[32] Of course, Allen did not mention that AIOC, not the Iranian government, had dictated the timing and the terms of the deal. The shah also feared that American companies no longer had an incentive to develop the Baluchistan concession, which the Iranians had long sought to barter. Allen insisted that in such an unlikely event, other American companies besides Stanvac would step into the picture.

The ambassador's comments made good politics, but poor oil economics. Either out of ignorance or out of his wish to placate the shah, Allen had misrepresented the American attitude toward Iranian oil. At least for the near future, no American company was likely to have any incentive to invest capital in the development of new Iranian fields. A. A. Curtice explained to the State Department that the new contract would increase Iran's share of existing world markets, but also that it accounted for as much oil as those markets could presently absorb. A new concession would not materially increase Iran's share. As a result, Curtice doubted that any American company would have any interest in a Baluchistan concession, because it could not easily sell what it produced. The AIOC contract, no matter what Allen claimed, had deprived Iran of one of its major diplomatic levers.[33]

ACT THREE: THE IRANIAN-SOVIET OIL DEAL

By December the Truman administration had determined to oppose the Iranian-Soviet oil deal. Before then, the State Department had recognized at least in principle the Soviet Union's right to obtain a concession. Allen had not been willing to encourage the Iranians to reject the concession outright, because he realized that the "normal outlet for northern Iranian oil is the USSR." But the fall of Pishevari loosened the Soviet grip on that region. And through the Stanvac-AIOC deal the United States had found a back door into Iranian oil. By emphasizing the private nature of the contract, the State Department could argue the opposite side of the coin that Allen had presented the shah—that the American government had no direct stake in Iran's oil. That made the American position categorically different from the Soviet one, though in fact the contract had received official endorsement. Ambassador Bedell Smith had warned from Moscow that "We have no doubt that the Kremlin will resume attempts to encroach on Iranian sovereignty and that it will continue to encroach on Turkish sovereignty." A. A. Curtice reaffirmed for the State Department its belief "that any type of concession granted to the Russians in the north will be very dangerous for Iranian sovereignty."[34]

Such warnings made the State Department much more reluctant to see the Russians establish a permanent position in Iran. By January the political climate in Iran had changed appreciably. With Qavam showing less sympathy for the Soviet Union and leftist factions, the Soviet oil deal no longer seemed to be a foregone conclusion. George Allen detected signs that the Iranian government might actually reject the agreement.[35]

Ironically, the reoccupation of Azerbaijan had weakened Qavam as he entered the elections for the Fifteenth Majles. The Tudeh Party no longer supported him. Rightists and royalists dominated the newly formed provincial governments in northern Iran. At least two of the major factions facing Qavam, the shah and his followers and the pro-British conservatives, opposed the Soviet oil deal. In addition, many nationalists such as Mohammad Mossadeq had become outspoken critics of Qavam's oil policy. They preferred granting no concessions to foreigners—negative equilibrium—to Qavam's notion of a deal with the Soviets balanced by new ties to the United States—positive equilibrium. When Qavam achieved only a slim majority in the Fifteenth Majles, he realized that he could not survive politically and honor his pledge to the Russians. Even though he continued to push for approval, he did not push hard. He gave equal attention to securing commitments from the United States to cushion the blow should the Majles vote against the oil deal.[36]

Shortly after the elections, President Truman announced in March 1947 the administration's determination to send economic and military aid to Greece and Turkey. Not only had the United States committed itself to fight communism by intervening in Greece's internal affairs, it had also publicly affirmed its role as the major power in the eastern Mediterranean. The Truman Doctrine seemed to vindicate the wisdom of Iran's efforts to court the United States rather than Great Britain, although Truman had said nothing about Iran in his speech or in the aid bill he had sent to Congress. Despite Iran's repeated requests for military and economic assistance, the United States had pledged support only to Greece and Turkey, even though U.S. policymakers saw a direct link between the pressures on Iran and those on its two northern-tier neighbors. In fact, administration spokesmen would assure Congress that the request for funds for Greece and Turkey did not imply a more global commitment of American resources. As a consequence, the Truman Doctrine made substantial American aid to Iran even less likely than it had been.[37]

The shah soon summoned Allen to the palace to find out why President Truman had ignored Iran. Did not his country face as severe a threat as Greece or Turkey? Allen replied that as much as the Truman administration valued Iran, it did not consider its danger as immediate. As long as Iran was willing to defend itself, Allen believed the shah could count on American support. That was not what either the shah or Qavam wished to hear. They continued to press for some tangible evidence of what their ties to the United States might mean. Qavam asked for assistance on a par with Greece and Turkey. When no American aid materialized, Qavam found another way to present his case. He informed Allen that the Russian ambassador had pointedly criticized Iran's pro-American and anti-Soviet policies. These remarks anticipated renewed Russian pressures on Iran, Qavam insisted. By making Iran an exception in relation to her Turkish and Greek neighbors, the United States had invited Russian aggression.[38]

The State Department appreciated the thrust of Qavam's argument. Though State could not offer the level of assistance Iran was seeking, Assistant Secretary Dean Acheson was working with Loy Henderson to devise a policy that would allow Iran to reject the concession without provoking a Soviet attack. They decided that either direct military aid to Iran or diplomatic pressure might push Moscow too far. At the same time, the pending oil agreement contained insufficient safeguards to protect Iran from Soviet ambitions, which were, in the eyes of Iranian and American policymakers alike, clearly political, not economic. At a minimum, Acheson told Secretary of State George Marshall, the Russians hoped to keep foreign powers out of the north. He therefore recommended that the United States leave the final decision on the oil agreement in Iranian hands. If the Iranians did reject it, the United States would ask the United Nations to respond to any Russian threat. Acheson had no special regard for the effectiveness of the United Nations. Rather, he hoped to minimize the danger to Iran and to avoid the escalation of any new crises. To placate the Russians, the United States could urge Iran to close the north to foreign development. Secretary of State Marshall endorsed Acheson's recommendations.[39]

That decision ended the immediate possibility of large-scale military assistance to Iran. Allen informed Qavam in June that Congress would not legislate the arms program he had requested. Instead, Secretary Marshall urged Qavam to rely on the Security Council. An arms program or diplomatic arm-twisting in Moscow could only provoke Soviet hostility. Besides, the State Department believed that while Greece and Turkey maintained no pretenses of friendship with the Soviet Union, Iran maintained ostensibly cordial relations with its neighbor. To Ambassador Allen, Marshall speculated privately that Qavam was up to another of his subterfuges. Why else would he make such unreasonable demands of the United States? When the State Department turned him down, Qavam could then claim that without American aid he had no choice but to grant the oil concession.[40]

As before, the tone of Allen's messages to Qavam belied the real anxiety in the State Department, where the idea of a Soviet oil company in Iran had become a nightmare. Ambassador Bedell Smith in Moscow, conjuring up one of the dark images that troubled American policymakers, warned that "we should certainly not encourage the concession on the mistaken notion that the Kremlin will be quietly satisfied. In organisms of this kind appetite and capacity grow with the eating." Assistant Secretary of State Robert Lovett expressed a similar concern in less graphic language. He told Allen that the department had no doubt that the Soviets would use a concession to control Iran "by devious means of infiltration, pressure etc." He assigned to Allen an almost impossible mission. The ambassador had to do nothing that would indicate that the United States was using its influence to defeat the concession. At the same time he was not to give the Iranians the sense that the United States favored approval of the concession.[41]

The Soviets vacillated between intimidation and seduction, as they waited for Qavam to present the oil bill to the Majles. Periodically Ambassador Sadchikov would remind Qavam in no uncertain terms that the decision had been delayed for far too long. Rumors of unrest in Azerbaijan added weight to such warnings. But the Soviets also made positive gestures. In July, for example, they announced the end of their control over air facilities and air routes in northern Iran. Given the American preoccupation with civil air agreements, that should have eased tensions. Allen, who always looked any Russian gift horses in the mouth, dismissed that gesture as a ploy to promote goodwill on behalf of the concession.[42]

Nevertheless, sometimes the Soviets could be frighteningly blunt. At one August meeting Sadchikov warned Qavam that failure to act on the oil agreement might endanger, not only Iran, but his personal safety as well. A visibly shaken prime minister rushed off to Allen with that harrowing tale. Allen assured him as always that he could appeal to the United Nations should the Soviet Union actually try to wrest by force what it could not win by intimidation. A month later Sadchikov combined both the carrot and the stick. He told Qavam, "If Majles approval is obtained for the agreement you will be considered among the most sincere friends of the USSR and will be helped financially, morally, and in every other respect." Then he added ominously, "If you refuse, you will be regarded as our most bitter enemy and treated as such."[43]

The British proved to be more clumsy than either the Americans or the Russians. On most issues they sided with the Americans, but the Russian oil concession confronted them with a special problem. Tory elements in Parliament joined the directors of AIOC in arguing that the rejection of the Iranian-Soviet agreement posed an indirect threat to their concession. If the Soviet Union had a similar stake in Iran, Radio Moscow could no longer accuse AIOC of "stealing the resources of the Iranian people." The Labor Party under Clement Attlee had no wish to provoke a confrontation with the Soviet Union, and the Foreign Office had accordingly instructed Ambassador Le Rougetel to urge Iran "to keep the door open" to the Russian concession.[44] That position may well have sealed the fate of AIOC's monopoly over Iranian oil. Qavam warned his followers that Iran could expect no support from Great Britain if the Russians resorted to strong-arm tactics. In Iranian eyes, the AIOC concession had become a political liability as well as a device of imperialistic exploitation.

By contrast George Allen exceeded departmental orders by openly siding with the shah, who favored outright rejection of the Russian concession. As of August, both the shah and Qavam had indicated that Iran would not accept the oil agreement in its original form, but Qavam argued for further negotiations. Allen warned that unless Iran followed the shah's course, negotiations would drag on. He assured Qavam that, while he respected Iran's sovereign right to make a decision, he believed that no terms with the Soviets would guarantee adequate safeguards. Even Qavam agreed with Allen's contention that all the Soviet officials assigned to the oil company would be political agents.[45]

For Allen, a bold position in words was not the same as speaking in deeds. As the parliamentary showdown on the oil agreement neared, the shah and Qavam complained that they were reluctant to stake Iran's future on the United Nations, as Secretary Marshall urged. What if the United Nations failed, the shah asked Allen at one meeting. Later the shah became even more explicit: the United Nations was a "fiasco," he told Allen. Iran needed a dependable aid program such as the ones Greece and Turkey had received. Allen was almost equally candid. If the shah was angling for a bilateral alliance, he should know that the American people would never sustain it. But under almost any circumstances the Americans would support the United Nations, and it, therefore, was Iran's safest course.[46]

No matter how many times he made those arguments, Allen did not altogether believe them himself, and he feared that without a more tangible show of American resolve, Iran might understandably succumb to Soviet pressures. The thought that the Russians might in that way gain control of the Persian Gulf oil basin horrified him. So without any authorization from Washington, he publicly implied that the United States opposed the oil agreement and would back Iran in turning it down. The occasion for this remarkable breach of the chain of command came in an address Allen delivered on 12 September to the Iran-American Society. He criticized nations who made proposals "accompanied by threats of intimidation." When such methods were employed, "doubt is cast on the value of the proposals themselves." While not so reckless as to make concrete commitments, Allen did conclude that "patriotic Iranians, when considering matters affecting their national interest, may therefore rest assured that the American people will support fully their freedom to make their own choice."[47]

Allen had not actually said anything new, but timing and circumstances are often as consequential as substance in speechmaking. Allen delivered his speech soon after the conference in which the shah criticized the United Nations. The day before Allen spoke, a member of the Majles had come secretly to warn him that the concession seemed certain to pass. That had fixed his decision to act without formal authorization. Since he had never before aired his views publicly, Allen obviously hoped the Iranians would treat his remarks as a new policy. That in turn might strengthen the resolve of Majles factions who opposed the Russian concession. Secretary of State Marshall was sufficiently disturbed by Allen's temerity to demand an explanation for his actions. Henderson again defended his protégé to Marshall's satisfaction. It did not hurt that whatever the secretary thought about Allen's behavior, he accepted his definition of American policy.[48]

After almost a year and a half of maneuvering the stage was finally set for

Qavam to present the Iranian-Soviet pact to the Majles. On 22 October he explained to the representatives that his decision to sign an agreement "was in the best interest of the country, and any other patriot in [his] place in those days would have inevitably ageed to such a suggestion." In essence he defended his own actions without asking the Majles to accept the agreement. Even the members of his Democrat Party joined almost the entire Majles in rejecting the oil concession by a vote of one hundred to two. The deputies apparently accepted Qavam's rationalization of his actions, for they did not invoke the provision of the 1944 law that could have sent him to prison for three to eight years.[49]

Defeat in the Majles did not immediately topple Qavam's government. Nationalists softened their criticism of him when the Soviet Union made Qavam the target of its wrath. Qavam further courted nationalist sympathies by publicly attacking Iran's arrangement with AIOC under the 1933 contract. Indeed, the Majles had not simply rejected the Soviet oil pact; it had also authorized Qavam to renegotiate the terms of the AIOC concession. Still, he had suffered mortal political wounds. His party was in shambles and his opponents smelled blood. When one group of royalists moved to impeach him, Qavam decided instead to resign, bringing to a close a major era in Iran's political history.[50]

And what about the assumptions of the American cold war consensus? If those were to be proven correct, the Soviet army would have poured across the border into Azerbaijan. Barring such an extreme response, at the least pro-Soviet mobs should have taken to the streets. Qavam, the shah, and many of the Majles delegates should have gone in fear for their lives. In fact, nothing happened. The Soviet ambassador did only what he had done for months. He made ominous threats, complained about the inequities of Iranian oil policy, and demanded that Iran honor its pledge. American policymakers had exaggerated both the nature and the strength of Soviet ambitions. In the two years following World War II, the relative positions in Iran of the United States and the Soviet Union had been reversed. The Russians had lost three of the instruments through which they could directly influence Iran's internal affairs. First the Red Army troops had left, then Pishevari had fallen, and now the concession had been defeated. The *de facto* Iranian-American alliance was far stronger, not because the United States had assumed a larger role, but because its Soviet rival was so much weaker. Furthermore, Greece and Turkey stood securely outside the Soviet orbit. Despite all the dire predictions, the Soviet Union took no aggressive steps to redress a balance of power that left its southern border dangerously exposed. Could it be seriously argued that the United States, if comparably threatened through Mexico or Cuba, would have shown similar restraint?

Here was a position of strength from which the State Department might have felt free to negotiate for some easing of tensions. The United States had succeeded in Iran with almost no expenditure of political, economic, or diplomatic capital. Iran had chosen to rely on its ties to the United States to protect its future independence. The Soviet Union posed no immediate threat to the Middle East. Yet, as we shall see, American policymakers did not reconsider any of their assumptions. Their mistrust of Soviet intentions remained as profound as ever. They faced the future of Iranian-American relations with the cold war consensus fully intact, even though the United States held the Middle East balance of power almost completely in its own hands. The shah would soon emerge as the crucial agent for maintaining American gains in the region.

NOTES

1. FO371/45464, notes by Bullard, 5/25/45.

2. State Department petroleum adviser Charles Raynor was one of the few policymakers who argued that the Soviets might actually want oil. For his view, see SD 891.6363/12–1145, "Oil Concessions and the Problem in Iran," memo by Raynor. For the evidence that the Soviets actually had done test drilling, see SD 891.6363/10–3145, 136; 146, 11–1545; 163, 11–2645; and 184, 12–1045; all cables from Murray to Secretary of State. Obviously the test drilling could have been a ploy to persuade skeptical Iranians of the Soviets' intentions to develop the economic potential of a concession. I am inclined to believe that the Soviet Union wanted to acquire foreign sources of oil, just as the United States did. For a summary of U.S. security evaluations of the eastern Mediterranean, see FR, 1947, 5, "The Pentagon Talks of 1947," p. 514. On postwar American oil policy and national security factors, see also Stoff, *Oil, War, and American Security,* ch. 7.

3. SD 891.00/6–646, Allen to Henderson.

4. George Allen, "Mission to Iran," (unpublished manuscript), Harry S Truman Library, Independence, Missouri. Hereafter cited as Allen Diaries. Allen's account adds some interesting dimensions to the materials in the *Foreign Relations* volumes. It must be treated with some caution since Allen misplaced several key events by as much as a year. Other documents make it possible to correct these errors and existing documents corroborate most of Allen's recollections.

5. Allen Diaries, pp. 51–65. SD 891.00/6–846, 817, Allen to Secretary of State.

6. SD 891.105A/5–646, 647, Allen to Secretary of State; SD 891.00/6–646, Allen letter; and FR, 1946, 7, p. 504 and 504n.

7. For the best analysis of Qavam's political strategy, see Abrahamian, *Iran Between Two Revolutions,* pp. 229–37.

8. FR, 1946, 7, pp. 505–6 and 503n. See also SD 891.00/7–1146, 981, Allen to Secretary of State.

9. FR, 1946, 7, pp. 510–15; Allen Diaries, pp. 52–54.

10. FR, 1946, 7, p. 512, and pp. 521–22.

11. Ibid., pp. 540n. and 510–15; ibid., pp. 523–28 and Allen Diaries, pp. 52–57.

12. SD 891.00/10–1846, NEA memorandum "Implementation of U.S. Policy Towards Iran," and cover letter by Loy Henderson. See also Allen Diaries, p. 111. Allen devotes considerable attention to the air transportation issue, but he has the chronology wrong, placing it much later than it occurred.

13. SD 891.00/10–1846.

14. FR, 1946, 7, p. 515 and pp. 529–32.

15. Ibid., pp. 529–33.

16. This question was posed by Rouhallah Ramazani, who sees Qavam as the key actor in this shift. See Ramazani, *Iran's Foreign Policy,* pp. 148–50, for an able analysis. An even more thorough explanation, though largely complementary, is Abrahamian, *Iran Between Two Revolutions,* pp. 235–39. Both Abrahamian and Ramazani see George Allen and the United States as crucial but not deciding factors in Qavam's change of course. Bruce Kuniholm, *The Origins of the Cold War in the Near East,* pp. 384–92, still emphasizes the collaboration between George Allen and the shah as decisive. That is based on information from Allen and the embassy's political officer, Robert Rossow. Kuniholm does recognize the same combination of events that Ramazani and Abrahamian treat. I think the American sources tend to overstate the impact Allen had. Qavam undoubtedly weighed domestic events even more heavily.

17. See FR, 1946, 7, pp. 516–17; SD 891.00/11–645, 2062, Allen to Secretary of State; and Abrahamian, *Iran Between Two Revolutions,* p. 235.

18. Allen Diaries, pp. 111–125; FR, 1946, 7, pp. 537–39. See also Kuniholm, *Origins of the Cold War in the Near East,* pp. 388–92 for a more detailed recreation of the events. I do not agree with Kuniholm's conclusion that the shah and Allen forced Qavam into an action he might not otherwise have taken. In that, Ramazani's conclusion seems more persuasive.

19. FR, 1946, 7, pp. 544–49; Ramazani, *Iran's Foreign Policy,* pp. 154–66.

20. FR, 1946, 7, pp. 547–56. Allen Diaries, pp. 57–60. The diaries are a bit sketchy on this period.

21. Allen Diaries, pp. 60–67. Abrahamian, *Iran Between Two Revolutions,* pp. 239–40. See also Sephir Zabih, *The Communist Movement in Iran* (Berkeley, 1966), pp. 111–22. The *New York Times,* December 12–16 covered events after Clifton Daniels had been sent to Iran. See also Rossow, "The Battle for Azerbaijan," pp. 30–31. On the fate of the Kurdish Republic, see Eagleton, *The Kurdish Republic of 1946,* pp. 101–32.

22. For an example of a historian arguing this line, see Gabriel Kolko, *The Politics of War,* pp. 295–300. See also Joyce and Gabriel Kolko, *The Limits of Power* (New York, 1972), pp. 336–42, and 417–20.

23. Stoff, *Oil, War, and American Security,* ch. 7, especially p. 195. See also Mosley, *Power Play,* pp. 156–63, and Miller, *Search for Security,* ch. 6.

24. Stoff, *Oil, War, and American Security,* pp. 178–95.

25. Ibid., pp. 195–208; see also Miller, *Search For Security,* pp. 158–62. The most thorough account of American oil in the postwar Middle East is to be found in Irvine Anderson, *Aramco, the United States, and Saudi Arabia* (Princeton, 1981).

26. SD 891.6363/2–1446, 198, Murray to Secretary of State; SD 891.6363/5–2046, 452, Byrnes to Allen.

27. SD 891.6363/3–2046, memorandum by Loftus, "British Oil Position in Iran." On American views of the oil agreement, see Stoff, *Oil, War, and American Security,* pp. 184–95.

28. SD 891.6363/2–2546, Edwin Pauley to Byrnes. Truman appointed Pauley under secretary of the navy, a position with important influence over oil policy. Pauley was an independent oil operator who raised campaign contributions from oil company coffers. His appointment was the final straw that drove Ickes out of Truman's cabinet. On the Iranian approach to oil concessions, see R. W. Ferrier, "The Development of the Iranian Oil Industry," in Hossein Armisadeghi and R. W. Ferrier, *Twentieth Century Iran* (London, 1977), pp. 93–127. See also Robert Stobaugh, "The Evolution of Iranian Oil Policy," in George Lenczowski, ed., *Iran Under the Pahlevis* (Stanford, 1978), pp. 201–52.

29. SD 891.6363/8–2346, 709, Acheson to Teheran, and SD 891.6363/8–3046, 729, Acheson to Teheran.

30. SD 891.6363/12–3146, 13, J. A. Loftus (Petroleum Adviser) to Allen; and SD 891.6363/12–3146, Byrnes to Teheran, 1/8/47. The contract did not specifically obligate AIOC to provide any amount of oil from Iran.

31. Stoff, *Oil, War, and American Security,* pp. 195–208. Stoff points out that the abrogation of the Red Line agreement also embittered the French government, which only had a small stake in IPC. It, along with Calouste Gulbenkian, should have been a big loser, but the companies once again worked out a deal that satisfied French objections.

32. SD 891.6363/12–2946, 1636, Allen to Secretary of State; SD 891.6363/1–847, 14, Allen to Secretary of State.

33. SD 891.6363/1–2847, "Petroleum Negotiations in Iran," memorandum by H. B. Minor.

34. FR, 1947, 7, pp. 2–3, Bedell Smith to Secretary of State, 1/8/47; SD 891.6363/1–2747, memorandum by Minor.

35. FR, 1947, 7, p. 894, Allen to Secretary of State, 1/28/47.

36. Abrahamian, *Iran Between Two Revolutions,* pp. 240–42; see also Ramazani, *Iran's Foreign Policy,* pp. 167–70.

37. For a good general discussion of the Truman Doctrine and its origins, see Richard Freeland, *The Truman Doctrine and the Origins of McCarthyism* (New York, 1972). For a brief analysis, see LaFeber, *America, Russia, and the Cold War,* pp. 49–59. For an analysis of the relationship of the Truman Doctrine to strategy in the northern tier and some analysis of the historical controversy, see Kuniholm, *Origins of the Cold War in the Near East,* pp. 410–31. On the problem of an open-ended commitment, see U.S. Senate Committee on Foreign Relations, "Legislative Origins of the Truman Doctrine, *Hearings,* S.938, 80th. Cong., First Sess., pp. 1–26. See appendix B for a copy of Truman's speech.

38. FR, 1947, 7, p. 901, Allen to Secretary of State, 3/27/47; ibid., pp. 906–7 and pp. 914–15.

39. Ibid., pp. 902–4, Acheson to Marshall, 4/4/47; and pp. 904–5, Marshall to Acheson, 4/10/47.

40. Ibid., pp. 914–15, Allen to Marshall, 6/16/47; ibid., pp. 916–18, Marshall to Allen, 6/21/47.

41. Ibid., p. 924, Smith to Secretary of State, 7/28/47; ibid., pp. 934–36, Lovett to Allen, 8/18/47.

42. See, for example, ibid., pp. 900–907, 910–11, p. 913, and p. 921, all from Allen to Secretary of State.

43. Allen Diaries, pp. 128–30; FR, 1947, 7, pp. 932–33, p. 945, and p. 956, all Allen to Secretary of State.

44. SD 891.6363/8–2047, "Soviet-Iranian Oil Agreement," memorandum by Henderson; SD 891.6363/9–1747, 5030, Allen to Secretary of State. See also FR, 1947, 8, p. 892, p. 925, pp. 936–37, and pp. 947–49. See also Allen Diaries, 130–31; and Abrahamian, *Iran Between Two Revolutions*, pp. 244–45.

45. FR, 1947, 8, p. 922, pp. 922–23, and pp. 929–30, all Allen to Secretary of State.

46. Ibid., pp. 936–37, pp. 939–41, and pp. 948–49.

47. Allen Diaries, pp. 132–37.

48. Allen Diaries, 137–39.

49. FR, 1947, 8, p. 969. Ramazani, *Iran's Foreign Policy*, pp. 167–70.

50. Abrahamian, *Iran Between Two Revolutions*, pp. 244–45.

12 *The Oil Nationalization Crisis*

On 4 October 1951 the once unthinkable had come to pass. The Anglo-Iranian Oil Company had been expelled from Iran by the National Front government of Mohammed Mossadeq. Henry Longhurst, the historian of AIOC, caught the flavor of that moment as the British staff of the Abadan refinery gathered to board a Royal Navy ship:

> The ship's band "correct" to the end, struck up the Persian national anthem and the launches began their shuttle service. . . . The cruiser *Mauritius* steamed slowly away up the river with the band playing, the assembled company lining the rails and roaring in unison the less printable version of "Colonel Bogey." . . . The greatest single overseas enterprise in British commerce had ground to a standstill.[1]

In Tehran that day, British Ambassador Sir Francis Shepard sped through the streets in the embassy car, the conspicuous Union Jack expressing his contempt for the "lunatics" who had subjected his nation to such a humiliation.

Historians have recognized the oil nationalization crisis not only as a turning point in British-Iranian relations, but also as the episode that forged the Iranian-American alliance. American diplomats had sought since 1941 to maintain an independent Iran as a barrier to Soviet expansion. After the Majles rejected the Iranian-Soviet oil concession in 1947, the objective of that policy seemed almost assured. The State Department came to see internal unrest, more than any immediate danger from the Soviet Union, as a threat to American national security interests. For four years, as the Iranian government staggered from one economic or political crisis to another, the Soviets had maintained an ominous distance. At the same time they had expanded their control over Hungary and Czechoslovakia. In 1949, a year of poor harvests in Iran and an assassination attempt on the shah, China had fallen to the communists and radioactive ash in the Pacific revealed the successful detonation of a Soviet atom bomb. A year later came the Korean War.

With cold war tensions deepening, the Truman administration feared that Mossadeq's decision to expel the British might afford the Soviet Union a new opportunity to make gains in Iran at American expense. American policymakers accepted Mossadeq so long as he seemed in control of the volatile factions. But as chaos threatened to engulf Iran, the fear of communist penetration once again dictated a more active American intervention. The Eisenhower-Dulles decision to undertake "Operation Ajax," in order to ensure Mossadeq's overthrow, marked a significant departure from the more restrained policy that had been pursued by President Truman and Secretary of State Dean Acheson. All the same, Acheson had grown ever more fearful of rising communist influence in Iran and in his memoirs he expressed no regret over the outcome.[2]

Historians must wonder whether circumstances justified the decision to overthrow Mossadeq; an act that would poison American-Iranian friendship over the next twenty-five years. What if the United States had given Mossadeq more assistance? Might he not have launched a liberal national movement that would have resulted in the progressive Iranian state Americans had previously envisioned? And by the summer of 1953 was it not likely that Mossadeq's government would have collapsed on its own, the victim of the factionalism that had dominated Iran's politics since the fall of Reza Shah in 1941? Equally important, was American intervention needed to prevent Iran from falling into Moscow's orbit? After all, the overthrow of Mossadeq coincided with the death of Stalin. Was the Soviet Union likely to embark on political adventurism in the Middle East during the transition to a new regime? Although history seldom allows us to answer such questions with any certainty, recent scholarship suggests that as much as "Operation Ajax" gave birth to the Iranian-American alliance, it also guaranteed its ultimate demise as well.[3]

TOWARD NATIONALIZATION

The oil nationalization crisis pitted the economic interests of Great Britain against the cold war politics of the United States. From 1947 through 1951 the British were willing to redefine the terms of the 1933 agreement under which AIOC operated, as long as the company remained profitable and the sanctity of the concession went unchallenged. American diplomats wanted AIOC to provide Iran with more of the financial resources the shah and his prime ministers needed to embark on a modernization program. Improvement in the material condition of Iran's impoverished masses would deny the communists an opportunity to play upon popular discontent. AIOC and its supporters believed the Americans expected them to give more than Britain could afford. American diplomats were sharply critical of AIOC's failure to see that its future survival required them to make far greater concessions than the company was willing to make.[4]

We should recall that when the Majles rejected the Soviet oil agreement, it also instructed Qavam to negotiate the revision of the AIOC concession. On several occasions in 1944 and again in 1947 Iranian officials had floated proposals that would have given Iran a greater share of the revenues from AIOC, but more important, they would have given Iran greater participation in the operation of its oil fields. Mohammed Mossadeq had hoped in each instance to shift Iran away from its historic policy of "positive equilibrium" to the strategy of "negative equilibrium" he favored. This kind of program meant more than merely restricting foreign influences by rejecting the Soviet demand for a concession. It also meant the reduction of British influence and a corresponding rise in Iran's control over its own resources. Only reluctantly would Mossadeq favor the continuation of the United States' third power role.

Mossadeq's evangelical Iranian nationalism attracted the support of the Islamic clergy who feared the corrupting influence of the west, and by 1948 the nationalization movement had become irresistible to significant political factions, who saw AIOC as the symbol of all Iran had suffered from foreign intrusions. British policy contributed heavily to the Iranians' determination to revise the AIOC concession. The company realized too late that imperial hubris did not serve its interests well. As negotiations began, the Iranians introduced a list of twenty-five demands that went well beyond economic questions. Just as galling as its unfavorable royalty schedules was AIOC's refusal to allow Iranians to hold important jobs or learn sophisticated technical skills in oil production. In addition, many Iranians had felt betrayed by the British government's soft posture on the Soviet oil concession. They believed that the United States, not Great Britain, was the friend Iran needed to secure its future independence.[5]

Cold war tensions shaped American policy for Iran. By 1947 national defense planners had determined that Soviet domination of the eastern Mediterranean and the Middle East would mean "retreat to the Western Hemisphere" and "the prospect of a war of attrition which could spell an end to the American way of life." Few doubted that the Soviet Union had aspirations in that direction. To forestall such a grim scenario, it became American policy to contain Soviet expansion in the region, "to promote directly and indirectly the political and economic development of the peoples of the Middle East," and to guarantee the independence of all the nations of the region, with special concern for Greece, Turkey, and Iran.[6] It was less clear to planners how to achieve these goals. What level and what form of American assistance would stabilize the Middle East? What role would the British be able to play in light of their economic distress and of rising third world nationalism? Would the United Nations serve as an effective deterrent to Soviet pressures on countries like Iran and thereby limit the commitment of American political and economic resources?

Iran raised some difficult problems for the Truman administration. By early 1949 the State Department feared that internal instability and vulnerability to attack by the USSR made Iran "the weakest link in the chain of independent states along the Soviet border in the strategically important Middle East."[7] Most western observers assumed Iran's economy would soon collapse. The unsuccessful attempt of a Muslim fundamentalist to assassinate the shah in February 1949 only emphasized the unsettled state of Iranian politics.

In addition, as of March 1949 Ambassador Wiley was so certain of the imminence of Soviet aggression that he warned the State Department, "in my opinion the Soviet return to Iran is not a question of 'if' but is solely a question of 'when.' " The evidence he cited was more circumstantial than substantive. Still he gave Secretary of State Dean Acheson one-in-three odds that the Soviet Union would "nip off all or part of the northern provinces" within the year. The Near East Division did not share Wiley's alarm. Indeed they worried that he would unduly frighten the Iranians to the point that they might seek to appease the Soviet Union. At the Near East Division's urging, Acheson informed Wiley that the Soviets did not then seem likely "to risk war in the near future. . . ." Both Acheson and Truman had warned the Soviets publicly against any incursions into Turkey, Greece, or Iran. The secretary concluded that the Soviets would not now go beyond pressure and subversion in their attempt to bring Iran into their orbit.[8]

In the face of internal unrest and Soviet pressures American planners had to search for a balance. What was the minimum aid the United States could provide without sending the Soviets a false signal about its interest in Iran? Too little aid might imply a lack of resolve. Too much aid might be both provocative and a drain on the United States' overtaxed equipment reserves. In addition, the State Department doubted Iran's capacity to absorb significant American funds. Corruption was so rampant in the Iranian government that members of the State Department described grants to Iran as "money down a rat hole." Still, if the Iranians were to receive far less than they requested, they might lose their pro-western orientation and their will to resist Soviet pressures. American diplomats remained overly sensitive to any Iranian tilt toward Moscow, no matter how slight or expedient such a move might be. For their part the Iranians in the royalist and court factions complained incessantly, as they had since 1941, about inadequate American aid in general and paltry military aid in particular.[9]

With the fall of Qavam in 1947, the shah had emerged as the central figure in Iranian political life. Factionalism within the Majles allowed the royalists to play a decisive role there. More important, the shah had benefited from the expansion of the armed forces made possible by limited American assistance. Morale rose in the wake of the successful military interventions in Azerbaijan and Kurdistan. But the shah had an even grander design. He envisioned an American-equipped army of 300,000 that would serve as the first line of defense against Soviet aggression in the Middle East. Not coincidentally, that would make the shah's authority in Iranian politics almost absolute.[10]

The State Department had always considered a large Iranian army an unnecessary extravagance. American military advisers had recommended the provision of a small, efficient force designed and equipped to maintain internal security, because no Iranian army could offer more than token resistance to a Soviet invasion. Thus American diplomats resisted the shah's pressures for military assistance on a par with Turkey. The shah made no secret of his desire to acquire advanced military equipment, such as tanks and jet aircraft. American Ambassador John Wiley found it necessary "to dampen his enthusiasm without discouraging him," but in his report to the State Department Wiley remarked that "[the shah's] thinking in that regard is strictly in never-never land."[11]

Besides the development of his army, the shah had ambitious dreams of economic modernization. The Iranian government accordingly hired an American consulting firm to draw up an economic development plan, undoubtedly on the assumption that recommendations from American experts would unleash American dollars. OCI (Overseas Consultants Inc.) had also disappointed Iranian expectations. Iran wanted a program for industrialization; OCI recommended programs to build a social infrastructure, improve public health, raise literacy standards, and reform agriculture. Small programs under President Truman's Point Four Technical Assistance program made more sense than massive U.S. loans and grants.[12]

The shah had gone ahead with a seven-year, $650 million dollar economic development plan, financed largely through oil revenues. In an effort to attract American support for his ambitious military development programs, the shah visited Washington in November 1949. To better defend Iran, he thought the United States might either extend Truman Doctrine aid to his country or enter with it into a regional defense pact similar to NATO. All of those requests would be fulfilled after 1953 by the Eisenhower administration. Secretary of State Dean Acheson, however, did not share John Foster Dulles's pactomania, nor was he eager for the United States to assume the British responsibility for the stability of the Middle East. The shah would be welcomed; he would be honored; but he would go home empty-handed. Washington would give him words, not money. A Near East Division memorandum captured the essence of American diplomacy in 1949: "The shah must be convinced that we have a genuine interest in his country and that we are prepared to assist it within reasonable and practical limits, and he must also be convinced that when we reject his requests we do so for sound logical reasons rather than out of any prejudice against Iran or in favor of other countries."[13]

What the State Department found "reasonable and practical" was a far cry from what the shah and members of his government thought Iran needed and deserved. Ambassador Wiley urged Washington to approach the matter in a political rather than a narrowly economic or military light. To avoid grave disappointment, Wiley thought a way should be found to at least give the shah some advanced recoilless rifles and tanks. Acheson warned the shah that too much military spending might undermine economic reforms, leading Iran down the path of Chiang Kai-Shek's nationalist China. The shah heard Acheson, but insisted that the comparison of China to Iran had no relevance. But for Acheson and the State Department, the lesson of China overshadowed their response to events in Iran. Corruption, concentration on military rather than economic development, and the demoralization of impoverished masses had opened China to the communists.[14]

The refusal of the United States to finance the shah's ambitious plans was one factor that spurred the Iranians toward the nationalization of AIOC. Iran needed more revenues for its ambitious development schemes, to stabilize its currency, and to cope with the sources of popular discontent. To make matters worse, poor harvests in 1949 had almost crippled the economy. Nationalists like Mohammed Mossadeq blamed the British and AIOC for all the ills Iran had suffered in the twentieth century. For them Iran could not be independent until nationalization became a reality.[15]

The State Department had no desire to see the British driven out of Iran. In discussions with high-level British officials, American diplomats and military leaders stressed that British forces still served as the first-line defense against Soviet aggression in the Middle East. From 1948 on the State Department urged AIOC and the British government to reach a settlement. That meant that AIOC would have to offer more generous terms than it finally agreed to in July of 1949. Under the 1949 Supplemental Agreement, Anglo-Iranian offered to raise Iran's royalties to 30 percent and make a lump sum payment, without otherwise altering the terms of the concession, which ran until 1993. In offering only a monetary settlement, AIOC ignored the nationalists' demand that Iran control its own oil. As American diplomats pointed out to the British, all the Middle Eastern rulers were aware of Venezuela's fifty-fifty contract and of a similar arrangement pending between Saudi Arabia and Aramco. The State Department also emphasized to the British that Iran's increased revenues from oil concessions would limit demands on the United States to make loans or grants to the Middle East, in that way financing the stability of the region through the sale of oil rather than by pumping in taxpayers' dollars. When AIOC negotiators held firm, the Fifteenth Majles closed without taking any action on the supplemental agreement. Mossadeq and his supporters urged nationalization instead.[16]

A number of factors frustrated American attempts to mediate the dispute between Iran and Great Britain. Most historians and participants have agreed that Anglo-Iranian Oil and the British government showed remarkable ineptitude in dealing with the Iranian nationalists. Dean Acheson subsequently observed that Mossadeq's political fortunes were greatly abetted "by the unusual and persistent stupidity of the company and the British government in their management of the affair." One liberal member of the British Foreign Office complained of the "shortsightedness and lack of political awareness" demonstrated by AIOC. In particular, he faulted AIOC chairman Sir William Fraser "as a thoroughly second rate intellect and personality." Fraser, he suggested, "had all the contempt of a Glasgow accountant for anything which cannot be shown on a balance sheet."[17]

Above all Fraser failed to recognize that the postwar weakness of Great Britain had made the AIOC monopoly of Iranian oil anachronistic. While he was willing to compromise on questions of money, he was determined to hold firm on questions of management and control. By 1950 AIOC had locked the British government into supporting the supplemental agreement, despite the overwhelming evidence that the Majles would never accept its terms. No amount of friendly American persuasion or urgent pleading led the British to offer terms that the nationalists might actually accept. The British defended their position on three grounds. They argued that they could not afford to pay what the Iranians were demanding. In addition, they complained that the Middle Eastern governments were forever escalating their demands on the oil companies. If AIOC did not resist in Iran, the greed of Middle Eastern leaders would know no bounds. Finally, the AIOC representatives pointed out that the Iranian government had never been clear about what it actually wanted the British to offer.[18]

American oil executives dismissed at least two of these arguments. AIOC had been paying dividends of about 30 percent for much of the postwar period. The company clearly had the means to offer more generous terms and to make prepayments without in any way damaging its financial position. Moreover, the terms Iran had asked for were not out of line with those that other oil-producing nations were then negotiating. Even knowing that, Secretary Acheson told Ambassador Wiley in June of 1950 that the State Department would not put additional pressure on the British government or AIOC, "since it has now gone considerably further in this direction than contemplated six months ago and has made its views thoroughly known to high UK officials including Bevin."[19]

But the British were undoubtedly correct when they complained that it was difficult to understand just what the Iranians wanted. Who, after all, actually spoke for Iran? The shah, who seemed to endorse the terms of the Supplemental Agreement? Prime ministers who negotiated the terms, but feared to present them to the Majles? Or the rabid nationalists who insisted that Iran should own and sell its own oil? To better understand the British predicament, we should recall the wartime American experience in such negotiations with Iran. The United States and Iran never successfully reached an agreement covering the presence of the Persian Gulf Command. The status of the American advisory missions remained forever uncertain. On even the most trivial matters, Iranian officials seemed to prevaricate, procrastinate, and equivocate. That typically Persian style drove western diplomats to despair.

Moreover, many Iranian officials suffered from a provincialism that left them with an inflated sense of the value of Iran's oil to the west. In the late 1940s oil surpluses threatened to upset market structures. AIOC had access to the vast resources of Kuwait (then estimated to be higher than Saudi Arabia's) as well as of Iran. As Acheson and others tried to impress on Mossadeq, the United States and Britain would never agree to a settlement that might undermine the world oil industry, even if that meant losing Iran to the communists.[20]

Yet a realistic political sense underlay what often struck westerners as irrational behavior. Iran generally entered into negotiations from a position of weakness. Not only was Iran at a disadvantage vis-à-vis the big powers, but so too the shah and the cabinets seldom operated from a strong domestic political base. Adverse popular reaction to any agreement with a foreign power could bring down a weak government. In such a political environment, no terms the State Department could devise could have resolved the impasse between Iran and AIOC.

American policy toward Iran began to shift during 1950. The State Department became more critical of the shah and of the inadequacies of his leadership. Early in the year he had suspended the anticorruption campaign "for reasons of state." In place of the respected Mohammed Saed he had named as prime minister Ali Mansur, a reactionary best known for his venality. One State Department official on a visit to Iran described the situation as "dangerous and explosive." Confusion reigned within government circles. The Tudeh Party was increasing its public activities and the economic depression was worsening. Within the State Department, irritation surfaced over the incessant and unrealistic Iranian demands for American aid.[21]

By July of 1950 Secretary Acheson feared that internal political weakness aggravated by AIOC's intransigence would encourage renewed Soviet pressures on Iran. The State Department became more determined than ever that Iran should have a stable government with a pro-western orientation. This was after all the period during which the National Security Council issued NSC–68, which framed cold war strategy and declared that "a defeat of free institutions anywhere is a defeat everywhere." The fall of China to the communists and the Soviet explosion of an atomic bomb in 1949 had raised cold war tensions to new heights. In February a little known U.S. senator from Wisconsin told an audience in Wheeling, West Virginia, that the State Department was riddled with communists. The combination of China's fall and McCarthy's assault had left the State Department beleaguered, its credibility eroded. On 25 June 1950 troops from North Korea swept across the thirty-eighth parallel. The cold war had suddenly become hot.[22]

Before June of 1950 American intelligence analyses had not anticipated any renewed Soviet pressure on Iran. With the invasion of South Korea, it now seemed all too possible that the Soviet Union would not passively wait until Iran collapsed under the weight of internal disorder before trying to extend its influence there. A July policy analysis supposed that the Soviets might decide to invade under the 1921 treaty by claiming that Iran had become an American base directed against their country. "It is known that the Soviet Union is militarily prepared for an Iranian adventure at any time," Assistant Secretary of State George McGhee told Dean Acheson.[23]

McGhee was constructing a worst-case scenario for planning purposes, not predicting the imminence of an invasion. For that reason he did not suggest that current circumstances required a sudden shift in American policy beyond the strengthening of intelligence activities in Iran. At the same time, however, his analysis left no doubt that after Korea the State Department had become more persuaded of the Soviet Union's aggressive intentions against Iran, which still appeared to policy planners as the most vulnerable link in the west's security perimeter.

As a promiment Texas oilman, George McGhee well understood the strategic value of petroleum in the Middle East. His father-in-law, Everett DeGolyer, was the eminent oil geologist who in 1943 had led an American survey team that had predicted that the future of the world's oil industry lay in the Persian Gulf basin. McGhee, therefore, stressed the link between Iran's independence, Middle Eastern oil, and the security of the noncommunist world. Iran alone produced 6 percent of world oil supplies, the same level as the Soviet Union. AIOC's refinery at Abadan remained the largest in the world. The Middle East supplied 75 percent of Europe's demand, over half the oil for Africa and South Asia, and almost all that used in the Near and Middle East. Within a few years its production would outstrip the combined volume of all American producers and its reserves were clearly far larger. Middle East oil also cost far less. An average American well pumped about twelve barrels per day; an Iranian or Arab well produced around five thousand. Even with the imposition of nine thousand miles of freight costs, Suez Canal tolls, and American import taxes, the competitive price of Middle Eastern crude had a deflationary impact on the price American consumers paid for energy. Just by rupturing the flow of that oil, the Soviet Union could cripple the United States and its allies.[24]

The Korean War compounded the danger. As of September 1950, the oil companies warned that "Iranian oil *could not be replaced* [State Department's emphasis]."[25] Wartime demand had turned surpluses into shortages, even though the United States, Venezuela, and the Middle East were producing at record levels. Under those circumstances, the State Department thought the British Foreign Office should accept Iran's most recent demands for revisions of the terms of the 1949 Supplemental Agreement. Since AIOC operations were still highly profitable, the company could afford the financial terms, while the prepayment of royalties would strengthen the likelihood of Majles approval. Nor did the State Department find the Iranians unreasonable in asking for such nonfinancial provisions as a ten-year program to train Iranians in key jobs, examination of AIOC books to ensure Iran's share of profits, oil prices for Iran as low as those given any other purchaser (e.g., the British navy), and inspection of the oil exported.[26]

Political developments in Iran had persuaded the State Department that an agreement was now both necessary and possible. In June the Majles had entrusted evaluation of the agreement to a special oil commission. At the same time the shah had heeded American urgings to name a strong prime minister by replacing Mansur with Army Chief of Staff Ali Razmara, who favored a compromise settlement with AIOC.[27]

Razmara's determination to exercise total control over the army and his criticisms of the court had strained his relations with the shah until the two joined ranks to protect the army from its enemies. Razmara was on generally good terms with the volatile tribal groups. Toward the old rich factions and the court establishment he harbored the animus of a self-made man, sharpened by the politics of his leftist wife. He sought to settle the dispute with AIOC, not because he was in any way pro-British, but because he wanted the revenues to promote development. To gain the backing in the Majles needed to reach an agreement, he wooed the noncommunist left with a package of taxes on the rich, with administrative decentralization, with investigations into corruption, and with the distribution of state lands to the peasants. Ambassador Henry Grady, who came to Iran from the embassy in Greece, told the State Department that the best line for the United States was to "help Razmara get strength to settle the matter [with AIOC]."[28]

Razmara's efforts to win Majles approval of the supplemental agreement only swelled the ranks of his opposition. Passions in the Majles ran too high for any settlement that left AIOC in control of the concession. Grady complained that the "real problem is the irrational, nationalistic Majles which has a standoff attitude toward Razmara."[29] Nor did American policy much help his cause. Iran continued to receive far less aid than either the shah or Razmara requested, since no one in the Defense or State Departments believed that the Iranian Army had any function beyond internal security. Thus the United States sent aid only to boost Iranian morale, but not to create the army of the shah's grand vision.

Some of Razmara's overtures to the left backfired. To placate pro-Russian elements, he refused to send an Iranian military force to Korea. In November, his government cancelled BBC and Voice of America relays broadcasting into the Soviet Union, while the Iranian press adopted an increasingly hostile tone toward the United States. When Soviet overtures to Iran led to the signing of a trade agreement, Secretary Acheson warned that attempts to appease the Soviet Union would jeopardize Iran's friendship with the United States. At the same time, the leftist National Front deserted Razmara over the oil question. Demands he had made that struck AIOC and the British government as excessive outraged the nationalist factions as not going far enough. By late 1950 they insisted that any settlement must involve nationalization in some form. With Razmara under attack from both the left and the right, Grady notified Washington that powerful forces were trying to undermine the general.[30]

No one had anticipated the degree to which the oil question would mobilize Razmara's opposition, which refused to consider any other issues. In February, Mossadeq had dismissed land redistribution as irrelevant to the problems of poverty and unemployment. "The chief cause of all these miseries is the oil situation," he insisted. His obsession with AIOC deflected public attention away from the issues of internal political and economic reform that Razmara urged as the way to overcome Iran's backwardness. The general did not believe Iran had the technical and marketing resources to make nationalization a success. And by February 1951, AIOC indicated privately that it would discuss a settlement along the lines of the fifty-fifty agreement just signed between Aramco and Saudi Arabia. While he did not reveal the extent of the British offer, Razmara pleaded with the special Majles Oil Commission to allow him to negotiate the most favorable settlement.[31]

Time had run out for both the general and AIOC. On 6 March the Oil Commission endorsed nationalization. The next day, as Razmara left Tehran's central mosque, a young assassin sent by the Feda'iyan Islam, an extremist religious sect, gunned him down. Public rejoicing followed his death. Terrorists of the right vied with leftists for control of the streets. When the Majles chose Hoseyn Ala as prime minister, he, too, was swept along with the political tide. By 20 March both houses of the Majles had approved nationalization in principle. Although Ala no doubt opposed such an extreme measure, he did nothing to restrain Mossadeq and his followers.[32]

In April the Tudeh Party emerged as a major force behind the political disorder. The spread of Tudeh-backed strikes from the oil installations at Abadan to other cities forced Ala to declare martial law. As his political support dissolved, the majority in the Majles offered the premiership to Mossadeq, who took office on 28 April. Four days later he nationalized the AIOC concession.

MOSSADEQ

While the Truman administration was no friend of nationalization, it did not initially oppose Mossadeq. Dean Acheson harbored genuine good feelings toward the man who would become known for his public weeping and his pajama suits. Indeed, many western diplomats seemed to find Mossadeq's eccentric behavior more disconcerting than his policies. In his memoirs Acheson recalled his first meeting with the newly appointed prime minister: "He was small and frail with not a shred of hair on his billiard-ball head; a thin face protruded into a long beak of a nose flanked by two bright, shoe-button eyes." As he left his train Mossadeq moved with the cautious frailty of an old man. First appearances proved deceptive, for, as Acheson recalled, "Spotting me at the gate, he dropped his stick, broke away from his party, and came skipping along ahead of the others to greet us."[33] From this meeting Acheson concluded that a rational politician lurked behind the emotional exterior that sometimes led Mossadeq to his fits of public weeping. Acheson's appraisal contrasted sharply with that of most of the British diplomats, who contemptuously dismissed Mossadeq as a fanatic or a lunatic.

Neither Mossadeq's appointment as prime minister nor the nationalization of AIOC led to a major revision of American policy. As it had before, the Truman administration continued to seek some means for bringing Iran and AIOC to a settlement. All along the State Department had tended to view the key issues as more economic than symbolic. As a consequence, many American diplomats did not seem to appreciate how wide a gulf separated the British from the Iranian nationalists. The Americans thought the British could deal with Mossadeq; the British believed his only goal was to rob AIOC. Acheson and McGhee were convinced that fifty-fifty was AIOC's only hope; the champions of AIOC saw it as an illegitimate way to destroy the company. To encourage successful negotiations, the Truman administration was willing to increase aid to Iran, but it refused to offer aid as an alternative to oil revenues. In that way Iran would be forced to bargain, without becoming so desperate that a move toward the left and the Soviet Union would become attractive. A Soviet-Iranian alliance struck American policymakers as far more threatening than nationalization. The State Department insisted only that Iran pay "fair market value" for the properties it had expropriated.[34]

The British government and the oil companies took a much harder line. Over the spring and summer, the Labor government of Clement Attlee reinforced the British naval units in the Persian Gulf and its army units on Cyprus. At the same time, planning commenced on a covert operation to overthrow the National Front and promote a government receptive to a settlement on British terms. AIOC suspended all royalties payments, it organized a worldwide boycott of oil produced in Iran, and three thousand British employees refused to accept contracts from the Iranian government. When all the major oil companies agreed to respect AIOC's legal claims to Iranian oil, Mossadeq found his exports reduced to a trickle and the treasury running on empty. Just the problem of paying the seventy thousand Iranian employees of AIOC would threaten to bankrupt his government.[35]

Secretary of State Acheson was horrified at the prospect of a British military intervention. At a July meeting in Washington, he told British Ambassador Oliver Franks in no uncertain terms that the United States opposed the use of force. A British military expedition might ultimately lead to Soviet intervention as well. Acheson concluded that "we might end up with the British out and the Russians in. In short, armed intervention offered nothing except great trouble."[36] As an alternative, he decided to send Averell Harriman to Tehran in hopes that Harriman could convince both parties to resume negotiations. American opposition was a key factor in the British decision to exercise restraint.

Harriman's grave reservations about his mission proved fully warranted. Neither side was willing to compromise on critical points. The British would accept nationalization only if they received adequate compensation for the loss of the ownership of the concession's oil and production facilities. They insisted too that they retain control over production and marketing. The basis for such compensation, according to the British, would include future earnings as well as existing physical facilities. Mossadeq refused to consider any solution that left so much control in British hands. As the negotiations bogged down over seemingly narrow differences. British-Iranian tensions rose. Harriman could not persuade Mossadeq that Abadan could be run only by a sophisticated organization, not by uncoordinated specialists. Nor would Iran have ready markets for the oil it produced, since without compensation to AIOC, potential customers would view Iran's actions as "confiscation rather than nationalization." Despite Harriman's efforts and the arrival of a mission from the World Bank, Iran took over the Abadan refinery in September and shortly thereafter Mossadeq ordered all the British technicians out of the country.[37]

Although Harriman had failed to achieve a settlement, he returned convinced that the nationalization movement had wide popular support in Iran. A British show of force would only create greater antagonism, thus driving Iran toward the Soviet Union. In fact, Harriman's arrival had been greeted, not by Iranians cheering this show of support from the United States, but by jeering Tudeh mobs protesting his presence. Mossadeq's warning of a communist threat to Iran supported Harriman's belief that the British hard line would play into Soviet hands. For the British, that danger was not a sufficient reason to sacrifice AIOC. For the United States, however, Iran's strategic importance had far greater value than British oil interests. The Truman administration would sympathize with Iran's aspirations as long as Mossadeq's National Front steered away from the Tudeh Party or a pro-Soviet foreign policy.[38]

Mossadeq soon revealed that there was almost no basis upon which he could agree to a settlement with AIOC. Extremists of the left and the right criticized his every move. In October he momentarily distracted his opponents by personally presenting Iran's response to a British complaint before the Security Council. So skillfully did he argue for his nationalization policy that the Tehran press almost universally applauded his efforts. The State Department took advantage of his presence in the United States to try once again to bring the adversaries to the bargaining table. These efforts too ended in an impasse, in large part because a Conservative government under Winston Churchill had replaced Attlee. The new government was even less disposed to compromise Britain's economic interests than the old had been. As Acheson observed, Anthony Eden, like his predecessor, seemed to take all his cues on Iran from the reactionaries at AIOC. So Mossadeq left New York with nothing resolved, telling American negotiators that he was better off that way. "Don't you realize that returning to Iran empty-handed, I return in a much stronger position than if I returned with an agreement which I had to sell to my fanatics?" he asked Harriman's translator Vernon Walters.[39]

Mossadeq's government rested on two pillars: the prime minister's charismatic appeal and nationalism. His battle against AIOC had temporarily established a coalition of radicals from the left and right, including religious fundamentalists and Marxist ideologues. All the same, a Shiite leader like Ayatollah Kashani could not long remain linked to westernized radicals. Underestimating the force of Mossadeq's popular appeal, the British and the Americans both generally believed that to maintain power Mossadeq would have to make inroads on Iran's mounting economic crisis. Only with a resumption of oil revenues or an infusion of American aid could he keep the Iranian economy afloat or carry out his modernization programs.

There was really no possible policy that could satisfy the latent conflicts within Mossadeq's National Front coalition and at the same time establish a basis for a settlement with AIOC and the British government. The British promised to be even more hard-line with Eden and Churchill in power. Secretary Acheson appreciated the difficulty of Mossadeq's situation. "If he were doing things that were sensible, I think he would run even greater dangers," Acheson told a congressional committee in January 1952.[40]

Throughout 1952 Mossadeq found himself checked on many political fronts, both domestic and foreign. His desire to increase his power put him at odds with the shah, the military, and pro-British conservatives. At the same time, Mossadeq's popularity with the people was so high that his opponents seldom dared to attack him openly, resorting instead to more indirect tactics such as denying him the broad authority he requested to deal with the economic crisis. British sympathizers and agents stirred discontent.

THE CONVERGENCE OF ANGLO-AMERICAN POLICY

July 1952 brought what Roger Louis has identified as the turning point in the nationalization crisis. Mossadeq had insisted on exercising his constitutional authority to name a minister of war sympathetic to his policies. When the shah refused to accept such a hostile appointment, Mossadeq resigned and took his case to the streets. The Majles quickly chose Ahmad Qavam to replace Mossadeq. The British were betting that Qavam could rework the magic that had extracted Iran from its confrontation with the Soviet Union in 1947. More important, they hoped he would arrange a settlement favorable to AIOC. But the magic was gone. Widespread demonstrations and Tudeh-instigated riots greeted the new prime minister. The shah deployed the army in a futile attempt to quash the demonstrations. Mossadeq's appeal proved too powerful. Five days after Mossadeq resigned, a badly shaken shah had to ask him to form a new government.[41]

Success often obscures signs of underlying weakness. That was certainly the case with Mossadeq in the summer of 1952. His power did not rest on the constitution, his National Front coalition, or any other major body. It stemmed from his ability to stir the volatile passions of the urban masses. Nor did his political victory in any way enhance his ability to resolve the economic crisis. Iran's oil remained in the ground, because AIOC was intimidating potential purchasers. American aid remained limited largely to military and technical assistance. Deepening divisions within the national front coalition severely limited his ability to govern. As a result, Mossadeq concentrated his energies on consolidating his political power. He purged the army of hostile officers, reduced its size, and cut its budget. Twice he persuaded the Majles to grant him short-term emergency powers with which he attacked the political and economic bases of the traditional ruling elite. That effort further aroused American fears about his leftward tilt. In addition, Mossadeq successfully attacked the royal court and the shah. Historian Ervand Abrahamian has observed that "by May of 1953, the Shah had been stripped of all the powers he had fought for and recovered since August 1941."[42]

The rift between the British and the Americans had shielded Mossadeq from more hostile foreign interference. After the outburst of rioting in July, Anglo-American diplomats came to a common understanding regarding the threat that Iran's instability posed. Loy Henderson had recently been appointed American ambassador. No sooner had he arrived than he warned that recent events had so demoralized the shah that all that stood between Iran and communism was Mossadeq—from Henderson's point of view a most unreliable ally. Spurred on by the gloomy news from Tehran, Acheson resolved to make yet another attempt to end the British-Iranian impasse. The United States would grant Iran $10 million; the British would buy all the oil currently stored in Iran; and Mossadeq would agree to have an international commission determine the price Britain would receive as compensation. Neither side would budge.[43]

Now, however, the British were more persuaded that the communists might capture Mossadeq's movement. When Winston Churchill assumed Anthony Eden's role in negotiating with the United States on the Iranian question, he proved more adept at creating at least an illusion of cooperation. American and British policy began to converge. Both accepted the need for a policy that would prevent a communist takeover. For the British, that meant Mossadeq must go. The Americans still believed that he was the only Iranian leader who could establish a stable government.[44]

As the United States and Great Britain moved closer together, Mossadeq became more intransigent on the issue of AIOC. In September, he rejected a joint communiqué from Churchill and President Truman that embodied much of Acheson's earlier proposal. Iran would have to receive $49 million in back taxes and royalties before Mossadeq would even agree to talk. Recent talks with W. Alton Jones, president of Cities Service Oil Company and a confidant of Republican presidential candidate Dwight D. Eisenhower, though they had led nowhere, seemed to have persuaded Mossadeq that he could market Iranian oil without settling with AIOC. By October his government had even expelled the British diplomatic mission from Iran.[45]

It was no small matter that former General of the Army Eisenhower had become even indirectly connected with the crisis in Iran. President Truman had already announced his decision not to seek reelection. Bogged down in Korea, hectored by Senator McCarthy and his anticommunist cohorts, battling rising inflation, and tarnished with scandals, the Democrats knew they could not repeat the election miracle of 1948. So did the British and the Iranians, and both sides believed that Eisenhower would afford them a better opportunity to bargain. Neither was correct. The new administration would resolve the crisis on its own terms. The British would get less than they demanded and more than they deserved. Mossadeq would receive a lesson in cold war politics, Republican style.

The uncertain fortunes of Mossadeq's government had been apparent as early as January 1953. By that time the focus of Iran's politics had shifted largely from the Majles to the streets. Mossadeq had insisted on an extension of his emergency powers. The panic-stricken shah had adopted what could be seen either as a form of Islamic protest or as a concern for his personal safety—he threatened to withdraw into exile. Royalist and Tudeh-inspired mobs took to the streets. When one mob stormed Mossadeq's house, the resourceful prime minister fled over his garden wall clad only in his famous pajamas. He may have held power, but his authority rested on a crumbling foundation. A tone of desperation can be read into the prime minister's letter to President-elect Eisenhower asking for American assistance and support.[46]

Mossadeq could not have known that the Eisenhower administration had already involved itself in a plot to overthrow his government. Just before the American elections, British Intelligence had approached Kermit Roosevelt of the CIA with a plan to get rid of Mossadeq. Roosevelt had found that both the outgoing agency director, Bedell Smith, and the heir apparent, Allen Dulles, were sympathetic to the British proposal. All three assumed that the new administration would be more amenable to the idea than Truman and Acheson. Dulles and his staff were "eager to improve upon the record of their predecessors and to show that their fresh outlook could significantly advance the national interest." Dulles rose to the bait that Operation Ajax offered, much as John Kennedy would later walk almost blindly into the Bay of Pigs fiasco. As Roosevelt observed, "Ajax was sufficiently young and undeveloped so that Foster Dulles could quite properly claim it as his own."[47] He equally deserves all the criticism he has gotten for the enthusiasm with which he authorized unwarranted operations against sovereign states.

Would Acheson have approved of Ajax, if he had not been in a "lame duck" administration during the fall of 1952? His memoirs imply that in some form or other he knew about the British plan. He reports a communication from London that Mossadeq "was not so strong as he might appear"; only the Tehran mobs and the Tudeh Party kept him in power. British sources indicated that "other groups as yet inadequately organized were threatened by him and, in time, might be able to supercede him."[48] That was, of course, precisely what the British wished would happen, with Kermit Roosevelt and the CIA organizing the dissidents, especially those in the army, against Mossadeq.

Acheson gave no indication that he actually opposed the British plan. He had not endorsed such ideas in the past, but now since the Truman administration did not have time for the plan to mature, the discussion of it would have to await the incoming Eisenhower administration. Acheson instead continued his efforts to negotiate a settlement. Again he ran into the usual frustrations. The British behaved in such an obstructionist fashion that many American officials described their policy as one of "rule or ruin." Mossadeq practiced traditional Iranian equivocation, seeming sometimes to favor compromise, sometimes to oppose it. American Middle East oil companies were also reluctant to cooperate with the United States government in Iran, especially since the FTC was currently pressing an antitrust action against their collusive practices. Nor did they wish to profit from AIOC's misfortunes, which could easily befall them in the future. Moreover, they agreed with Anthony Eden and British Intelligence that Mossadeq's days were numbered.[49]

Nothing came of Acheson's long efforts to achieve a compromise. He left the State Department convinced that "Iran was on the verge of an explosion in which Mossadeq would break relations with the United States, after which nothing could save the country from the Tudeh Party and disappearance behind the Iron Curtain." In the end, Acheson believed that events had vindicated Eden and the British policy of avoiding a compromise on Mossadeq's terms. In that indirect way he indicated that he accepted the Eisenhower-Dulles decision to go ahead with "Operation Ajax." Certainly his alarm at the deteriorating political climate in Iran confirmed for the Dulles brothers their belief that American security required a quick end to Mossadeq and his flirtation with the Tudeh Party.[50]

EISENHOWER AND THE OVERTHROW OF MOSSADEQ

The events of early 1953 only hardened the Eisenhower administration's resolve to get rid of Mossadeq. The prime minister seemed to be threatening American interests on three grounds: He was increasingly estranged from the western powers, he appeared to have become dependent on the Soviet Union, and his grab for personal power had undermined the position of the shah. Given their obsession with the dangers of Soviet expansion, most American policymakers preferred an orderly despotism under the shah to the unruly democracy that kept Mossadeq in power. Certainly, Kermit Roosevelt, if not the other advocates of Ajax, had an almost boyish enthusiasm for the shah and for the monarchy in Iran. Roosevelt recalled in breathless prose his first meeting with "H.I.M.":

> I had no problem recognizing the finely drawn, distinctive regal features. And I was not surprised that H.I.M. recognized me immediately. (His memory for names, faces, facts and figures is truly remarkable . . .). When he had approached the car I could feel my heart pounding. Now the beat was even, my breathing regular. It was like a meeting of friends.[51]

Dulles saw Moscow's hand manipulating behind the scenes in Tehran. He feared that the political and social unrest Mossadeq had unleashed had created ideal conditions for a Soviet takeover. As Mossadeq became more dependent on the Tudeh Party, the Soviets would increase their control over his government. Dulles refused to sit idly by while Iran fell under the Kremlin's domination, "because a purely defensive policy never wins against an aggressive policy." Once again, the specter of Munich was haunting American foreign policy. No one chose to dispute the secretary of state's analysis, for, as Sherman Adams quipped, "How are you going to disagree with a man who has lived with a problem—for instance in respect to Iran—for longer than most of us knew there was such a country?" What Adams meant as a compliment to the worldly Dulles could equally well be treated as testimony to the ignorance of most of those in the Eisenhower administration who pondered Mossadeq's fate.[52]

Soon after Eisenhower's inauguration, the State Department turned aside, without answer, Mossadeq's request for increased American aid in favor of a British proposal for a negotiated settlement. Mossadeq rejected that solution because it required Iran to compensate AIOC. "What the Anglo-Iranian company did in southern Iran was sheer looting, not business," he told the Majles. But by May Mossadeq was more desperate for loans and for American assistance in establishing Iran's legitimate claims against the British and AIOC. In his appeal to President Eisenhower he warned that if Washington refused, Moscow would back his regime. He thus confirmed Dulles's assumption that he was an unreliable leader flirting dangerously with America's archenemy.[53]

For one month, Eisenhower made no reply. While Mossadeq waited, the "best and the brightest" met in Washington to consider a proposal from CIA agent Kermit Roosevelt, who since February had been working out the operations plan for Ajax. On 25 June the group that joined John Foster Dulles to hear Roosevelt's report included the secretary's brother, Allen, the new director of the CIA; Gen. Walter Bedell Smith, his predecessor and a former ambassador to the Soviet Union; Robert Murphy, the OSS operative for the North African landing and now director of political affairs at the State Department; H. Freeman Matthews, a State Department expert on Soviet affairs, Secretary of Defense Charles Wilson, and Ambassador to Iran Loy Henderson. No one in that august assemblage, with the exception of Henderson, had any real knowledge of Iran or about the current situation there. Perhaps that is why Henderson's views proved so persuasive.

Roosevelt himself was certainly no expert on Iran. Much of his knowledge of its history and culture came secondhand from UN Ambassador Ralph Bunche, who was no expert either, although intelligence work had given Roosevelt considerable experience in the Middle East and had led him to write a book on the Arabs and their oil. Once he had Allen Dulles's authorization to plan Ajax, Roosevelt did travel to Iran in order to familiarize himself with the situation and to contact his potential operatives. Virtually all his contacts were either westerners or Iranians sympathetic to the shah. As a result he came to the meeting convinced that the shah, his army, and the "overwhelming majority of the Iranian people" wished an end to Mossadeq and his flirtation with the communists.

If the group approved Ajax, Roosevelt planned to slip into Tehran where he would meet secretly with the shah. Once the shah had agreed, Ajax would proceed. Roosevelt's small band of American agents, working in concert with the British, would organize royalist support. The shah would order Mossadeq to resign in favor of former army chief Fazlollah Zahedi. In case Mossadeq and his followers resisted, the CIA-organized supporters of the shah would take their followers to the streets. It did not trouble Roosevelt that the British had imprisoned Zahedi during World War II because of his pro-Nazi sympathies. The general was the shah's choice and thus acceptable to Roosevelt. The Soviet Union, he predicted, would be helpless to intervene when it became apparent that the new regime and the shah had overwhelming popular support.

Having heard Roosevelt's plan, Secretary Dulles posed just two questions. What would the operation cost and what was the "flap" potential if the plan failed? The first question was easy. Roosevelt anticipated spending only a few hundred thousand dollars. The second question caused him to pause, but he concluded that the consequences of failure were little different than the dangers of inaction—either course might lead to a Soviet takeover. Thus assured, Dulles canvassed the group. All present with varying degrees of uncertainty gave their assent. Then it was Henderson's turn. For almost ten years he had warned about the Soviet menace to Iran and his recent experience had brought him in line with the British view of Mossadeq: "We are confronted by a desperate, a dangerous situation, and a madman who would ally himself with the Russians. We have no choice but to proceed with this undertaking. May God grant us success." Braced by Henderson's assessment, Roosevelt reaffirmed his faith in Ajax. John Foster Dulles evidently needed little persuading. "That's that, then," he announced. "Let's get going."[54]

What of President Eisenhower? Would he act as a brake on the excesses of his overzealous lieutenants? The masterminds of Ajax, Bedell Smith, the Dulles brothers, and Kermit Roosevelt worried little about what the president might think. Having served under Eisenhower in World War II, Smith could assure Roosevelt that "Ike will agree," to which the eager CIA operative assumed his superior would add "with whatever we tell him." In Roosevelt's account Eisenhower emerges almost as a patsy, easily manipulated by his hardboiled advisers. More recent scholarship would suggest, instead, that Smith and Dulles knew that Eisenhower agreed with their position, but that he did not want to be personally associated with the decision. Anthony Eden recalled that soon after his election, Eisenhower chafed at Truman's and Acheson's reluctance to intervene.[55]

On 29 June 1953 President Eisenhower struck the first blow in the Anglo-American operation against Mossadeq by rejecting the prime minister's request for aid. Iran could have all the funds it needed, Eisenhower noted, if it reached a reasonable settlement with the British and resumed marketing its oil. And in a statement remarkable both for its lack of candor and its largely unintentional irony, Eisenhower concluded, "I hope our future relationships will be completely free of suspicion, but on the contrary will be characterized by frankness and friendliness."[56]

News that the United States had turned down Mossadeq's plea sent communist-backed mobs into the streets. As chaos threatened to engulf Iran, Roosevelt returned to set his plan in motion. At the same time Mossadeq struggled desperately to strengthen his position. On 3 August he held a public referendum on his decision to dissolve the Majles and assume dictatorial powers. Not surprisingly, Mossadeq won some 95 percent of the votes by calling off the balloting before rural returns spelled defeat. He believed he had been forced to disrupt a liberal democratic process to achieve liberal democratic ends. His critics once again saw the danger of communist dictatorship threatening. On 16 August the shah left Tehran for a "rest cure" at a Caspian resort. Before leaving he issued a series of royal decrees ordering that Mossadeq resign in favor of General Zahedi. That phase of Roosevelt's plan was foiled because Mossadeq learned of the move and had the shah's messenger arrested. With pro-Mossadeq crowds swarming the streets, the shah fled the country. Where, Roosevelt worried, were the mobs his operatives had hired?

Now Loy Henderson played his crucial part. American diplomatic officers knew nothing about Roosevelt's operations and Henderson had at first purposely remained outside Iran. News of the turmoil had brought him rushing back to Tehran. With anti-Shah and anti-American mobs thronging the streets, Henderson went to Mossadeq demanding protection for American citizens. That forced Mossadeq to call out the army, the stronghold of his potential enemies, to clear the streets of his supporters. Roosevelt saw the opening he needed. The shah's loyalists and some hired mobs took over the streets from the Tudeh Party. By 19 August Mossadeq was under arrest, Zahedi was prime minister, and the shah was back on his throne. As a show of American support, Henderson was able to give the new government the $900,000 left in Roosevelt's operations fund and promised a $45 million emergency credit under Point Four.

In the midst of the planning for this operation, Roosevelt had assured the shah of U.S. support with a message that he claimed came from President Eisenhower, but which was his own improvised rendering of the president's views: "If the Pahlevis and Roosevelts working together cannot solve this little problem there is no hope anywhere." Thus, when the shah returned he offered a toast to Roosevelt, "I owe my throne to God, my people, my army, and to you."[57] The future of the Pahlevis had become inextricably tied to the United States. The shah might never in any sense become an American puppet, indeed he would act with great autonomy, but the Iranian-American alliance had been born. That did not mean that the forces Mossadeq had led or the emotions he had called forth had been forever silenced. In 1978 the secular intelligentsia and the radical Muslim fundamentalists would once again join together to rid Iran of an intrusive foreign influence.

Eisenhower's role in the overthrow of the Mossadeq government should stand as a corrective to recent attempts to refurbish his presidential reputation. Having once relegated him to the level of the passive chief executives like Calvin Coolidge, some scholars have found wisdom in his noninvolvement and his willingness to delegate authority. Eisenhower's style has become an attractive alternative to the abuses of power practiced by Kennedy, Johnson, Nixon, and most recently, and dramatically, the Reagan administration. Yet with the urging of his advisers, particularly John Foster Dulles, Eisenhower authorized a Central Intelligence Agency operation to support factions eager to replace Mossadeq with a premier more loyal to the shah, one who was willing to negotiate a settlement with AIOC, and, above all, one committed to the west in the cold war. Certainly, no one had anticipated the tyranny that would follow the shah's return, and Roosevelt had not made assassination a part of his plan. All the same, this was interventionism of the worst kind.[58]

The decision to participate in the overthrow of Mossadeq can be faulted on many levels. The new administration knew almost nothing about Iran nor about the dynamics of its internal politics. As a result, the United States associated itself with the downfall of one of the most revered Iranian leaders of the twentieth century and the return to power of one of the most widely disliked—Mohammed Reza Shah Pahlevi. Few Iranians ever viewed the Pahlevi regime as legitimate. They had respected Reza Shah out of fear, not out of devotion, and most neither respected nor feared his son.

After the CIA helped to restore his throne, the young shah would always seem beholden to the United States. Dreams of liberal reform would give way to grand visions of modernization and militarism. The fortunes of the shah and those of the United States in Iran would rise and fall together. American security interests in the Persian Gulf region became entangled in the affairs of a regime that was highly vulnerable to internal collapse either from its own corruption or from the factionalism that has long been a characteristic of Iranian society. The economic miracle of the 1960s would obscure the weaknesses of a regime dependent for its authority on the military and secret police, not on popular approval of its policies.

Worst of all, the overthrow of Mossadeq was probably unnecessary. By the summer of 1953 Mossadeq was in such a precarious political position that he would probably have fallen of his own weight. Disrupted by the oil boycott, the Iranian economy was in shambles. The Eisenhower administration's refusal to extend further American aid had probably doomed Mossadeq in any case. Although his popularity with the masses remained high, many of his political allies had deserted from his National Front coalition, most notably the Ayatollah Kashani and the traditional Islamic radicals, along with the noncommunist middle-class factions led by the bazaar merchants. And though there exists a remote possibility that the Tudeh Party could have capitalized on his downfall to seize power, the forces on the right were in a much better position to replace Mossadeq than the ones on the left. The United States would most likely have achieved a similar outcome by simply doing nothing.[59]

NOTES

1. Henry Longhurst, *Adventure in Oil: The Story of British Petroleum* (London, 1959), p. 508. On Sir Francis Shepard, see William Roger Louis, *The British Empire in the Middle East, 1945–1951*, pp. 638–42, and p. 689. I have benefited enormously from Louis's account of British policy from 1949 to 1951, which has allowed me to flesh out my own account.

2. See Dean Acheson, *Present at the Creation* (New York, 1969), pp. 872–73. One source of evidence for the shift comes from the person who helped orchestrate Mossadeq's overthrow—Kermit Roosevelt. Anyone familiar with *Countercoup* (New York, 1979) is probably aware of the controversy that surrounded its publication. To save British Intelligence from unwanted publicity, Roosevelt attributed their activities to AIOC; see, for example, *Countercoup*, p. 3, pp. 107–8, and p. 119. In response, AIOC threatened legal action against Roosevelt and his publisher, McGraw-Hill. The book was withdrawn from the bookstores and a sanitized version was later published. I am citing the first, unsanitized edition. Though we have reason to distrust Roosevelt, I suspect that on matters of politics in which intelligence sources are not involved he has been reasonably candid. See *Countercoup*, pp. 94–95, for his view of the shift between Acheson and Dulles on Iran.

3. My account of the period from 1948 to 1953 is not as detailed as my treatment of the earlier years. In particular there remain restrictions on both British and American sources from 1952–53. While completing this manuscript I had the unusual good fortune to receive a number of papers from the Conference on Iranian Nationalism and the International Oil Crisis of 1951 organized by Prof. James Bill and the Center for Middle Eastern Studies at the University of Texas at Austin, September 1985. I have profited enormously from reading these papers. Anyone interested in seeing them might contact the scholars directly. R. W. Ferrier, "The British Government, the Anglo-Iranian Oil Company and Iranian Oil"; William Roger Louis (University of Texas), "Mussadiq, Oil, and the Dilemmas of British Imperialism"; Farhang Rajaee, "Islam, Nationalism and Mussadiq's Era: The Perspective of the Islamic Republic of Iran"; Homa Katouzian (University of Kent, at Canterbury), "The Strategy of Non-Oil Economics: Economic Policy and Performance under Mussadiq"; F. Azimi (St. Anthony's College, Oxford), "Profile of a Democratic Nationalist: Dr. Muhammad Mussadiq"; Shahrough Akhavi (University of South Carolina), "The Role of the Clergy in Iranian Politics, 1949–1954"; Richard Cottam (University of Pittsburgh), "Nationalism in Twentieth Century Iran"; Irvine Anderson (University of Cincinnati), "The American Oil Industry and the 'Fifty-Fifty Agreement' of 1950"; George McGhee, "Recollections of Dr. Muhammad Musaddiq." McGhee's views are available in his *Envoy to the Middle World* (New York, 1983). For other published analyses, see Ramazani, *Iran's Foreign Policy*, pp. 181ff. and Barry Rubin, *Paved With Good Intentions*, pp. 29–90. A detailed and enlightening analysis of Iran's domestic policy during the period is available in Abrahamian, *Iran Between Two Revolutions*, pp. 242ff. See also Abrahamian's comprehensive analysis of the Tudeh Party, pp. 281–415.

4. Louis, *The British Empire in the Middle East*, pp. 54–73.

5. Louis, *The British Empire in the Middle East*, pp. 633–40. Ramazani, *Iran's Foreign Policy*, ch. 8.

6. On the British situation in 1947, see FR, 1947, 5, "Pentagon Talks of 1947," pp. 510–13 and pp. 547–49. For quoted passages, see p. 577. One interesting aspect of these talks was the American recognition that the United States needed British military assistance in the Middle East. Despite its postwar prosperity, the United States did not possess the resources to "go it alone" in the region. The large increase in defense spending that attended NSC–68 and the Korean War was a thing of the future. On AIOC, see Mosley, *Power Play*, pp. 198–201. On the opening of negotiations between AIOC and the Iranian government, see FR, 1948, 5, pt. 1, p. 49.

7. SD 711.91/2–149, Policy Statement on Iran. See also FR, 1949, 6, pp. 474–75, for the first sections. See also pp. 477–86, for report on the failed assassination and the shah's response.

8. Ibid., pp. 514–22, Wiley to Acheson, 4/29/49; memorandum by Satterthwaite, 5/3/49; and Acheson to Wiley, 5/16/49.

9. For a good review of Iran's aspirations for American military aid, see Ramazani, *Iran's Foreign Policy,* pp. 154–62. A large portion of the documents in *Foreign Relations* pertaining to Iran deals with the problem of military assistance.

10. On the shah's political role, see Abrahamian, *Iran Between Two Revolutions,* pp. 245–47.

11. See FR, 1949, 6, pp. 471–72, editorial note, and pp. 470–593 and passim. The issue of military assistance underlay much of the diplomatic correspondence for the year.

12. On the clash between OCI and Iran, see Ramazani, *Iran's Foreign Policy* pp. 162–66; see also FR, 1949, 6, pp. 477n., p. 513, p. 521, p. 526, pp. 566–67. OCI once again brought Max Thornburg into Iranian affairs, since he was a vice-president of the company. The British believed, perhaps correctly, that he thought the Americans could profit from AIOC's difficulties.

13. Ibid., pp. 569–71, memorandum by McGhee, 11/17/49.

14. On the shah's visit, see ibid., pp. 572–93. See also Rubin, *Paved With Good Intentions,* pp. 40–42. To appreciate how the China analogy could affect American thinking, see the column by Joseph Alsop in the *Washington Post,* 30 July 1952. "[The United States] may be faced with the choice of allowing Iran to go the way of China, or intervening forcefully to support any anti-Communist forces in Iran, however reactionary and blindly nationalist."

15. See FR, 1949, 6, pp. 141–42, Wiley to Secretary of State, 7/21/49 and p. 142n. See SD 891.6363/7–2849, 965, Wiley to Secretary of State, and SD 891.6363/7–3149, Wiley to Secretary of State. See also FR, 1950, 5, p. 82.

16. John Blair has shown how the State and Treasury Departments in 1950 concocted an ingenious tax scheme that allowed the oil companies to meet the demand from Ibn Saud and other Middle East leaders for greater revenues. By treating royalty payments as taxes, the companies avoided tax payments to the treasury. The loss to the U.S. government became gain for the oil companies and the host countries. In that way, two executive departments circumvented the congressional control of the nation's purse strings and were able in effect to increase foreign aid without a congressional appropriation. For a fuller explanation, see Blair, *The Control of Oil,* pp. 195–203; and Anthony Sampson, *The Seven Sisters,* pp. 126–34. The most scholarly treatment is in Irvine Anderson, *Aramco, the United States and Saudi Arabia* (Princeton, 1981). In his paper, "The American Oil Industry and the 'Fifty-Fifty Agreement' of 1950" Anderson argues persuasively that the National Security Council had no role in the agreement as Blair suggested. See also Louis, *The British Empire in the Middle East,* pp. 632–37, and for the effect of fifty-fifty elsewhere in the Middle East, pp. 595–600. See Keddie, *Roots of Revolution,* pp. 132–34, for the influence of fifty-fifty on Iran.

17. For Acheson's views, see Dean Acheson, *Present at the Creation* (New York, 1969), p. 646. For the view of one critical English observer, see Anthony Sampson, *Seven Sisters,* pp. 135–140. For an example of the role assumed by the State Department prior to nationalization, see FR, 1950, 5, pp. 13–15. Roger Louis is kinder to Fraser in his treatment, *The British Empire in the Middle East,* pp. 643–47.

18. On the role of the British government and AIOC from the American records, see FR, 1950, 5, p. 460, pp. 530–31, p. 545, p. 547, p. 567, p. 570, p. 576, pp. 580–81, and pp. 595–96.

19. Ibid., pp. 562–63 and p. 576.

20. George McGhee, "Recollections of Dr. Muhammad Musaddiq," pp. 4–6; see also Vernon Walters, *Silent Mission* (New York, 1978), pp. 246–63. From Yonah Alexander and Allan Nannes, eds., *The United States and Iran: A Documentary History,* pp. 221–22, letter from Harriman to Mosaddeq, 9/15/51.

21. FR, 1950, 5, pp. 490–99.

22. Ibid., pp. 569–70. It is interesting to compare this note from Acheson of July 14, 1950, to his note three weeks earlier to the embassy in Iran (see pp. 562–63). After July, references to Soviet intentions become far more common as a backdrop for questions of aid and the resolution of Iran's conflict with AIOC. For a good discussion of the general cold war background, see Gaddis, *Russia, the Soviet Union, and the United States,* pp. 193–204, and LaFeber, *Russia, America, and the Cold War,* pp. 75–127.

23. FR, 1950, 5, pp. 572–74, McGhee memorandum for Acheson, 7/21/50.

24. Ibid., pp. 76–96, "Middle East Oil." This paper was prepared for McGhee by an assistant, but there is no question of his central role in petroleum policy analysis and planning. Anyone interested in oil policy will find this paper most informative.

25. Ibid., pp. 97–99, memorandum by Funkhouser and McGhee, 9/14/50.

26. Ibid., pp. 97–99.

27. Ibid., pp. 463–64, Wiley to Secretary of State, 1/30/50.

28. Ibid., pp. 581–83, Grady to Secretary of State, 8/15/50. See also Abrahamian, *Iran Between Two Revolutions*, pp. 263–64.

29. FR, 1950, 5, pp. 582, and pp. 605–6, Grady to Secretary of State, 10/12/50.

30. Ibid., pp. 615–16, Acheson to Grady, 11/20/50. See also ibid., p. 615n., 1 and 2 and pp. 630–32, Grady to Secretary of State, 12/14/50.

31. Mossadeq, quoted in Ramazani, *Iran's Foreign Policy*, p. 196. See also Dean Acheson, *Present at the Creation*, p. 649.

32. For good analyses of the internal events leading up to nationalization, see Ramazani, *Iran's Foreign Policy*, pp. 194–97 and Abrahamian, *Iran Between Two Revolutions*, pp. 263–67.

33. Acheson, *Present at the Creation*, pp. 650–51. Again I draw readers' attention to the paper by F. Azimi, "Profile of a Democratic Nationalist: Dr. Muhammad Musaddiq," as well as to sketches by McGhee in *Envoy to The Middle World* and Vernon Walters in *Silent Missions*. Azimi draws an especially favorable portrait of Mosaddeq, who appears as one of the great patriotic and humane leaders of the twentieth century.

34. Louis, *The British Empire in The Middle East*, pp. 654–57 and Alexander and Nannes, eds., *The United States and Iran*, pp. 223–24, memorandum for the Secretary of Defense from the Joint Chiefs of Staff, 10/10/51.

35. Mosley, *Power Play*, pp. 203–7; Ramazani, *Iran's Foreign Policy*, pp. 198–206; Acheson, *Present at the Creation*, pp. 653–54. Roger Louis ascribes the inspiration for covert planning to Persian scholar Ann Lampton, who served in the Tehran Embassy during the war. See Louis, *The British Empire in The Middle East*, pp. 658–61.

36. Acheson, *Present at the Creation*, pp. 654–55. Louis, *The British Empire in The Middle East*, pp. 668–69.

37. Ramazani, *Iran's Foreign Policy*, pp. 206–14. See Alexander and Nannes, eds., *The United States and Iran*, pp. 221–22, Harriman to Mosaddeq, 9/15/51.

38. Acheson, *Present at the Creation*, pp. 654–57; Mosley, *Power Play*, pp. 207–8; U.S. Department of State, *Bulletin*, 621, 5/28/51, p. 851; 622, 6/4/51, pp. 891–92; 628, 7/9/51. See also Ferrier, "The British Government, The Anglo-Iranian Oil Company and Iranian Oil," pp. 25–27.

39. Vernon Walters, *Silent Mission*, pp. 259–63; Acheson, *Present at the Creation*, pp. 658–59; Ramazani, *Iran's Foreign Policy*, pp. 213–18.

40. On Mossadeq's domestic situation, see Abrahamian, *Iran Between Two Revolutions*, pp. 257–61, and pp. 267–70. See also Acheson, *Present at the Creation*, pp. 865–67.

41. Abrahamian, *Iran Between Two Revolutions*, pp. 270–72. See also William Roger Louis, "Musaddiq, Oil, and the Dilemmas of British Imperialism," pp. 15–17.

42. Abrahamian, *Iran Between Two Revolutions*, pp. 272–73.

43. Acheson, *Present at the Creation*, pp. 865–67.

44. Louis, "Musaddiq, Oil, and the Dilemmas of British Imperialism," pp. 26–27.

45. Acheson, *Present at the Creation*, pp. 867–68; Mosely, *Power Play*, pp. 209–11.

46. Barry Rubin, *Paved With Good Intentions*, p. 78. See also Kermit Roosevelt, *Countercoup*, pp. 114–35, and Mosley, *Power Play*, pp. 209–15, for other accounts of this period.

47. Roosevelt, *Countercoup*, pp. 107–26. This is a section in which Roosevelt substitutes AIOC for British intelligence. See also Rubin, p. 77.

48. Acheson, *Present at the Creation*, p. 868.

49. Ibid., pp. 868–70.

50. Ibid., pp. 870–72.

51. For the flavor of Roosevelt's near hero worship of the shah, see *Countercoup*, pp. 155–68. Roosevelt himself seems largely unselfconscious about his relish for contact with a monarch.

52. On Dulles and foreign policy, see LaFeber, *America, Russia, and the Cold War*, pp. 139–44 and 153. See also Townsend Hoopes, *The Devil and John Foster Dulles*, (New York, 1973) for a perhaps somewhat overcritical treatment of Dulles.

53. Mosley, *Power Play,* pp. 211–12; U.S. Department of State, *Bulletin,* 734, 7/29/53, pp. 73–74.

54. Roosevelt, *Countercoup,* pp. 3–18. See also Kermit Roosevelt, *Arabs, Oil, and History* (New York, 1949).

55. Roosevelt, *Countercoup,* p. 116. Stephen Ambrose, *Eisenhower: The President* (New York, 1984), p. 111. An important discussion of Eisenhower's role in foreign policy is George C. Herring and Richard Immerman, "Eisenhower, Dulles, and Dienbienphu: 'The Day We Didn't Go To War' Revisited," *Journal of American History,* 71, 2 (September 1984): 349–51, 362–63. In their analysis, Herring and Immerman see much of the confusion surrounding both policy and process as intentional. Of course, there is no definite reason to assume that Eisenhower saw Iran in the same light as he saw Indochina, but the parallels are striking, with similar concerns about cooperation with allies and the dangers of inaction in the face of a communist threat. See also Anthony Eden, *Full Circle* (Boston, 1960), p. 227.

56. U.S. Department of State, *Bulletin,* 734, 7/23/53, pp. 73–74. For Mossadeq's quote, see Mosley, *Power Play,* pp. 211–12.

57. For Roosevelt's description of his operation, see *Countercoup,* chs. 9–12. For the quotes see p. 168, pp. 199–200. Other good brief accounts are Abrahamian, *Iran Between Two Revolutions,* pp. 278–80; and Rubin, *Paved With Good Intentions,* pp. 81–90. Both Rouhollah Ramazani and Rubin agree that the Mossadeq overthrow and the reinstallation of the shah marked the beginning of an Iranian-American alliance. See Ramazani, *Iran's Foreign Policy,* ch. 11 and Rubin, *Paved With Good Intentions,* ch. 4.

58. For one good reevaluation of Eisenhower's foreign policy, see Robert Divine, *Eisenhower and the Cold War* (New York, 1981). A good discussion of the historiographic issues is in George C. Herring and Richard Immerman, "Eisenhower, Dulles, and Dienbienphu: 'The Day We Didn't Go to War' Revisited," pp. 363, and especially p. 344.

59. For some examples of such scholarly reaction, see Abrahamian, *Iran Between Two Revolutions,* pp. 278–80; Richard Cottom, *Nationalism in Iran,* p. 229; Rubin, *Paved With Good Intentions,* pp. 87–90. Rubin wrote, "Overthrowing Mossadeq had been like pushing on an already open door." See also Ramazani, *Iran's Foreign Policy,* pp. 248–50. Ramazani tends to accept Anthony Eden's view that Eisenhower's refusal to send aid doomed Mossadeq. See Anthony Eden, *Full Circle* (Boston, 1960), pp. 222–26. The view that the CIA's role was decisive comes largely from Eisenhower's memoirs, *Mandate for Change,* pp. 160–66, where he claims credit for saving Iran from communism. See also a similar view from Allen Dulles, *The Craft of Intelligence* (New York, 1963), p. 224. Certain writers have agreed. See, for example, Richard Barnett, *Intervention and Revolution* (New York, 1969), pp. 226–27, and Andrew Tully, *CIA, The Inside Story* (New York, 1962), p. 96. It is interesting that while in his narrative of events Kermit Roosevelt sees Ajax as largely determining the outcome, in his conclusions he emphasizes the circumstances peculiar to Iran at that time that allowed Ajax to succeed where similar operations in other countries would end in disaster or farce.

Epilogue

When Kermit Roosevelt returned to Washington after his Iranian adventure, the "best and brightest" met once again to analyze the outcome of the operation. Dulles had obviously concluded that the CIA's success vindicated his faith in an offensive American policy wherever Soviet-directed communism threatened. He radiated self-congratulatory pleasure as he listened to Roosevelt's account of Ajax. "His eyes were gleaming; he seemed to be purring like a giant cat," Roosevelt recalled. "Clearly, he was not only enjoying what he was hearing, but . . . planning as well." Fearful that Dulles might miss the point of his presentation, Roosevelt emphasized the special circumstance that had favored Ajax. The CIA had correctly gauged popular disenchantment with Mossadeq. "The people and the army came, overwhelmingly, to the support of the Shah," Roosevelt observed, but then added to make his point, "If our analysis had been wrong, we'd have fallen flat on our, er, faces."[1]

Dulles chose not to heed Roosevelt's warning. The idea that other crises involving leftist or nationalist discontent might not lend themselves to an Iranian-style solution did not penetrate Dulles' thoughts. A few weeks later the secretary asked Roosevelt if he would head a CIA operation in Guatemala, "already in preparation." After a few inquiries had persuaded Roosevelt that Guatemala was not another Iran, he declined the invitation. The operation went ahead anyway, as would an even more ill-conceived CIA plan at the Bay of Pigs a few years later. Covert operations had become an accepted part of the American cold war arsenal.[2]

For Dulles, as for the Truman administration, Iran had served as a test case of cold war assumptions and policies. In Iran, in Korea, in Vietnam, and in other third world areas the Kremlin had revealed its plan "to accelerate Communist conquest of every country where the Soviet government could make its influence felt." Dulles made no attempt to appreciate Mossadeq's policy of "negative equilibrium," which was as much anti-Soviet as anti-British. He may not even have realized that Mossadeq had cancelled the Soviet Union's Caspian fishing concession shortly after he nationalized AIOC. Nor did it matter that Mossadeq had a wide popular following or that his overthrow in no way stilled the anti-foreign sentiments that his leadership symbolized for many Iranians. Mossadeq had become in Dulles' eyes an instrument of the Kremlin's strategy of confusion and subversion, so he had to go.[3]

The Eisenhower administration moved quickly to ensure that the CIA's success did not come undone. That did not mean a total reversal of policy or major new initiatives. American economic aid, although it was increased, remained at relatively modest levels. Between 1953 and 1957 the Zahedi government received about $145 million in emergency funds from the United States. But the key to Iran's future lay in its oil fields. Before Iranian crude would flow into world markets, a number of obstacles had to be removed. The British had not yet renounced their claims against Iran. At the same time, the shah and Zahedi had no intention of reestablishing the British monopoly over Iranian oil. An alternative had to be found. Into the breach stepped an old player in the game of Iranian oil, Herbert Hoover, Jr.[4]

Hoover had a good idea on how to break the impasse caused by Britain's desire for a return to the *status quo ante* and Iran's determination to end the AIOC monopoly and assume ownership of its oil. Several times in the past the Iranians had proposed the idea of a multinational consortium with a role for their own state oil company and, perhaps, even one for the Russians. Hoover now revived the idea of a consortium in which the American "sisters" would assume a central role. That would seem to confirm a revisionist interpretation of the coup against Mossadeq: Political explanations masked the Eisenhower administration's determination to open Iran to American oil companies. However, such an *ex post facto* argument confuses effect with cause. While the coup did let American oil companies acquire a major share of Iranian oil production, that was not necessarily the original intention of the CIA planners.

In fact, we have seen repeatedly that the Truman and Eisenhower administrations had subordinated the interests of the oil companies to national security concerns whenever the two conflicted. Most often, of course, they did not, but in this case they did. Dulles wanted to foreclose any possibility that the shah might actually make good his invitation to the Russians to send in oil negotiators. As Leonard Mosley has concluded, "the U.S. government wanted to make sure that Iranian oil was kept out of Russian hands."[5] The British government was equally determined to have revenues from Iran's oil and to get a share of the compensation the consortium members would pay AIOC. Thus both governments pressured the oil companies to agree to a settlement.

The companies had little immediate interest in joining the Iranian consortium. AIOC's disaster had been a bonanza for Aramco and the other Persian Gulf producers, whose market shares had increased dramatically. The renewed flow of Iranian oil threatened to force cuts in production and revenues upon other Gulf states. Since it did not work out that way, it is tempting to assume that the oil companies knew how rapidly world markets would expand, that they feigned reluctance to join the consortium only to improve their bargaining position. If so, their strategy worked. Only after the Justice Department had agreed to waive any further antitrust actions against the "sisters" and AIOC had given its blessing was Hoover able to entice Standard Oil of New Jersey, Mobil, Socal, Texaco, and Gulf Oil to share a 40 percent interest. The new partners pledged to compensate AIOC for its lost facilities. AIOC retained a 40 percent interest, while 14 percent went to Royal-Dutch Shell and 6 percent to Compagnie Française des Pétroles. That settlement did nothing to ease antitrust grievances against the major oil companies. As a sop to the smaller producers, a group of American independents later received a token 5 percent share, leaving the majors with 7 percent interests.[6]

The terms worked out over the summer of 1954 fulfilled three foreign policy goals that Iran had pursued intermittently since 1940. The AIOC monopoly had ended; the United States had a major interest in Iran and its oil; and Iran now had established title to its oil while realizing a far greater share of the oil revenues. Over the first three years of the consortium's operation, Iran received some $500 million in royalties. That money helped the shah launch his modernization campaign that would eventually lead western observers to describe Iran's economic growth as a third world miracle. Economic recovery also helped the shah consolidate his power with the help of SAVAK and a greatly expanded military. By the 1960s the shah had become the United States' major ally in one of the most strategically vital areas of the world. Only with his collapse would the underlying weaknesses of the Iranian-American alliance become more obvious.[7]

Of course, all political successes inevitably prove transitory. The American policymakers who forged the Iranian-American alliance between 1941 and 1953 can hardly be faulted for its collapse in 1979. Or can they? It has been one purpose of this study to show that the Iranian-American alliance always contained the seeds of disaster. It involved for the United States a strategic entanglement in an area of the world that Americans little understood and where they had little desire to commit their economic or political resources. Only since the OPEC crisis of 1973–74 and the 1978 Iranian Revolution have most Americans realized what it means to be dependent on a foreign oil supplier under the control of unstable governments whose proximity to the Soviet Union gives the Russians a clear-cut tactical advantage in any confrontation. That, however, was something that policymakers understood in 1943 when advisers and oil companies deepened the American involvement in Iran; in 1946, when American diplomacy helped Iran survive a confrontation with its northern neighbor; and in 1953 when Kermit Roosevelt and the CIA helped to return the shah to his throne. In each instance, American policymakers sought to maintain Iran as a pro-western barrier against possible Soviet ambitions in the oil-rich Persian Gulf region.

Did the Soviet Union have a carefully conceived plan to extend its orbit into the Persian Gulf? Insofar as Iran is a representative case, the answer is a qualified no. Certainly American policymakers had cause for suspicion and concern. Soviet foreign policy followed few of the rules that generally governed the behavior of the western powers. And there can be little question that the Soviet Union envisioned a dependent Iran as one of the spoils of war. But once again we should recall Firuz Kazemzadeh's observation that the Soviets would never take major risks, much less invite war, to realize their objectives in Iran. That suggests that the United States did not have to resort to an interventionist policy in order to maintain Iran as an independent buffer state.

A viable alternative always did exist. Henry Stimson and Walter Lippmann had both implicitly recognized it in 1944. The United States should have fostered Iranian neutrality. That was part of the somewhat muddled policy John Jernegan had proposed in his 1943 memorandum. By removing Iran from the arena of big power conflict, the United States could have relieved one of the major sources of tension in the Middle East. Nor did the United States have to threaten the Soviet Union so directly by reaching for an ally within a traditional Russian sphere of influence. But U.S. involvement in Iran coincided with two monumental shifts in the world situation in relation to the United States. The powers that had once held the Soviet Union in check—Great Britain, Germany, and Japan, in particular—had been devastated by war. That inspired the State Department to conceive, even as the war raged, of a system of containment in which Iran was a crucial link. At the same time, American oil companies assumed a dominant position in the newly developed Persian Gulf oil fields. As we have seen, almost all Washington policymakers appreciated the relationship of that oil to future national security and to the United States' role as a world power. They came to view the Iranian-American alliance as one way to guarantee access to Middle East oil while denying the Soviet Union entry into the region. Iranian neutrality involved too many risks for policymakers who assumed that national security should be one of the fruits of an American victory in both World War II and the cold war.

Still, we must go beyond circumstances and the strategies of containment to explain why the Truman and Eisenhower administrations did not heed Walter Lippmann's timely warning against an alliance with Iran. Certainly geopolitical conditions during the war created both an opportunity and a rationale for closer American-Iranian ties. After 1943, American diplomats believed that the waning of British power in the region created a vacuum that it was in the interest of the United States to fill. And no explanation that ignores the attraction of Middle Eastern oil for both oil executives and national security managers can be satisfactory. But we should also return to the three more general themes offered earlier in this study—bureaucratic or organizational rivalries, traditional anti-Soviet obsessions, and American exceptionalism—to understand the origins of the Iranian-American alliance.

As this study has tried to show, the organization that took the lead in forging that alliance—the State Department—seldom controlled either the resources or the policy areas most crucial to realizing its objectives. During the war Harold Ickes as petroleum administrator, President Roosevelt, the oil companies, the British government in combination with AIOC, and the military, with control over strategic materials, all contended with State to determine foreign oil policy. Once the State Department had decided to carve out an important American role in Iran, it had to depend on various civilian and military agencies for the personnel and materials with which to implement its programs. Even the adoption of the cold war consensus under which an independent Iran was seen as vital to American security did not guarantee the State Department the resources it needed to carry out its programs. Other agencies had their own priorities for containing the Soviet Union.

As a consequence, organizational rivalries encouraged those involved with Iranian policy to exaggerate the Soviet threat. The more immediate or grave the peril, the more Iran would command economic or military assistance. I do not mean to suggest that people like Wallace Murray, Loy Henderson, or George Allen acted cynically or even with self-conscious political motives when they evoked the specter of Soviet communist imperialism. Anyone who reads State Department files knows how dedicated these men were in their anti-Soviet convictions. Indeed, it was their passion that made them so persuasive. At the same time, however, this passion often warped their judgment. They could not easily question assumptions that they held deeply and that also helped them persuade reluctant organizations to support programs the department viewed as vital to American security. Cold War rhetoric proved to be good institutional politics as well.[8]

Iran could have served those policymakers as a test case of quite another kind. Here we should again recall Lloyd Gardner's observation that the Iranian crisis of 1945–1947 showed it was possible to extend American influence to the border of the Soviet Union without effective challenge. Between 1941 and 1953 the United States virtually replaced the Soviet Union and Great Britain in Iran. AIOC was no longer Iran's second major employer. The Russians had gradually lost or given up all the major instruments of their policy—their occupation forces in March 1946, the Azeri and Kurdish separatists in December 1946, an oil concession in October 1947, and after the fall of Mossadeq, the Tudeh Party. Where then was the "carefully prepared and implemented program" to control Iran that Dulles, Acheson, and the veterans of the Soviet Service had anticipated? Modest American aid combined with diplomatic support had proved sufficient to keep Iran outside the Soviet orbit. Policymakers might just have realistically concluded that Iran need not be a point of conflict, that negotiations or accommodations were possible, and that a neutral Iran would have better served the goal of a stable peace. These are the conclusions that this study supports.

Policymakers could have adopted them only if they had hoped to resolve Soviet-American conflict over Iran. But as Walter LaFeber has observed, few Americans "wanted specific issues negotiated. . . ." They demanded instead "that the entire broad conflict with the Soviet Union be settled." And he might have justly added, settled on American terms. Faith in their exceptionalism convinced most Americans not only that they could win in the struggle against the communist menace, but that they *ought* to win. Nothing in their World War II experience gave them any reason to doubt their national virtue. The war had confirmed that abundance, success, and innocence were theirs as the rewards of divine favor, sacrifice, and character.[9]

C. Vann Woodward has identified that faith with two major strands of postwar foreign policy. On the one hand it has caused many Americans to prefer unilateral to multilateral policies. They "insist that America must be strong enough to carry her way by economic coercion or force," regardless of world opinion or the reservations of our allies. James Byrnes did not go to the United Nations in March 1946 to guarantee the future effectiveness of that multilateral organization. He went to "give it to [the Russians] with both barrels." The United Nations became a forum in which to embarrass his enemy while demonstrating his own toughness. As much as American diplomats might urge Iranian leaders to see the United Nations as guarantor of their independence, they themselves largely ignored the organization. They preferred to rely on an Iranian-American alliance as a means of promoting American security in the Persian Gulf region.[10]

When a Qavam or a Mossadeq tried to operate outside that alliance, American policymakers became either suspicious or hostile. Within the cold war crusade, dissent from the American way was treason, because, as Woodward has argued, the second strand of American policy is a moral one. Americans feel themselves bound "to liberate the enslaved peoples of the earth, punish the wicked oppressors, and convert liberated people to our way of thought." In the postwar era there has been only one true oppressor—"Soviet directed world communism."[11] To cooperate with Moscow or the Kremlin's agents was to traffic with the devil. Tudeh Party members could not legitimately join a cabinet, no matter how stabilizing their presence might be. Nationalization by leftists was unacceptable whenever it threatened American interests, even if it offered foreign leaders the only means of controlling their nations' futures.

Exceptionalism has often led American policymakers into postures that defeat the larger goals of American foreign policy. In the competition for the "hearts and minds" of nations like Iran, many Americans would, in Woodward's view, "urge upon them institutions and abstract ideas of our own that have little or no relevance to their real needs and circumstances." In that way the United States set about nation-building in Iran during World War II. Few policymakers questioned the relevance of western technology or economic institutions for a traditionial Islamic society. Nor did they care that the aspirations of the westernized elite had little meaning to the impoverished masses. Instead they sympathized with the shah's desire to modernize his nation. They did not much object when the army, the secret police, or corrupt elites became the shah's instruments for realizing his goals. Nor were they much concerned about the opposition of the Islamic clergy and their followers, whose strange ways were at such odds with the American gospel of progress. The U.S. alliance with the shah had come to symbolize the enlightened American presence, not just in Iran but throughout the third world. In a perceptive essay on American cold war ideology, Nagai Yonosuke, a political scientist at the Tokyo Institute of Technology, observed in a vein similar to Woodward, "This tendency of Americans to project their democratic experience universalistically has another tendency as its corollary: the tendency to draw abstract generalizations and to derive broad principles from special problems and unique experiences."[12]

By seeking to establish a neutral Iran, the United States might have avoided the disaster of 1979 and still have maintained an effective barrier to Soviet ambitions. One less point of tension along the Soviet border would have reduced the potential for Soviet-American conflict. In addition, Soviet leaders would have had less cause to oppose the many postwar Iranian governments that tied their fortunes to an alliance with the United States. Leaders like Mossadeq would have been less vulnerable to the factionalism that beset Iran after 1941. Greater stability within Iran would have reduced the possibility of big power interventions. That, too, would have made Iran less of a cold war trouble spot.

Iranian neutrality might also have had another benefit for the United States. Iranian leaders operating with greater autonomy would have been less likely to excite the anti-foreign hysteria that has always been a recurrent phenomenon in Iran's political life. When and if it arose, the ire of Ayatollah Khomeini and others might have been directed against the Soviet Union or its Iraqi and Syrian allies rather than the United States. To achieve Iranian neutrality American policymakers did not have to ignore Iran. They had only to sacrifice a degree of influence that they never used very effectively anyway. Without the Iranian-American alliance, Iranian-American friendship might have been more enduring.

NOTES

1. Kermit Roosevelt, *Countercoup,* pp. 209–10.

2. Ibid. pp. 209–10. On covert activities as instruments of foreign policy, see also John Lewis Gaddis, *Strategies of Containment,* pp. 158–59 and 180–81.

3. John Foster Dulles, "Speech to the American Society of International Law, April 27, 1950," Department of State, *Bulletin,* 22, May 8, 1950; quoted in Gaddis, *Strategies of Containment,* p. 140.

4. For a good analysis of the negotiations from Iran's vantage point, see Ramazani, *Iran's Foreign Policy,* pp. 264–72; see also Abrahamian, *Iran Between Two Revolutions,* pp. 419–20.

5. Mosley, *Power Play,* p. 223.

6. Accounts of the American approach to the oil negotiations are found in Blair, *Control of Oil,* pp. 43–47; and Mosley, *Power Play,* pp. 219–29. See also Sampson, *The Seven Sisters,* pp. 153–63. See also U.S. Senate Committee on Foreign Relations, (the Church Committee), *Hearings,* "Multinational Corporations and United States Foreign Policy," Part 8 (Washington, 1975).

7. On the shah's consolidation of power and development programs see Abrahamian, *Iran Between Two Revolutions,* pp. 419–46. On the shah's views of the alliance with the United States, see Ramazani, *Iran's Foreign Policy,* ch. 11. See also Rubin, *Paved With Good Intentions,* ch. 4.

8. For a parallel argument, see Paul Hammond, "NSC–68, Prologue to Rearmament," in W. Schilling, P. Hammond, and G. Snyder, *Strategy, Politics, and Defense Budgets* (New York, 1962).

9. Walter LaFeber, "American Policy-Makers, Public Opinion, and the Outbreak of the Cold War, 1945–50," in Nagai Yonosuke and Akira Iriye, eds., *The Origins of the Cold War in Asia* (New York, 1977), p. 58.

10. Woodward developed those ideas in his essay "The Irony of Southern History," in

The Burden of Southern History (Baton Rouge, La., 1977). See especially pp. 187–94. Diplomatic historians would profit from Woodward's perspective as a regional historian. More recently Theodore Draper has discussed those ideas in an attack on revived "neoconservative" history. See Theodore Draper, "Neo-conservative History," *New York Review of Books*, 32, 21/22, (January 1986): 5–15.

11. On American strategy see FR, 1947, 5, "Pentagon Talks of 1947," pp. 510–77. For Byrnes quote see FR, 1947, 7, editorial note, pp. 346–48.

12. Nagai Yonosuke, "The Roots of Cold War Doctrine," in Yonosuke and Iriye, eds., *Origins of the Cold War in Asia*, p. 38.

Bibliography

ARCHIVES, PUBLIC AND PRIVATE PAPERS

ACHESON, DEAN. Papers. Harry S. Truman Library, Independence, Mo.
ALLEN, GEORGE. Papers. Harry S. Trumàn Library, Independence, Mo.
ATKINS, PAUL. Papers. Yale University Library, New Haven, Conn.
BARUCH, BERNARD. Papers. Princeton University Library, Princeton, N.J.
BOWLES, CHESTER. Papers. Yale University Library, New Haven, Conn.
British Foreign Office, Class F.O. 371, Public Records Office, London, England.
British War Cabinet Minutes, CAB 65, Public Records Office.
BYRNES, JAMES F. Clemson University Library, Clemson, S.C.
FEIS, HERBERT. Papers. Manuscript Division, Library of Congress, Washington, D.C.
Foreign Economic Administration (Lend-Lease), RG 169, National Archives, Suitland, Md.
FORRESTAL, JAMES V. Papers. Princeton University Library. Princeton, N.J.
GREW, JOSEPH C. Papers. Houghton Library, Harvard University, Cambridge, Mass.
HOPKINS, HARRY. Papers. Franklin D. Roosevelt Library, Hyde Park, N.Y.
HULL, CORDELL. Papers. Manuscript Division, Library of Congress, Washington, D.C.
HURLEY, PATRICK J. Papers. University of Oklahoma Library. Normaw, Okla.
KENNAN, GEORGE F. Papers. Princeton University Library, Princeton, N.J.
KNOX, FRANK. Papers. Manuscript Division, Library of Congress, Washington, D.C.
LEAHY, WILLIAM. Papers. Manuscript Division, Library of Congress, Washington, D.C.
Modern Military Records Branch. RG 218 and Combined Chiefs Files, National Archives, Washington, D.C.
PATTERSON, ROBERT: Papers. Manuscript Division, Library of Congress, Washington, D.C.
Office of Strategic Services (OSS), RG 226, Research and Analysis File(R&A), National Archives.
PASVOLSKY, LEO. Papers. Manuscript Division, Library of Congress, Washington, D.C.
Persian Gulf Service Command, MMRB, National Archives.
Petroleum Administration for War, RG 253, National Archives.
President's Soviet Protocol Committee, Franklin D. Roosevelt Library, Hyde Park, N.Y.
ROOSEVELT, FRANKLIN D. Map Room File, Official File (OF), President's Secretary's File (PSF), President's Personal File (PPF), Franklin D. Roosevelt Library, Hyde Park, N.Y.
ROSENMAN, SAMUEL. Papers. Franklin D. Roosevelt Library, Hyde Park, N.Y.

STEINHARDT, LAWRENCE. Papers. Manuscript Division, Library of Congress, Washington, D.C.

STETTINIUS, EDWARD. Papers. University of Virginia, Charlottesville, Va.

STIMSON, HENRY L. Papers. Yale University Library, New Haven, Conn.

U.S. Army, Operations Division (OPD), National Archives.

U.S. Army, Military Intelligence and Adjutant General, National Archives, Suitland, Md.

U.S. Department of State, RG 59, National Archives.

INTERVIEWS AND CORRESPONDENCES

Ball, George
Bohlen, Charles
Blum, John M.
Cohen, Benjamin V.
Henderson, Loy
Hiss, Alger
Jernegan, John
Kazemzadeh, Firuz
Matthews, H. Freeman
Rostow, Eugene

PUBLISHED PUBLIC DOCUMENTS

Commission for the Publication of Diplomatic Documents. *Correspondence Between the Chairman of the Council of Ministers of the USSR and the Presidents of the of the USA and the Prime Ministers of Great Britain During the Great Patriotic War of 1941–45*. Moscow, 1957; New York, 1965.

DEGRAS, JANE, ed. *Soviet Documents on Foreign Affairs*. vol. 3, 1938–1941. London, 1951.

CORDIER, A.W., and W. FOOTE, eds. *Public Papers of the Secretaries-General of the United Nations*. Vol. 1, Trygve Lie, 1946–53. New York, 1969.

ETZOLD, THOMAS H., and JOHN L. GADDIS, eds. *Containment: Documents on American Policy and Strategy, 1945–1950*. New York, 1978.

Great Britain, *Hansard's Parliamentary Debates*, 5th Series, 1941–1953.

HUREWITZ, J. C., ed. *Diplomacy in the Near and Middle East: A Documentary Record, 1914–1956*. Princeton, 1956.

MOTTER, T. H. VAIL, *The United States Army in World War II: The Middle East Theater, the Persian Corridor and Aid to Russia*. Washington, D.C., 1952.

Public Papers of the Presidents of the United States: Harry S. Truman, 1945–53. Washington, D.C., 1961–66.

———. *Dwight D. Eisenhower, 1953–1954*. Washington, D.C., 1960–61.

SONTAG, RAYMOND, and JAMES BEDDIE, eds. *Nazi-Soviet Relations, 1939–1941: Documents from the Archives of the German Foreign Office*. Washington, D.C., 1948.

United Nations. *United Nations Security Council Journal*. First year, Series 1, Meetings 1–42, 17 January–26 June 1946. New York, 1946.

———. *United Nations Security Council Official Records*. First Year, Series 2, Meetings 50–88, 10 July–31 December 1946. New York, 1946.

———. *Yearbook of the United Nations, 1946–47*. New York, 1947.

U.S. Bureau of the Census. *Historical Statistics of the United States: Colonial Times to 1957*. Washington, DC, 1960.

U.S. Congress. *Congresional Record*. 1941–1954.

———. Senate. Committee on Foreign Relations. *Anglo-American Oil Agreement. Report to Accompany Executive H.* 80th Congress, 1st Session, 1947.

———. Senate. Committee on Foreign Relations. *Legislative Origins of the Truman Doctrine: Hearings Held in Executive Session*. 80th Cong., 1st Sess., Washington, D.C., 1973.

———. Senate. Small Business Committee. *The International Petroleum Cartel*. Staff Report of the Federal Trade Commission, 82nd Cong., 2nd Sess., 1952.

———. Senate, Special Committee Investigating Petroleum Resources. *American Petroleum*

Interests in Foreign Countries. Hearings, Petroleum Resources of the United States. 79th Cong., 1st Sess., 1945.

———. Senate. Special Committee Investigating Petroleum Resources. *Hearings, American Petroleum Interests in Foreign Countries.* 79th Cong., 1st Sess., 1945.

———. Senate Special Committee Investigating Petroleum Resources. *Hearings, Petroleum Requirements—Postwar.* 79th Cong., 1st Sess., 1946.

———. Senate. Special Committee Investigating the National Defense Program. *Hearings, Part 41, Petroleum Arrangements with Saudi Arabia.* 80th Cong., 1st Sess., 1948.

———. Senate. Subcommittee on Multinational Corporations and Foreign Policy. *A Documentary History of the Petroleum Reserves Corporation.* 93rd Cong., 2nd Sess., 1974.

———. Senate. Subcommittee on Multinational Corporations and Foreign Policy. *Hearings, Multinational Petroleum Corporations and Foreign Policy.* 93rd Cong., 2nd Sess., 1974.

———. Senate. Subcommittee on Multinational Corporations and Foreign Policy. *Report on Multinational Petroleum Corporations and Foreign Policy.* 93rd Cong., 2nd Sess., 1975.

U.S. Department of State, *Bulletin,* 1935–1957.

———. *Papers Relating to the Foreign Relations of the United States, 1933–1952/54.* Washington, D.C., 1949–1979.

———. *The Conference of Berlin* (The Potsdam Conference), 2 vols., 1945. Washington, D.C., 1960.

———. *The Conferences at Cairo and Tehran, 1943.* Washington, D.C., 1961.

———. *The Conferences at Malta and Yalta, 1945.* Washington, D.C., 1955.

NEWSPAPERS AND PERIODICALS

Chicago Tribune
Christian Science Monitor
Collier's
Current Digest of the Soviet Press
Daily Worker
The Economist
Fortune
Los Angeles Times
The Manchester Guardian
Nation
New Republic
New Statesman
Newsweek
New York Times
PM
Salt Lake City Chronicle
San Francisco Chronicle
Saturday Evening Post
The Times (London)
Time
Wall Street Journal
War and the Working Class
Washington Post

PETROLEUM INDUSTRY JOURNALS

International Oil and Gas Development. Austin, Texas.
International Oilman. (*Oil Forum* after 1947). N.Y./Ft. Worth, Texas.
National Petroleum News. Cleveland, Ohio.
Petroleum Times. London.
Oil and Gas Journal, Tulsa, Oklahoma.
The Oil Trade, New York.
The Oil Weekly. (*World Oil* after 1947). Houston, Texas.
World Petroleum. New York.

BOOKS, DISSERTATIONS, AND ARTICLES

ABELL, TYLER, ed., *Drew Pearson: Diaries, 1949–1959*. New York, 1974.

ABRAHAMIAN, ERVAND. *Iran Between Two Revolutions*. Princeton, 1982.

ACHESON, DEAN. *Present at the Creation*. New York, 1969.

ADELMAN, KENNETH. *The World Petroleum Market*. Baltimore, 1972.

AGABEKOV, SERGE. *OGPU: The Russian Secret Terror*. New York, 1931.

ALLEN, GEORGE V. "Mission to Iran." Unpublished manuscript, Harry S. Truman Library, Independence, Mo.

ALLILUYEVA, SVETLANA. *Twenty Letters to A Friend*. Translated by Priscilla McMillan. New York, 1967.

ALLISON, GRAHAM, T. *Essence of Decision: Explaining the Cuban Missle Crisis*, Boston, 1971.

ALPEROVITZ, GAR. *Atomic Diplomacy: Hiroshima and Potsdam*. New York, 1967.

AMBROSE, STEPHEN. *Rise to Globalism: American Foreign Policy Since 1938*. Baltimore, 1970.

AMIRSADEGHI, HOSSEIN. *Twentieth Century Iran*. London, 1977.

ANDERSON, IRVINE. *The Standard-Vacuum Oil Company and United States East Asian Policy*. Princeton, 1975.

———. *Aramco, the United States, and Saudi Arabia*. Princeton, 1981.

ANDERSON, TERRY H. *The United States, Great Britain, and the Origins of the Cold War, 1944–47*. Columbia, Mo., 1981.

ARFA, HASSAN. *Under Five Shahs*. London, 1964.

ARKES, HADLEY. *Bureaucracy, the Marshall Plan, and the National Interest*. Princeton, 1972.

ARMAJANI, YAHYA. *Iran*. Englewood Cliffs, N.J., 1972.

ARNOLD, THURMAN. *Fair Fights and Foul*. New York, 1965.

ARON, RAYMOND. *The Imperial Republic: The United States and the World, 1945–1973*. Englewood Cliffs, N.J., 1974.

ART, ROBERT. "Bureaucratic Politics and American Foreign Policy: A Critique." *Policy Sciences* 4 (December 1973): 467–90.

ATIYEH, GEORGE N. *The Contemporary Middle East, 1948–1973: A Selective and Annotated Bibliography*. Boston, 1975.

AVERY, PETER. *Modern Iran*. New York, 1965.

BAILEY, THOMAS. *America Faces Russia*. Ithaca, N.Y., 1950.

BANANI, AMIN. *The Modernization of Iran, 1921–1941*. Stanford, 1961.

BARNET, RICHARD J. *Intervention and Revolution*. New York, 1968.

———. *Roots of War*. Baltimore, 1972.

BEISNER, ROBERT. *Twelve Against Empire*. New York, 1968.

BEITZELL, ROBERT. *The Uneasy Alliance: America, Britain, and Russia, 1941–1943*. New York, 1972.

BERLE, BEATRICE, and TRAVIS BEAL JACOBS, eds. *Navigating the Rapids, 1918–1971: From the Papers of Adolf A. Berle*. New York, 1973.

BERNSTEIN, BARTON J. "Cold War Orthodoxy Restated." *Reviews in American History* 1 (December 1973): 453–62.

———. "Roosevelt, Truman, and the Atomic Bomb, 1941–1945: A Reinterpretation." *Political Science Quarterly* 90 (Spring 1975): 23–69.

———, ed. *Politics and Policies of the Truman Administration*. Chicago, 1970.

———, ed., *Towards a New Past*. New York, 1968.

BIALER, SEWERYN, ed. *Stalin and His Generals: Soviet Military Memoirs of World War II*. New York, 1969.

BILL, J. *The Politics of Iran: Groups, Classes, and Modernization*. Columbus, Ohio, 1972.

BLUM, JOHN M. *V Was for Victory*. New York, 1976.

———, ed. *From the Morgenthau Diaries: Years of War, 1941–1945*. Boston, 1967.

———, ed. *The Price of Vision: The Diary of Henry A. Wallace*. Boston, 1973.

BLUM, ROBERT M. *Drawing the Line: The Origin of American Containment Policy in East Asia*. New York, 1982.

BOHLEN, CHARLES. *The Transformation of American Foreign Policy*. New York, 1969.

———. *Witness to History, 1929–69*. New York, 1973.

BOROWSKI, HARRY R. *A Hollow Threat: Strategic Air Power and Containment Before Korea*. Westport, Conn., 1982.

BOWLES, CHESTER. *Promises to Keep.* New York, 1971.
BRODIE, BERNARD. *Foreign Oil and American Security.* New Haven, Conn., 1947.
BUHITE, RUSSELL. *Patrick J. Hurley and American Foreign Policy.* Ithaca, N. Y. 1973.
BULLARD, SIR READER. *Britain and the Middle East.* London, 1951.
———. *The Camels Must Go.* London, 1961.
BURNS, JAMES MACGREGOR. *Roosevelt: The Lion and the Fox.* New York, 1956.
———. *Roosevelt: The Soldier of Freedom.* New York, 1970.
BYRNES, JAMES F. *Speaking Frankly.* New York, 1947.
———. *All in One Lifetime.* New York, 1958.
CAMPBELL, JOHN C. *Defense of the Middle East: Problems of American Foreign Policy.* New York, 1960.
———. "The Soviet Union in the Middle East." *Middle East Journal* 32 (Winter 1978): 1–12.
CAMPBELL, THOMAS and GEORGE C. HERRING, ed. *The Diaries of Edward Stettinius, Jr., 1943–1946.* New York, 1975.
CANTRIL, HADLEY. *Public Opinion, 1935–1946.* Princeton, 1953.
CHESTER, EDWARD W., *United States Oil Policy and Diplomacy.* Westport, Conn., 1983.
CHUBIN, S. and SEPEHR ZABIH. *The Foreign Relations of Iran.* Berkeley, 1974.
CHURCHILL, WINSTON. *The Grand Alliance.* Boston, 1950.
———. *The Hinge of Fate.* Boston, 1950.
———. *Closing the Ring.* Boston, 1951.
———. *Triumph and Tragedy.* Boston, 1953.
CLEMENS, DIANE S. *Yalta.* New York, 1970.
COHEN, BERNARD. *The Public's Impact on Foreign Policy.* Boston, 1973.
COHEN, WARREN I. *America's Response to China.* New York, 1971.
COLE, WAYNE S. *Roosevelt and the Isolationists, 1932–1945.* Lincoln, Neb., 1983.
CORSON, WILLIAM R. *The Armies of Ignorance: The Rise of the American Intelligence Empire.* New York, 1977.
COTTAM, RICHARD W. *Nationalism in Iran.* Pittsburgh, 1964.
———. "The United States, Iran, and the Cold War." *Iranian Studies* 3–4 (Winter 1970): 2–22.
CUMINGS, BRUCE. *The Origins of the Korean War.* Princeton, 1982.
DALLEK, ROBERT. *Franklin D. Roosevelt and American Foreign Policy, 1932–1945.* New York, 1979.
DALLIN, DAVID. *The Rise of Russia in Asia.* New Haven, 1949.
———. *The Soviet Union at the United Nations.* New York, 1962.
DANIELS, JONATHAN. *The Man of Independence.* Philadelphia, 1950.
———. *White House Witness.* New York, 1975.
DAVIES, JOSEPH, *Mission to Moscow.* New York, 1941.
DAVIS, LYNN ETHERIDGE. *The Cold War Begins.* Princeton, 1974.
DEANE, JOHN R. *The Strange Alliance: The Story of Our Efforts at Wartime Cooperation with Russia.* New York, 1947.
DENOVO, JOHN. *American Interests and Policies in the Middle East.* Minneapolis, 1963.
DEUTSCHER, ISAAC. *Stalin: A Poltical Biography.* New York, 1949.
———. *Ironies of History: Essays of Contemporary Communism.* London, 1966.
DIVINE, ROBERT A. *The Reluctant Belligerent.* New York, 1965.
———. *A Second Chance: The Triumph of Internationalism in America During World War II.* New York, 1971.
———. *Eisenhower and the Cold War.* New York, 1983.
DIXON, PIERS. *Double Diploma: The Life of Sir Pierson Dixon.* London, 1968.
DJILAS, MILOVAN. *Conversations with Stalin.* New York, 1962.
DOENECKE, JUSTUS D. "Revisionists, Oil, and Cold War Diplomacy." *Iranian Studies* 4 (Winter 1970): 23–33.
———. "Iran's Role in Cold War Revisionism." *Iranian Studies.* 6 (Spring-Summer 1972): 96–106.
DONOVAN, ROBERT J. *Conflict and Crisis: The Presidency of Harry S. Truman, 1945–1948.* New York, 1977.
DOUGLAS, ROY. *From War to Cold War.* New York, 1981.
DUCE, JAMES TERRY. *Middle East Oil Developments.* New York, 1952.

DULLES, ALLEN W. *The Craft of Intelligence*. New York, 1963.
DULLES, JOHN FOSTER. *War or Peace*. New York, 1950.
EAGLETON, WILLIAM, JR. *The Kurdish Republic of 1946*. London, 1963.
EDEN, SIR ANTHONY. *Full Circle*. Boston, 1960.
———. *The Reckoning*. Boston, 1965.
EISENHOWER, DWIGHT D. *The White House Years: Mandate for Change, 1953–1956*. New York, 1963.
ELWELL-SUTTON, L. P. "Political Parties in Iran." *The Middle East Journal* (January 1949): 45–62.
———. *Persian Oil: A Study in Power Politics*. London, 1955.
ENGLER, ROBERT. *The Politics of Oil*. New York, 1961.
FANNING, LEONARD M. *American Oil Operations Abroad*. New York, 1947.
———. *The Rise of American Oil*. New York, 1948.
———. *Foreign Oil and the World*. New York, 1954.
FATEMI, NASROLLAH. *Oil Diplomacy: Powderkeg in Iran*. New York, 1954.
FEIS, HERBERT. *Petroleum and American Foreign Policy*. Stanford, Calif., 1944.
———. *Three International Episodes Seen from EA*. New York, 1946.
———. *The China Tangle*. Princeton, 1953.
———. *Churchill-Roosevelt-Stalin: The War They Waged and The Peace They Sought*. Princeton, 1957.
———. *Between War and Peace: The Potsdam Conference*. Princeton, 1960.
———. *The Atomic Bomb and the End of World War II*. Princeton, 1966.
FERRELL, ROBERT. *George C. Marshall*. Vol. 15, The American Secretaries of State Series, edited by Robert Ferrell. New York, 1966.
GALLUP, GEORGE. *The Gallup Poll: Public Opinion, 1935–71*. Vol. 1, New York, 1972.
GARDNER, LLOYD. *Economic Aspects of New Deal Diplomacy*. Madison, 1964.
———. *Architects of Illusion*. Chicago, 1972.
———, ARTHUR M. SCHLESINGER, JR., and HANS MORGENTHAU. *Origins of the Cold War*. Waltham, Mass., 1970.
GARDNER, RICHARD N. *Sterling-Dollar Diplomacy*. New York, 1956.
GARTHOFF, R. L. *Soviet Strategy in the Nuclear Age*. New York, 1962.
GHRISHMAN, R. *Iran*. Middlesex, U. K., 1961.
GORDON, DAVID. *Self-Determination and History in the Third World*. Princeton, 1971.
GRADY, HENRY. "Real Story of Iran." *U.S. News and World Report*. 19 October 1951.
———. "What Went Wrong in Iran?" *Saturday Evening Post*. 5 June 1952.
GREAVES, R. L. *Persia and the Defense of India*. Athlone, U. K., 1959.
GREENFIELD, KENT R. *American Strategy in World War II: A Reconsideration*. Baltimore, 1973.
GREW, JOSEPH. *Turbulent Era: A Diplomatic Record of Forty Years, 1904–1945*. 2 vols. Boston, 1952.
GROSECLOSE, ELGIN. *Ararat*. New York, 1939.
———. *Introduction to Iran*. New York, 1947.
GULBENKIAN, NUBAR. *Pantaraxia*. London, 1965.
GUPTA, RAJ NARAIN. *Iran: An Economic Study*. New Delhi, 1947.
HAAS, WILLIAM. *Iran*. New York, 1946.
HALIFAX, EDWARD, EARL OF. *Fullness of Days*. London, 1957.
HALLE, LOUIS J. *The Cold War as History*. New York, 1967.
HALLIDAY, F. *Iran: Dictatorship and Development*. New York, 1979.
HAMBY, ALONZO. *Beyond the New Deal: Harry S. Truman and American Liberalism*. New York, 1973.
HAMMOND, PAUL Y. *Organizing for Defense*. Princeton, 1961.
———. *Cold War and Détente: The American Foreign Policy Process Since 1945*. New York, 1975.
HAMZAVI, A. H. K. *Persia and the Powers, 1941–1946*. London, 1946.
HARKNESS, RICHARD and GLADYS. "The Mysterious Doings of the CIA." *Saturday Evening Post,* 6 November 1954, 34–35.
HARRIMAN, W. AVERELL, and ELIE ABEL. *Special Envoy to Churchill and Stalin, 1941–1946*. New York, 1975.

HARTSHORN, J. E. *Oil Companies and Governments.* London, 1962.

HASSEMAN, HEINRICH. *Oil in the Soviet Union.* Princeton, 1953.

HATHAWAY, ROBERT M. *Ambiguous Partnership: Britain and America 1944–1947.* New York, 1981.

HAWLEY, ELLIS. *The New Deal and the Problem of Monopoly.* Princeton, 1966.

HERKEN, GREGG. *The Winning Weapon.* New York, 1980.

HERRING, GEORGE. *Aid to Russia, 1941–46.* New York, 1973.

———. *America's Longest War.* New York, 1979.

HERZ, MARTIN, *Beginnings of the Cold War.* Bloomington, 1966.

HESS, GARY. "The Iranian Crisis of 1945–46 and the Cold War." *Political Science Quarterly* 89 (March 1974): 117–46.

HEWINS, RALPH. *Mr. Five Per Cent: The Story of Calouste Gulbenkian.* New York, 1958.

HEWLETT, RICHARD G., and OSCAR E. ANDERSON, JR. *The New World: 1939–1946.* University Park, Penn., 1962.

HEWLETT, RICHARD and FRANCIS DUNCAN. *Atomic Shield: 1947–52.* University Park, Penn., 1969.

HIPPLE, PETER. *The Petroleum Industry of the United Kingdom.* London, 1966.

HOOPES, TOWNSEND. *The Devil and John Foster Dulles.* Boston, 1973.

HORELICK, ARNOLD, and MYRON RUSH. *Strategic Power and Soviet Foreign Policy.* Chicago, 1966.

HOROWITZ, DAVID. *Free World Colossus.* New York, 1965.

———, ed. *Containment and Revolution.* Boston, 1968.

HOSKINS, HALFORD L. *The Middle East Problem Area in World Politics.* New York, 1964.

HOWARD, MICHAEL. *Studies in War and Peace.* New York, 1971.

HUGHES, EMMET JOHN. *The Ordeal of Power: A Political Memoir of the Eisenhower Years.* New York, 1963.

HULL, CORDELL. *The Memoirs of Cordell Hull.* 2 vols. New York, 1948.

HUREWITZ, JACOB C. *Middle East Dilemmas: The Background of United States Policy.* New York, 1953.

———. *Soviet-American Rivalry in the Middle East.* New York, 1969.

IATRIDES, JOHN. *Revolt in Athens.* Princeton, 1972.

ICKES, HAROLD L. *Fightin' Oil.* New York, 1943.

———. "We're Running Out of Oil." *American Magazine,* January 1944, 26–27.

———. "Persian Gulf Oil Furnishes Great Backlog for U.S. Reserves." *Oil Weekly,* 6 March 1944, 13–15.

———. "Oil and Peace." *Collier's,* 2 December 1944, 21.

IRANI, R. "The United States Involvements in Iran, 1942–1944." *Iranian Review of International Relations* 7 (1976): 136–61.

JACOBS, NORMAN. *The Sociology of Development; Iran as a Case Study.* New York, 1967.

JACOBY, NEIL. *Multinational Oil: A Study in Industrial Dynamics.* New York, 1974.

JONES, JOSEPH. *The Fifteen Weeks.* New York, 1964.

KAPLAN, FRED. *The Wizards of Armageddon.* New York, 1983.

KAOUR, H. *Soviet Russia and Asia, 1917–1927: A Study of Soviet Policy Toward Turkey, Iran, and Afghanistan.* New York, 1969.

KAUFMAN, BURTON I. *The Oil Cartel Case,* Westport, Conn., 1978.

KAZEMZADEH, FIRUZ. *Russia and Britain in Persia, 1864–1914.* New Haven, 1968.

———. "The Soviet Union and Iran Since World War II." Manuscript in author's possession.

KENNAN, GEORGE. *American Diplomacy, 1900–1950.* Chicago, 1951.

———. *Memoirs, 1925–50.* Boston, 1967.

———. *Memoirs, 1950–63.* Boston, 1972.

———. *The Nuclear Delusion.* New York, 1983.

———. *Russia and the West Under Lenin and Stalin.* New York, 1961.

KEVLIS, DANIEL J. *The Physicists.* New York, 1977.

KHRUSHCHEV, NIKITA. *Khrushchev Remembers.* Boston, 1970.

KIRK, GEORGE. *The Middle East in the War, 1939–1946.* London, 1952.

———. *Survey of International Affairs. The Middle East, 1945–1950.* London, 1954.

KIRKENDALL, RICHARD S., ed., *The Truman Period as a Research Field: A Reappraisal, 1972*. Columbia, Mo., 1974.

KOLKO, GABRIEL. *The Politics of War*. New York, 1968.

———. *The Roots of American Foreign Policy*. Boston, 1969.

KOLKO, JOYCE and GABRIEL KOLKO. *The Limits of Power: The World and United States Foreign Policy, 1945–1954*. New York, 1972.

KRASNER, STEPHEN D. *Defending the National Interest: Raw Materials Investments and U.S. Foreign Policy*. Princeton, 1978.

KROCK, ARTHUR. *Memoirs: Sixty Years on the Firing Line*. New York, 1968.

KUNIHOLM, BRUCE R. *The Origins of the Cold War in the Near East: Great Power Conflict and Diplomacy in Iran, Turkey, and Greece*. Princeton, 1980.

LAFEBER, WALTER. *The New Empire*. Ithaca, 1963.

———. "American Policy-Makers, Public Opinion, and the Outbreak of the Cold War, 1945–50," in *The Origins of the Cold War in Asia,* edited by Y. Nagai and A. Iriye, Tokyo/New York, 1977.

———. *America, Russia, and The Cold War*. 4th ed. New York, 1980.

———. *Inevitable Revolutions: The United States in Central America*. Enlarged ed. New York, 1984.

LAMPTON, ANNE K. S. *Landlord and Peasant in Persia*. London, 1953.

LAQUEUR, WALTER. *Communism and Nationalism in the Middle East*. New York, 1956.

LASCH, CHRISTOPHER. *The Agony of the American Left*. New York, 1968.

———. "The Cold War Revisited and Re-Visioned." *New York Times Magazine*. 14 January 1968.

LEAHY, WILLIAM. *I Was There*. New York, 1950.

LEBKICHER, ROY. *Aramco and the World*. New York, 1952.

LEDEEN, MICHAEL and WILLIAM LEWIS. *Debacle: The American Failure in Iran*. New York, 1981.

LEDERER, IVO, and WAYNE VUCINICH, eds. *The Soviet Union and the Middle East: The Post World War II Era*. Stanford, 1974.

LEFFLER, MELVYN. "The American Conception of National Security and the Origins of the Cold War, 1945–48." *American Historical Review* 89 (April 1984): 346–81.

LENCZOWSKI, GEORGE. *Russia and the West in Iran, 1918–1948*. Ithaca, 1949.

———. *Oil and State in the Middle East*. Ithaca, 1960.

———. "United States Support for Iran's Independence and Integrity, 1945–1959." *The Annals of the American Academy of Political and Social Sciences* 401 (May 1972): 45–55.

———. ed. *Iran Under the Pahlevis*. Stanford, 1978.

LEUCHTENBERG, WILLIAM. *Franklin D. Roosevelt and the New Deal*. New York, 1963.

LEVERING, RALPH. *American Opinion and the Russian Alliance, 1939–1945*. Chapel Hill, 1976.

LEVIN, GORDON. *Woodrow Wilson and World Politics*. New York, 1968.

LIDDELL HART, BASIL. *The History of the Second World War*. New York, 1971.

LIE, TRYGVE. *In the Cause of Peace*. New York, 1954.

LINK, ARTHUR. *Wilson the Diplomatist*. Baltimore, 1957.

LIPPMANN, WALTER. *U.S. Foreign Policy: Shield of the Republic*. New York, 1943.

———. *U.S. War Aims*. Boston, 1944.

———. *The Cold War,* New York, 1947.

LOEWENHEIM, FRANCIS, ed., *Roosevelt and Churchill: Their Secret Wartime Correspondence*. New York, 1975.

LOHBECK, DON. *Patrick J. Hurley*. Chicago, 1956.

LONGHURST, HENRY. *Adventure in Oil: The Story of British Petroleum*. London, 1959.

LONGRIGG, STEPHEN. *Oil in the Middle East*. London, 1954.

LOUIS, WILLIAM ROGER. *Imperialism at Bay: The United Sates and The Decolonization of the British Empire, 1941–1945*. New York, 1978.

———. *the British Empire in the Middle East, 1945–1951*. New York, 1985.

LUKACS, JOHN. *A New History of the Cold War*. Rev. ed. Garden City, N.Y., 1966.

LYTLE, MARK H. "American-Iranian Relations and the Redefinition of National Security, 1941-1947." Ph.D. Diss., Yale University, 1973.

———. "Thurman Arnold and the Wartime Cartels." unpublished manuscript in the Papers of John M. Blum, Yale University Library.

MCCLELLAN, DAVID. *Dean Acheson: The Department of State Years.* New York, 1976.

MCNEILL, WILLIAM H. *America, Britain, and Russia: Their Cooperation and Conflict, 1941–1946*. Reprinted, New York, 1974.

———. *The Pursuit of Power: Technology, Armed Force, and Society Since A.D. 1000.* Chicago, 1982.

MADDOX, ROBERT J. *The New Left and the Origins of the Cold War.* Princeton, 1973.

MAIER, CHARLES S. "Revisionism and the Interpretation of Cold War Origins," in *Perspectives in American History.* vol. 4, 313–347. Cambridge, Mass., 1970.

MAISKY, IVAN. *Memoirs of a Soviet Ambassador: The War, 1939–1943*. New York, 1967.

MACKINTOSH, J. *Strategies and Tactics of Soviet Foreign Policy.* New York, 1962.

MARK, EDUARD. "Allied Relations in Iran, 1941–1947: The Origins of a Cold War Crisis." *Wisconsin Magazine of History* 59 (Autumn 1975): 51–63.

———. "The Question of Containment: A Reply to John Lewis Gaddis." *Foreign Affairs* 56 (January 1978): 430–40.

MARCHETTI, VICTOR, and JOHN MARKS. *The CIA and the Cult of Intelligence*. New York, 1974.

MARLOWE, JOHN. *Iran*. London, 1963.

MASTNY, VOJTECH. *Russia's Road to Cold War: Diplomacy, Warfare and the Politics of Communism*. New York, 1979.

MAY, ERNEST. *American Imperialism: A Speculative Essay.* New York, 1968.

———. *"Lessons" of the Past: The Use and Misuse of History in American Foreign Policy.* New York, 1973.

MAYER, ARNO. *Politics and Diplomacy of Peacemaking.* New York, 1969.

———. *Wilson Versus Lenin: The Political Origins of the New Diplomacy, 1917–18.* Cleveland, 1964.

MEDVEDEV, ROY. *Let History Judge*. New York, 1971.

MEISTER, IRENE. "Soviet Policy in Iran, 1917–1950: A Case Study in Techniques." Ph.D. Diss., Fletcher School, Tufts University, 1954.

MESSER, ROBERT. "Paths Not Taken: The United States Department of State and Alternatives to Containment." *Diplomatic History* 1 (Fall 1977): 297–319.

———. *The End of an Alliance: James F. Byrnes, Roosevelt, Truman and the Origins of the Cold War* (Chapel Hill, 1982).

MIKDASKI, ZAHAYER. *A Financial Analysis of Middle Eastern Oil Concessions, 1901–1965.* New York, 1966.

MIKESELL, RAYMOND, and HOLLIS CHENERY. *Arabian Oil: America's Stake in the Middle East.* Chapel Hill, 1949.

MILLER, AARON D. *Search for Security: Saudi Arabian Oil and American Foreign Policy, 1939–1949*. Chapel Hill, 1980.

MILLIS, WALTER, ed. *The Forrestal Diaries.* New York, 1951.

MILLSPAUGH, ARTHUR. *The American Task In Persia.* New York, 1925.

———. *American in Persia.* New York, 1946.

MORAN, LORD CHARLES. *Churchill: The Struggle for Survival.* Boston, 1966.

MORISON, ELTING E. *Turmoil and Tradition: A Study of the Life and Times of Henry L. Stimson*. Boston, 1960.

MOSELEY, P. E. *The Kremlin and World Politics.* New York, 1961.

MOSLEY, LEONARD. *Power Play: Oil in the Middle East*. New York, 1973.

MULLER, EDWIN. "Behind the Scenes in Azerbaijan." *American Mercury.* vol. (June 1946): 696–703.

MURPHY, ROBERT. *Diplomat Among Warriors.* New York, 1965.

NAGAI, YONUSUKE, and AKIRA IRIYE, eds. *The Origins of the Cold War in Asia.* Tokyo/New York, 1977.

NASH, GERALD. *United States Oil Policy, 1890–1964*. Pittsburgh, 1968.

NIRUMAND, BAHMAR. *Iran: The New Imperialism in Action*. New York, 1969.

NOLLAU, GUNTHER, and HANS WIEHE. *Russia's South Flank: Soviet Operations in Iran, Turkey, and Afghanistan*. New York, 1963.

NOTTER, HARLEY. *Postwar Policy Preparation, 1939–1945*. Washington, 1949.

O'CONNER, HARVEY. *The Empire of Oil.* New York, 1962.

ODELL, PETER. *Oil and World Power.* New York, 1970.
OSGOOD, ROBERT. *Ideals and Self-Interest in America's Foreign Relations.* Chicago, 1953.
PAHLEVI, MOHAMMED REZA SHAH, *Mission for My Country.* London, 1961.
PAINTER, DAVID. *Oil and the American Century.* Baltimore, 1985.
PATERSON, THOMAS. *Soviet-American Confrontation: Postwar Reconstruction and the Origins of the Cold War.* Baltimore, 1973.
———. *On Every Front: The Making of the Cold War.* New York, 1979.
———, ed. *Cold War Critics.* Chicago, 1971.
———, ed. *The Origins of the Cold War.* Lexington, Mass., 1974.
PATERSON, THOMAS and LES ADLER. "Red Fascism." *American Historical Review* 85 (April 1984): 1046–64.
PATTERSON, JAMES T. *Mr. Republican: A Biography of Robert A. Taft.* Boston, 1972.
PENROSE, EDITH. *The Large International Firm in Developing Countries: The Petroleum Industry.* Cambridge, 1968.
Petroleum Industry War Council. *A National Oil Policy for the United States.* Washington, 1945.
PFAU, RICHARD. "The Legal Status of American Forces in Iran." *Middle East Journal* 28 (Spring 1974): 141–53.
———. "The United States and Iran, 1941–1947: Origins of a Partnership." Ph.D. Diss., University of Virginia, 1975.
———. "Containment in Iran, 1946: The Shift to an Active Policy." *Diplomatic History* 1 (Fall 1977): 359–72.
PHILLIPS, CABELL. *The Truman Presidency.* New York, 1966.
POGUE, FORREST C. *George C. Marshall: Organizer of Victory.* New York, 1973.
POLENBERG, RICHARD. *War and Society: The United States, 1941–1945.* New York, 1972.
———. *One Nation Divisible.* New York. 1980.
POLK, WILLIAM. *The United States and the Arab World.* 3rd. ed., Cambridge, Mass., 1975.
PONOMARYOV, B., A. GROMYKO, and V. KHVOSTOV, eds. *History of Soviet Foreign Policy, 1917–1945.* Moscow, 1969.
———, eds. *A History of Soviet Foreign Policy, 1945–1970.* Moscow, 1974.
POPPLE, CHARLES S. *Standard Oil Company (New Jersey) in World War II.* New York, 1952.
PRATT, JULIUS. *Cordell Hull, 1933–1944.* 2 vols., New York, 1964.
PRATT, WALLACE. *Our Petroleum Resources.* Washington, 1945.
RAMAZANI, ROUHALLAH. *The Foreign Policy of Iran; A Developing Nation in World Affairs, 1500–1941.* Charlottesville, Va., 1966.
———. *The Northern Tier: Afghanistan, Iran, and Turkey.* Princeton, 1966.
———. *Iran's Foreign Policy, 1941–1973: A Study of Foreign Policy in Modernizing Nations.* Charlottesville, Va., 1975.
———. "The Autonomous Republic of Azerbaijan and the Kurdish People's Republic: Their Rise and Fall." In *The Anatomy of Communist Takeovers.* edited by Thomas Hammond, New Haven, 1975.
———. *The United States and Iran: The Patterns of Influence.* New York, 1982.
RAPAPORT, ANATOL. *The Big Two: Soviet-American Images of Foreign Policy.* Indianapolis, Ind., 1971.
REES, DAVID. *The Age of Containment: The Cold War 1945–1965.* New York, 1968.
ROGOW, ARNOLD. *James Forrestal: A Study in Personality, Politics, and Policy.* New York, 1963.
ROOSEVELT, ARCHIE, JR. "The Kurdish Republic of Mahabad." *Middle East Journal* 1 (July 1947): 247–69.
ROOSEVELT, ELLIOT. *As He Saw It.* New York, 1946.
ROOSEVELT, KERMIT. *Arabs, Oil, and History: The Story of the Middle East.* New York, 1949.
———. *Countercoup: The Struggle for Iran.* (First version), New York, 1979.
———. "How the CIA Brought the Shah to Power." *Washington Post,* 6 May 1979.
ROSE, LISLE. *Dubious Victory: The United States and the End of World War II.* Kent, Ohio, 1973.
———. *After Yalta: The United States and the Origins of the Cold War.* New York, 1973.
ROSENAU, JAMES, ed. *Domestic Sources of Foreign Policy.* New York, 1967.

ROSENBERG, DAVID. "American Atomic Strategy and the Hydrogen Bomb Decision." *Journal of American History* 66 (1979–80): 62–87.

ROSSOW, ROBERT. "The Battle for Azerbaijan, 1946." *Middle East Journal* 10 (Winter 1956): 17–32.

ROSTOW, EUGENE. *A National Policy for the Oil Industry.* New Haven, 1948.

RUBIN, BARRY. *The Great Powers in the Middle East, 1941–1947: The Road to the Cold War.* London, 1980.

———. *Paved With Good Intentions: The American Experience and Iran.* New York, 1980.

SACHAR, HOWARD. *Europe Leaves the Middle East.* New York, 1972.

SAID, EDWARD, *Orientalisms.* New York, 1977.

———. *Covering Islam.* New York, 1981.

SAIKAL, A. *The Rise and Fall of the Shah.* Princeton, 1980.

SAMPSON, ANTHONY. *The Seven Sisters: The Great Oil Comapnies and the World They Shaped.* New York, 1975.

SANGHVI, RAMESH. *Arayamehr: The Shah of Iran.* London, 1968.

SCHALLER, MICHAEL. *The U.S. Crusade in China, 1938–1945.* New York, 1979.

SCHILLING, WARNER, PAUL Y. HAMMOND, and GLENN SNYDER. *Strategy, Politics, and Defense Budgets.* New York, 1962.

SCHLESINGER, ARTHUR, JR. "Origins of the Cold War." *Foreign Affairs* 46 (October 1967),: 22–52.

———. *The Imperial Presidency.* New York, 1974.

SCHULZE-HOLTHUS, BERNARD. *Daybreak in Iran: A Story of the German Intelligence Service.* London, 1954.

SCHULZINGER, ROBERT D. *The Making of the Diplomatic Mind.* Middletown, Conn., 1975.

SEARIGHT, SARAH. *The British in the Middle East.* London, 1969.

SHEEHAN, MICHAEL K. *Iran: The Impact of United States Interests and Policies.* New York, 1968.

SHERRY, MICHAEL. *Preparing for the Next War.* New Haven, 1977.

SHERWIN, MARTIN. *A World Destroyed.* New York, 1975.

SHERWOOD, ROBERT. *Roosevelt and Hopkins.* Rev. ed., 2 vols., New York: 1950.

SHULMAN, MARSHALL D. *Stalin's Foreign Policy Reappraised.* Cambridge, Mass., 1963.

———. *Beyond the Cold War.* New Haven, 1966.

SHUSTER, MORGAN. *The Strangling of Persia.* New York, 1912.

SHWADRAN, BENJAMIN. *The Middle East, Oil and the Great Powers.* 3rd. ed., revised and enlarged. New York, 1973.

SKRINE, SIR CLAREMONT. *World War in Iran.* London, 1962.

SLUSSER, ROBERT. "A Soviet Historian Evaluates Stalin's Role in History." *American Historical Review* 77 (December 1972): 1389–98.

SMITH, GADDIS. *Dean Acheson.* New York, 1972.

———. *American Diplomacy During the Second World War, 1941–1945.* 2nd. ed. New York, 1985.

SMITH, HARRIS. *OSS: The Secret History of America's First Central Intelligence Agency.* Berkeley, 1972.

SMITH, PERRY M. *The Air Force Plans for Peace, 1943–1945.* Baltimore, 1970.

SMITH, WALTER BEDELL. *My Three Years in Moscow.* Philadelphia, 1950.

SNELL, JOHN. *Illusion and Necessity: The Diplomacy of Global War.* Boston, 1963.

SPANIER, JOHN. *American Foreign Policy Since World War II.* 6th. ed. New York, 1973.

SPECTOR, IVAN. *The Soviet Union and the Muslim World, 1917–1958.* Seattle, 1958.

SPELMAN, WILLIAM. *The United States in the Middle East: A Study of American Foreign Policy.* New York, 1959.

STALIN, JOSEPH. *The Great Patriotic War of the Soviet Union.* New York, 1945.

STEEL, RONALD. *Pax Americana.* New York, 1967.

———. *Imperialists and Other Heroes: A Chronicle of the American Empire.* New York, 1979.

———. *Walter Lippmann and the American Century.* New York, 1980.

STETTINIUS, EDWARD R. *Roosevelt and the Russians: The Yalta Conference.* Garden City, N.Y., 1949.

STIMSON, HENRY L., and MCGEORGE BUNDY. *On Active Service in Peace and War.* New York, 1948.

STOCKING, GEORGE. *Middle East Oil.* Nashville, 1970.

STOFF, MICHAEL. *Oil, War, and American Security.* New Haven, 1980.

STUART, GRAHAM. *The Department of State: A History of Its Organization, Procedure, and Personnel.* New York, 1949.

STUECK, WILLIAM, JR. *The Road to Confrontation: American Policy Towards China and Korea.* Chapel Hill, 1981.

SULZBERGER, C. L. *A Long Row of Candles: Memoirs and Diaries, 1934–1954.* New York, 1969.

TANZER, MICHAEL. *The Political Economy of International Oil and the Underdeveloped Countries.* Boston, 1969.

TAYLOR, A. J. P. *Churchill Revised: A Critical Assessment.* New York, 1969.

THEOHARIS, ATHAN. *Seeds of Repression: Harry S. Truman and the Origins of McCarthyism.* Chicago, 1971.

THOMAS, LEWIS V., and RICHARD FRYE. *The United States and Turkey and Iran.* Cambridge, Mass., 1951.

THORNBURG, MAX W. *People and Policy in the Middle East: A Study of Social and Political Change as Basis for United States Policy.* New York, 1964.

TINKLE, LON. *Mr. Dee: A Biography of Everett Lee DeGolyer.* New York, 1970.

TRUMAN, HARRY S. *Memoirs: Year of Decisions.* Garden City, N.Y., 1955.

———. *Memoirs: Years of Trial and Hope.* Garden City, N.Y., 1956.

TRUMAN, MARGARET. *Harry S Truman.* New York, 1973.

TUCKER, ROBERT W. *The Radical Left and American Foreign Policy.* Baltimore, 1971.

TULLY, ANDREW. *The CIA: The Inside Story.* New York, 1963.

ULAM, ADAM. *The Bolsheviks: The Political History of the Triumph of Communism in Russia.* New York, 1965.

———. *The Rivals: America and Russia Since World War II.* New York, 1971.

———. *Stalin: The Man and His Era.* New York, 1973.

———. *Expansion and Coexistence: Soviet Foreign Policy, 1917–1973.* 2nd. ed. New York, 1974.

UPTON, J. *The History of Modern Iran: An Interpretation.* Cambridge, Mass., 1968.

VANDENBERG, ARTHUR H., JR., ed. *The Private Papers of Senator Vandenberg.* Boston, 1952.

VAN WAGENEN, RICHARD. *The Iranian Case, 1946.* New York, 1952.

VERNON, RAYMOND. *Storm Over the Multinationals: The Real Issues.* Cambridge, Mass., 1977.

VILLIERS, GERARD DE. *The Imperial Shah: An Informal Biography.* Boston, 1976.

VREELAND, HERBERT. *Iran.* New Haven, 1957.

WALKER, RICHARD. *E. R. Stettinius, Jr.* New York, 1965.

WALTERS, VERNON. *Silent Missions.* New York, 1978.

WALTON, RICHARD J. *Henry Wallace, Harry Truman, and the Cold War.* New York, 1976.

WEIGLEY, RUSSELL. *The American Way of War.* New York, 1973.

WELCH, WILLIAM. *American Images of Soviet Foreign Policy.* New Haven, 1970.

Index